The Cambridge Companion to the Concerto

No musical genre has had a more chequered critical history than the
concerto and yet simultaneously retained as consistently prominent
a place in the affections of the concert-going public. This volume,
one of very few to deal with the genre in its entirety, assumes a broad
remit, setting the concerto in its musical and non-musical contexts,
examining the concertos that have made important contributions
to musical culture, and looking at performance-related topics.
A picture emerges of a genre in a continual state of change,
re-inventing itself in the process of growth and development and
regularly challenging its performers and listeners to broaden the
horizons of their musical experience.

The Cambridge Companion to the

CONCERTO

....

EDITED BY

Simon P. Keefe

CAMBRIDGE
UNIVERSITY PRESS

CAMBRIDGE UNIVERSITY PRESS
Cambridge, New York, Melbourne, Madrid, Cape Town, Singapore, São Paulo

CAMBRIDGE UNIVERSITY PRESS
The Edinburgh Building, Cambridge CB2 2RU, UK
Published in the United States of America by Cambridge University Press, New York

www.cambridge.org
Information on this title: www.cambridge.org/9780521542579

First published 2005

Printed in the United Kingdom at the University Press, Cambridge

A catalogue record for this book is available from the British Library

ISBN-13 978-0-521-83483-4 hardback
ISBN-10 0-521-83483-X hardback
ISBN-13 978-0-521-54257-9 paperback
ISBN-10 0-521-54257-X paperback

In memory of
John Daverio (1954–2003)

Contents

Notes on contributors

Timothy Day is Curator of Classical Music Recordings at the British Library. He has contributed to two other Cambridge Companions, on Elgar and on singing, and is the author of *A Century of Recorded Music: Listening to Musical History* (2000). In 1999 he established the British Library's Saul Seminar series, 'Studies in Recorded Music', and in 2000 inaugurated the Edison Fellowship scheme, to assist scholars who wish to carry out intensive work on the Library's collections of recordings of Western art music.

Tia DeNora teaches Sociology at Exeter University. She is author of *Beethoven and the Construction of Genius* (1995), *Music in Everyday Life* (2000) and *After Adorno: Rethinking Music Sociology* (2003). Her current research focuses on two areas, material culture in Beethoven's Vienna, and music therapy and the mind–body debate in sociology.

Cliff Eisen teaches at King's College London. He has published numerous articles on Mozart and late eighteenth-century music generally and is currently working on an annotated translation of Hermann Abert's classic *W. A. Mozart* as well as an edition of selected Mozart letters.

Simon P. Keefe is Professor of Music and Head of Department at City University London. He is the author of *Mozart's Piano Concertos: Dramatic Dialogue in the Age of Enlightenment* (2001) and of numerous articles on late eighteenth-century topics and is editor of *The Cambridge Companion to Mozart* (2003).

Stephan D. Lindeman is Associate Professor of Theory in the School of Music at Brigham Young University, Provo, Utah. His publications include *Structural Novelty and Tradition in the Early Romantic Piano Concerto* (1999), an article on Felix Mendelssohn's concerted works in *The Cambridge Companion to Mendelssohn* (2004) and several articles in *The New Grove Dictionary of Music and Musicians Revised Edition* (2001) related to the concerto genre in the nineteenth century. Lindeman's research interests also include jazz and he is active as a jazz composer and pianist.

David Rowland is Senior Lecturer in Music at the Open University and Director of Music at Christ's College, Cambridge. He has made frequent broadcasts and recordings as an organist, harpsichordist and fortepianist and as conductor of Christ's College Choir and the National Youth Choir of Wales. He has written extensively on the history of the piano, its performance and repertory, including *A History of Pianoforte Pedalling* (1993) and *Early Keyboard Instruments: a Practical Guide* (2001), and is editor of *The Cambridge Companion to the Piano* (1998).

David E. Schneider teaches music history and theory at Amherst College. His work has appeared in *Studia Musicologica*, *Journal of the American Musicological Society*, *Bartók and his World* (ed. Peter Laki), and the *International Journal of Musicology*. His book *Bartók, Hungary and the Renewal of Tradition* is scheduled for publication by the University of California Press in 2005. A professional clarinettist, he has recorded Copland's Clarinet Concerto on the AFKA label.

Robin Stowell is Professor and Head of Music at Cardiff University. Much of his career as a musicologist is reflected in his work as a performer (violinist/ Baroque violinist). His first major book *Violin Technique and Performance Practice in the Late Eighteenth and Early Nineteenth Centuries* (1985) was a pioneering work in its field, and he has since published numerous chapters/ articles in a wide range of books, dictionaries and journals. His most recent major publications include a Cambridge Handbook on *Beethoven's Violin Concerto* (1998), *The Early Violin and Viola: a Practical Guide* (2001) and a co-authored volume (with Colin Lawson) entitled *Historical Performance: an Introduction* (1999), these last two publications forming part of a series of 'Cambridge Handbooks to the Historical Performance of Music' of which he is co-editor. He is music consultant for and chief contributor to *The Violin Book* (1999) and editor of *Performing Beethoven* (1994); he is also editor/principal contributor to the Cambridge Companions to the Violin (1992), the Cello (1999) and the String Quartet (2003).

Michael Talbot is Emeritus Professor of Music at the University of Liverpool and a Fellow of the British Academy. He has published extensively on Italian music of the first half of the eighteenth century and takes a special interest in the life and music of Vivaldi. He has edited several of Vivaldi's sacred vocal works for the New Critical Edition published by Ricordi.

R. Larry Todd is Professor of Music at Duke University. He has published widely on music of the nineteenth century, including, most recently, *Mendelssohn: a Life in Music*, named best biography of 2003 by the Association of American Publishers. He is currently writing a new biography of Mendelssohn's sister, Fanny Hensel.

Arnold Whittall is Professor Emeritus of Music Theory and Analysis at King's College London. The author of *Exploring Twentieth-Century Music* (2003) and *Musical Composition in the Twentieth Century* (1999), he has contributed to several Cambridge Companions, including those on Berg, Britten, Debussy, Stravinsky, and Twentieth-Century Opera.

David Yearsley is the author of numerous articles on seventeenth- and eighteenth-century music as well as the book, *Bach and the Meanings of Counterpoint* (2002). Associate Professor of Music at Cornell University, Yearsley's recordings, including the recent *Bach, Scarlatti, Handel: the Great Contest*, are available on the Loft label.

Acknowledgements

The contributors to this volume receive my sincere gratitude for the timely delivery of their chapters and for their prompt responses to my queries – I have greatly enjoyed our conversations about the concerto. Cliff Eisen's lucid advice on concerto-related topics has been invaluable throughout; I owe him many (more) pints of beer in London pubs. My wife, Celia Hurwitz-Keefe, and children, Abraham and Madeleine, have helped in numerous ways, large and small, not least in encouraging me to keep the rigours of academic work in perspective.

When I began to canvas support for this volume among British and North American scholars in Autumn 2002 I could hardly have foreseen the awful turn of events that would lead me to dedicate it to the memory of one of its prospective contributors, John Daverio, who died in tragic circumstances in Boston in March 2003. As those of us who benefited from his masterly tutelage at Boston University will attest, he was an exemplary scholar, teacher and friend. His extraordinary generosity, support and hospitality, especially when I first arrived in the US as a Master's student in 1991, is something for which I shall always be grateful and remember with great fondness. It is entirely fitting that this modest, mild-mannered yet wonderful virtuoso – a highly talented violinist as well as academic – should be the volume's dedicatee. He is sorely missed.

SIMON P. KEEFE
City University London

The concerto: a chronology

SIMON P. KEEFE

The following list of concertos and concerto-related works is selective; the
majority of works here are discussed – in varying degrees of details – in
Chapters 3–9. Dates cited are generally those of the composition of the
work(s) in question but, where these are uncertain or unknown, dates of
the first performance or publication are given instead. (In some cases,
discrepancies between composition, performance and publication dates
are noted.) Readers are referred to Stanley Sadie (ed.), *The New Grove
Dictionary of Music and Musicians Revised Edition* (29 vols. London,
2001) (*NG Revised*) for comprehensive composer work-lists.

Late sixteenth and seventeenth centuries

1587:   *Concerti di Andrea e di Gio[vanni] Gabrieli* (the earliest recorded
        musical use of the term 'concerto').

1602:   Lodovico Viadana, *Cento concerti ecclesiastici* (one to four voices
        and continuo)

1605:   Giovanni Paolo Cima, *Cento concerti ecclesiastici* (sacred works
        for voices and orchestra)

1613:   Giulio Belli, *Concerti ecclesiastici* (sacred works for voices
        and orchestra)

1636–9: Heinrich Schütz, *Kleine geistliche Konzerte* (sacred works for
        voices and orchestra)

1665:   Maurizio Cazzati, Sonatas, Op. 35 (including several for trumpets
        and strings)

*c.*1675: Petronio Franceschini, sonatas (including one for trumpet
        and strings)

*c.*1680: Domenico Gabrielli, six sonatas for one/two trumpets
        and orchestra

1690:   Giuseppe Maria Jacchini, *Sinfonia con tromba* (trumpet
        and strings)

1692:   Giuseppe Torelli, Concertos, Op. 5

1695:   Giuseppe Maria Jacchini, *Sonata con tromba* (trumpet
        and strings)

1696:   Giulio Taglietti, Concertos, Op. 2

1698: Giovanni Lorenzo Gregori, *Concerti grossi*, Op. 2

1698: Giuseppe Torelli, *Concerti musicali*, Op. 6

Eighteenth century

1700: Tomaso Albinoni, *Sinfonie e concerti a cinque*, Op. 2

1701: Giuseppe Maria Jacchini, Concertos, Op. 4

1707: Tomaso Albinoni, *Concerti a cinque*, Op. 5

1708: Giorgio Gentili, Concertos, Op. 5

1708: Benedetto Marcello, Concertos, Op. 1

c.1708–35 Georg Philipp Telemann, concertos for recorder, violin, oboe, oboe d'amore, flute, bass viol

1709: Giulio Taglietti, Concertos, Op. 4

1709: Giuseppe Torelli, Concertos, Op. 8

1710: Giuseppe Valentini, *Concerti grossi*, Op. 7

1711: Antonio Vivaldi, *L'estro armonico*, Op. 3

1712: Arcangelo Corelli, Concertos Op. 6 published in Amsterdam

1713: Giuseppe Matteo Alberti, *Concerti per chiesa e per camera*, Op. 1

1715: Tomaso Albinoni, Concertos, Op. 7

1716: Giorgio Gentili, Concertos, Op. 6

1716: Antonio Vivaldi, Concertos (*La stravaganza*), Op. 4

1717–23: Johann Sebastian Bach, Violin Concertos in A minor and E major, BWV 1041 and 1042, Concerto for Two Violins in D minor, BWV 1043

1719: Antonio Vivaldi, Concertos, Op. 6

1720: Antonio Vivaldi, Concertos, Op. 7

1721: Johann Sebastian Bach, Brandenburg Concertos, BWV 1046–51

1721: Pietro Locatelli, *Concerti grossi*, Op. 1

1722: Tomaso Albinoni, Concertos, Op. 9

1725: Antonio Vivaldi, *Le quattro stagioni* ('The Four Seasons'), as part of *Il cimento dell'armonia e dell' inventione*, Op. 8 (Nos. 1–4)

1727: Joseph Bodin de Boismortier, Flute Concertos, Op. 15

1728: Giuseppe Tartini, Concertos, Op. 1

1729: Antonio Vivaldi, Concertos, Opp. 10, 11, 12

1732: Francesco Geminiani, *Concerti grossi*, Opp. 2 and 3

1733: Pietro Locatelli, Concertos, Op. 3

c.1734: Giuseppe Tartini, Concertos, Op. 2

1734: Georg Frideric Handel, Concertos, Op. 3 (HWV 312–17)

1735:   Johann Sebastian Bach, *Concerto nach italiänischem Gusto* ('Italian Concerto') for solo harpsichord, BWV 971

1735–6:   Tomaso Albinoni, Concertos, Op. 10

1735–42:   Johann Sebastian Bach, concertos for one, two, three and four harpsichords, BWV 1054–65. (Most of these works probably originate from Bach's time in Cöthen, 1717–23.)

1737:   Jean Marie Leclair, Concertos, Op. 7 (violin concertos, except No. 3)

1738:   Georg Frideric Handel, Concertos for Organ, Op. 4 (HWV 289–94)

1739:   Georg Frideric Handel, Concertos, Op. 6 (HWV 319–330)

1740–51:   Georg Frideric Handel, Concertos for Organ, Op. 7 (HWV 306–11)

1740–62:   Carl Philipp Emanuel Bach, Concertos, H. 409–48

1741:   Johann Adolf Hasse, Concertos, Op. 3

1745:   Jean Marie Leclair, Concertos for Violin, Op. 10

c.1747:   Georg Frideric Handel, *Concerti a due cori* (concertos for two instrumental choruses), Opp. 1, 2, 3 (HWV 332–4)

1752:   Johann Joachim Quantz names Giuseppe Torelli as the inventor of the concerto genre

c.1752–63: Leopold Mozart, two concertos for horn, two for two horns, five for flute, and one each for trumpet, oboe and piano

c.1756–71: Joseph Haydn, concertos for violin, cello, baryton, flute, horn, organ/harpsichord

c.1757–85: Michael Haydn, concertos for violin, organ/harpsichord and viola, harpsichord, flute

1760–79:   Carl Ditters von Dittersdorf, concertos for violin, two violins, flute, oboe, oboe d'amore, harpsichord, horn, violin, viola, cello

1763:   Johann Christian Bach, Keyboard Concertos, Op. 1 (C49–54)

1765–78:   Carl Philipp Emanuel Bach, Keyboard Concertos, H. 465–78

1767:   Wolfgang Amadeus Mozart, arrangements of movements of keyboard sonatas by Carl Philipp Emanuel Bach, Johann Gottfried Eckard, Leontzi Honauer, Hermann Friedrich Raupach, Johann Schobert as keyboard concertos (K. 37, 39–41)

c.1768–82: Luigi Boccherini, *c*.11 cello concertos, and one each for harpsichord, violin and flute

1769–71:   Jean-Baptiste Davaux, four violin concertos

1770:   Johann Christian Bach, Keyboard Concertos, Op. 7 (C55–60)

1772:   Wolfgang Amadeus Mozart, arrangements of Johann Christian Bach's keyboard sonatas Op. 5, Nos. 2, 3 and 4 as keyboard concertos (K. 107i–iii)

1773–80:   Wolfgang Amadeus Mozart, four concertos for solo piano – K. 175 in D (1773), K. 238 in B flat (1776), K. 246 in C (1776), K. 271 in E flat (1777); one concerto for three pianos – K. 242 in F (1776); one concerto for two pianos – K. 365 in E flat (1780); five concertos for violin – K. 207 in B flat (1773), K. 211 in D (1775), K. 216 in G (1775), K. 218 in D (1775), K. 219 in A (1775); one concerto for bassoon – K. 191 in B flat (1774); two concertos for flute – K. 313 in G (1778), K. 315 in C (1780); one concerto for oboe/flute – K. 314 in C (1778); and one concerto for flute and harp – K. 299 in C (1778). All were written while Mozart was based in Salzburg.

1774–7:   Johann Samuel Schroeter, 12 keyboard concertos

1774–93:   Carl Stamitz, 15 concertos for violin, three for viola d'amore, eight for flute, ten for clarinet, and seven for bassoon, two for piano, and two for harp

1779–1813: Jan Ladislav Dussek, *c.*18 piano concertos, including publications Opp. 15, 20, 49, 50, 66.

1780–6:   Giuseppe Maria Cambini, three concertos for violin, one for viola, five for flute and three for harpsichord/piano

1781:   Joseph Haydn, Piano Concerto in G, Hob. XVIII:4

*c.*1782–1817: Giovanni Battista Viotti, 29 violin concertos

1782–91:   Wolfgang Amadeus Mozart, 17 concertos for solo piano – K. 413 in F (1782–3), K. 414 in A (1782), K. 415 in C (1782–3), K. 449 in E flat (1782–4), K. 450 in B flat (1784), K. 451 in D (1784), K. 453 in G (1784), K. 456 in B flat (1784), K. 459 in F (1784), K. 466 in D minor (1785), K. 467 in C (1785), K. 482 in E flat (1785), K. 488 in A (1786), K. 491 in C minor (1786), K. 503 in C (1786), K. 537 in D (1788), K. 595 in B flat (1788–91); four concertos for horn – K. 412 in E flat (1791), K. 417 in E flat (1783), K. 447 in E flat (*c.*1787), K. 495 in E flat (1786); and one concerto for clarinet – K. 622 in A (1791). All were written while Mozart was based in Vienna.

*c.*1782–1800: Ignace Joseph Pleyel, four concertos for cello, two for violin, one for bassoon, one for viola or cello, and one for clarinet, flute or cello

1783:	Joseph Haydn, Cello Concerto in D, Hob. VIIb:2
1783–*c.*1810:	Rodolphe Kreutzer, 19 violin concertos
1784:	Joseph Haydn, Piano Concerto in D, Hob. XVIII:11
1784–1800:	Leopold Kozeluch, 22 keyboard concertos
*c.*1788:	Ludwig van Beethoven begins his Piano Concerto No. 2 in B flat, Op. 19, revising it on and off over the next 10 years. (Publication, 1801)
1793:	Domenico Cimarosa, Concerto for Two Flutes in G
*c.*1794–1815:	Pierre Rode, 13 violin concertos
1795:	Ludwig van Beethoven, Piano Concerto No. 1 in C, Op. 15 (revised 1800; published 1801)
1795–1825:	Johann Baptist Cramer, eight piano concertos, Opp. 10, 16, 26, 38, 48, 51, 56, 70
1796:	Muzio Clementi, Piano Concerto in C
1796:	Joseph Haydn, Trumpet Concerto in E flat, Hob. VIIe:1
1796–1800:	Adalbert Gyrowetz, two piano concertos, Opp. 26, 49
1796–1820:	Daniel Steibelt, eight piano concertos
*c.*1797–1809:	Anton Eberl, three piano concertos, Opp. 32, 40, 45
1799–1822:	John Field, seven piano concertos

Nineteenth century

*c.*1800–03:	Ludwig van Beethoven, Piano Concerto No. 3 in C minor, Op. 37 (first performed 1803; published 1804)
1802–*c.*1820:	Pierre Baillot, nine violin concertos, Opp. 3, 6, 7, 10, 13, 18, 21, 22, 30
1802–44:	Louis Spohr, 15 violin concertos
1803:	Johann Nepomuk Hummel, Trumpet Concerto in E flat major
1804–7:	Ludwig van Beethoven, 'Triple Concerto' for Piano, Violin and Cello in C, Op. 56
1805–33:	Johann Nepomuk Hummel, piano concertos, Opp. 17, 34a, 73, 85, 89, 110, 113 and Opus post. 1
1805–06:	Ludwig van Beethoven, Piano Concerto No. 4 in G, Op. 58
1806:	Ludwig van Beethoven, Violin Concerto in D, Op. 61
1808–28:	Louis Spohr, four clarinet concertos in C minor, E flat, F minor and E minor
1809:	Ludwig van Beethoven, Piano Concerto No. 5 in E flat, Op. 73, 'Emperor'
1810–12:	Carl Maria von Weber, Piano Concerto No. 1 in C major, Op. 11, and No. 2 in E flat major

1811:	Carl Maria von Weber, Bassoon Concerto in F, Op. 75, Clarinet Concerto in F minor, Op. 73 and Clarinet Concerto in E flat major, Op. 74
c.1813:	Ferdinand Ries, Concerto No. 3 in C sharp minor, Op. 55
c.1815:	Nicolò Paganini, Violin Concerto in E minor
1815:	Carl Maria von Weber, Concertino in E, for Natural Horn and Orchestra, Op. 45
1816:	Nicolò Paganini, Violin Concerto No. 1 in E flat, Op. 6
1819–38:	Ignaz Moscheles, eight piano concertos, Opp. 45, 56, 60, 64, 87, 90, 93, 96
1821:	Carl Maria von Weber, *Konzertstück* in F minor for Piano and Orchestra, Op. 79. (Begun as Piano Concerto No. 3 in 1815.)
1822–4:	Felix Mendelssohn, concertos for violin (D minor), piano (A minor) and two pianos (E)
1823–4:	Ferdinand Ries, *Farewell to London* (piano concerto), Op. 132
1823–35:	Frédéric Kalkbrenner, piano concertos, Opp. 61, 80, 107, 125
1824:	Ferdinand Ries, *Salut au Rhin*, Op. 151
1826:	Nicolò Paganini, Violin Concerto No. 2 in B minor, Op. 7 and No. 3 in E major
1829:	Frédéric Chopin, Piano Concerto No. 2 in F minor, Op. 21
1830:	Frédéric Chopin, Piano Concerto No. 1 in E minor, Op. 11
1830:	Nicolò Paganini, Violin Concerto No. 4 in D minor and No. 5 in A minor
1831:	Felix Mendelssohn, Piano Concerto No. 1 in G minor, Op. 25
1832:	(Charles-) Valentin Alkan, *Concerto da camera* No. 1 in A minor, Op. 10
1834:	(Charles-) Valentin Alkan, *Concerto da camera* No. 2 in C sharp minor
1834:	Hector Berlioz, *Harold en Italie* (programmatic symphony for viola and orchestra), Op. 16
1835:	Clara Wieck (later Schumann), Piano Concerto in A minor, Op. 7
1835–55:	Franz Liszt, Piano Concerto No. 1 in E flat (sketches and piano score from 1832; work published 1857)
1837:	Felix Mendelssohn, Piano Concerto No. 2 in D minor, Op. 40
1839–61:	Franz Liszt, Piano Concerto No. 2 in A (published 1861)
1840–83:	Henry Vieuxtemps, seven violin concertos, Opp. 10, 19, 25, 31, 37, 47, 49

1844:   Felix Mendelssohn, Violin Concerto in E minor, Op. 64

1844:   Adolf Henselt, Piano Concerto in F minor, Op. 16

1844:   Henri Charles Litolff, *Concerto Symphonique* No. 2 (piano
           and orchestra), Op. 22

1845:   Robert Schumann, Piano Concerto in A minor, Op. 54
           (premièred by Clara Schumann)

1846:   Heinrich Wilhelm Ernst, *Concerto pathétique* in F sharp
           minor (violin and orchestra), Op. 23

*c.*1846:   Henri Charles Litolff, *Concerto Symphonique* No. 3 (piano
           and orchestra), Op. 45

1849:   Robert Schumann, *Konzertstück* in F (four horns
           and orchestra), Op. 86

1850:   Anton Rubinstein, Piano Concerto No. 1 in E minor, Op. 25

1850:   Robert Schumann, Cello Concerto in A minor, Op. 129

1851:   Franz Liszt adapts Franz Schubert's Piano Fantasy in
           C major (*Wanderer*), Op. 15/D760 (1822) into a piano
           concerto

1851:   Anton Rubinstein, Piano Concerto No. 2 in F major, Op. 35

1851–2:   Henri Charles Litolff, *Concerto Symphonique* No. 4 (piano
           and orchestra), Op. 102

1853:   Robert Schumann, Fantasy in C major for Violin and
           Orchestra, Op. 131 and Violin Concerto in D minor,
           WoO23 (premièred 1937)

1853:   Henryk Wieniawski, Violin Concerto No. 1 in F sharp
           minor, Op. 14

1853–4:   Anton Rubinstein, Piano Concerto No. 3 in G major, Op. 45

1858:   Camille Saint-Saëns, Piano Concerto No. 1 in D major,
           Op. 17 and Violin Concerto No. 2 in C major, Op. 58

1859:   Camille Saint-Saëns, Violin Concerto No. 1 in A major,
           Op. 20

1861:   Johannes Brahms, Piano Concerto No. 1 in D minor, Op. 15
           is published. (The work was composed between 1854 and
           1859.)

1862:   Henryk Wieniawski, Violin Concerto No. 2 in D minor,
           Op. 22

1864:   Anton Rubinstein, Piano Concerto No. 4 in D minor, Op. 70

1866:   Edvard Grieg, Piano Concerto in A minor, Op. 16
           (published 1872)

1867:   Max Bruch, Violin Concerto No. 1 in G minor, Op. 26

1868:   Camille Saint-Saëns, Piano Concerto No. 2 in G minor,
           Op. 22

1870:   Henri Charles Litolff, *Concerto Symphonique* No. 5 (piano and orchestra), Op. 123

1873:   Camille Saint-Saëns, Cello Concerto No. 1 in A minor, Op. 33

1874:   Anton Rubinstein, Piano Concerto No. 5 in E flat, Op. 94

1874–5:   Pyotr Il'yich Tchaikovsky, Piano Concerto No. 1 in B flat minor, Op. 23

1875:   Camille Saint-Saëns, Piano Concerto No. 4 in C minor, Op. 44

1876:   Antonín Dvořák, Piano Concerto in G minor, Op. 33

1876:   Xaver Scharwenka, Piano Concerto No. 1 in B flat minor, Op. 32

1876:   Pyotr Il'yich Tchaikovsky, Variations on a Rococo Theme in A major, Op. 33 (cello and orchestra)

1877:   Edouard Lalo, Cello Concerto in D minor

1878:   Johannes Brahms, Violin Concerto in D major, Op. 77

1878:   Max Bruch, Violin Concerto No. 2 in D minor, Op. 44

1878:   Pyotr Il'yich Tchaikovsky, Violin Concerto in D, Op. 35. (Published 1888)

1879:   Antonín Dvořák, Violin Concerto in A minor, Op. 53 (revised 1882)

1879–80: Pyotr Il'yich Tchaikovsky, Piano Concerto No. 2 in G major, Op. 44

1880:   Max Bruch, *Fantasie unter freier Benutzung schottischer Volksmelodien* ('Scottish Fantasy'), Op. 46 (violin and orchestra)

1880:   Camille Saint-Saëns, Violin Concerto No. 3 in B minor, Op. 61

1881:   Max Bruch, *Kol Nidrei*, Op. 47 (cello and orchestra)

1881:   Xaver Scharwenka, Piano Concerto No. 2 in C minor, Op. 56

1882:   Johannes Brahms, Piano Concerto No. 2 in B flat major, Op. 83

1882:   Anton Arensky, Piano Concerto in F minor, Op. 2

1882:   Edward MacDowell, Piano Concerto No. 1 in A minor

1882:   Richard Strauss, Violin Concerto in D minor, Op. 8

1882–3:   Nikolay Rimsky-Korsakov, Piano Concerto in C sharp minor, Op. 30

1883:   Richard Strauss, Horn Concerto No. 1 in E flat, Op. 11

1885:   Edward MacDowell, Piano Concerto No. 2 in D minor, Op. 23

1887:   Johannes Brahms, Concerto in A minor for Violin and Cello, Op. 102

1890–1:   Serge Rachmaninov, Piano Concerto No. 1 in F sharp
            minor, Op. 1
1891:   Max Bruch, Violin Concerto No. 3 in D minor, Op. 58
1893:   Wilhelm Stenhammar, Piano Concerto No. 1 in B flat
            minor, Op. 1
1895:   Antonín Dvořák, Cello Concerto in B minor, Op. 104
1896:   Camille Saint-Saëns, Piano Concerto No. 5 in F major,
            Op. 103 ('Egyptian')
1896:   Aleksandr Skryabin, Piano Concerto in F sharp minor, Op. 20
1898:   Ernst von Dohnányi, Piano Concerto in E minor, Op. 5
1898–9:   Amy Beach, Piano Concerto in C sharp minor, Op. 45
1898:   Moritz Moszkowski, Piano Concerto in E major, Op. 59

Twentieth and twenty-first centuries

1901:   Serge Rachmaninov, Piano Concerto No. 2 in C minor, Op. 18
1904:   Ferruccio Busoni, Piano Concerto, Op. 39
1904:   Aleksandr Glazunov, Violin Concerto in A minor, Op. 82
1904:   Jean Sibelius, Violin Concerto in D minor, Op. 47
1904–7:   Wilhelm Stenhammar, Piano Concerto No. 2 in D minor,
            Op. 23
1906:   Mily Balakirev, Piano Concerto No. 2 in E flat major, Op. posth.
            (The first movement and sketches for the second and third
            originate from the early 1860s.)
1907–8:   Béla Bártok, Violin Concerto No. 1
1908:   Max Reger, Violin Concerto in A, Op. 101
1908:   Xaver Scharwenka, Piano Concerto No. 4 in F minor, Op. 82
1909:   Serge Rachmaninov, Piano Concerto No. 3 in D minor, Op. 30
1910:   Edward Elgar, Violin Concerto in B minor, Op. 61
1910:   Max Reger, Piano Concerto in F minor, Op. 114
1912:   Serge Prokofiev, Piano Concerto No. 1 in D flat, Op. 10
1912–13:   Serge Prokofiev, Piano Concerto No. 2 in G minor, Op. 16
1914:   Ernst von Dohnányi, *Variations on a Nursery Song*, Op. 25
            (piano and orchestra)
1915:   Frederick Delius, Double Concerto for Violin and Cello
1916:   Frederick Delius, Violin Concerto
1916:   Karol Szymanowski, Violin Concerto No. 1, Op. 35
1917:   Serge Prokofiev, Violin Concerto No. 1 in D, Op. 19
            (premièred 1923)
1918–19:   Edward Elgar, Cello Concerto in E minor, Op. 85
1921:   Frederick Delius, Cello Concerto

1921:   Serge Prokofiev, Piano Concerto No. 3 in C, Op. 26

1922:   Hans Pfitzner, Piano Concerto in E flat, Op. 31

1923:   Hans Pfitzner, Violin Concerto in B minor, Op. 34

1923–4:   Igor Stravinsky, Concerto for Piano and Winds

1924:   Arthur Honegger, Piano Concertino

1924:   Kurt Weill, Violin Concerto

1925:   Jacques Ibert, Cello Concerto

1925:   Alfredo Casella, Partita for Piano and Orchestra, Op. 42

1925:   Ernest Bloch, Concerto Grosso for String Orchestra and Piano obbligato

1925:   George Gershwin, Concerto in F (piano and orchestra)

1926:   Béla Bartók, Piano Concerto No. 1

1926:   Aaron Copland, Piano Concerto

1926:   Manuel de Falla, Harpsichord Concerto

1926:   Carl Nielsen, Flute Concerto

1926:   Serge Rachmaninov, Piano Concerto No. 4 in G minor, Op. 40

1926–31: Ralph Vaughan Williams, Piano Concerto in C

1927–64: Darius Milhaud, five concertos for piano, three for violin, two for viola, two for cello, and one each for flute and violin, clarinet, oboe and harpsichord

1928:   Carl Nielsen, Clarinet Concerto, Op. 57

1928:   Francis Poulenc, Harpsichord Concerto

1928:   Henry Cowell, Piano Concerto

1929:   William Walton, Viola Concerto

1929–30: Maurice Ravel, Piano Concerto for the Left Hand

1930–5:   Roger Sessions, Violin Concerto

1931:   Béla Bartók, Piano Concerto No. 2

1931:   Serge Prokofiev, Piano Concerto No. 4, Op. 53 (published 1966)

1931:   Maurice Ravel, Piano Concerto in G

1931:   Igor Stravinsky, Violin Concerto in D

1931–2:   Serge Prokofiev, Piano Concerto No. 5, Op. 55

1931–4:   Anton Webern, Concerto for Nine Instruments, Op. 24

1932:   Arnold Bax, Cello Concerto

1933:   Dmitry Shostakovich, Concerto for Piano, Trumpet and Strings in C minor, Op. 35

1933:   Karol Szymanowski, Violin Concerto No. 2, Op. 61

1934:   Serge Rachmaninov, *Rhapsody on a Theme of Paganini*, Op. 43 (piano and orchestra)

1935:   Alban Berg, Violin Concerto

1935:   Hans Pfitzner, Cello Concerto No. 1 in G, Op. 42

1935:   Serge Prokofiev, Violin Concerto No. 2 in G minor, Op. 63

1966: Dmitry Shostakovich, Cello Concerto No. 2 in G

1967: Hans Werner Henze, Piano Concerto No. 2

1967: György Ligeti, Cello Concerto

1967: Dmitry Shostakovich, Violin Concerto No. 2 in C sharp minor, Op. 129

1969: Elliott Carter, Concerto for Orchestra

1969: Iannis Xenakis, *Synaphaï* (piano and orchestra)

1969–70: Hans Werner Henze, *Compases para preguntas ensimismadas* (viola and 22 instruments)

1969–70: György Ligeti, Chamber Concerto

1969–70: Witold Lutosławski, Cello Concerto

1971: Hans Werner Henze, Violin Concerto No. 2

1972: Morton Feldman, *Cello and Orchestra*

1972: György Ligeti, Double Concerto (flute, oboe and orchestra)

1972–3: Luciano Berio, Concerto for Two Pianos and Orchestra

1975: Morton Feldman, *Piano and Orchestra*

1975–81: Michael Finnissy, seven piano concertos

1976: Luciano Berio, *Il ritorno degli snovidenia* (cello and small orchestra)

1976: Harrison Birtwistle, *Melencolia I* (clarinet, harp and two string orchestras)

1976–7: Krzysztof Penderecki, Violin Concerto No. 1

1978: Morton Feldman, *Flute and Orchestra*

1978–9: Michael Tippett, Concerto for String Trio and Orchestra

1980–8: György Ligeti, Piano Concerto

1981: Hans Werner Henze, *Le miracle de la rose* (clarinet and chamber ensemble)

1984–5: Alfred Schnittke, Concerto for Mixed Chorus

1985: Peter Maxwell Davies, Violin Concerto

1985: Alfred Schnittke, Viola Concerto

1986: Iannis Xenakis, *Keqrops*

1986–96: Peter Maxwell Davies, 'Strathclyde' concertos (nine concertos for various instruments and a Concerto for Orchestra)

1987: Elliott Carter, Oboe Concerto

1987: Philip Glass, Violin Concerto

1988: Witold Lutosławski, Piano Concerto

1988: Peter Maxwell Davies, Trumpet Concerto

1989–93: György Ligeti, Violin Concerto

1990: Elliott Carter, Violin Concerto

1990: Jonathan Harvey, Cello Concerto

1991: Magnus Lindberg, Piano Concerto

1992–3:   John Adams, Violin Concerto
1992–5:   Krzysztof Penderecki, Violin Concerto No. 2
1996:   John Adams, *Gnarly Buttons* (clarinet, piano and orchestra)
1996:   Elliott Carter, Clarinet Concerto
1997:   John Adams, *Century Rolls* (clarinet, piano and orchestra)
1997:   Peter Maxwell Davies, Piccolo Concerto and Piano Concerto
1999:   György Ligeti, Horn Concerto
1999:   Magnus Lindberg, Cello Concerto
2000:   Elliott Carter, *ASKO Concerto*
2001:   Elliott Carter, Cello Concerto
2001:   Jonathan Harvey, *Bird Concerto with Pianosong*
2002:   Elliott Carter, *Boston Concerto*
2002:   Magnus Lindberg, Clarinet Concerto
2003:   Magnus Lindberg, Concerto for Orchestra

Abbreviations

Books

NG	Stanley Sadie (ed.), *New Grove Dictionary of Music and Musicians* (20 vols., London, 1980)
NG Revised	Stanley Sadie (ed.), *New Grove Dictionary of Music and Musicians, Revised Edition* (29 vols., London, 2001)

Journals

AM	*Acta Musicologica*
AmZ	*Allgemeine musikalische Zeitung*
EM	*Early Music*
JAMS	*Journal of the American Musicological Society*
JM	*Journal of Musicology*
JRMA	*Journal of the Royal Musical Association*
ML	*Music & Letters*
MQ	*The Musical Quarterly*
MT	*The Musical Times*
PRMA	*Proceedings of the Royal Musical Association*

Introduction

SIMON P. KEEFE

In a famous, oft-repeated British TV comedy sketch, first broadcast on 25 December 1971, the classic duo of Eric Morecambe and Ernie Wise wreak havoc in a performance of the opening of Edvard Grieg's Piano Concerto in A minor, conducted by André Previn. Pianist Morecambe and his 'manager' Wise make a string of ridiculous demands: they want to perform what Morecambe calls a 'special arrangement' of the concerto with the orchestra playing the opening flourishes and the piano the main theme (Previn reluctantly agrees); they deem the new orchestral introduction 'too short' and suggest contacting Grieg to get him to lengthen it; and, after missing Previn's cue on account of a poor sight-line to the conductor, ask him either to wear high heels or to 'jump up in the air' in order to be visible. Finally entering at the appropriate moment at the third attempt, Morecambe delivers a grotesquely butchered version of the main theme. Reprimanded by Previn for 'playing all the wrong notes', Morecambe purses his lips, grabs his conductor by the lapels and, with the exquisite timing that made him one of Britain's greatest post-war comedians, delivered his *coup de grace*: 'I'm playing all the *right* notes, but not *necessarily* in the right order'.[1]

In some respects, Morecambe's comic character is an archetypal arrogant diva (with good, old-fashioned buffoonery thrown in). He is self-regarding and disdainful of the accompanying orchestra ('Is this the band? . . . I've seen better bands on a cigar'), assumes the violins are to blame as Previn approaches him horrified at the distortion of the main theme, and is condescending towards the conductor, dismissing him with the claim that 'For another £4 we could have got [then UK Prime Minister and music aficionado] Edward Heath'. In other respects, however, his actions and behaviour can be taken to represent several of the different strains of criticism levelled specifically against the concerto during its protracted and controversial history. His disregard for the orchestra and blinkered self-interest encapsulate the consistently articulated critical view that concertos are primarily vehicles for compositional and soloistic self-promotion rather than for genuine audience edification. Just as Morecambe considers his orchestra more-or-less irrelevant to the musical experience at hand, so critics collectively condemn countless concerto composers for treating their accompanying orchestras in just this way. While Morecambe is no piano virtuoso (quite the contrary), he neatly sums up the troubled,

[1]

ambiguous reaction to concerto virtuosity in the collective critical consciousness. After Previn performs the correct version of the piano's ostentatious opening salvo, Morecambe is visibly awestruck by the technical skill involved. Composing himself for a few seconds, he finally utters the single word 'Rubbish!' and heads off stage. In short, Morecambe's comedic alter ego is a symbolic critic of the very same genre in which he is an all-too-eager participant.

No musical genre has had a more chequered critical history than the concerto but has simultaneously retained as consistently prominent a place in the affections of the concert-going public. Historically speaking, concertos have had a more polarizing effect than any other kind of musical work. The inherent virtues of a wide range of concertos are now of course taken for granted – and such works are as firmly entrenched as their symphonic counterparts in both critical and performance canons – but established concertos even today inspire widely diverging responses. While most of an audience may swoon at, say, the flamboyant virtuosity of Rachmaninov's Piano Concerto No. 3, self-professed *cognoscenti* often recoil at it. Nothing is more likely to fill a packed performance venue with a buzz of excitement than a concert featuring one of the nineteenth-century 'warhorse' concertos performed by a world-renowned soloist, for example, and nothing more likely to induce weary resignation among musical 'highbrows'. Indeed, the concerto remains an active battleground for musical tastes, continuing to use tensions inherent in polemical reactions to old and new works as fuel for the development of an art form that is as vibrant as ever 400 years or so into its history.

The vitality and longevity of the concerto must also be attributed to the genre's considerable ability both to encourage thinking about issues that reach beyond the narrow confines of the music itself and to engage directly with (and influence directly) prevailing performance trends. This volume therefore assumes a broad remit, including but not limiting itself to consideration of the concertos that have made – and continue to make – such important contributions to musical culture. Part I sets the concerto in its musical and non-musical contexts, surveying theories that surround perceived positive and negative features of the genre and exploring socio-musical factors that bear upon our perception of the concerto (and, indeed, music in general). Following detailed study of concerto repertories in Part II, Part III turns to performance-related topics, examining qualities historically associated with the virtuoso, as well as performance practice trends in the eighteenth and nineteenth centuries as they relate to the genre, and the productive relationship the concerto has enjoyed with the recording industry. A picture emerges of a genre in a continual state of change, reinventing itself in the process of growth and development and regularly challenging its performers and listeners to broaden the horizons of their musical experience. There is every reason to believe that concertos will be written for centuries to come as so many of the fundamental issues with which they engage – including the status of the 'star' performer and the understanding of how individuals and groups interact – have perennial social and musical relevance. By engaging in our own considerations of the genre – as composers, performers, scholars, critics, music-lovers and concert-goers – we contribute actively to the concerto's colourful history and help to shape its future.

PART ONE

Contexts

1 Theories of the concerto from the eighteenth century to the present day

SIMON P. KEEFE

Discussing his G major Piano Concerto early in the last century, Maurice Ravel writes that it 'is a concerto in the strictest sense of the term'.[1] At approximately the same time, the critic F. Bonavia explains that Beethoven's Violin Concerto represents 'no conscious departure from the accepted criterion of what a concerto should be'.[2] But what is the 'strictest sense' of concerto and the 'accepted criterion' of its ontological status? At one level, the concerto is all-too-easy to define, at another level, intractably difficult to pin down. In broadest terms a concerto from the eighteenth century through to the present day is expected to feature a soloist or soloists interacting with an orchestra, providing a vehicle for the solo performer(s) to demonstrate their technical and musical proficiency; in practical terms, concertos demonstrate multifarious types of solo–orchestra interaction and virtuosity, often provide as much of a showcase for the orchestra as for the soloist(s) and sometimes dispense altogether with the hard-and-fast distinction between soloist(s) and orchestra. Given the extraordinary diversity of works labelled concertos, it is no wonder that critics, composers and musicologists – indeed, musicians of all shapes and sizes – have on the whole steered clear of systematic theorizing about the genre. The concerto's capacity for reinvention over its venerable 400-year history – even in 1835 a reviewer for the *Gazette musicale* praised Chopin's E minor Piano Concerto for 'rejuvenating such an old form'[3] – has ensured its fundamental elusiveness, its longevity as a genre and, in all likelihood, its deeply ingrained popularity with the musical public at large.

While protracted theorizing about the concerto is rare, aside from on technical matters such as form,[4] there is no shortage of opinion about the genre's aesthetic status and about prerequisites for composing popular and musically successful works. The wide diversity of theoretical and critical views over the last two centuries focuses in particular on two perennially controversial topics that lie at the heart of the concerto: the nature of the interaction among participants, solo and orchestral alike, and, by extension, the function of the 'accompanying' orchestra; and the nature of the music given to the soloist(s). Theoretical and critical debate on these topics influences and is influenced by compositional practice, thus making a highly significant contribution to the continued vitality, transformability and popularity of the concerto genre.

Virtuosity and the interaction of the soloist and orchestra in the eighteenth and nineteenth centuries

Throughout the eighteenth and nineteenth centuries respected theorists and critics castigate excessive virtuosity in concertos, believing that it detracts unequivocally from a listener's aesthetic experience. Johann Georg Sulzer's influential *Allgemeine Theorie der schönen Künste* (*General Theory of the Fine Arts*, 1771–4) contains several swipes at the concerto on account of purportedly extreme virtuosity; Heinrich Christoph Koch (1787) explains that composer-performers 'stuff their concertos with nothing but difficulties and passages in fashion, instead of coaxing the hearts of their listeners with beautiful melodies'; and Johann Karl Friedrich Triest (1801) neatly sums up the received wisdom of his age in claiming that 'hardly one in a hundred [concertos] can claim to possess any inner artistic value' representing the 'special proving ground for virtuosity' instead.[5] Later writers continue this critical trend: reviewers for *La Revue et Gazette musicale de Paris* repeatedly stress in the second and third quarters of the nineteenth century that bravura passages with meagre accompaniment will in no way suffice for concertos; writers on early performances from the 1830s and 1840s of Chopin's piano concertos – by no means the most technically challenging of early nineteenth-century virtuoso works – criticize the 'unprecedented and unjustified' difficulties and 'extravagant passages', asking 'what more do the hands need?' and the composer and critic Robert Schumann offers 'a special vote of thanks' in 1839 to 'recent concerto composers for no longer boring us with concluding trills and, especially, leaping octave passages' as they had earlier in the century when excessive virtuosity was *à la mode*, coming down heavily on virtuoso-composers whom he likens to popular entertainers.[6] Indeed, late eighteenth- and nineteenth-century writers, not just Schumann, often equate virtuosos – including writers and performers of concertos – with non-aesthetic phenomena, Sulzer and Koch likening solo roles in many concertos to those of acrobats, Friedrich Rochlitz claiming that virtuosos 'are interested only in the good or bad execution of difficulties and so-called magic tricks, just as tightrope walkers are interested only in keeping their balance on the high wire' and James W. Davidson asserting that for the virtuosos 'repose is nauseous – unless it be the repose indispensable to a winded acrobat'.[7] Davidson continues in this vein with an uproarious account of Anton Rubinstein's performance of a Mozart piano concerto in 1858, clarifying in no uncertain terms that the virtuoso's self-aggrandizement ruined the listener's experience of the work:

> A 'lion' in the most leonine sense of the term, he treated the concerto of
> Mozart just as the monarch of the forest, hungry and truculent, is in the habit

of treating the unlucky beast that falls to his prey. He seized it, shook it, worried it, tore it to pieces, and then devoured it, limb by limb. Long intervals of roaring diversified his repast. These roarings were 'cadenzas'. After having swallowed as much of the concerto as extended to the *point d'orgue* of the first movement, his appetite being in some measure assuaged, the lion roared vociferously, and so long, that many ... admitted that, at all events, a 'lion' could be heard from the 'recess' in St. James's Hall. Having thus roared, our 'lion's' appetite revived, and he ate up the slow movement as if it had been the wing of a partridge. (Never did the slow movement so suddenly vanish.) Still ravenous, however, he pounced upon the finale – which having stripped to the *queue* ('*coda*'), he re-roared, as before. The *queue* was then disposed of, and nothing left of the concerto.[8]

Late eighteenth- and nineteenth-century writers often consider active interaction between the concerto soloist and the orchestra an ideal foil for 'excessive' solo virtuosity. While Koch, for example, is as willing as Sulzer to point the finger at empty virtuosity in late eighteenth-century concertos, he is unwilling to condemn the entire genre to aesthetic oblivion as a result, mounting a spirited defence of its genuine aesthetic qualities in the hands of practitioners such as C. P. E. Bach and Mozart. For Koch, the accompanying voices in the best concertos 'are not merely there to sound this or that missing interval' but rather to engage in a 'passionate dialogue' with the soloist, expressing approval, commiseration and comfort.[9] Forcefully countering the prevailing distrust of the concerto, Koch's remarks also foreshadow nineteenth-century concerns. Schumann describes the 'severing of the bond with the orchestra' in many early nineteenth-century works, bemoans the possibility that piano concertos with orchestra could become 'entirely obsolete' and issues a clarion call for 'the genius who will show us a brilliant way of combining orchestra and piano, so that the autocrat at the keyboard may reveal the richness of his instrument and of his art, while the orchestra, more than a mere onlooker, with its many expressive capabilities adds to the artistic whole'.[10] The ideal concerto for writers at *La Revue et Gazette musicale* also focuses on 'equality and dialogue between the solo instrument and the orchestra' rather than on issues such as the showcasing of the soloist or form.[11] Indeed, dialogue has served as one of the most popular metaphors for productive exchange between the soloist and the orchestra over the last 200 years, from Koch's comments on C. P. E. Bach and Mozart and Schumann's on Ignaz Moscheles through to the proliferation of twentieth-century references by composers, critics and performers as diverse as Donald Tovey, Elliot Carter, Joseph Kerman and Glenn Gould.[12] For Carl Dahlhaus, solo–orchestra dialogue is 'a sine qua non of the traditional concerto movement'.[13]

Symphonic dimensions to concertos, as recognized by nineteenth-century writers, also depend upon protracted interaction between the soloist and the orchestra (albeit not necessarily of a co-operative kind) and prominent roles for the orchestra. Whereas in 1800 a writer for the *Allgemeine musikalische Zeitung* (presumably the editor Friedrich Rochlitz) distinguishes Mozart's symphonies and concertos on account of the 'grandeur' of the former and the 'intimacy' (close to the spirit of his quartets) of the latter,[14] subsequent critics draw attention in a positive way to the symphonic attributes of concertos. Thus, nineteenth-century French writers praise Henri Litolff for 'absorbing the virtuoso', which duly 'gained, rather than lost, in power' in his *Concerto symphonique* No. 4, Op. 102, and Brahms for a 'greater fusion within the whole' in the Piano Concerto No. 1 that results in 'a more elevated musical interest than the technical feats which are the essence of the non-symphonic concerto'.[15]

At the heart of orchestral involvement in concertos is the issue of *how* they interact with the soloist(s), of what the interaction of the protagonists represents in anthropomorphic terms. Ultimately, the rich hermeneutic tradition in regard to solo–orchestra relations has its origins in the uncertain etymology of the term 'concerto', which derives in all likelihood from the Latin *concertare* (to agree, act together), the Italian *concertare* (to compete, contend), or the Latin *conserere* (to consort).[16] Embracing this ontological imprecision brings to the fore contrasting co-operative and competitive types of interaction. Critics in the eighteenth century, for example, are collectively attuned to both types of motivation. Johann Mattheson (1713) describes a scenario whereby 'each part in turn comes to prominence and vies, as it were, with the other parts', subsequently (1739) drawing attention to the 'contest, from which all concertos get their name',[17] Johann Gottfried Walther speaks of the 'rivalry' between concerto protagonists[18] and Augustus Frederick Christopher Kollmann (1799) suggests that the concerto is capable of representing the kind of confrontation witnessed in C. P. E. Bach's famous trio sonata, 'A Conversation between a Cheerful Man and a Melancholy Man'.[19] Other eighteenth-century critics, in contrast, paint pictures of collaboration, Johann Joachim Quantz (1752) explaining that each orchestral participant 'must regulate himself in all cases by the execution of the soloist, ... always do his share' and yield to the soloist's tempo when he or she 'gives a sign to that effect' and Heinrich Koch (1793) identifying sentiments such as 'approval', 'acceptance', 'commiseration' and 'comfort' on the part of the orchestra.[20] Confrontation tends to dominate nineteenth-century discourse on interaction and is often linked to the symphonic qualities of concertos. Thus, Joseph Hellmesberger and Bronislaw Hubermann debate whether Brahms's Violin Concerto, Op. 77, is *for* the orchestra and *against* the soloist or vice versa (Hubermann suggests that the violin 'wins'), and Maurice Bourges argues that Beethoven's Piano Concerto No. 4 in G is *against* the soloist on account of the orchestra's 'sudden interruptions' and brusque curtailment of solo passages.[21] In a letter to Nadezhda von Meck from 1880, Tchaikovsky offers a famously uncompromising interpretation of solo–orchestra confrontation in the piano concerto. Maintaining that the tone of the piano renders it incapable of blending with that of the orchestra, he identifies

> two forces possessed of equal rights, i.e. the powerful, inexhaustibly richly coloured orchestra, with which there struggles and over which there triumphs (given a talented performer) a small, insignificant but strong-minded rival. In this struggle there is much poetry and a whole mass of enticing combinations of sound for the composer ... To my mind, the piano can be effective in only three situations: (1) alone, (2) in a contest with the orchestra, (3) as accompaniment, i.e. the background of a picture.[22]

Virtuosity and the interaction of the soloist and orchestra in twentieth-century writings

Twentieth-century writings continue to focus on themes prevalent in the nineteenth century. Criticisms of excessive virtuosity are not uncommon even in scholarly discourse of the last thirty years or so: John Warrack talks disparagingly, for example, of the 'finger music of [Weber's] First [Piano] Concerto and its passages in which the virtuoso is clearly meant to be seen at least as much as heard'.[23] Equally, critics are often eager to stress that a particular work transcends the status of straightforward, solo-dominated display piece; thus, in Schumann's Violin Concerto, 'Specific virtuoso styles ... are not invoked for their own sake, but are rather put to the service of a specific musical function' and in Dvořák's Cello Concerto, the composer's intentions are not 'to dazzle' but rather 'focused much more on the expansion of timbre and the interaction between the cello and the other instruments'.[24] On the whole, however, recent scholarship is marked by a greater receptivity to the aesthetic virtues of virtuosity than in earlier scholarly eras; a good case in point is Joseph Kerman's careful broadening of the concept to include *virtù*, with its constituent bravura, mimetic and spontaneous qualities.[25]

Not surprisingly, given the diversification of the genre to include works such as concertos for orchestra, twentieth-century composers and critics also put significant emphasis – like their nineteenth-century counterparts – on the symphonic dimension of works. Karol Szymanowski writes that his Violin Concerto No. 1, Op. 35, is 'really ... a symphonic work for quite large orchestra with solo violin'.[26] Bartók describes his Concerto for Orchestra as 'symphony-like' and David Cooper claims it can be situated in the nineteenth-century symphonic tradition.[27] Georges Enescu baldly describes Beethoven's Violin Concerto as 'a great symphony. The violin has a leading voice, but it is merely one of the many orchestral voices which make up the whole.'[28] And Sibelius explains a Prokofiev violin concerto (probably No. 1) as 'a symphonic unity where the violin plays a subordinate role'.[29] While the origins and development of the symphonic concerto remain a matter of scholarly debate – Dahlhaus goes against the grain, for example, in considering it 'foolish' to describe Beethoven's concertos as precursors and Schumann's as prototypes[30] – neither its important generic status nor its implications for prominent orchestral involvement and interaction with the soloist(s) are in doubt. Even those who disapprove of symphonic characteristics in concertos (in both the nineteenth and the twentieth centuries) clarify that the balance of soloist(s) and orchestra – and by implication their interaction – is paramount: Carl Czerny, likening the orchestra to 'inferior objects in a picture, which are merely introduced for the purpose of setting the principal object in a clearer light' counsels against 'an overladen accompaniment' since it 'only creates confusion, and the most brilliant passages of the pianist are then lost'; Donald Tovey is adamant that the opening orchestral section of a Classical concerto 'remains truly a ritornello and does not merge into pure symphonic writing' but also maintains that this section prevents the orchestra from seeming 'unnaturally repressed' after the entry of the soloist, transcending mere 'support'; and Sibelius dislikes the symphonic qualities of Prokofiev ('Quite the opposite of my view') on account of the subordination of the soloist.[31]

In a similar fashion to their nineteenth-century predecessors, twentieth-century composers and critics regularly highlight contrast, conflict and struggle in the concerto, imbuing these types of interaction with symbolic social significance.[32] Thus, Richard Strauss describes his Cello Concerto, which survives only as sketches for a three-movement work (1935/6), as a 'struggle of the artistic spirit [the cello] against pseudo-heroism, resignation, melancholy [the orchestra]', and John Cage explains his Concerto for Prepared Piano and Chamber Orchestra (1950–1) as an opposition of 'the piano, which remains romantic, expressive, and the orchestra, which itself follows the principles of oriental philosophy', simultaneously representing the contrasting phenomena of control and freedom.[33] Nicky Losseff's explanation of the broad-ranging musical and social significance of confrontation and opposition in the concerto – supporting and supported by the long-standing tradition of anthropomorphic description of interaction – reflects a substantial body of twentieth-century opinion: 'The dualities and oppositions inherent in the virtuoso piano concerto makes it the most suitable genre in which to explore the struggle of subjectivity against the external world, since the encounter between lone soloist and orchestra is in more than one sense representative of conflict: between the single, elite individual and the group, and between a single instrumental part which yet constitutes "half" of the music against the very large collection of colours and timbres which collectively form its complement'.[34] In a description from 1974 of his Concerto for Orchestra, Elliott Carter returns to the idea of contrasting types of interaction co-existing in a work, again assigning social significance to the roles of the orchestral protagonists. Explaining that he '[extends] to the orchestra the kind of individualization of instruments ... tried for the four players of [the] Second Quartet', in which individuals in the group 'are related to each other in what might be metaphorically termed three forms of responsiveness: discipleship, companionship and confrontation', Carter '[treats] the orchestra as a crowd of individuals, each having his own personal expression'.[35]

Twentieth-century theories of solo–orchestra interaction and its social significance, however, are not limited to *ad hoc* commentary. Anglophone critics have paid serious scholarly attention to the hermeneutic and semantic resonance of concerto interaction since Donald Tovey's seminal essay 'The Classical Concerto' from 1903. With characteristic eloquence, Tovey links the oppositional nature of the concerto to a compelling social scenario:

> Nothing in human life and history is much more thrilling or of more ancient
> and universal experience than the antithesis of the individual and the crowd;
> an antithesis which is familiar in every degree, from flat opposition to
> harmonious reconciliation, and with every contrast and blending of emotion,
> and which has been of no less universal prominence in works of art than in life.[36]

Solo–orchestra interaction is inherently dramatic for Tovey, since the concerto itself is a 'highly dramatic and poetic art form'.[37] Thus, the soloist '[thrusts] the orchestra into the background, while at the same time the orchestra has ... its say and need not seem unnaturally repressed as it probably would seem (supposing it to be at all powerful) if it were employed only to support the solo'. In short, 'the solo should first be inclined to enter into dialogue with the orchestra – the speaker should conciliate the crowd before he breaks into monologue'.[38]

Like Tovey, later writers on concerto interaction recognize the powerful dramatic impact and the historical and contextual significance of solo–orchestra interaction in eighteenth-century repertories such as Bach's Brandenburg Concertos and Mozart's piano concertos.[39] (Analogies with drama, for Mozart's works at least, extend back to the late eighteenth and nineteenth centuries as well, finding their original inspiration in Koch's aforementioned descriptions of dialogue in the Classical concerto, which he likens to that of ancient tragedy.[40]) Two recent, socially motivated readings of Mozart's concertos, by Susan McClary and Joseph Kerman, are especially provocative (and problematic). Both explain piano/orchestra relations in metaphorical terms – Kerman as 'a composite metaphor for Mozart and his audience and *their* relationship' and McClary as 'a soloist and a large communal group, the orchestra ... [enacting] as a spectacle the dramatic tensions between individual and society'[41] – but fail to marshal convincing stylistic and historical evidence in support. Kerman regards the Piano Concerto No. 24 in C minor, K. 491, as a 'deeply subversive work' where 'power relations are in doubt', concluding by implication that Mozart must have felt alienated from his audience at this stage.[42] But Mozart finished K. 491 on 24 March 1786, only three weeks after completing his less demonstrative Piano Concerto No. 23 in A, K. 488, a work that surely upholds Kerman's 'tacit contract'[43] between composer and audiences; thus, a fundamental shift in Mozart's mindset in the short intervening period is unlikely. Moreover, the highly sophisticated solo–orchestra dialogue in the solo exposition and recapitulation sections of K. 491/i and powerful confrontation in bars 330–45 of the development are better understood as intensifications of pre-existent processes of exchange from his thirteen preceding Viennese piano concertos (1782–6), rather than as departures from his stylistic *modus operandus*.[44] McClary also allows metaphorical interpretation to cloud analytical judgement, overstating her claim for piano/orchestra opposition in K. 453/ii. In order to recognize the piano after the pauses in bars 33–4 as either 'the individual voice, heroic in its opposition to the collective orchestral force' or 'flamboyant, theatrical, indulgent in its mode of self-presentation',[45] for example, we have to overlook the co-operative dialogue in which they engage moments later (bars 42–7). Similarly, McClary's interpretations of the beginning of the recapitulation – 'Just at the moment at which the soloist seemed hopelessly lost in despair, the orchestra valiantly salvages the situation, returns the piece to the comfort of "rationality"' and 'It could just as easily seem ... that the organic necessities of the individual are blatantly sacrificed to the overpowering requirements of social convention' – rest on her questionable claim that the tonic C major is the product of an 'irrational' modulatory process in the orchestra (bars 86–90).[46] In fact, the modulation from C sharp to C is achieved with arpeggiated material that grows directly from the end of the piano's preceding phrase (bar 186) – suggesting 'rational' engagement with, not disengagement from, the soloist – and with an entirely comprehensible $G\sharp - g\sharp - E^7$ $(III^7) - G^7$ $(V^7) - C$ (I) chord progression.[47] Ultimately, Kerman's and McClary's articles offer a salutary lesson: socially charged readings of concertos, while true to the prevailing spirit of anthropomorphic interpretation, only hold scholarly water if supported by sufficiently nuanced analytical, stylistic and contextual arguments.

Kerman offers a more protracted, and more satisfying, account of the concerto genre – with interaction at its core – in his book, *Concerto Conversations*.[48] Proceeding empirically rather than systematically, he usefully explains and sets in musical context phenomena associated with interaction such as 'particularity', 'the distinctive characteristics of the solo and the orchestra in any particular context', 'polarity', a type of 'duality' in which engagement between protagonists is lacking, and 'reciprocity', marked by solo–orchestra engagement and by processes of 'replay', 'counterplay' and 'coplay'.[49] But his critical acceptance of a plethora of possible roles for soloist and orchestra that includes 'eavesdropper, tease, survivor, victim, mourner or pleurant, minx, lover, critic, editor', and that provokes a free-wheeling 'relationship story' for Tchaikovsky's Violin Concerto, gives pause for thought.[50] Is the identification and application of a wide range of roles for concerto participants a legitimate hermeneutic practice in the present scholarly era, when not accompanied by thorough consideration of the historical, contextual or critical implications of each role? Critical justification of distinctions between types of solo–orchestra behaviour – especially finely refined types – provides a formidable challenge. But the rigorous explanation and justification of concepts and phenomena used to describe solo–orchestra interaction is surely one of the pressing hermeneutic concerns for twenty-first-century concerto criticism. Advances in this area will ensure the continued relevance of creative, anthropomorphic interpretation to scholarly debate.

Theories of form in the Classical concerto

The most popular topic in critical discourse on concertos – especially those of the late eighteenth and early nineteenth centuries – is first-movement form. While formal designations have varied considerably over the last 200 years, formal theories have remained closely linked to the underlying aesthetic currents of concerto criticism discussed above. This is especially apparent in explanations of works from the Classical period, a crucial juncture in the aesthetic and formal history of the genre encapsulating both the emergence of the concerto as a credible aesthetic force after overwhelming critical condemnation and the vivid confluence of old and modern formal practices (ritornello and sonata).

Formal descriptions of the first movements of Classical concertos often recognize, implicitly or explicitly, a hybrid of sonata and ritornello structures. In the late eighteenth century, Koch, the era's most influential writer on instrumental form, identifies four ritornello and three solo sections that appear alternately (three ritornellos and two solos in the later *Musikalisches Lexikon* of 1802), equating the latter with the three principal sections of a symphonic movement (designated exposition, development and recapitulation in the nineteenth century).[51] Two hundred years later, most critics still write in a similar way, freely combining ritornello and sonata designations. A good case in point is Daniel N. Leeson and Robert D. Levin's intelligent codification of Mozart's piano concerto first movements into opening ritornello, solo exposition, middle ritornello, development, recapitulation, ritornello-to-cadenza and final ritornello sections.[52] In between, a predominantly symphonic conception of concerto form takes root. Beginning in the mid-nineteenth century with Carl Czerny's inference of close thematic correspondences between the first tutti and first solo sections and Adolf Bernard Marx's appropriation of sonata and first-movement concerto forms, and culminating at the end of the century with Ebenezer Prout's interpretation of the first two sections as a 'double exposition',[53] formal theories are closely aligned with general commentary on the symphonic attributes of works.

Above all, descriptions of first-movement concerto form have consistently overlapped with perceptions of solo–orchestra interaction in the concerto and with emphasis placed upon the active involvement of the orchestra. Two of the earliest writers on concerto form, Quantz (1752) and Joseph Riepel (1755), encourage judicious inclusion of small-scale tuttis in solo sections – as well as describing large-scale ritornello–solo alternation – thus implicitly acknowledging lively solo–orchestra interaction: Quantz writes that 'The best ideas of the ritornello must be dismembered, and intermingled during or between the solo passages'; and Riepel advocates the inclusion of fragmented or altered versions of ritornello motifs in solo sections.[54] Riepel's admission that he 'now and again . . . [borrows] a few measures from the solo, that is, measures that have already been heard in the solo'[55] to begin the second tutti also points towards a transmission of material from soloist to orchestra that will result in active exchange between protagonists. In a similar vein to Quantz and Riepel, Kollmann (1799) suggests that the first solo 'is occasionally relieved by short Tuttis, to keep up the grandeur of the piece',[56] imbuing orchestral involvement in this section with a vital function. Koch formalizes this kind of orchestral participation as fervent solo–orchestra interaction: 'As a segment of the whole . . . [the orchestra] is involved in the passionate dialogue and has the right to show its feelings concerning the main part through short phrases. To this end, these voices do not always wait for the conclusion of the incise or phrase in the principal part, but throughout its performance may be heard alternately in brief imitations.'[57] Thus, 'passionate dialogue' comprises both evolving solo–orchestra relations across a concerto as a whole – 'Now in the allegro it tries to stimulate his noble feelings still more; now it commiserates, now it comforts him in the adagio'[58] – and immediate give and take in individual solo sections.

Two of the most influential twentieth-century Anglophone writers on the Classical concerto, Tovey and Rosen, also draw attention to the interdependence of formal shape and solo–orchestra interaction and relationships. Tovey explains that the first-movement arrangement of an opening ritornello section for the orchestra followed by a section highlighting the soloist is musically and affectively intuitive, since it 'brings out the force of the solo in thrusting the orchestra into the background'.[59] The forms of the concerto, moreover, express the antithesis of individual and crowd 'with all possible force and delicacy'.[60] For Rosen, 'the latent pathetic nature of the form' comprises 'the contrast and struggle of one individual voice against many'; furthermore, the 'dynamic contrast between soloist and orchestra' best exhibited in Mozart's and Beethoven's works contains many 'formal and coloristic possibilities'.[61]

Tovey and Rosen's discussion of form as it relates to the role of the orchestra also resonates with earlier writings on the Classical concerto in the formal and affective function assigned to the initial orchestral ritornello/exposition. Both critics argue that it is a predominantly preparatory section; it has 'much the effect of an *introduction*' for Tovey and 'always conveys an introductory atmosphere' for Rosen since what is 'most important ... about concerto form is that the audience waits for the soloist to enter, and when he stops playing they wait for him to begin again'.[62] Introductory qualities have been assigned to this section from the late eighteenth century onwards,[63] but rarely in a way that downplays its formal significance. In fact, this orchestral section fulfils an essential role in introducing the content of the movement. As Koch asks rhetorically, implicitly recognizing its structural importance: 'does not the first ritornello of a concerto have just the same relationship with the contents of the solo part as the introduction of a speech with its contents?'[64] Critics such as Kollmann who demand concision – 'nothing should be introduced in it, but Subjects or Passages, which are to be elaborated in the course of the movement' – also acknowledge that the section as a whole has a vital formal function, exhibiting 'the number and sort of instruments that shall be used in the Concerto; and ... [impressing] on the ear of the hearer the Key and Mode, the principal Subjects and the Character of the Movement'.[65] The 'double-exposition' theoretical model, moreover, could be interpreted as the initial orchestral section transcending its introductory function, even assuming the status of 'primary' exposition.[66]

One recent interpretation of first-movement form in the Classical concerto, dividing it into four main periods '[articulated] into a hierarchy of parts' in line with Koch's theory of 'punctuation', explains that the first orchestral section (period one), subsequent solo section (period two), and recapitulation (period four) can be thought of as a tripartite narrative in which 'the orchestra tells the story as it knows it', the soloist then 'tells his version' and the soloist and orchestra finally 'reconcile and synthesize their two versions'.[67] Irrespective of how we understand the formal significance of the orchestra's initial section, it would seem that concerto form actively encourages this kind of narratological speculation, just as solo–orchestra interaction encourages anthropomorphic interpretation. The rich hermeneutic potential that derives from the synergy of form and interaction in the Classical concerto – and from analogous synergies in earlier and later works as well – will no doubt ensure enlightening and provocative interpretations of concertos, as well as of their aesthetic and theoretical foundations, for generations to come.

2 The concerto and society

TIA DENORA

As something 'that people do',[1] music shapes and takes shape in relation to the social settings where it is produced, distributed and consumed. Within those settings, music may provide exemplars and resources for the constitution of extra-musical matters. Through the confluence of performance and reception, musicking makes and partakes of values, ideas and tacit or practical notions about the social whole, agency and social relations; in this respect, music is an active ingredient of social life.[2]

The concerto – the form par excellence of *contrast* – provides a useful case in point for socio-musical exploration. Following its vicissitudes will reveal music's role as a medium of social values and as a medium enabled and constrained by practical, conventional, material and organizational factors. This chapter explores the concerto and its link to society from two interrelated perspectives, the focus on local and pragmatic features of musicking and music's role as a meaningful medium and a medium of social change. I use three case studies to explore the concerto's social features, in especial relation to the keyboard concerto – Bach's Brandenburg No. 5, Mozart's career as a concerto composer/performer in 1780s Vienna, and Beethoven's innovations in keyboard performance and their connections to the gendering of the repertory during the early nineteenth century.

Case study one: Bach's Brandenburg Concerto No. 5

J. S. Bach's six Brandenburg Concertos, written separately but collected as a set and dedicated to Christian Ludwig, Elector of Margrave, Brandenburg, in 1721, constitute a milestone in the concerto's history,[3] not least because of the degree of virtuosity they displayed and demanded of the players. The fifth Brandenburg, for a combination of flute, violin and harpsichord, merits special attention, not only because it 'marks the beginning of the harpsichord concerto as a form'[4] but because it opens up a range of themes within music sociology. It has already been the subject of socio-cultural analysis[5] and this account can be used as a springboard for further exploration of the concerto as a social medium.

The stylistic strategies Bach appropriated in this work, Susan McClary argues, can be read as embodying social values.[6] In particular, his adoption of the Italian concerto style, via Vivaldi, makes greatest use of what McClary sees as the bourgeois properties of tonality more generally ('values … held most dear by the middle class: belief in progress, in expansion, in the ability to attain ultimate goals through rational striving, in the ingenuity of the individual strategist operating both within and in defiance of the norm') so as to depict and celebrate values associated with the new individualism ('virtuosity, dissonance and extravagant dynamic motion').[7]

In Brandenburg No. 5, which begins ostensibly as a concerto for flute and violin, the harpsichord is initially presented as a 'darkhorse competitor for the position of soloist'.[8] During the course of the first movement, the harpsichord comes to occupy an extreme foreground position in the extended cadenza ('delivered by a frenzied continuo instrument'),[9] the longest cadenza then known, lasting roughly a quarter of the entire movement's length. As McClary puts it: '[T]he harpsichord, which first serves as continuo support … then begins to compete with the soloists for attention … and finally overthrows the other forces in a kind of hijacking of the piece'.[10]

McClary's essay illustrates an interesting and important analytical approach to the Concerto–Society topic, namely, narrative analysis. She considers in particular the disruption of convention, represented by the prominence of the harpsichord as a solo instrument (the harpsichord had hitherto played the background role of continuo, namely blending into the background to provide harmonic and rhythmic stability). By bringing this 'service' instrument to the limelight and allowing it to indulge in 'one of the most outlandish displays in music history',[11] Bach, McClary argues, musically presents (and in an extreme form) then-emerging notions of individual freedom of expression:

> In the eighteenth century, most musical genres testify to a widespread interest in integrating the best of both those worlds into one in which social harmony and individual expression are mutually compatible. The concerto, the new formalized opera aria, and the later sonata procedure all are motivated by this interest.[12]

As McClary observes – and this is at the heart of her semiotic method – the strategies of an individual piece (such as in Brandenburg No. 5) can only be perceived as significant if they are held against a backdrop of musical norms and conventions. Such a method, she observes, is:

> both ad hoc … and dialectical in so far as its strategies take shape in relation to the specific demands of particular compositions and in so far as the method seeks to account for the ways that particular compositions relate to the norms and conventions that enable and constrain the compositional process.[13]

All methods of analysis reveal and conceal, and semiotic methods are by no means immune to this predicament. The semiotic toolkit consists of a catalogue of conventions, an understanding of the history of ideas, politics, economics and some astute interpretative observation. At the same time, the analytic strategy of reading musical works may promote a kind of theorizing that is disconnected from the *actual* mechanisms through which music plays a mediating role in social life. Elsewhere, I have suggested that semiotics is useful but not sufficient as a method of socio-musical analysis and that semiotic analytical strategies occupy what the novelist and philosopher Iris Murdoch has described as 'a wrong level of generality',[14] one that foregrounds analytical concepts such as style, compositional strategy and idea but leaves in shadow the rather more 'down-home', and more overtly sociological, matters of music's material culture and physical practice, custom and local meanings, networks, occupational worlds and structures, and pragmatic and mundane matters.[15]

In short, reading music for its ideological content implies a conception of the music–society nexus in terms of homological relationships between *macro* historical trends and developments in musical *works*. However, social life (for example, what Bach did in Brandenburg No. 5) happens in the here-and-now and is embedded in local conditions. It is at this *local* level that large-scale social trends are *mediated* by what is 'do-able'[16] – by material culture, by the specific concerns of patrons and other local contextual issues such as occasion and dedicatee, and by an individual composer's particular appropriation of ideas, models and working materials.

In short, there is no one-to-one connection between musical forms and the world of ideas (for how does the genie of 'The Social' actually get into the music and how, even more complicatedly, does the music inform the social – what are the *mechanisms*?). Rather, there are always a multiplicity of connections and possibilities and it is only at this level of actual doing that what we describe as social structure is produced and reproduced.[17] The particular pathway through these possibilities taken by a particular composer at a particular time is thus shot through with layers of significance that cannot be reduced to the history of ideas. It is only through an appreciation of the myriad conditions of a work's genesis (and regenesis via performance, reception, scholarship and other cultural practices) that it is possible to begin to describe how it is *actually* linked to society.

Again, Brandenburg No. 5 provides a case-in-point. Looking closely at the specific features of Bach and the local musical worlds in which he operated extends our understanding of music–society connections by helping to explain why, *in this case*, Bach came to position the harpsichord so prominently in the musical limelight.

Prior to his move to Cöthen, Bach's experience at Arnstadt (1703–7), Mülhausen (1707–8) and Weimar (1708–17) was – in both church and court contexts – as an organist. As such, Bach was intimately acquainted with musical instrument technology. He was frequently called upon, for example, to test new organs, such as the one in Halle in 1716 about which, in company with Johann Kuhnau and Christian Friedrich Rolle, he produced a highly detailed report.[18] Bach was also familiar with the convention of dedicating a new instrument; he was present for the dedication of the Halle organ (two weeks after the report was filed), and he served as the soloist at other organ dedications.

On such occasions, flamboyant display was *de rigueur*, so as to display the instrument's capacities and, as a by-product of that primary display, inevitably also the capabilities of the performer. Also, during these years just prior to the composition of Brandenburg No. 5, musical skill was conceived as a kind of sport; Bach took part or was scheduled to take part in various musical tournaments for the amusement of aristocratic patrons. Improvisation would be fundamental to both types of occasion and, of course, Bach was a master improviser, praised by virtually all who came into contact with his art.

> Enter the arrival of a new harpsichord in 1719:
> On 1 March 1719 Bach travelled to Berlin to acquire a splendid new harpsichord for the Köthen court – 'The great harpsichord or Flügel with two keyboards, by Michael Mietke'. It has been suggested that he may have had this instrument in mind when he conceived two of his most brilliant harpsichord works – Brandenburg Concerto No. 5 in D major BWV 1050, and the Chromatic Fantasia and Fugue in D minor BWV 903. . . . According to Forkel, 'When he played from his fancy, all the 24 keys were in his power. . . . All his extempore fantasies are said to have been of a similar description'.[19]

Christoph Wolff has also suggested that Brandenburg No. 5 was written to inaugurate the new harpsichord, as has Malcolm Boyd, who reasons that, '[p]ossibly it was with this new and unprecedentedly elaborate cadenza that Bach celebrated the arrival of the new instrument from Berlin'.[20]

Bach spent a good deal of time in Berlin negotiating for the new harpsichord (between June 1718 and March 1719). During this time he played for and came to know Christian Ludwig, Elector of Margrave, to whom Bach dedicated the Brandenburg Concertos in 1721. The harpsichord would have loomed large for Bach during this phase of his life and it seems reasonable to suggest that it would have loomed not only as a 'dark horse' figure in Concerto No. 5 (possibly the last to have been composed)[21] but behind the entire set on which he worked during these years.

In this context, and bearing in mind Bach's intimate knowledge of keyboard instrument technology, the predominant display of the harpsichord no longer seems, in McClary's terms, 'deviant' but rather, within the musical culture of Bach's world, appears as a fitting practice, one devoted to celebrating the new instrument. This would have been even more the case if the first performance were indeed the instrument's 'inauguration', where an extended unaccompanied frenzy would allow the instrument to be put through its paces (simultaneously allowing Bach, who apparently premièred the work, to display his own abilities). And indeed, the *type of frenzy* in that extended cadenza (numerous scales up and down the keyboard, the chromatic passages) seems precisely to place on public trial the instrument's capacities, testing its entire range. Set against the 'self-contained' character of the ritornello,[22] this trial is made ever more celebratory, entirely fitting, in other words, for the local occasion. And the otherwise inexplicable way in which the cadenza 'blurs almost entirely the sense of key'[23] also makes good local sense, displaying the instrument from the full gamut of harmonic perspectives.

In sum, one can imagine how Bach took advantage, in this case, of an emerging rhetorical strategy (the solo concerto), gave it a new twist (as a keyboard concerto) that was charged with a frisson (that unruly keyboard!) in a way that was wholly appropriate and meaningful as an occasioning device under the local conditions of musical culture at Cöthen. The form that emerged from these local circumstances, practices and resources was eventually bequeathed as a 'work' that could be read (by variously located readers) as historically significant (for example, McClary's reading). To provide a reading, however, is to engage in situated meaning-making. It is also a very different activity from the gathering of information about the local environment of production, distribution and reception/use.

In short, as the music sociologist Antoine Hennion has observed, by merely reading musical works we risk providing just one more in 'a long line of Bach interpretations'.[24] (Indeed, music criticism can be understood as involved in the *performance* of meaning.[25]) By contrast, we need to consider works from a range of perspectives including: cultural trends (new rhetorics, values, devices, discourses); large-scale events (including natural disasters, political change, economic developments); features of the worlds[26] in which music is made (conventions, technology, support personnel, funding, performance practices, reputation, distribution structures); local events (occasions, situations, news, local history, events); and reception (time after time as the meaning of works is recursively established and modified, in their own time and later, by musicians, critics, scholars, listeners, patrons and others). In short, the question of 'how' musical meaning is possible needs to focus on the complexity of situated meaning production and the status of this production as a form of interpretative 'work',[27] that is as culture creation. Such an approach has affinities with the study of the everyday and with ethnography of history and cultural experience.

Case study two: occupational structure and local Enlightenment culture in Mozart's Vienna

During the eighteenth century concert life was transformed across Europe. This transformation involved a shift from private to public funding for music. In Vienna and the German-speaking lands, the old Hauskapelle (house ensemble) was abandoned and musicians increasingly had to build careers in a nascent freelance economy.[28] This inevitably involved compiling an income from teaching and touring, private commissions and private concertizing in the salons, and from benefit concerts. The new system meant that reputation took on heightened salience – to live, and to have enough work, a musician had to become known. As Moore has observed, this shift towards a 'star system' worked well for some musicians, some of the time.[29] However, it was antithetical to most musicians, most of the time.

For a while, during the 1780s, the system worked well for Mozart. In 1784, describing a series of highly successful subscription concerts, he wrote exuberantly to his father: 'The first concert ... went off very well. The hall was overflowing; and the new concerto [possibly K. 449] I played won extraordinary applause. Everywhere I go I hear praises of that concert.'[30]

Next to opera, the piano concerto was one of 'the two worlds in which Mozart was supremely predominant' during these, his 'golden years'.[31] Between 1782 and December 1786, Mozart introduced a total of fifteen concertos to the Viennese public, nearly all of which he premièred himself. This was his heyday for the piano concerto (he subsequently introduced only two more between 1787 and 1791).

This choice was first of all pragmatic. Johann Schönfeld's *Jahrbuch*[32] lists 167 virtuoso and amateur performers. Of these, seventy (41 per cent) were keyboard players. During the 1780s the keyboard was a 'hot' instrument: it was undergoing technological development as keyboard artists increasingly used it as a means for display. (During the 1760s and 1770s the most popular instruments for concerto treatment were the violin and flute.[33]) It was also an instrument of conspicuous consumption (expensive and like a piece of furniture) and, related to this, an aristocratic instrument. To distinguish oneself as a keyboard virtuoso was simultaneously to enhance one's chance of recruiting wealthy pupils. In addition, one can find signs of a growing trend towards musical display all over Europe during these years. As Morrow has observed, concertos were the 'central showcase' within which musicians' talents could be displayed.[34] 'For Beethoven as for J. C. Bach, Mozart and Clementi before him and Hummel, Moscheles, and Liszt after him', writes Leon Plantinga, 'the concerto was mainly a personal vehicle for the composer-virtuoso's performances, a means for displaying new musical ideas of which a central feature was his own distinctive style of playing'.[35]

In Josephinian Vienna, *c*.1784, the 'new musical ideas' elaborated in the concerto genre resonated with new, 'enlightened' ideas and practices – liberalism, toleration, the suppression of aristocratic powers (via a refusal to rule through the Hungarian and Bohemian Diets),[36] the lifting of censorship and, to some degree, economic resurgence. All of these ideas were forcefully promulgated by writers such as Josef Sonnenfels and his notion of the 'mittleren Klassen', whose desires and aspirations could, with care, be aligned with the needs of the state. In short, it is in Mozart's Vienna that we can observe a prime example of what has been termed the emergence of the public sphere.[37]

Central to the Enlightenment notion of the public sphere was the idea that individual will could be brought into convergence with (be constructed as) public opinion, via various forms of discussion and cultural persuasion. It is during this period, throughout Europe, that social thinkers (Locke and Rousseau, for example) began to concern themselves with the concept of moral, as opposed to political, law. Echoing Rousseau, Sonnenfels wrote: 'the most important aim is to ensure the uniting of the individual with the general good … through which the individual citizen is bonded to society as a whole, bringing the understanding of the honourable citizen to enlightenment, and at the same time ensuring that his own desires are met'.[38]

It is at this time that the arts, in particular those art forms that depicted action and experience over time (as opposed to the static arts of painting and sculpture), took on a new social function, the moulding not so much of public opinion, but of two other Enlightenment inventions, subjectivity and the self. As George Eliot came to put it, some time later and in reference to a fictional character, 'Hetty had never read a novel: how then could she find a shape for her expectations?'[39] In the late eighteenth century numerous fictional and non-fictional pamphlets were produced and circulated, in which the individual's role was modelled. Similarly, in the dramatic arts, and, perhaps most kinaesthetically, in opera, social relations were performed for widening audiences, and for some of these less literate audiences, the performing arts would have been the primary contact with the new imagery – models – of agency and social being. This imagery was Rousseauian; it depicted an individual who, via his desires and passions, could be bound to the needs and structures of the whole.

One of Mozart's most significant contributions to the history of the concerto was his conceptualization of the relationship between soloist and orchestra. From 1784 onwards technical difficulties increase, enhancing the drama of the form. Also at this time the orchestra comes to be used in a wider variety of ways than hitherto, as Simon P. Keefe has observed, sometimes in dialogue with the soloist, via individual instruments and collectively.[40]

Thus the concerto – the form of figure–ground, solo–tutti – was a highly charged form, one that was produced and received as an object lesson in new forms of agency. '[I]t is not fanciful', Till observes, 'to hear in Mozart's piano concertos a representation of this dynamic relationship; a progressive dialogue between the individual expressive voice of the soloist and the wider "community" of the orchestra, the former distinguished from the latter, yet frequently drawing from the same fountainhead of ideas, and both ultimately uniting in joyous unanimity'.[41]

As Keefe has observed, the concerto was much more than a metaphor, whether for Mozart's audiences or for the readings provided by today's music analysts and critics. Understood in the context of dramatic theory as circulating in Mozart's Vienna, Mozart's concertos can be seen to provide templates against which knowledge about social relations could be produced.[42] They carried (or may be explored as having carried), in other words, intellectual significance for their recipients:

> Following every stage in the process of relational change in each movement would have been a highly demanding exercise for a contemporary listener; Mozart's concertos would certainly have provided a prime example of the kind of instrumental music that, according to Adam Smith, can 'occupy, and as it were fill up completely the whole capacity of the mind so as to leave no part of its attention vacant for thinking of anything else'. By engaging the listener in a challenging intellectual pursuit, Mozart offered him or her an excellent vehicle for learning about cooperation (or, more precisely, the quest for cooperation), a value deeply cherished in the age of Enlightenment. Mozart's concertos thus fulfilled the single most important requirement for all late-eighteenth century music and drama: the general instruction of the listener-spectator.[43]

In other words, music was not merely 'about' an abstract correlation between sonic structure and social structure. Rather, as we have seen in the case of Brandenburg No. 5 above, we risk, in Hennion's and Fauquet's words, providing yet another 'in a long line'[44] of interpretations if we confine our analytical attention to 'readings' of music's social significance. By contrast, a more nuanced understanding of music's connections to social structure and social action can be achieved by situating that analysis in the context of the music's contemporary contexts of production, distribution and consumption. Considering the interaction between musical practice and other cultural practices of the time and place is part of this project as is the often-overlooked topic of music's material practice. These topics are considered in the next case study.

Case study three: gendering the piano concerto

At a time when all music was performed live, musical performance was always, and at least implicitly, a visually dramatic event, one that inevitably involved bodily procedures, strictures about comportment and, at times, choreography. To speak of these matters is to deconstruct the technical neutrality of musical performance, and to recognize by contrast how musical performance may itself provide significant factors in the overall understanding of works and their perceived meanings. Here, much more than mere phrasing is at stake. More significantly, it is the performance *of* performance that is at issue. Music may, for example, make demands upon the body. It may be used by performers, as implicitly described above, for embodied display. In these respects, music performance is dramaturgical: the practices of performing may delineate various meanings.[45]

Circa 1800, there was probably no realm within musical performance as charged with social meaning as the keyboard. The piano in late eighteenth- and early nineteenth-century Vienna was at the heart of debates over aesthetic practice, a site at which new and often-competing aesthetics were deployed and defended, at times through the overt medium of the 'piano duel'.[46]

Enter Beethoven and the piano performing body. Using the Concert Calendars in Morrow's study of Viennese musical life as a database,[47] we can determine that between 1793 and 1810 – during which time Beethoven was perhaps the most frequently performed composer for fortepiano in Vienna – his works were performed most often by men: 79 per cent of performances of *all* his piano works were performed by men and 21 per cent by women; and 84 per cent of his concertos by men, 16 per cent by women. This contrasts dramatically with the proportion of male performances of Mozart: 26 per cent of all his piano works were given by men and 74 per cent by women; and 27 per cent of his concertos performed by men during the years 1787–1810 and 73 per cent by women.

Between 1803 and 1810 the number of performances of Beethoven's concertos was increasing. The number of performers who played his concertos (particularly after he retreated from performing them himself as his hearing failed) was also growing. And yet, there would appear to be no extant evidence of a female performance of a Beethoven concerto in Vienna after 1806 and before 1810, a time during which men increasingly took up his works. (Once a concerto was published, Beethoven tended not to perform it again himself.) Never before had women and men been divided within the piano repertory in this way, at a time when women continued to be active (Josepha Auernhammer, Frauline Kurzbeck, Baroness Ertmann, Countess Anna Marie Erdody and others were all featured on the concert stage at this time). Indeed, women would appear to have given as many and sometimes more performances of piano concertos than men during these years.

Why then, this segregation? Elsewhere I have suggested, tentatively, that Beethoven's music made new demands upon the piano performing body in terms of how it was to be performed – it required a more visceral keyboard approach, and more demonstrative physical action (the choreography associated with this action was sometimes lampooned as the century progressed).[48] For women, bodily composure was doubly important because of the risk not only of transgressing one's social status, but also one's femininity and propriety. Speaking of the oboe, for example, John Essex described it in 1722 as, 'too Manlike … [looking] indecent in a Woman's Mouth'.[49]

Thus, the physicality demanded by Beethoven's music was incompatible with late eighteenth-century piano technology. It was also in opposition to strictures about appropriate feminine comportment – whether at the piano or elsewhere. But it was linked to the ways in which Beethoven cast himself within the form. As Plantinga notes: 'In his concertos, Beethoven typically cast himself as a leader; the concerto was for him mainly a youthful preoccupation intimately bound up with his prowess and ambition as a public pianist'.[50]

In short, and delineated through the material-practical realm of piano performance, Beethoven's concertos introduced a new (visceral and heroic) role for the soloist and also provided an exemplar of a new type of individual and his (sic) relation to the social whole. Beethoven's concertos provided a vocabulary of gestures and a compendium of movement styles associated with powerful individualism and with struggle. In this respect he pioneered strategies later exploited by Liszt, Chopin and

Paganini. As Charles Rosen observes, describing the athletics of double-octave effects:

> The true invention of this kind of octave display – or at least, the first
> appearance of a long and relentlessly fortissimo page of unison octaves in
> both hands – is to be found in the opening movement of Beethoven's Emperor
> Concerto. It marks a revolution in keyboard sonority. . . . It is initially with the
> generation of composers that followed Beethoven that the performer must
> experience physical pain with such octaves, starting with Liszt.[51]

Speaking of how music in the nineteenth century came to involve a
'look' as well as sonority, Richard Leppert has suggested that, 'more than
ever before, performers' bodies, in the act of realizing music, also helped
to transliterate musical sound into musical meaning by means of the
sight – and sometimes spectacle – of their gestures, facial expressions
and general physicality'.[52]

Is it possible to explore more specifically the kind of meaning that the
material performance of Beethoven concertos helped to delineate? It is
worth pausing here to reconsider Kant and the ways in which his notion
of the sublime came to be linked to instrumental music in general, and to
Beethoven in particular during the early nineteenth century. As Christine
Battersby tells us, Kant's conception both of the sublime and of the genius
was gendered, something clarified only in his less central texts. As Kant
put it: 'Strivings and surmounted difficulties arouse admiration and
belong to the sublime. . . . Laborious learning or painful pondering,
even if a woman should greatly succeed in it, destroy the merits that are
proper to her sex.'[53]

As it was elaborated in and through musical performance practices,
the Beethoven imago came to be associated with a visual imagery. It also
resonated with new ideas about the connections between appearance and
social capacity and with configurations of social agency. At the same time,
not everyone could occupy the new socio-musical spaces that the
Beethoven imago implied. This is to say that the form of pianistic display
that came to be associated with heroism, and with the ability to resist
nature, was not only a masculine attribute but also one associated with a
particular kind of male performer. This imagery was consequential for
then-emerging conceptions of gender and sexual difference, for masculin-
ity as well as femininity.

This gender divide widened over the course of the nineteenth century
and throughout Europe as musical practice provided object lessons in
gender-linked modes of agency. As Katharine Ellis has described it, during
the nineteenth century musical life was increasingly characterized by,
'a stereotypically feminine world of decorative and sweetly plaintive

expression, contrasting with the gigantic outbursts of Beethoven or the dazzling virtuosity of Liszt and Thalberg'.[54] The new forms of musical display, and the agencies they implied, not only excluded women from the heart of the musical canon; they also celebrated a currency of bodily capital (appearance, physique, comportment and temperament) that was not equally available to all men. Indeed it is during these years and shortly later that the discourse of piano playing begins to engage in gender stereotyping, Kalkbrenner's music, for example, being described as requiring 'muscular power' (and thus essentially better suited to male performers) as opposed to the 'grace' required for the performance of Chopin's works.

Ellis observes, with regard to mid-nineteenth-century France, that female pianists were, 'caught in a web of conflicting ideas concerning the relative value of particular keyboard repertoires that were themselves gendered, either explicitly or implicitly'.[55] (Parisian critics during this period were concerned not only with repertory, but also with the use of the body, with feminine 'attitudes' at the keyboard and with what was considered to be the 'appropriate' level of acting in performance.) From the perspective of French observers, the chief problem with women on the concert stage c.1844–5 (a time in which there was an influx of female performers) was that the vision of a woman at the keyboard, engaging in showmanship and physical power, was in direct conflict with Parisian mores concerning feminine conduct (mores reinforced by the Napoleonic Code of 1804 but stretching back to Rousseau's 'Lettre à M. D'Alembert'). No woman was to make, as Ellis observes, 'a spectacle of herself'[56] and it was for this reason that women came to be associated with the 'sweeter' and more delicate music of earlier times.

In short, women came to be marginalized in relation to the canon as a result of Beethoven's incorporation into his concertos (as well as into his other piano works) of particular types of bodies and bodily habits. As the century waned, and musical discourse (and musical technology) further reinforced these notions, it is possible to see the gender segregation of musical life being institutionalized through discourse and performance practice. The concerto, c.1803–10, played a significant role in this process.

The late nineteenth century and beyond – future directions for socio-musical research

As a culturally 'live' or 'hot' form, the heyday of the concerto occurred during the nineteenth century. Over half of the concertos performed in Vienna between 1800 and 1810 were performed by musicians who were not their composers.[57] By the early twentieth century, the concerto was an institution of musical life, more a performer genre than a composer-performer genre, and the soloist–orchestra relationship has been explored in a wide variety of manners. Concerto strategies have ranged from emphasis on the whole orchestra, allowing each section a turn for display, to conflict between soloist and group, to forms that play with audiences' pre-conceptions of the solo-instrument's properties and also with conventions about a concerto's length.[58] The form has also been appropriated for comic effect, as in Kleinsinger's *Tubby the Tuba*, where a stereotypically 'clumsy' instrument is featured as soloist (in turn helping to illuminate the ways in which instruments and their musical assignment itself reproduces social stereotypes),[59] in the antics of Victor Borge and in pieces such as Leroy Anderson's *Typewriter Concerto*. At the same time, preference for flamboyant and dramatic solo forms has been cited as a marker of social standing, at least in Paris.[60]

Within music sociology directions for future research would include the following interrelated topics: performance practice, in particular how soloists employ various performing strategies as part of their on-going professional identity construction, and also for the production of other forms of identity – gender identity, class, race and age (and including attention to embodied conduct as described above and also decisions concerning phrasing, tempo, instrumentation);[61] solo competitions and the production of musical judgement; cinematic depictions of concerto performance, rehearsal or composition; listening practices and consumption patterns; further analysis of musical-critical discourse; and, finally, the ways in which the concerto may come to be 'active' in extra-musical realms, how it may be drawn into interaction with other cultural practices and thereby come to provide resources for knowledge production.[62]

PART TWO

The works

3 The Italian concerto in the late seventeenth and early eighteenth centuries

MICHAEL TALBOT

The early history of the concerto is intimately linked to the early history of the orchestra in the modern sense of that word: an ensemble in which each of the string parts is taken by several players. What instrumental compositions termed concerto written before 1700 have in common, despite their great variety of structure and style, is suitability for performance with doubled parts. This suitability was not – and should not today be misinterpreted as – an explicit compulsion to perform early concertos with massed strings, but it set the defining parameters. In brief, the nascent concerto acquired defining features that drew it apart from its parent genre, the sonata. By the first decade of the eighteenth century, it had made a sufficient impact on the musical scene to become the object of transcriptions for organ by J. S. Bach's cousin Johann Gottfried Walther. Bach continued the practice himself in the following decade, and the logical point of arrival was his *Italian Concerto*, published in 1735: a concerto for a solo instrument (two-manual harpsichord) that mimics a solo concerto for violin in every respect except scoring.

Much ink has been spilled over the etymology and semantic ramifications of the word *concerto*.[1] It goes back ultimately to the Latin verb *concertare*, the primary meaning of which is 'to compete'. As used in Italian, however, the same word has the radically different meaning of 'to agree', a sense that survives in such cognate English phrases as 'in concert' or 'a concerted effort'. This second meaning dominates the early use of the derived noun, *concerto*, which occurs most often in connection with sacred works for voices with added instruments, such as Giovanni Paolo Cima's *Cento concerti ecclesiastici* (1605) or – using the same word in its German form – Heinrich Schütz's *Kleine geistliche Konzerte* (1636–9).[2] Even there, however, the older Latin sense exerts a background influence, for agreement presupposes the existence of different parties, whose harmonious conjunction cannot be assumed beforehand. In this respect, *concerto* has always been an apt term for any kind of ensemble music where the participants are diverse in nature (as in the sacred concerto) or differentiated in function (as in the solo concerto). In Italian the same word can also mean a consort (a set of instruments belonging to the same family), an ensemble, a concert or simply music-making in general. This spectrum of overlapping concrete and abstract meanings often makes for vagueness or ambiguity in the primary sources.

Most historians of music are agreed that the cradle of the concerto was the collegiate church of San Petronio in Bologna, a city that belonged to the Papacy but by geography and culture was linked more strongly to the states of the Italian north and north-east: Lombardy and Venice. Enjoying the status of a basilica (it was also the main civic church), San Petronio maintained a large permanent orchestra, which was augmented by specially hired players on the occasion of the annual patronal festival. In the vast, resonant spaces of the church, whose nave has a reverberation time of twelve seconds,[3] a special and in some respects novel kind of music was needed: broad in effect, slow in harmonic rhythm and robust in tone. The result was the creation, around 1660, of a new sub-genre: the sonata (or sinfonia) for one or more trumpets and massed strings.

Such purely instrumental pieces could be used to introduce, conclude or punctuate solemn services.[4] Dispensing with intricate counterpoint, they relied on the principle of *concertato*: the call-and-response technique that pitted the lightly accompanied trumpet against the full string ensemble, bringing the two groups together at climactic points. In internal slow movements, where the trumpet usually paused,[5] the principal violin (the contemporary term for the leader) was sometimes given the opportunity to play a showy solo episode in quicker tempo, which produced a tripartite (slow–fast–slow) structure. Prominent cultivators of the trumpet sonata in Bologna before 1700 were the *maestri di cappella* Maurizio Cazzati (1616–78) and Gian Paolo Colonna (1637–95), the cellists Petronio Franceschini (1651–80), Domenico Gabrielli (1659–90) and Giuseppe Maria Jacchini (1667–1727), and, most importantly, the violinist and viola player Giuseppe Torelli (1658–1709).

When two instruments of different kind share material, it is always the more versatile – here, the violin – that mimics the less versatile – here, the trumpet. Via this process the violin learned, through its partnership with the trumpet (which occurred principally in the keys of C major and D major, in which the latter was pitched), to assimilate certain prominent features of the *stile tromba*: the striding broken-chord figures; the rapid note-repetitions; the scale-passages in the second octave above Middle C. So successfully did the violin (and the lower members of its family) assimilate this trumpet-like idiom that it soon became part and parcel of the violin style itself. For this purpose, copious use was made of the instrument's open strings, which in weight of sound and sometimes also (coincidentally) in pitch correspond to important notes in the trumpet's overtone series, both in C and in D.

The time was bound to arise when composers would attempt what one might term a 'trumpet sonata without the trumpet' – in other words,

a concerto. Because so much of the seventeenth-century musical repertory was transmitted in highly perishable manuscript form, it would be
unwise to attempt to identify the composer of the first concerto for strings
and continuo alone. There can be no doubt, however, that Giuseppe
Torelli was the first composer to popularize the new form. Writing over
sixty years later, the theorist Johann Joachim Quantz named him as its
reputed inventor,[6] and it seems certain that the six four-part concertos
contained in his Op. 5 of 1692, which alternate with an equal number of
three-part sinfonias (that is, trio sonatas), were the earliest specimens of
the genre to appear in print.

To contrapose sonatas of traditional type to these newfangled concertos was a method, to be copied by Taglietti and Albinoni a few years
later, of setting in relief the second genre's original features. In a preface
Torelli advises players of the concertos (but not of the sonatas) to 'multi-
ply all the instruments': that is, to perform them orchestrally. Such
instructions should not be taken as a prohibition of performance with
one instrument to a part (Baroque performance practice is rarely so
prescriptive) but, rather, as information on the conditions that gave rise
to the concertos and in which they make their best effect.

The design of the concertos, which contain upwards of three movements, has not yet parted company with that of the sonatas. Both always
end with a fast movement, and may begin either with a slow movement (a
preferred option for works performed in churches, expressing the dignity
of the occasion) or a fast movement. The internal movements alternate
slow and quick tempo. However, the concertos are noticeably more
concise than the sonatas, especially in their internal slow movements,
which are often no more than short postludes to the preceding fast
movement or preludes to the incoming one (the slow movement of
Bach's Brandenburg Concerto No. 3, which consists merely of two
block chords, is the descendant of these rudimentary links found in
Torelli's early concertos). Two concertos (Nos. 2 and 5) already sport
the three-movement fast–slow–fast design that a little later became norm-
ative, although at this stage it is merely the simplest of many possible
options.

The addition of a viola part goes hand in hand with the orchestral
conception. Italian composers of the late Baroque tend to use violas as
'fillers' that plug a gap in the texture and pick up the harmonic leavings of
the other parts. Torelli, who himself played the instrument at San
Petronio, is more generous than most, allowing the instrument moments
of imitation and dialogue with the violins, although the surest evidence of
importance – the possession of the leading-note at cadences – is generally
withheld.

Torelli's Op. 5 concertos grapple with the central problem of the early concerto: how to construct an Allegro movement of reasonable length without resorting either to imitation or to dialogue as the controlling feature. True, both devices retain a foothold. In the finale of the third concerto (in D major and dominated by the *stile tromba*) Torelli presents snatches of canon between the three upper parts. But this is decorative play, not a structural feature. More significant is the dialogue between the two violin parts in the finale of the sixth concerto. This is a new, more flexible version of the old dialogue between trumpet and violin in the Bolognese trumpet sonata. The composer and theorist Johann Mattheson was probably thinking of this kind of interplay when in 1713 he gave as one definition of concertos 'works for violin that are composed in such a way that at the appropriate moments each part comes into prominence and vies with the other parts'.[7]

However, most of the time the essential structure of a concerto fast movement is fully visible from the first violin part alone (unlike in a trio sonata, where imitation is more pervasive and discontinuities occur in every part). In effect, this part absorbs imitation and dialogue into its own essence: it becomes self-imitating and self-dialoguing. The result is that thematic recurrence becomes concentrated in this single upper part. This occurs both at short range (in immediate repetitions and sequences) and at long range (in restatements of primary material at significant junctures, such as after a main cadence). Torelli's style is conservative in that head-motifs – the 'mottos' that lead off a musical sentence, or period – are much more often subjected to requotation than either the material that follows on immediately from them (generally taking the form of passage-work, with liberal use of sequence) or the cadential phrases. The problem with both of the latter is that they are too unmemorable, too little different from their counterparts in other movements, to become effective reference points.

Another conservative and limiting aspect of Torelli's musical language at this point in his career is that the periods from which a movement is formed are predominantly 'open': they end in a key different from the one in which they began. Conversely, 'closed' periods begin and end in the same key. Since the field of modulation is restricted to keys that (to use modern terminology) have a key signature that differs from that of the home key by no more than a single sharp or flat, the composer soon uses up his stock of available modulations and has to return to the tonic to close the movement. The result is a 'motto' form, usually comprising three to five periods, that places the head-motif at the head of each successive period, usually in the key of the preceding cadence.[8] To some extent, Torelli retains the seventeenth-century fondness for 'sequential' modulation, in which movement along the circle of fifths (for example, from C major to G major) is continued by analogy in the same direction (thus from G major to D major). But this is a minor element that in any case does not carry on into the musical language of the late Baroque. A symptom of Torelli's awkwardness in handling tonality in these early concertos (and of his desperation to secure sufficient length) is the relative frequency with which keys are visited a second time, a procedure that tends to induce shapelessness.

Indeed, in Torelli's Op. 5 it is difficult to tell apart short-range and long-range restatements, with the result that the periodic structure is sometimes unclear. Greater transparency is achieved, however, in its sequel, a set of twelve *concerti a quattro* (entitled *Concerti musicali*) published in Augsburg in 1698 and quickly reprinted in Amsterdam. (To explain: The Italian terms 'a quattro' and 'a cinque' refer to the number of obbligato parts (respectively, four and five) in addition to the continuo. Most *concerti a quattro* were concertos for four-part strings without a separate part for principal violin (so-called 'ripieno' concertos); most *concerti a cinque* were concertos for solo violin.) It is interesting to note that Op. 6 was brought out in Germany and not in Bologna, a leading centre of music printing, on account of the fact that between 1695 and 1701 the San Petronio orchestra was disbanded in order to finance repairs to the basilica's roof. The temporary dispersal of its musicians, several of whom (including Torelli) spent time in northern Europe, played a significant part in introducing the concerto to Germany, which was soon to become a significant centre of concerto composition.

Op. 6 moves beyond Op. 5 in other ways, too. Some (though far from all) of the slow movements have a strong melodic profile that almost qualifies them for the description of 'singing Adagio' – the type that was very soon to become prevalent. In three movements – the outer movements of No. 6 and the last movement of No. 12 (two concertos, not by coincidence perhaps, that are in three movements) – Torelli inserts into some of the central periods certain passages marked 'solo' that are to be played by the principal violin, accompanied only by continuo. (There are also brief solos for players taken from both violin parts in the opening Adagio of the tenth concerto.) Although these have no real structural significance, they mark the birth of the solo concerto and, equally importantly, the introduction of a form of accompaniment to the solo that was to remain the favoured option for some while: plain continuo. In this instance, one could speak of the embedding of a 'sonata' texture within the concerto: such cross-fertilization of concerto and sonata is a constant feature of the parallel evolution of the two genres during the late Baroque period. These two works correspond to Mattheson's description of a second variety of concerto, 'where only the first [violin] dominates, and where among many violins one called *Violino concertino* stands out by virtue of its especial rapidity'.[9]

In his preface to Op. 6 Torelli offers a little more information about the size of the ensemble. He writes that where 'solo' appears only one violin should play (a necessary precaution, seeing that such variation of scoring was foreign to the sonata tradition), and that as many as three or four instruments may otherwise play each of the parts.

Torelli says nothing about the locale of concerto performance. Given the preference for orchestral performance, one may assume that concertos were most often performed in churches, in theatres (as *entr'acte* music) or in the recreational setting of music societies (*accademie, collegia musica*, etc.). Many large ensembles were made up – perforce – of players of different ability levels. Virtuosos mingled with rank-and-file players, professionals with amateurs. From the beginning, therefore, there was an incentive to mirror this inequality in the structure of the music. The 'classic' differentiation is between solo and tutti (or, in the Roman repertory, to which we shall turn shortly, between *concertino* and *ripieno*). In some contexts, not only a principal violin (or two) but also a principal cellist is singled out; when distinct from continuo parts (labelled *basso, basso continuo, cembalo, organo*, etc.), cello parts seem often to be intended for a single player – several early concertos (for example, Giuseppe Maria Jacchini's Op. 4 concertos of 1701 and Giorgio Gentili's unpublished Op. 6 concertos of 1716) make copious use of solo cello, alone or in combination with other solo instruments, without aspiring to the status of full-blown cello concertos. However, the same sort of stratification extends to the tutti itself: the first violin part is likely to be more taxing than the second, and the second more taxing than the viola. In that sense, a *concerto a quattro* in which the first violins are kept busy may express the spirit of the early concerto as perfectly as a *concerto a cinque* with a challenging solo part.

Between Torelli's Op. 5 and Op. 6 two further collections were published: a set of six concertos and four sinfonias (sonatas), Op. 2, by the Brescian composer Giulio Taglietti (Venice, 1696), and a set of ten Concerti grossi by the Lucchese composer Giovanni Lorenzo Gregori (Lucca, 1698). These two publications show how rapidly the concerto genre was gaining favour across northern Italy. Gregori's recourse to the expression Concerti grossi in a title prompts a reflection on the use of the term in historical and analytical writing today. It means, quite simply, 'large ensemble', and by extension 'works (concertos) for large ensemble'. As employed by Gregori and Baroque composers in general, it has nothing to do with the use, or non-use, of soloists, or with the number of soloists.

It is really not a technical term at all, but simply conveys the idea that many players participate. So the opposition between a 'concerto grosso' (with plural soloists) and a 'solo concerto' (with only one) is unfortunate in terminological respects, even though the differentiation itself may be valid for purposes of analysis.

In his fourth concerto Gregori innovated by supplying a separate part for orchestral first violins (the principal violin plays from the main part-book). This made it possible for the orchestral players to accompany the principal violin in solos and thereby provided alternatives to simple continuo accompaniment. For obvious reasons, it was necessary to simplify the texture when accompanying the soloists, but this could be effected in various ways without silencing the orchestra: by interspersing rests among the chords; by bringing parts together in unison; by eliminating the middle (viola) or the bass (continuo, cello and sometimes viola) of the texture.

We now switch to Rome, where a very different kind of evolution was producing pieces similarly called 'concertos', elements of which would in time become assimilated into the mainstream concerto that we have been discussing. Rome, with its vast clerical population and pockets of great wealth among nobles and prelates, was an early centre of orchestral performance in Italy. Indeed, in the 1670s, the period of Alessandro Stradella's maturity and Arcangelo Corelli's arrival on the scene, Roman orchestras pioneered the modern form of orchestra in which the violins are divided into two parts and the violas are reduced to a single part. However, these orchestras were assembled in a special way that, initially at any rate, reflected the origin and status of their members. Their core was a group of four players – two violinists, a cellist (or lutenist) and a keyboard player – who were often co-extensive with the household musicians employed by a patron (such as the cardinals Benedetto Pamphilij and Pietro Ottoboni) and were precisely the forces needed for a trio sonata. These formed the *concertino*, or small ensemble. All the other musicians recruited to make up the orchestra, who included viola players, joined the *concerto grosso* (or *ripieno*), the large ensemble. The scores on which the music for such ensembles was written had seven staves: three for the *concertino* and four for the *ripieno*. This did not predetermine in a rigid way how the music was to be conceived – it was always possible to make a *concertino* part double its *ripieno* equivalent and thereby suppress its separate identity. But the typical manner of treatment, which is also the most common one in Corelli's twelve Concerti grossi, Op. 6, which constitute the *locus classicus* of the style, is to use the opposition between the constituent ensembles for effects of light and shade or for quick-fire *concertato* exchanges. Remarkably, Corelli's concertos in their published form can be played, as the title-page mentions, by the *concertino* alone. This entails the sacrifice of much interesting detail and compels the cello to play imitative entries for the viola as well as its own, but is nevertheless a viable option that tells us a lot about the pragmatic attitudes of both composers and publishers.

Since his comfortable existence in the service of Cardinal Pietro Ottoboni put little pressure on him, Corelli (1653–1713) spent many years polishing these concertos before sending them in 1712 to the publisher Estienne Roger in Amsterdam. Some of them may be based on the orchestral works heard in Rome by the German composer Georg Muffat in 1681 and imitated one year later in his own *Armonico tributo* sonatas. The basic model for the Concerti grossi is that of the trio sonata, in either its 'church' variant (adopted for the first eight concertos) or its 'chamber' variant (adopted for the last four).[10] However, the church concertos resemble the solo sonatas of Corelli's Op. 5 (1700) in finding room for an extra fast movement (the fourth concerto, with its S–F–S–F–F design, offers a good illustration). Hints of the trumpet sonata also survive, as in the opening of the twelfth concerto, where the first *concertino* violin mimics the brass instrument. Finally, there are occasional signs that Corelli wishes to flatter the north Italian solo concerto by imitation; in the movement just described the first *concertino* violin sometimes breaks loose from its companions to become, in effect, a soloist.

How does one account for the evergreen reputation of these concertos? Many commentators, including the pioneering music historians Charles Burney and John Hawkins, have emphasized their classic purity, their avoidance of excess. However, these qualities are perhaps not the cause but only the precondition of their attraction (indeed, the 'off the peg' appearance of many passages can even irritate). Corelli's genius lies, rather, in his ability to achieve satisfying forms without resorting to rigid templates, his skill at juxtaposing contrasted ideas (the high incidence of composite movements and of *attacca* continuations in the concertos plays to this strength), his exquisite aural imagination, and his moments – more numerous than commonly supposed – of tonal or harmonic boldness. Among the unforgettable moments in the Concerti grossi are the biting suspensions and eerie octave-doublings in the second Adagio of the fourth concerto and the magical switch from minor to major at the start of the *Pastorale* concluding the eighth concerto. An optional movement, the *Pastorale* is intended for performance on Christmas Eve. It mimics the sound of shawm (*ciaramella*) and bagpipe (*piva*) proper to the folk pastorale.

In Corelli's footsteps there emerged a flourishing Roman school of concerto composers, whose members included Antonio Montanari (1676–1737), Giovanni Mossi (1680–1742), Giuseppe Valentini

(1681–1753) and Pietro Locatelli (1694–1764). All of these men – except Locatelli in *L'arte del violino*, Op. 3, which has a specifically Venetian connection – retained the Roman orchestral layout with seven parts.[11] However, their style of composition converged increasingly with that of the mainstream, lessening the musical relevance of the *concertino–ripieno* distinction. Corelli gained more faithful adherents in northern Europe, where in England Geminiani and Handel, and in Germany Muffat and Telemann (in a few works), produced concertos that may aptly be called 'neo-Corellian' – Geminiani (1687–1762) even arranged Corelli's Op. 5 violin sonatas as concerti grossi in order to gratify the English taste for his former teacher's music. Differently from Rome, in northern Europe the *concertino–ripieno* division had no social basis: its *raison d'être* was purely stylistic. Hence, perhaps, the tenacity with which it survived there.

The evolution of the north Italian concerto continued with the Venetian amateur composer Tomaso Albinoni (1671–1751), whose early music owes a lot to Torelli and the Bolognese school and just as much to his experience as a composer of opera. Unlike most composers of his time (his close contemporary and fellow Venetian Vivaldi is a striking exception), Albinoni put equal effort during his career into vocal (operas, cantatas) and instrumental (sonatas, concertos) composition, his music being noteworthy for its cross-fertilization of vocal and instrumental practices. Albinoni's second opus, a mélange of sonatas and concertos entitled *Sinfonie e concerti a cinque*, appeared in Venice in 1700. The partbooks, which number seven, include one specifically for principal violin (even if it doubles the orchestral first violin part most of the time), one for a second viola (*tenore viola*) and one for obbligato cello.[12] Several features of the concertos in the collection are innovative. All are in three movements: this plan is no longer only one among several but has become the fixed norm. The periodic structure of the fast movements is less chaotic than in Torelli and is delineated with almost excessive neatness. Strongly etched mottos, often stated twice in succession, in different keys, lead off each period. The central portion of the periods is given over to busy passage-work, occasionally assigned to the principal violin. There is some evidence that Albinoni is attempting, influenced by the example of the operatic sinfonia, to impart a distinct, lighter character to the finale. All six are in triple or compound metre (as opposed to the common time of the opening movements), and four of them (Nos. 1, 3, 4 and 5) substitute binary form for motto form. Unlike most composers of his time, Albinoni is reluctant to accompany passage-work with continuo alone. Instead, he uses light, well-spaced tutti chords.

The slow movements are less progressive. Two of them (Nos. 3 and 6) revert to a common Bolognese model by inserting a fast central episode with passage-work for the principal violin. Otherwise, the middle movements consist of slowly moving chords that feature either repetitive melodic-rhythmic patterns or an imitation of vocal polyphony. However, in the sequel to Op. 2, the *Concerti a cinque*, Op. 5 (Venice, 1707), Albinoni introduces four lyrical slow movements (Nos. 2, 5, 8 and 11) that mark a qualitative step forward. These movements are based on a model already used in his sonatas (Op. 2, Sonata V). Another 'import' from the sonata is the fugal character of all twelve finales. These buoyant fugues with short *concertante* episodes spawned many imitations in the Baroque concerto literature.

Quantz was right to identify Albinoni, alongside Vivaldi, as an 'improver'.[13] Albinoni was too idiosyncratic in style to found a school (as an amateur musician of relatively low social status, he was not in the best position to take pupils), but his consolidation of Torelli's foundations and anticipation of some of Vivaldi's innovations ensure his historical importance. More will be said later about his mature concertos.

In the same decade we see the rise of a distinctly Venetian school of concerto composers. Besides Albinoni, there were Giorgio Gentili (born *c.* 1669), a colleague of Vivaldi's father in the orchestra of the ducal church of San Marco, and the noble amateur Benedetto Marcello (1686–1739). Concertos by both men appeared, as Op. 5 and Op. 1, respectively, in 1708. Gentili, a minor talent, follows in the footsteps of Albinoni. Marcello is more individual, but it is impossible, unfortunately, to evaluate his first concertos adequately, since the sole surviving source lacks a principal violin part![14]

Antonio Vivaldi (1678–1741) began writing concertos well before his first, and most influential, set of concertos, *L'estro armonico*, Op. 3, came out in 1711. In 1703 he was appointed violin master, and *de facto* director of instrumental music, at the Ospedale della Pietà, the famous Venetian institution for foundlings. The Pietà maintained a choir and orchestra, which were staffed entirely by its female wards (nearly all the males left at the age of eighteen). At the time when the concerto came into being, the Pietà was acquiring a Europe-wide reputation as a centre of orchestral excellence: its performance standards were exceptionally high; it made a special point of collecting and cultivating such uncommon instruments as the chalumeau, clarinet, viola d'amore and viol; and the egalitarian ethos of the institution encouraged the wide distribution of solo roles, whether vocal or instrumental. In other words, it was the ideal laboratory for a composer, like Vivaldi, who relished virtuosity, instrumental colour and experimentation of every kind.

Few concertos by Vivaldi composed in the first decade of the century survive (it was only towards the end of the next decade that he began to stockpile his instrumental compositions systematically).[15] They suffice, however, to show that close to the start of his career he took a radically new approach to the genre. In the solo concerto, which henceforth was to constitute the dominant type,[16] the role of the soloist was changed from decorative and structurally unimportant to fundamental and structurally dominant. To achieve this, the layout of a fast movement has to be based not on a succession of open periods but on the alternation of closed and open periods in patterns such as COCOC or COCOCOC. Among other things, this process tends to extend the length of a movement, since the limited stock of foreign keys to be visited is used up less quickly. Vivaldi was no slave to routine, and his concerto movements often deviate from the principle of strict alternation. For example, extra closed periods can be added at either end of the movement, or consecutive open periods can appear in the centre. The scheme just described should therefore be viewed as an abstract point of reference against which to assess the plans adopted in individual movements.

Coincident with the alternation of closed and open periods was that of ritornellos (or tutti sections) and episodes (or solo sections). A ritornello section, which stabilizes a tonal area, exposes the primary thematic material, and treats the audience to a full orchestral sound, is an assembly of thematic units that recurs, generally in closed periods, in at least three tonalities (including a final tonic statement). Unlike the refrain of a rondo, a ritornello is a highly flexible structure amenable to modification on any restatement. It can be shortened by losing its beginning, middle or end; its units can be shuffled around or presented in new forms; it can be supplemented by newly introduced material. Generally speaking, Vivaldi likes to make the first ritornello statement the longest, and to find various ways of abridging the remainder.

Alternating with the ritornellos, generally in open periods, are the episodes, in which the soloist, or soloists, play continuously with light orchestral or continuo accompaniment. They serve to connect one tonal plateau to another and to showcase the virtuoso and expressive abilities of the soloist. The technical demands made on the soloist by Vivaldi represented a quantum leap forward. Into the solo parts for his own instrument he introduced bowing and articulation of unprecedented sophistication, complex arpeggiation, inventive multiple-stopping and – not least – moments of passionate lyricism. Vivaldi was a pioneer of the 'singing Allegro' (as opposed to the 'singing Adagio'), even though, particularly in his early concertos, the lyrical moments are brief oases amid the sparkling passage-work. He ventured into higher regions than anyone before him, reaching the fifteenth position (the note a$''''$) in the concerto RV 212, which was written for the celebration of the feast of the Holy Tongue of St Anthony of Padua (in the basilica dedicated to the saint in Padua itself) in 1712 and is Vivaldi's earliest precisely dated instrumental work in manuscript. In thematic respects, Vivaldi's solo episodes demonstrate absolute freedom. They quote freely from ritornello material (dashes of which the accompanying instruments may also insert) but also introduce new melodies as well as the inevitable quotient of 'abstract' display writing.

One innovation made by Vivaldi, important for the later history of the concerto, was to introduce a cadenza just before the final ritornello. It is normal in Vivaldi's fast movements in ritornello form for the episodes to increase in length as the movement proceeds. Often the last episode, or its conclusion, is heard over a pedal-point. From there it is only a short step to the independent, unaccompanied long cadenza (for which other composers, such as Locatelli, often used the term 'capriccio'). Several Vivaldi concerto movements come to a halt during what promised to be the final ritornello: the composer inserts a fermata and a direction such as 'Qui si ferma a piacimento' ('Pause here, if you like'), which is the cue for a cadenza. A few written-out examples by the composer survive (for example, for the outer movements of the concerto RV 212, mentioned above); they show that, in this early period, thematic connection between the cadenza and the main movement was not sought.

Whereas few fast movements in solo concertos by Vivaldi depart from ritornello form (here and there, and particularly in finales, one finds fugues, variation movements or binary structures), his central slow movements explore a greater number of formal options. Full-blown ritornello form is difficult to achieve, unless the sections are miniaturized (as happens occasionally). More often, the orchestral ritornello is reduced to a frame around a central long solo, or even to a simple introduction or conclusion. Binary form is also extremely common, especially when the orchestra is silent and the one or more soloists play in 'sonata' style just with the continuo. The solo parts of Vivaldi's concertos are typical for their time in the amount of scope they give to a performer who wishes to elaborate them with ornaments; that is, they present in places a surprisingly simple, even skeletal, outline that cries out for extra notes (Bach duly obliged when he transcribed several early Vivaldi concertos for harpsichord at Weimar). When he wished, Vivaldi could, however, create a *fioritura* for violin (or another instrument) of unbelievable complexity. A case in point is the version of the slow movement of the violin concerto in C major with two orchestras, RV 582, that Vivaldi created for his pupil and protégée at the Pietà, Anna Maria, around 1726. This outdoes in exuberance the ornamented versions of the slow movements in Corelli's Op. 5 violin sonatas, today believed to be authentic, published by Roger in 1710.

Just as important as Vivaldi's pioneering efforts with form was his creation – and we are not exaggerating here – of a new musical language. He rediscovered the power of simplicity: the way in which the simplest scales, arpeggios, unisons, sequences and cadences are able, in combination with artful vertical spacing, to produce not weary banality but

Example 3.1 Vivaldi, Op. 3, No. 8, 1st movement, bars 1–16

electrifying excitement. The keyword is 'juxtaposition'. Take, for example, the opening of the well-known eighth concerto from Op. 3 (RV 522), shown as Example 3.1.

This ritornello begins with a 'three hammer-blows' motif in crotchets. It is significant that the motif has the shape of an emphatic cadence. In Vivaldi's

music sectional beginnings and endings are often linked by their common
cadential character, a property that can be exploited to increase thematic
coherence or provide useful connection points. A rushing downward scale
then brusquely imparts a new vitality and clarifies the tonal context. Bars
2 and 3 'play' with scales in attractively contrasted melodic and rhythmic
configurations: descending in the bass, ascending in the unison violins. This is
not imitation as ordinarily understood, but the listener senses the congruity
and relatedness of treble and bass lines. The immediate repetition of the
scale-motifs is what Arthur Hutchings, author of the first full-length survey in
English of the Baroque concerto, aptly termed 'kinetic recurrence' – a device
corresponding to the rhetoricians' *analepsis*.[17]

On the first beat of bar 4 an emphatic half-close provides an opportunity to introduce new material. In bars 4 and 5, using a similar *analepsis*,
Vivaldi marks time by 'playing' with tonic and dominant harmonies: the
alternation of the two chords is mirrored by the imitation at the unison of
the two violins, which toss snippets (contrasting greatly with the previous
longer phrases) at each other. The very inconsequentiality of these
exchanges generates tension and the expectation of dramatic change.
This duly arrives in bars 6–8, where we find a classic Vivaldian sequence
based on seventh chords moving backwards diatonically through the
circle of fifths. In this sequence the violins, the viola and the bass move
at different, regular rates. Individually, each rhythm is almost childishly
simple: together, they create something much more fascinating. Vivaldi
lends interest to his quaver arpeggiations by allowing the second part to
'climb' over the first. The free interweaving of the violins is in fact a
characteristic feature of his style. Note, too, how the semiquavers preceding the broken chords intensify the 'auxiliary (neighbour) note' figure
introduced in bar 4 and constituting a speeded-up inversion of the
violins' 'hammer-blow' motif. Vivaldi's unforced achievement of thematic coherence points to an important truth: the simpler the building
blocks, the easier and more natural it is to place them in a variety of
situations and thereby secure unity.

Half way through bar 9 Vivaldi comes to rest on a dominant-seventh
chord, which, on account of being sustained for three whole bars, could
be described as a 'pedal-chord'. This sudden 'freezing' of the texture in
rhythmic as well as in harmonic respects makes a striking effect. Over it,
Vivaldi reiterates, as if in a trance, notes of the same chord (plus a grating
minor ninth – one of his harmonic specialities). The slurred phrasing of
the quavers is a new element that heightens the strangeness of the passage.
The listener knows that there must be at some point an escape from this
stasis – but when and how? The answer comes in the vigorous 'trademark'
cadence in bar 13.

Most listeners hearing this ritornello for the first time would be satisfied for it to end there. But Vivaldi has another trick up his sleeve. Because his method of composition is modular and paratactic (placing units next to one another instead of relating them syntactically), he is always able, whether on impulse or through prior calculation, to append or intercalate extra ideas. In this instance, the (apparently) concluding cadence is reinforced by an extra cadential phrase that for the first time – and therefore with heightened emotional power – subverts the diatonic world of A minor. In bar 14 we have a 'Neapolitan' chord; in bar 15, a major chord of A that seems to prepare a tonicization of D (a possibility sidestepped by the downward motion of the bass to C♮). This capacity to do 'more than the strictly necessary' is a quality that places Vivaldi among the great composers.

Vivaldi has traditionally been seen as a prime mover in the 'flight from counterpoint' leading first to the *galant* and later to the Classical style. It is untrue that he did not practise his contrapuntal skills (his *concerti a quattro*, in particular, contain some magnificent fugues, and he knew how to combine contrasted motifs very effectively), but it is true that he subordinated them to his quest for a direct, transparent and, above all, malleable musical language.

By a strange irony, *L'estro armonico*, which Vivaldi entrusted to the Amsterdam publisher Roger, thereby ensuring a Europe-wide circulation for his collection, came to be seen as a paradigm of ritornello form, of writing for the solo violin, and of Vivaldi's musical language *tout court*, even though it is, as a whole, fairly atypical of the composer's practice *c.*1710. Vivaldi, incidentally, was the first Italian composer to entrust concertos directly to Roger (who would, in any case, have 'pirated' them sooner or later from any earlier Italian edition). Roger's editions had the advantage of greater clarity – they were engraved rather than typeset – but they also circulated internationally, whereas Italian publishers had no transalpine sales outlets. Op. 3 comprises four 'solo' concertos for violin, four 'double' concertos (among which is RV 522, just discussed) and four concertos for four violins. Some concertos use obbligato cello, and there are two separate viola partbooks for the sake of the relatively few instances where the violas are divided. In fact, for almost the only time in his life Vivaldi employs a 'Roman' orchestral layout, even if this has little relevance for the solo concertos.

His purpose in publishing such an elaborate collection was probably to outdo his rivals and precursors. In 1709 Torelli's Op. 8, a collection containing six solo concertos for violin and six 'double' concertos, had appeared posthumously in Bologna. These concertos, which are much more mature than those of Op. 6 and make tentative moves towards ritornello form, are the first published specimens of the 'double' concerto, and show how the two solo instruments can variously reinforce, accompany and dialogue with each other. Equally impressive were the Concerti grossi, Op. 7, of Giuseppe Valentini, which appeared in Bologna in 1710 but conform in layout to the Roman model. Valentini's eleventh concerto has four obbligato violin parts; Vivaldi took from him the effective idea of organizing solos in 'chains' passing from one violin to the next.[18] Vivaldi's ambition is also evident from his choice of dedicatee, Grand Prince Ferdinando of Tuscany (1663–1713). Since, if he lived to succeed his father Cosimo III, the prince would be styled Ferdinando III, it became a fashion among composers (inaugurated by Torelli in 1687) to dedicate their third opus to him. Unfortunately, by 1711, when *L'estro armonico* came out, Ferdinando was bedridden with syphilis and no longer in a position to offer the composer active patronage.

In Holland and Germany, and then soon in the whole of northern Europe, the concertos of Vivaldi's Op. 3, their sequels in Op. 4 (1716), Op. 6 (1719) and Op. 7 (1720), and the considerable quantity of manuscript copies brought back, or ordered, from Venice by visitors and then often repeatedly recopied, took the musical world by storm. Telemann, Heinichen, Meck, Bach and a host of others adopted their form and style, tempered as always by a Germanic sense of decorum and orderliness. In Vivaldi's own later violin concertos a degree of conformity to habit is undeniable, but this predictability has its positive side – it supplies a sturdy framework within which interesting details can be elaborated – and in any case falls far short of what his harshest critics (who included the composers Luigi Dallapiccola and Igor Stravinsky) at one time alleged.

In Italy, Vivaldi had fewer direct imitators, especially among composers who had become involved with the concerto at an earlier stage. The case of Albinoni is instructive. His Op. 7 concertos (1715) persist in preferring unreconstructed motto form to ritornello form, and when Albinoni seeks a more expansive design for the four concertos for oboe (another four are for two oboes), he finds it in certain procedures of the operatic aria, to which his melodic style remains close; prominent among these features is the *Devise*, Hugo Riemann's term for an interrupted preliminary statement of the soloist's first theme. Albinoni's Op. 9 (1722), which reproduces the formula of Op. 7, is considerably richer in content, but one now begins to feel that the form is no longer adequate to the content, a shortcoming only aggravated in his late concertos for strings alone (Op. 10, *c*.1735).[19] Vivaldi's one relatively epigonic early Italian follower was the Bolognese composer Giuseppe Matteo Alberti (1685–1751), whose *Concerti per chiesa e per camera*, Op. 1 (1713), and their sequels presented the public with a watered-down version of the master's form and language – a version that amateur players welcomed.[20]

Vivaldi's opportunity to compose for the orchestra of the Pietà, and later for other large ensembles, such as the Saxon Hofkapelle at Dresden and the orchestras of Cardinal Pietro Ottoboni in Rome and Count Wenzel von Morzin in Prague, stimulated his inventiveness in the choice of both solo and supporting instruments. His 320-odd fully extant solo concertos include examples for bassoon (thirty-seven), cello (twenty-seven), oboe (twenty), flute (fourteen), viola d'amore (six), recorder (five), and mandolin (one). Of these, the flute concertos must be singled out. The six concertos in Vivaldi's Op. 10 (1729) were the first for solo flute to be published by an Italian composer; they inaugurated a fashion for flute concertos that did not abate until well after the middle of the century.

A handful of solo concertos, including *Le quattro stagioni* (*The Four Seasons*, Op. 8, Nos. 1–4), have an illustrative or (more rarely) narrative content. Vivaldi's experience at composing operatic music, and his brief exposure to the countryside during 1718–20, when he served the Mantuan court, stimulated his taste for pictorialism. It is noteworthy, however, that he rarely allowed a programmatic content to affect the musical structure: the content was draped around the form rather than the reverse (the two concertos entitled *La notte* – RV 104/439 for flute and RV 501 for bassoon – are an arguable exception).

The double concertos total almost fifty; three-quarters are for two like instruments (twenty-five for violins), and the remainder mix unlike instruments, often very inventively, as in RV 540, for viola d'amore and lute, and RV 545, for oboe and bassoon. A further thirty-odd are 'ensemble' concertos for three or more instruments, mixed or unmixed. In some of these Vivaldi anticipates the orchestral practices of the Classical period, giving such instruments as horns or oboes obbligato parts that are not 'solo' in nature but serve to reinforce and colour the orchestral texture. Four concertos, all written for the Pietà, employ a double orchestra.

Vivaldi also invented a new kind of concerto: the 'chamber' concerto for a group of three or more solo instruments and continuo.[21] He may have been inspired to write works of this kind by the sojourn in Venice, in 1716–17, of an élite group of Dresden musicians who accompanied the electoral prince to Italy; they included the violinist Johann Georg Pisendel (1687–1755), who became Vivaldi's pupil and promoted his mentor's music on his return to Dresden. These sparkling works, of which over twenty survive, derive their identity as concertos from their use of ritornello form and their *concertante* style. They apparently had no successors in Italy, but German composers imitated them very eagerly not only in actual concertos but also in the so-called 'concerto-like sonatas' (*Sonaten auf Concertenart*). The *quadro* genre, which enjoyed great popularity in the middle of the eighteenth century at the hands of such composers as Quantz and Telemann, also owes much to them.

In the mid-1720s a new generation of Italian concerto composers that one may describe as 'post-Vivaldian' came to the fore. Out of the rich stockpot of forms and scorings that made up Vivaldi's contribution it selected the relatively few options that a kind of natural selection had privileged.[22] From Locatelli and Tartini (1692–1771) the line of descent advances via Pietro Nardini (1722–93) to Giovanni Battista Viotti (1755–1824) – and that is to ignore the developments on the European plane that took leadership in the concerto, as in instrumental music as a whole, away from Italy and placed it in the hands of German and French composers. Locatelli refined the violinistic technique used in the solo episodes (the twenty-four *capricci* used as cadenzas in his Op. 3 of 1733 are still valued today as free-standing studies), whereas Tartini's violin concertos are noteworthy for their cantabile writing for the soloist.[23] The style of both composers was informed by the fussily nuanced *galant* style that spread from Naples in the mid-1720s. In his later concertos Vivaldi tried with difficulty to keep up with his younger rivals; the accompaniment to the soloist on two violins (a feature adopted also by Albinoni in his Op. 10) encountered in the late violin concerto RV 552 (1740) is a device clearly borrowed from Tartini.

In any synoptic account of an entire genre in a whole country over a wide span of time one is inevitably torn between the desire to work in as many names and compositions as possible for the sake of completeness and the desire to focus on those few composers and works regarded as pivotal historically or of outstanding artistic merit. The inevitable result is a compromise that does full justice to no single aim. To foreground Vivaldi, and to a lesser extent Torelli, Corelli and Albinoni, seems justified, however, on both historical and musical counts. The period of Italian primacy in the concerto, approximately 1690–1740, was not long enough to give rise to more than a handful of dominant figures, among whom Vivaldi stood out. But it was long enough for the broad character of the genre to become fixed – and the fact that today most concertos are still in three movements and organize their form in each movement around a 'balanced opposition' between soloist and orchestra shows how deep it sank its roots.[24]

4 The concerto in northern Europe to *c*.1770

DAVID YEARSLEY

The Italian concerto was brought north across the Alps by travelling virtuosos and touring princes; it was further disseminated by enterprising publishers and through the avid sharing of manuscript copies among musicians; and by the 1720s it was everywhere. The best northern composers, many of whom had never been to Italy, contributed prolifically to the genre and stamped it with their own creativity; indeed, the hundreds of concertos produced in northern Europe in the first half of the eighteenth century represent a vast, and largely unexplored, treasury.

The importance of the concerto to northern musical culture is perhaps best exemplified by the repertory produced and performed by members of the Saxon court orchestra in Dresden, arguably the best in Europe in the first half of the eighteenth century.[1] From the Kapellmeister Johann David Heinichen (1683–1729), who had himself been to Venice, some two dozen wonderful concertos survive, works that were often performed for the Saxon elector and his entourage as they celebrated a successful day of hunting in the antler-bedecked dining hall of their country castle, the Moritzburg. The heroic horn calls and pressing ritornellos of Heinichen's allegros recall the excitement of the hunt, while their arcadian slow movements evoke the bucolic aspect of the surrounding countryside. The Dresden first violinist, Johann Georg Pisendel (1687–1755), had studied with Torelli in Germany and later with Vivaldi in Venice; only seven of his concertos survive, but this mere remnant demonstrates how well Pisendel had learned his lessons from the Italians, and how creatively he engaged with the genre. More than imitations of Italian models, Pisendel's concertos are ambitious and often unlikely; the first movement of his D major Concerto, for example, begins with a fast Vivaldian ritornello in triple time, only to be followed at the solo violin entry by a lilting duple-metre Andante flirting pathetically with the minor mode. With this restrained, lyrical entrance, the great violinist seems to claim that he can impress as much through intimate expression as with the bravura technical display for which he was famous.

The spectacular Italian violinist Francesco Maria Veracini (1690–1768) spent a number of years in Dresden around 1720; only five thrilling concertos survive from what was presumably a much larger number. The flautist Johann Joachim Quantz (1697–1773) was a member of the Dresden orchestra from 1728 until 1741, when he received his lucrative appointment as flute master to Frederick the Great in Berlin; over the course of his long career in the two great German musical capitals Quantz composed more than 300 concertos.[2] Johann Adolph Hasse (1699–1783) took up the post of court Kapellmeister at Dresden on returning from Italy in 1731 and, aside from a vast output of operatic and sacred music, provided at least two dozen concertos for the court. This is to say nothing of the untold number of now-lost concertos by these and other members of the band. Meanwhile, composers from across Europe sent their concertos to the Dresden court – most famously Vivaldi who, late in life, provided autograph copies of six lavishly scored concertos (RV 224, 240, 260, 552, 558, 585) for Dresden, where they became a staple part of the repertory.

The cultivation of the concerto in Dresden was rivalled only by the Berlin court establishment, whose musicians, assembled by Frederick the Great (himself an avid composer and performer of concertos), included Karl Heinrich Graun, Johann Gottlieb Graun, Franz Benda, Quantz and Carl Philipp Emanuel Bach. Ironically, Frederick's harpsichordist, C. P. E. Bach, was the greatest concerto composer in residence, yet his concertos were never heard at court.

The cosmopolitan at home: J. S. Bach and the Italian concerto

The allure of the concerto for northern composers, even for those – or perhaps *especially* for those – who had never been to Italy, can be sensed in the autobiography of the organist and theorist Johann Gottfried Walther (1684–1748), Johann Sebastian Bach's kinsman and, from 1708 to 1717, his colleague in the central German city of Weimar. Walther describes what amounts to an obsession with the Italian concerto, proudly claiming to have transcribed no fewer than seventy-eight concertos, among them works by Vivaldi and Torelli.[3] J. S. Bach's own engagement with the concerto began in the same place, and at the same time, as Walther's; both composers' interest in setting Italian concertos for the keyboard was fuelled by the young, musical Duke of Weimar, Johann Ernst, who, as a student in the Netherlands, sent home to his court musicians copies of the latest Italian concertos, most importantly Vivaldi's *L'estro armonico* (published in Amsterdam in 1711).

The young duke wanted not only to have his Weimar musicians play Vivaldi's concertos, but also to compose such pieces himself – most likely with the help of his court organist J. S. Bach, who then arranged them for the keyboard. Although Ernst's concertos are the work of a princely dilettante, they possess a vibrancy that immediately brings Italy to mind. When Bach performed these pieces on the organ, Ernst – and Bach for that matter – must have caught a whiff of Venice, a connection with the latest trends in music, the spirit of a wider Europe. Indeed, the adoption of an Italian pose was a luxury that the German-bound Bach and others afforded themselves; thus in several copies of his concertos Bach is styled 'Giov. Seb.'

The appeal of the concerto for young musicians across Germany emerges also from a letter of April 1713 by Bach's pupil Philipp David Kräuter, in which Kräuter requests further financial support from the Augsburg city authorities for an extension of his stay in Weimar; the young duke, explains Kräuter, 'will return from Holland after Easter [and] I could then hear much fine Italian [music], which would help me especially in the composition of concertos'.[4] Kräuter goes on to mention that he will also have the chance to hear Bach play again on the soon-to-be renovated chapel organ; undoubtedly Bach's performances there included his concerto transcriptions.

Print copies from Amsterdam were just one source of the latest concertos from Italy; the wild-fire dissemination through personally exchanged manuscript copies was another. For example, Bach's setting of Vivaldi's Op. 7/ii, No. 5 (published in Amsterdam between 1716 and 1721), is in fact based on a manuscript that circulated north of the Alps prior to the publication of the piece.[5] While Bach's study of the Italian concerto through transcription concentrated on Vivaldi, it paid attention also to other Italian masters such as Alessandro and Benedetto Marcello (see Bach's transcriptions, BWV 974 and 981). Torelli was another early and important influence, and here again the routes of dissemination are interesting: in March 1709 Pisendel, who had studied with Torelli in Ansbach, passed through Weimar, and later that year he performed a violin concerto by Torelli in Leipzig.[6] Practically every facet of Bach's composing and performing life would draw on the lessons he learned from Italian concertos – especially those of Vivaldi, with their ritornello construction, movement layout and motoric energy. Yet Bach infused these elements with his own comprehensive and infinitely adaptable mastery of counterpoint.

Vivaldi's concertos mostly eschew counterpoint, but not all are without it, as illustrated by the D minor Concerto for two violins and cello continuo from *L'estro armonico* (Op. 3, No. 1), transcribed for the organ by Bach (BWV 596). After the first movement's canonic opening section, which he set as an ethereal dialogue between two manuals above a pulsing pedal-point, Bach – the newly minted student of the Italian concerto – was privileged to have the chance to transcribe Vivaldi's electrifying fugue in four-part invertible counterpoint. Here was the kind of learning and energy that would mark so many of Bach's own concertos, and that likely confirmed Bach's suspicion that the Italian concerto could be a vehicle for his own compositional research – that there could be more to the genre than fire and pathos.

In general Bach adopted the Vivaldian approach to ritornello construction with its three essential parts, often referred to in the musicological literature as *Vordersatz* (a strongly profiled head-motif which establishes the tonality), *Fortspinnung* (a forward-pressing section which involves harmonic sequences), and *Epilog* (which emphatically confirms the key at the close of the ritornello). Bach subjects this tripartite scheme to his own intellectual rigours:[7] each part can in turn be constructed of detachable sub-units, and these intricately constructed ritornellos are then segmentalized throughout a movement, the constituent parts presented on their own, and often divided up in ingenious ways between the soloist(s) and tutti.

This last point brings us to a hallmark of Bach's concertos. One of the crucial lessons to be learned from the Italian concerto was, of course, the opposition between the tutti statements of the ritornello and the solo episodes that modulate between them. A great deal of the motivic power of Vivaldi's concertos derives from the polarity between the ritornellos and the episodes; this opposition is built up not only through thematic differentiation – the tutti is charged with the ritornellos and the solo instrument(s) with the independent episodes – but also through a contrast of texture achieved chiefly through the virtuoso demands placed on the soloist(s).[8] Bach did not accept this dichotomy as a requisite feature of the genre, and instead continually pursued his own kind of integration between solo and tutti elements. To be sure, Bach's concertos are often difficult to play and impressive to watch and listen to, but there is rarely a sense that the *raison d'être* of these works is the hegemony of the soloist(s). (The indisputable dominance of the soloist(s) over the rest of the orchestra only emerges in the rare instances in which Bach introduces lengthy cadenzas, as in the Brandenburg Concerto No. 5, BWV 1050 and the D minor Harpsichord Concerto, BWV 1052.) Instead, Bach willingly sacrifices the contrast between tutti and soloists by ingeniously assigning ritornello elements traditionally associated with the tutti to the soloist(s), and, in turn, allowing the tutti to take on soloistic attributes; furthermore, the accompanying material of the episodes often draws on thematic material from the ritornello. Adopting a more fluid and highly wrought approach to the tutti–solo relationship, Bach gives us a richly interwoven texture brimming with energy and intellect. Although his detailed craftsmanship did not drain his concertos of their Italian excitement, Bach imbued the genre with an unprecedented complexity.

After his initial study of the Italian concerto through transcription, probably around 1713, Bach's next extended engagement with the genre appears to have taken place in Cöthen between 1717 and 1723, where one of the composer's principal duties was the production of chamber music. Unfortunately many of these must be assumed to be lost; two concertos for solo violin (in A minor and E major, BWV 1041–2) and another for two violins in D minor (BWV 1043) survive in their Cöthen versions.[9] The other surviving concertos from the Cöthen period constitute one of the greatest monuments to the genre, in modern times far surpassing the popularity held by Vivaldi's *L'estro armonico* in Bach's age. In 1721 he collected six concertos (BWV 1046–51) for 'diverse instruments' in a beautifully prepared autograph that he sent to the Margrave of Brandenburg. The Brandenburg Concertos represent Bach's only unified, if self-consciously varied, concerto collection.

The set boasts a vast array of forms and instrumental combinations. The first concerto is scored for two horns, three oboes, bassoon, violino piccolo, strings and continuo; Bach's idiosyncratic approach to the genre announces itself in the opening bars with the raucous triplet horn calls that intrude over what appears initially to be a conventional semiquaver ritornello. Neither the use of oboes and bassoon nor the inclusion of hunting horns in such concertos was without precedents. What makes Bach's approach in Brandenburg No. 1 so unexpected, however, is the initial sense that the horns are not integrated into the orchestral texture; it is as if they are calling from the hunt itself instead, from outside the walls of the princely music room. Yet Bach goes on to collapse this distance by progressively integrating the horns into the episodes, where they enmesh themselves contrapuntally with the other members of the *concertino*, and take on ever more soloistic (and strenuous) tasks. Thus, the transformation of Vivaldian concerto principles – that is, the breakdown of the tutti and *ripieno* distinction – happens before our very ears as the unruly horns are domesticated into the spirited ensemble colloquy.[10]

In the Brandenburg Concerto No. 1 Bach also strays from the three-movement plan to which he otherwise adhered; he appends a minuet, which is itself interleaved with three trio movements, diverse in their scoring and affects. Among these trios is a polonaise, which nicely rounds out what amounts to a European tour of Italy (the concerto allegro), France (the minuet and its first trio, set for the Lullian group of two oboes and bassoon), and Germany (the mixed taste in general and the contrapuntal episodes of the first movement) with a trip to Poland. (This was the kind of sampling and synthesis of national styles and tastes for which Bach's friend Georg Philipp Telemann (1681–1767) was justifiably renowned. Telemann's 125 concertos are Italianate works, but with northern touches: the frequent use of rondo form in his finales shows a personal affinity for France; and the introduction of polonaise and mazurka rhythms reflects a fascination with Polish music.) That the abundant musical feast of Brandenburg No. 1 stands at the entrance to Bach's great collection of orchestral music is no coincidence; it is an emblem of his engagement with the musical world beyond his native land, and the unquenchable desire to mould musical imports not only to German customs, but also to his own critical faculties.

The wonderfully heterogeneous *concertino* of Brandenburg No. 2, consisting of oboe, trumpet, violin and recorder, is yet another example of the kind of musical universalism Bach pursues in the set as a whole. Likewise, the slow movements of the Brandenburg concertos are remarkable for their variety. Two of these (Nos. 2 and 5) set members of the *concertino* in sonata-like textures, without the tutti. In the slow movement of No. 5, however, the harpsichord not only provides continuo accompaniment but is also afforded spacious solo obbligato interludes. The slow movement of Brandenburg No. 1 has a *concertino* group of oboe, violino piccolo and the continuo instruments; the florid solo lines ride above a brooding passacaglia-like bass, and once each of the soloists has performed an individual episode they begin to participate in rich contrapuntal dialogue, with dark commentary from the tutti. In the middle movement of Brandenburg No. 4 the solo group of recorder and violin inexorably echoes the two-bar 'theme' of the tutti; only in the harmonic journey to the cadences is this predictable pattern spun out, ritornello-like, into longer harmonic gestures. The slow movement of Brandenburg No. 6 is a magnificent adagio, delivered elegiacally by the violas above the walking continuo line, and ending, uncharacteristically for Bach, in a different key from its opening. In contrast to all these carefully wrought movements, spanning the textural and affective range of Bach's concerto ensemble, the slow 'movement' of Brandenburg No. 3 humorously reduces the space between the outer movements to the two chords of a Phrygian cadence.

Diversity of scoring coupled with formal manipulation is an important theme in these concertos; diversity within apparent unity of scoring is another, one that Bach explored in two of the concertos (No. 3 and No. 6) for string orchestra without winds. These involve the unusual trinitarian instrumentation of No. 3 with its three violins, three violas, three cellos, and the use of only the lower members of the violin family (along with gambas) in No. 6. In the absence of the despotic violin in No. 6, the two violas have the rare chance to crown the musical texture: at the opening of the concerto the violas revel in canon above the low, lush homophony of the lower strings. What one might describe as the democratization of the orchestra, achieved not only by according instruments unusual roles but also by destabilizing formal boundaries, is one of Bach's major contributions as a concerto composer.

Perhaps the most celebrated example of this kind of reconfiguration is found in Brandenburg No. 5, whose magnificent cadenza has been held up as the birth certificate of the keyboard concerto. How unexpected it must have been around 1720 to hear the harpsichord emerge from its traditional role as a continuo instrument to join with the flute and violin in the *concertino* with its own glittering obbligato filigree, and then, late in the movement, liberate itself even from these partners and conquer the piece in the riot of self-indulgence and display that is the epoch-making cadenza. Here was devilish music whose flamboyance and eccentricity surpassed even the infernal displays of the great Italian violinists. With unprecedented daring Bach stamped his own compositional and performing virtuosity on this concerto and presaged the ultimate ascendance of the keyboard in the later history of the genre.

The keyboard concerto was the focus of Bach's attention when he returned to the genre with renewed energy after his assumption of the leadership of the Leipzig Collegium Musicum in 1729. Twelve concertos (BWV 1054–65) survive for between one and four harpsichords, almost all of them originally written in Cöthen, and reworked for Leipzig so as to feature Bach, his sons, and/or his pupils as soloists. Bach's cultivation of the keyboard concerto inspired those young musicians lucky enough to hear him play, or participate themselves in the performances, to write their own diverse concertos later on. As his sons learned first hand, J. S. Bach pursued with unmatched ingenuity the highest purposes of the genre.

The cosmopolitan abroad: Handel's concertos

For Bach's German contemporaries 'concerto' was a fairly stable generic term: it generally meant three movements in fast–slow–fast order typically maintaining the tutti/solo division. (From this perspective, Telemann's frequent inclusion of a slow introductory movement, a practice drawn from the so-called Italian church concerto, stands outside the German mainstream.) Georg Frideric Handel's prolific relationship with the concerto, by contrast, is marked by formal flexibility and a looseness with respect to overall design, the order and number of movements, and the relationship between tutti and solo. Handel was perhaps the age's greatest musical cosmopolitan and a flamboyant flouter of generic limitations. His dynamic approach was nurtured by immense gifts for the expansion of melodic material and for imbuing large-scale designs with a sense of spontaneity. Handel's concertos project both grandiosity and gracefulness, supreme confidence that nonetheless allows for intimacy, an oratorical logic that leaves room for the unexpected.

Handel came into direct contact with the latest Italian style probably in 1702 on a trip to Berlin. There he would have met the two great Italians then resident at the Prussian court, Attilio Ariosti and Giovanni Bononcini, both of whom would later join Handel in the London opera scene in the 1720s. This early brush with Italian musicians in the north could only have helped to kindle Handel's desire to find his way to Italy, and indeed, when he made his sojourn there between 1706 and 1710, he gained the kind of first-hand experience of Italian music that Bach never had: Handel met and played with Corelli in Rome, and would also have been exposed to Vivaldi's music, although the Venetian composer's influence on him proved much less decisive than that of Corelli. Handel greatly admired Corelli's music and it was his assimilation of this style that could be said to parallel Bach's engagement with the work of Vivaldi; on the broadest level, though, Handel was far more ecumenical in his conception of the concerto than Bach, who rarely strayed from the Vivaldian model even while he subjected it to his own artistic impulses.

Nonetheless, Handel's confrontation with the most modern trends in the concerto as developed by Vivaldi can be heard in the *sonata* from his oratorio, *Il trionfo del Tempo e del Disinganno* (HWV 46a) written for Rome in 1707; with its flashy solo organ part and clearly delineated episodes and tuttis the movement is a relatively straightforward explication of concerto principles of the latest vintage.[11] In the *sonata* Handel demonstrates his life-long penchant for using the concerto as a way to insert himself as a keyboard player into the forefront of a major vocal or orchestral work. This inspired musical opportunism is reflected most clearly in *Vo' far guerra*, the closing aria from the second act of *Rinaldo* (HWV 7), the opera with which Handel stormed London in 1711. In *Vo' far guerra* the tutti strings boil forth as the sorceress Armida stands on stage waiting, ready to proclaim the commencement of hostilities against her enemies; yet in the midst of this ritornello, before the character on stage is given the chance to voice her passions, Handel pushes himself into the centre of the action as a sorcerer of the keyboard, with a theatricality that must have astonished his London audience. The bravura harpsichord part sparkles with virtuoso figuration and shifting textures; the first episode, in flashing quavers, gives both the right and left hands their chance to shine separately before coming together for the rush to the cadence. The second episode relaxes slightly into more flowing triplet quavers. Elsewhere, Handel accords himself chances to play in counterpoint to, and in concert with, the singer. *Vo' far guerra* is both aria and a concerto, and must be seen – especially given the watershed nature of this first-ever Italian opera composed for the London stage – as a landmark in the history of the keyboard concerto, a star-vehicle that pre-dates Bach's own promotion of the erstwhile continuo instrument in his Brandenburg Concerto No. 5. Like Bach, Handel resourcefully – and unforgettably – exploited the potential of the concerto to enliven other genres.

This kind of generic mixing was the product of Handel's genius, but also the result of the practicalities of his musical life. At no point was the concerto an independent pursuit; most of his concertos were conceived as introductions or interludes to his vocal works rather than as independent works. (It is useful to remember though that this kind of cross-pollination, and recycling in different contexts, was also a hallmark of Bach's concertos, and indeed of Baroque musical practice more generally; concertos were adaptable to multiple contexts, in church, stage and in the chamber.)

Like the composer himself, Handel's concertos are a cosmopolitan mélange that resists easy classification. Not only did Handel draw on Roman and Venetian traditions, but he also integrated into his concertos such diverse elements as French overture, Italian sinfonia, fugues, and an array of dance types. Where Bach's concertos were almost exclusively in three movements, Handel's ranged from two movements to six, a fluid approach to the series of movements that betrays the influence of Corelli. Indeed, Handel's concertos reflect not only the English popularity of Corelli's music, but also his own debt to the composer, an admiration he expressed by assigning the opus number '6' to his 12 Grand Concertos (HWV 319–30) in what seems a clear tribute to Corelli's Op. 6 concertos. Handel's flexible approach to the genre is also evident in his first set of concertos, Op. 3 (HWV 312–17), which appeared in 1734.[12] The first concerto of the Op. 3 set, with its three-movement layout and the marked tutti/solo contrasts of the first movement, seems to appeal to Vivaldian ideals – and one could probably say that it is more Venetian than Roman. The second concerto, on the other hand, hearkens back to Roman practice, with its suite-like string of movements and, indeed, its strong thematic affinities throughout with Corelli's Op. 6, No. 8. Handel's Op. 3, No. 1, includes a fugue (third movement), a minuet (fourth movement), and a bourée with variations (fifth and last movement). By contrast, Op. 3, No. 6, has only two movements; after the allegro, which displays an almost Classical symmetry in the exposition, development and ultimate recapitulation of the opening, Handel introduces a concerted movement for organ solo. Here, once again, the Vivaldian division of tutti–solo is apparent, yet the eight-bar ritornello is itself based on one from Corelli's concerto Op. 6, No. 12.

This last movement of the Op. 3 concertos anticipates Handel's turn to the organ concerto. From 1735 on, his oratorio performances featured at least one organ concerto with the composer as soloist.[13] The first set of organ concertos appeared three years later in 1738, as Op. 4 (HWV 289–94), while the organ concertos performed by Handel in the 1740s were published posthumously as Op. 7 (HWV 306–11). Handel is right-fully given credit as the originator of the genre, which continued to enjoy popularity in England after his death, and inspired emulators such as Thomas Arne. Arne expanded the palette of virtuoso keyboard artifices, as in the Scarlattian hand-crossing of his G minor Concerto (from the set published in 1793), yet his fluid notion of the overall shape of a concerto points ultimately back to Corelli as well, and his fondness for opening a concerto with a French overture answers to English taste.

Yet the inventiveness and vigour of Handel's organ concertos were never surpassed. Handel's exploitation of the concerto cast him as one of the most successful public keyboard virtuosos of the age; the new key-board medium he essentially invented, allowed the performer to market himself and his other musical products, the oratorio performances, as well as prints of his concertos. As organ soloist at important musical events in a major European capital ten times the size of Leipzig, Handel set the course for the rise of keyboard virtuosos such as J. C. Bach and Mozart, for whom the concerto was a vital medium of self-promotion. With the publication of his organ concertos, Handel established the keyboard player/concerto composer as a market force.

But Handel's 'Grand Concertos' of Op. 6 represent his greatest con-tribution to the genre. The immediate impetus for these works was the public concerts Handel had planned to give in London in the winter of 1739–40. Indulging his habitual methods of borrowing from himself and others much less than he had in the composition of Op. 3, Handel completed the twelve concertos of Op. 6 in one month, between late September and late October 1739; as if to highlight his creative resolve, he entered the completion date of each concerto into his autograph score. In conceiving the collection, Handel was not only aiming to enliven his concerts with new music, but he also had in mind the publication of these new works, as the pattern of the organ concertos had already established.

Handel's Grand Concertos range from four to six movements; some show Vivaldian traits, although they betray a greater fondness for Corellian looseness with respect to the solo–tutti relationship, as well as the prevailing trio-sonata texture of the *concertino*. Like Bach, Handel introduces binary forms and in one case a combination of ritornello with da capo form (No. 11/v), neatly uniting the operatic and instrumental strands of his musical personality. There is a range of dance-like move-ments from lively gigues to stately sarabandes as well as French overture openings (Nos. 5 and 10). All but one concerto (No. 8) have a fugue, and these, too, treat a huge spectrum of characterful subjects, from the progressively faster repeated-note theme of No. 7/ii, to the harmonically baffling descending intervals of No. 3/ii, which recall the eccentric ascent of Scarlatti's 'Cat's Fugue', a piece published in London in the same year that Handel set to work on his Grand Concertos.

Handel's distinct musical character is ever present in the novel turns of his figuration, the vigour of his ritornellos, the never restrictive formal designs, and an unmatched ability to achieve a quasi-operatic projection of character in his instrumental music. The opening movement of Op. 6, No. 5, for example, is styled as a French overture, yet it begins with a short, urgent violin solo. Starting a concerto with a pre-emptive solo is a trick that Vivaldi had famously used in the first concerto of his *L'estro armonico*, but in Handel's hands the theatrical solo entrance not only thwarts deeply harboured expectations about the relationship between soloist and tutti, it also recasts the genre of the French overture before it begins – as if to suggest that the rhetorical power of a single player can equal, or even surpass, that of the orchestra itself. It is a small but telling detail, one of the myriad examples in this collection that demonstrate Handel's mastery of the moment, of the seemingly spontaneous utterance, even in the context of large-scale instrumental music.

In contrast to his own Op. 3 concertos, Handel's Op. 6 adopts the uniform scoring of Corelli's orchestra, with its four-part *ripieno* strings and a *concertino* of two violins and cello;[14] there is only one movement in the collection for violin soloist (No. 6/iv). Yet with this Corellian ensemble, Handel strides across a vast stylistic territory: the collection is a triumph of innovation and synthesis, and the music cannot be reduced to its influences or affiliations. Rome is here in the textural (and sometimes thematic) details and perhaps most clearly the *concerto da camera* succession of dances found in No. 8. A pastoral, but not unclouded, Poland is alluded to in the polonaise of No. 3. One might detect an 'Iberian flavour' in the Scarlattian allusions of the fugue movement just mentioned, and in the nagging humour and Scarlattian gestures of No. 5/v. Frenchness can be heard in the overtures, and in slow movements such as the mournful, sarabande-like 'Air' of No. 10. The fugues testify to Handel's place among the great German contrapuntists. The stylistic panorama presented by the Grand Concertos is a testament once again to the self-consciously pan-European quality of Handel's concertos, although the richness of this continental tapestry is far more complex and rewarding than this brief overview can convey.

Still busy with organ concertos in the late 1740s, not to mention his oratorios, Handel also contributed three works to the sub-genre of the concerto for two instrumental choruses (*Concerti a due cori*, HWV 332–4), the one chorus made up of strings, the other of winds. The opposition between two essentially equal yet distinct musical contingents lay at the heart of the concerto principle as articulated by Praetorius and as practised by the Gabrielis in Venice; Vivaldi had updated the principle to the Baroque concerto with his own *concerti a due cori*.[15] In Handel's three sprawling instrumental canvases, the composer updates the dialectic of competition and co-operation to the orchestral ensemble of the mid-eighteenth century.[16] The governing dichotomy in these concertos is the opposition between winds and strings, but Handel divides the wind group still further into its two constituent elements: the two oboes and bassoon contend or converse with the two horns. Handel manipulates the relationships between these orchestral groups to produce a constantly shifting musical scenery; the distinctive sonority and technical capabilities of each group provides the brilliant palette with which Handel paints one of the richest instrumental landscapes witnessed in eighteenth-century music.

Novel forms also abound in these *Concerti a due cori*; one memorable example is the rollicking ground bass of No. 2/v, a much expanded version of an earlier vocal work first used in the 1713 Birthday Ode for Queen Anne and reused again in the 1732 version of *Esther*. Handel was a master of the ground bass, a favourite medium for his keyboard improvisations and, given his all-embracing view of the concerto, it is not surprising that he let his fantasy loose on standard bass lines in the context of his late orchestral works; indeed, Handel had composed two of his finest ostinato movements for the organ concertos (HWV 306, 310) from the 1740s. In one sense, the harmonically static, cyclic nature of a ground bass is the polar opposite of the Italian allegro, with its dogged forward progress sign-posted by the modulations of its ritornello; yet the relentless, inventive optimism of Handel's ground-bass elaboration in the *Concerto a due cori*, No. 2/v, with its rich interplay of orchestral colour and the soaring contrapuntal trajectories of its distinct instrumental choirs, makes it as exciting as any teleologically driven Italian allegro. Why should Handel have denied himself the pleasure of indulging his love for such ground basses, simply because these did not accord with the mythical generic requirements of the concerto? Self-denial is not a Handelian attribute, much to the benefit of his concertos.

The French archangel: Leclair and the concerto

The lure of Italian instrumental music was equally strong for the French virtuosos, the first of whom to write and publish solo music under the title 'concerto' was Joseph Bodin de Boismoitier (1689–1755). But the greatest French master of the genre was Jean Marie Leclair (1697–1764). As it was for Handel, Italy was a goal for Leclair: he was in Turin in 1722 and again in 1726–7, when he met the touring Quantz. In Turin, Leclair studied with the Corelli student Giovanni Battista Somis, from whom he developed the fine sense of melodic line associated with Corelli; yet the principles of concerto construction employed by Leclair, and the nature of his ritornellos, would prove far more heavily indebted to Vivaldi. On his return from Italy, the Italianate flair of Leclair's performances was celebrated with great public enthusiasm in Paris; he subsequently travelled both to London and Kassel, where he met and played with another former student of Corelli, Pietro Locatelli.

Leclair published two sets of concertos: his Op. 7 of 1737 (violin concertos, with the exception of No. 3 which is scored for solo oboe or flute), and his Op. 10 of 1745 (all concertos of this set for the violin). His concertos are true virtuoso showpieces with expansive solo episodes that allow ample room for the hair-raising pyrotechnics from which Leclair derived the greater part of his fame: double- and triple-stops, arpeggios, double-trills, spectacularly awkward leaps, and lightning passage-work, which often requires the player to double the speed of an already brisk allegro set by the tutti. Though the virtuoso writing is itself enough to give Leclair's concertos a prominent place in the history of the genre, such displays should not draw attention away from Leclair's brilliant and varied use of Vivaldian ritornello principles. Like Vivaldi, Leclair favours the three-movement plan, and the tripartite nature of Vivaldi's ritornellos is often quite apparent, though Leclair's ritornellos tend to be more involved and longer.

Leclair's Op. 7, No. 2 is a good example of the richness of his ritornello constructions and his sense of large-scale drama. The concerto begins with an adagio introduction with staccato chordal statements in the *ripieno* between which the violin solo is given interludes with highly expressive (even chromatic) runs and arpeggios. Using a device favoured by Vivaldi (and, following Vivaldi, by Bach), the harmony is darkened with a mode shift to minor at the close, before a lush, and very French, chord progression leads to the half-cadence. The allegro ritornello begins as a double fugue with a rising cantus firmus-like scale against a cascading counterpoint. After all members of the *ripieno* have joined in this contrapuntal framework, Leclair pursues a Vivaldian *Fortspinnung* based on the material from the faster contrapuntal line. At its close this *Fortspinnung* shifts modes again to a minor *Epilog*; this phrase is echoed, Vivaldi-like, before the *forte* tutti plunges into a parenthetical *Fortspinnung* to a brusque cadence in octaves. Over the first solo episode, which extends to nearly a minute, the pyrotechnic violin finally winds its way to a tutti drawn from the learned – and very exciting – contrapuntal music of the opening part of the ritornello. The contrast between unbounded virtuoso display and penetrating counterpoint brings both elements into arresting relief. In its first two-and-a-half minutes this concerto presents a huge range of inspired technical and compositional ideas, which, after the poised introduction, are all delivered with breathless energy. The opening minutes of this great concerto also reflect a crucial feature of Leclair's writing, namely, that the violin is less a spirited and independent colla-borator, as in Vivaldi, than an often monomaniacal competitor.

The ritornello of Leclair's Op. 7, No. 6/i is still more ambitious than that of No. 2/i. The head-motif is Vivaldian in the way it outlines the tonic triad and then immediately repeats the idea as a sort of echo. Then comes the expected *Fortspinnung*, though here as elsewhere in Leclair's concertos the harmonic sequence has a suave and often unexpected harmonic rhythm that sets it apart from Vivaldi. A minor phrase seems to prepare the expected cadence and conclusion of the ritornello, but this is hi-jacked by another broad *Fortspinnung* section, which culminates in big jumps and syncopa-tions. This, too, sounds as if it should be the cadence, but is unexpectedly followed by a sprightly cadential unit that deflates the swashbuckling mood with a coy humour. As this description tries to suggest, the ritornello is not only complex, but extremely varied; on a larger scale, one hears clearly that it is made up of two balanced elements that look forward to the ritornellos of full-blown Classical concertos. The violin episode begins with a melodic inversion of the ritornello in similarly balanced phrases before quickly launching into unexplored territory.

Leclair's slow movements have a more distinctly French lineage, although these harmonic and rhythmic features are elaborated with masterful, florid ornamentation in Corellian style. Indeed, Leclair's con-certos are among the best of the cultural mixtures so effectively produced in the first half of the eighteenth century.

Two Bach sons and their concertos

Two of J. S. Bach's four musical sons will lead us into the second half of the eighteenth century. We turn first to C. P. E. Bach, who only now is being more fully appreciated as one of the great concerto composers. He wrote some fifty concertos spanning a creative career of half a century; this huge repertory has not been adequately studied, though it is thank-fully becoming more easily accessible on recordings, and the complete scholarly edition of C. P. E. Bach's works is finally underway. All of Bach's sons must have participated in the family concerto tradition, and it is therefore not surprising that C. P. E. Bach began composing concertos before he left his father's home in Leipzig in 1734. For C. P. E. Bach, as for his father, concertos remained a lofty artistic medium; indeed, his contributions to the concerto were so closely identified with his personal style that he published hardly any of them. A set of six (H. 471–6) appeared in Hamburg in 1772, and these were decidedly simpler than his larger, more challenging works, but even in this 'easy' set his stylistic inclinations are evident – the suddenly shifting affects, the unexpected breaks and syncopations, the bizarre shifts of register, and surprising harmonic turns. Of his large-scale concertos, only H. 414 and H. 429 were published under C. P. E. Bach's auspices (Nuremburg, 1745, 1752).[17]

During C. P. E. Bach's years in Berlin as accompanist to Frederick the Great, whose nightly diet of concertos was restricted to his own, those of Quantz and those of the Saxon Capellmeister, J. A. Hasse, Bach played continuo to the driving allegros and the pathetic, highly ornamented adagios favoured by the king. Quantz was a master of the adagio and of the buoyant concerto allegro in the *galant* style – an updating of the Vivaldian ideal he so admired to the stylistic proclivities of the Prussian court. But one should not overlook the more turbulent, searching side to Quantz's musical personality – a character that can be heard in his tempestuous and difficult Concerto for Flute in G minor (QV 5:196); under the aegis of his musical sovereign, the hugely prolific Quantz assiduously cultivated the concerto as a genre demanding lofty artistic ambition from both composer and performer. Like C. P. E. Bach, Quantz did not publish his concertos, although unlike Bach, Quantz's were composed above all for the edification of his royal employer, Frederick the Great.

Given the high standards of the concerto culture in Berlin, it is not surprising that C. P. E. Bach concertos strove with even greater intensity to uphold these ideals. The number and variety of the concertos – mostly for harpsichord, although C. P. E. Bach also produced some for the organ, the cello and flute – makes any attempt at a survey hazardous at best. In the earlier concertos (for example, H. 406, 411, 414) C. P. E. Bach generally adhered to a fairly stable division between solo and tutti; in the 1740s especially, he often shared musical material between these two groups, and even when there is rapid dialogue between solo and tutti there is little sense of conflict between them. Thus, the soloist is generally allowed spacious episodes, often with relatively non-intrusive commentary from the orchestra. In formal terms the concertos are conventional, although the idiosyncratic harmonic and registral moves are the opposite of predictable – and are almost always immediately identifiable as the work of C. P. E. Bach.

As Bach's career progressed, the textural juxtapositions and collisions in his concertos became more pronounced, and he increasingly favoured rapid-fire exchange that blurs the boundaries between soloist and tutti. This evolving style can be heard in the Concerto for Cello in A minor (H. 432) written around 1750, the year of J. S. Bach's death. As with several other concertos by C. P. E. Bach the piece exists in authentic versions for other solo instruments, in this case flute and harpsichord. One can hear in the tempestuous ritornello the lineage through J. S. Bach, back to Vivaldi, but this is a temperamental *Fortspinnung* given to extreme swings of mood. After the concerto's bold opening gesture, which yields to a dialogue between a low stentorian motto and high-voltage descending arpeggios, Bach develops the ritornello by visiting a quick succession of musical topics: contrapuntal motif in contrary motion, more traditional late Baroque sequences juxtaposed against insistent repeated-note figures, deceptive cadences evaporating into silence, Beethovenian melodies floating above insistent chordal accompaniments, then a return to the opening motto before a chromatic, syncopated cadence rendered in emphatic octaves.

After this manic ritornello the solo cello entry is almost subdued; on the one hand this seems an odd and extreme contrast, yet on the other, one might have expected (if familiar with C. P. E. Bach's music) the antics of the tutti only to mask a deeper melancholy. Over the course of this long episode the soloist is left for the most part free from orchestral interventions, though the tutti offers some supportive gestures derived from the opening motif. But near the end of the episode the orchestral interjections become more pressing. With its second episode the cello enters as a changed character: here is music that is suddenly fast and turbulent, even though it occasionally gravitates back towards the opening pathos. In the next episode the cello takes up a repeated-note figure from one of the elements of the ritornello, giving it a more optimistic presentation in the major mode. But this too spins off into revelatory virtuoso outpourings. Now the orchestra begins increasingly to intrude, sometimes with jolting arpeggios, sometimes with doubting pizzicatos. The stability of the tutti-solo shatters, and the cadenza and final ritornello can only appear to restore some sense of order.

There is much more to say about the way C. P. E. Bach segments his ritornello in this concerto movement and deploys it in both the tutti and solo. The manner in which the solo line seems to manifest the complicated and difficult character of the ritornello over the course of the piece is even more fascinating, as if the opening ritornello were a prologue – or as in the eighteenth-century novel, an argument – to the turbulent narrative that ensues. Failing a more thorough examination of this fascinating piece, suffice it to say that it is brilliant, highly wrought and troubled enough to unsettle the very foundations of the concerto principle. In pushing the genre inherited from his father and nourished by his Berlin colleagues to its furthest extreme, C. P. E. Bach created a body of work that, with our increasing awareness of it, will long reward the engagement of players, listeners and scholars.

J. S. Bach's youngest son, J. C. Bach, represents a fundamentally different approach to the concerto from that found in the masterful corpus of his elder half-brother C. P. E. Bach. J. C. Bach was the only member of his family to leave Germany, following Handel's path first to Italy and then to London. He had already begun to compose keyboard concertos indebted to C. P. E. Bach during his stay with him in Berlin between 1750 and 1755. But it was J. C. Bach's exposure to Italian opera in its native land that formed his concerto aesthetic, one in which the high artistic vision of his brother had no place. Indeed, C. P. E. Bach dismissed his half-brother's music as shallow; it is an opinion I share, although I appreciate the ingratiating ease of J. C. Bach's work, whose qualities the Mozarts famously admired. This is a music of clarity, of stability devoid of any sense that musical problems need to be constructed and then conquered.

It is true that the balanced structure of the ritornellos and their tonally formalized placement throughout the course of a movement, as well as the stable relationship between soloist and orchestra, provided the basis for the further development of the concerto in Vienna. Unlike the concertos of C. P. E. Bach, J. C. Bach's were for public consumption both in the concert hall and on the printed page. J. C. Bach published two volumes of keyboard concertos: Op. 1 in 1763 (already reissued by 1765) and his Op. 7 in 1770. And unlike the connoisseurs' concertos of C. P. E. Bach, J. C. Bach's music could be – and was – played by amateurs. The aesthetic orientation towards unchallenging entertainment is perhaps best heard in the last movement of the concluding concerto of Op. 1 – a set of variations on 'God Save the Queen'. This charming and never-too-demanding movement encapsulates J. C. Bach's geographic and musical distance not only from the traditions of his own family, but also from Handel, who had died only six years earlier. The symmetry and poise of J. C. Bach's music points towards a new and important path for the concerto, away from the myriad technical and formal adventures pursued by the best northern concerto composers in the first half of the eighteenth century.

5 The concerto from Mozart to Beethoven: aesthetic and stylistic perspectives

SIMON P. KEEFE

Wolfgang Amadeus Mozart (1756–91) and Ludwig van Beethoven (1770–1827), names writ large in histories of the concerto, dominate critical discourse on late eighteenth- and early nineteenth-century works. Their status as the pre-eminent concerto practitioners of the period was enshrined right from the outset. Theorists August Frederick Christopher Kollmann and Heinrich Christoph Koch cite Mozart as the exemplary concerto composer in influential writings from 1799 and 1802 respectively.[1] In addition, the *Allgemeine musikalische Zeitung* of Leipzig, published from 1798 onwards and destined to become a significant barometer of nineteenth-century musical opinion, initially accords Mozart highest honours, subsequently placing Beethoven on the same pedestal. Superlatives for Mozart's concertos flow freely: the Piano Concerto No. 24 in C minor, K. 491, and one of the E flat works (No. 9, K. 271; No. 14, K. 449; or No. 22, K. 482) performed at Leipzig concerts in late 1800 are among his most excellent and thus, by definition, among the best concertos ever written;[2] the 'famous grand ... concerto in D minor', No. 20, K. 466, is one of the most admirable works in the genre;[3] and his piano concertos as a whole are 'unsurpassed',[4] intimidating, even, for those 'estimable' composers who are not as talented as Mozart.[5] Beethoven's Piano Concerto No. 3 in C minor, Op. 37, and Piano Concerto No. 5 in E flat, Op. 73 ('Emperor'), soon elicit a similar level of praise: the C minor Concerto 'in regard to its intended spirit and effect ... is one of the most outstanding of all that have ever been written', possessing a second movement that is 'assuredly one of the most expressive and emotionally rich instrumental pieces' of all time;[6] and the 'Emperor' is one of the musical world's most imaginative and original concertos.[7] To be sure, Beethoven's concertos are also criticized in the early nineteenth century, exemplifying the 'awed but skeptical' attitude towards Beethoven in the *AmZ* at this time.[8] In the 'Triple Concerto' for Piano, Violin and Cello, Op. 56, Beethoven 'has loosed the reins of his rich imagination, all too ready to luxuriate exuberantly in its richness, as he has scarcely yet done anywhere else' incorporating 'scarcely playable and at times even ineffectual difficulties'[9] and in the Violin Concerto in D, Op. 61, writes music with 'many beautiful qualities' but 'often [seeming] completely disjointed'.[10] Nevertheless, the die had been cast: writers firmly established Mozart and Beethoven as the supreme concerto composers of their era during the first two decades of the nineteenth century and bequeathed a powerful legacy to generations of performers, critics and composers.

Setting aside issues of musical quality, it must be recognized that Mozart's concertos – including twenty-seven for piano, five for violin, four for horn, two for flute, and one each for bassoon, oboe, clarinet and flute and harp – and Beethoven's concertos – an early piano concerto in E flat as well as Nos. 1–5, the Violin Concerto and the 'Triple Concerto' – represent only a tiny fraction of the total output of concertos from the Classical era.[11] Other works popular across Europe in the late eighteenth century and first decade of the nineteenth include (to cite only a few by well-known composers) about eleven cello concertos by Luigi Boccherini (1743–1805), four violin concertos by Jean-Baptiste Davaux (1742–1822), about eighteen piano concertos by Jan Ladislav Dussek (1760–1812), twenty-two keyboard concertos by Leopold Kozeluch (1747–1818), twelve keyboard concertos by Johann Samuel Schroeter (*c*.1752–88) and twenty-nine violin concertos by Giovanni Battista Viotti (1755–1824), as well as numerous works for a diverse range of solo instruments by illustrious figures such as Giuseppe Maria Cambini (1746–1825), Carl Ditters von Dittersdorf (1739–99), Joseph Haydn (1732–1809), Michael Haydn (1737–1806), Ignace Joseph Pleyel (1757–1831) and Carl Stamitz (1745–1801). The ever-popular *sinfonia concertante* or *symphonie concertante*, moreover, provided performers and public alike with a plethora of concerto-type works.[12]

Above all, a concerto written at the end of the eighteenth or beginning of the nineteenth century offered its composer an ideal opportunity to demonstrate high-level musicianship as both a composer and a performer. For the majority of concertos from this era were intended – at least initially – as solo vehicles for their composers;[13] thus, concerto outputs usually reflect instrumental expertise. Several composers who wrote most of their concertos for one particular instrument were among the most acclaimed virtuosos of their era, including Boccherini (cello), Viotti (violin) and Dussek, Mozart and Beethoven (piano). Their performances of their own concertos, moreover, were often high-profile events, proving critically and commercially successful: Mozart wrote twelve piano concertos (K. 449–503) to perform at subscription concerts and grand academy events in Vienna between 1784 and 1786; Viotti played his violin concertos to considerable acclaim at the Salomon Concerts and 'Opera Concert' series in London in 1793–5; and Beethoven gave a number of performances of his early piano concertos at prominent public concerts in Vienna and across Europe between 1795 and 1800.[14]

In spite of the popularity of concertos among composers of this period, writers often viewed concertos with considerable suspicion, even outright derision, routinely criticizing excessive technical virtuosity as a means of dazzling the audience rather than providing them with an aesthetically edifying experience. But this critical posture represents only one part of the historical equation. The aesthetic situation pertaining to the concerto merits more detailed consideration, since it offers insight not only into prevalent stylistic features of works from this period, but also into the privileged critical status of Mozart's and Beethoven's works.

The aesthetics of the concerto, *c.*1770–1810

The confluence of three aesthetic phenomena, the grand (with a related idea of nobleness), the virtuoso (including, but not limited to, brilliance) and the intimate, accounts for the unique position of the Classical concerto among late eighteenth-century instrumental genres. As an orchestral piece it is required to demonstrate grandeur; as a piece featuring a soloist (or soloists) it must provide a vehicle for virtuosity. Kollmann, who regards grandeur as 'one of the principal characteristics of Concertos',[15] neatly accounts for this dual requirement in distinguishing the 'grandeur of Harmony' and 'fullness' of orchestral tuttis from the 'brilliant passages' and 'nicety' of solo sections.[16] Above all, a balance must be struck between grandeur and brilliance. Pierre-Louis Ginguené, co-editor of and contributor to the *Encyclopédie méthodique: musique* (1791), clarifies that the greatest exponents of the mid to late eighteenth-century concerto, including Carl Stamitz (1745–1801), do precisely this, providing (in Stamitz's case) 'force and ... majesty' in tuttis as a complement to fiery, original and cutting solos.[17] Intimacy, a third aesthetic dimension that intersects with grandeur, comprises delicate, elegant and subtle writing for the soloist and the orchestra individually and, above all, in interaction with each other. Koch observes in 1793, for example, that a 'well-worked out concerto' will feature 'a passionate dialogue between the concerto player and the accompanying orchestra'. This consists of an expression of feelings from the soloist and a signalling 'through short interspersed phrases sometimes approval, sometimes acceptance of his expression' from the orchestra, who are likened to a symbol of nobility, the chorus of Ancient Greek tragedy. Koch continues by explaining solo–orchestra exchange in terms of both nobility and intimacy: 'Now in the allegro [the orchestra] tries to stimulate his noble feelings still more; now it commiserates, now it comforts him in the adagio'.[18] In short, Koch associates solo–orchestra exchange with a quality best described as *intimate grandeur*, one that co-exists with the more emphatic grandeur exemplified by orchestral tutti sections.[19] For one *AmZ* critic writing on Mozart's works in October 1800, intimacy in the concerto is in fact more prominent than the grandeur associated with sonic force: 'the concerto is the greatest *from the point of view of intimacy* [*im Zarten*], in contrast to the symphony which is the greatest *where grandeur is concerned* [*im Grossen*]'.[20]

Even when not explicitly mentioning grandeur, intimacy and virtuosity, contributors to early issues of the *AmZ* clarify that concertos must balance solo virtuosity and orchestral involvement, reconciling brilliant and expressive solo writing with active orchestral participation. Without an appropriate level of orchestral engagement, after all, grandeur and the intimate grandeur of interaction would be beyond a composer's reach. Reviewers of concertos often pay close attention to the role of the orchestra, and in so doing implicitly acknowledge dynamic orchestral involvement as a *sine qua non* of a successful work. In his Flute Concerto Op. 16, August Eberhard Müller (1767–1817) is praised for writing a diligent and brilliant accompaniment that utilizes trumpets and timpani to produce a full effect; on one occasion Dussek includes an accompaniment that is rich but not so rich that it obscures the soloist and on another includes orchestral writing that is one of the work's best features; and in a violin concerto, Viotti's orchestral writing helps to elevate the soloist in a very effective fashion.[21] Praise for wind writing is also forthcoming in the *AmZ*, often implying intimate roles for these instruments: in Pierre Rode's Violin Concerto No. 7, they engage in echoes, lending already attractive melodies extraordinary charm; in Ignaz Fränzl's Violin Concerto No. 7 well-chosen wind solos render tutti sections extremely diverse and engaging; and in Anton Eberl's Concerto for Two Pianos in B flat the wind instruments are used with great discernment and with refined taste.[22] But orchestral wind parts in concertos are sometimes a disappointment: one writer bemoans the fact that they are often given 100, 120 or 130 bars rest and only heard in tutti sections; another draws attention to the excellent use of wind instruments in Ignaz Fränzl's Violin Concerto No. 6 in G minor, explaining that such treatment is regrettably uncommon in violin concertos of the period.[23]

Just as writers for the *AmZ* focus on the active involvement of the accompanying orchestra, so they also pay close attention, of course, to the nature of the concerto soloist's material. It emerges with considerable regularity that brilliance is insufficient in itself as a representation of instrumental virtuosity; carefully crafted expression and brilliance must co-exist. Viotti is frequently lauded in this respect. One *AmZ* reviewer of a Viotti violin concerto explains in 1799 that ample opportunities are given to the soloist to display versatility and strength of bowing technique as well as appropriate expression, with brilliant passages suitably blended into the musical fabric;[24] another (1808) describes Viotti transcending all-consuming technical virtuosity by writing profound, content-rich music that still retains a pleasant and charming liveliness in its Allegro movements.[25] London-based reviewers of Viotti's solo performances of his violin concertos in the 1790s are especially effusive in their praise of his broad-ranging virtuosity. On 10 March 1794, the *Morning Chronicle* comments: 'The grand mistake of musicians has been the continued effort to excite amazement. VIOTTI, it is true, without making this his object, astonishes his hearer; but he does something infinitely better – he awakens emotion, gives a soul to sound, and leads the passions captive'.[26] For a reviewer (1799) of a flute concerto by Christian Westerhoff (1763–1806), an appreciation of musical rhetoric is crucial. Knowledge not only of harmony and modulation, for example, but also of a musical oration allows the concerto composer to write in a forceful, entertaining way that impresses the listener with more than just the technical difficulties of the solo part.[27]

The idea that solo virtuosity should incorporate expressiveness as well as brilliance and that the orchestra should participate actively in the work, attests to the balanced stylistic approach required of a concerto composer at the turn of the nineteenth century. Invariably, positive reviews of concertos in the *AmZ*, such as Fränzl's Violin Concertos Nos. 6 and 7 in 1804, praise both solo and orchestral writing. The opening movement of No. 6 is serious and weighty, with powerful tutti sections, brilliant writing for the soloist and a practical accompaniment, as well as the first-rate use of winds cited above; No. 7 employs its wind section excellently and, if the solo part is performed with force, certainty and clarity in addition to taste and charm, has a splendid overall effect.[28]

The integration of lively orchestral participation (including engagement with the soloist) and judicious virtuosity and the related assimilation of grand, brilliant and intimate qualities are readily found in the late eighteenth-century concerto repertory. Viotti's violin concertos offer good cases in point, even though Viotti is rarely praised for his orchestral writing. (One *AmZ* review of No. 27 in C remarks matter-of-factly that orchestral writing is 'well known not to be Viotti's strength'.[29]) His best-known concerto, No. 22 in A minor (*c.*1793–7), scored for a large orchestral contingent of flute, two oboes, two clarinets, two bassoons, two horns, two trumpets and strings, marshals orchestral support effectively in the service of aesthetic and stylistic equilibrium. The onsets of the second and third ritornellos (bars 160 and 281) in the first movement, for example, manifest a striking grand force on account of contrasts engendered with the light orchestral scoring (excluding winds) from the

immediately preceding display passages. Far from demonstrating a neg-
ligent attitude to orchestration, the thin scoring (including a lengthy
absence of winds) followed by the emphatic re-entry of the full orchestra
underscores two complementary aesthetic phenomena: solo brilliance
that shows off the violinist to best advantage as it is unobscured by the
orchestra; and forceful grandeur articulated by the orchestra. The intimate grandeur characteristic of solo–orchestra dialogue reappears soon
after the opening of Ritornello 2; the first and second violins (bars 180–4,
joined by the flute in bar 182) present material that is subsequently used
by the solo violin to initiate Solo 2 (bars 184–8). Viotti pays attention
elsewhere in the movement as well to the orchestra's role as a three-
dimensional musical protagonist. The diverse wind sonorities in
Ritornello 1, for example, demonstrate sensitive handling of orchestral
texture and complement showings of force in the *ff* tutti passages; as in
Ritornello 2, intimate and forceful orchestral writing co-exists.

Joseph Haydn's works, especially the Cello Concerto in D, Hob VIIb:2
(1783) and the Piano Concerto in D, Hob XVIII:11 (1784), also reveal a
balanced mixture of solo brilliance and active orchestral participation.
The Cello Concerto has come in for its fair share of criticism. In 1895
Eduard Hanslick calls it 'an old-fashioned, insipid, occasional or courtesy
piece', drawing attention to the poor quality of both the orchestral
and solo writing when explaining that 'No brilliant orchestral
ritornello awakens us from the light slumber of this violoncello solo'.[30]
H. C. Robbins Landon is harsher still, on account of the work's 'extraordinary
lack of tension' and its excessively brilliant writing: the concerto 'has been
the delight of cellists the world over – less the delight of audiences, who
are obliged to listen to passages of fabulous virtuosity which are the pride
of the soloists and anathema to any except the highly trained listener'.[31]
To be sure, the work is a highly advanced display piece for cellists, one of
the most technically challenging concertos in the cello repertory. But
criticism of the work's technical brilliance misses an important aesthetic
point, namely that the large amount of brilliant passage-work in the first
and third movements is complemented by frequent solo–orchestra dialogue that manifests intimate grandeur. In the solo exposition (Solo 1)
and development (Solo 2) of the first movement, the orchestra often
segues between the end of one solo phrase and the beginning of the next
(a form of dialogue) and, in tutti interjections such as bars 39–40 and
45–7, incorporates more dialogue with the solo cellist. Informed by late
eighteenth-century criticism, we could argue that the cello's ascending
semiquaver/demisemiquaver scales (bars 44–5) become more than just
hollow displays of solo brilliance by virtue of the dialogue in which they
engage with the violins' ensuing brilliant scales (bar 47). At any rate, tutti

interjections similar to those found in this solo exposition fulfil the function – following A. F. C. Kollmann – of '[keeping] up the grandeur of the
piece'.[32]

Dialogue in the development and recapitulation sections of the first
movement of Haydn's D major Cello Concerto also attests both to the
active role of the orchestra and to the lively engagement of solo and
orchestra as stylistic foils for solo brilliance. The first violin at the opening
of the tutti section that immediately precedes the recapitulation (see bars
128–30) grows out of demisemiquaver material in the cello (bars 121, 124,
127), bringing brilliance into the realm of dialogue-orientated intimate
grandeur in a similar fashion to the aforementioned bars 44–7. In the
recapitulation, dialogue additional to that witnessed in the solo exposition is heard, reinforcing the reciprocal bond between soloist and orchestra by elaborating their interaction: the strings and oboes' scalar sextuplet
semiquavers in bar 146 merge into the cello's scalar sextuplet semiquavers
in bar 147; and the main theme is split between the orchestra and the cello
in bars 168–72.

Haydn's D major Piano Concerto, Hob XVIII:11, like his D major
Cello Concerto, emphasizes complementary aesthetic and stylistic qualities. The first movement features less ostentatiously virtuoso solo writing
than the corresponding movement of the Cello Concerto, and less elaborate solo–orchestra dialogue, implicitly recognizing that brilliance and
intimate grandeur are mutually dependent in the context of a stylistically
balanced Allegro. Even though the winds are used sparingly, they fulfil an
aesthetically significant function. The only substantive wind contribution
to the solo exposition in bars 69–72, for example, underscores dialogue
between piano and full orchestra that represents forceful rather than
intimate grandeur on account of the contrasting material presented by
the two protagonists. The presence of the wind for a full-orchestra *forte* at
the beginning of the recapitulation (bar 175) accentuates the grandeur of
orchestral participation, whereas the exchange of the main theme from
orchestra (bars 175–80) to piano (180–6) highlights the intimate grandeur of
dialogic engagement (see Ex. 5.1). Forceful and intimate grandeur are
consequently combined in the context of a recapitulation that begins with
adapted versions of bars 7–12 (opening ritornello) and bars 54–60 (solo
exposition); an important formal function (integrating material from the
opening ritornello and solo exposition in the recapitulation) thus coincides with an important aesthetic function (integrating complementary
qualities). The corresponding recapitulation passage in the 'Un poco
Adagio' slow movement (see Ex. 5.2) also fulfils a crucial formal and
aesthetic role, bringing back the orchestra–solo main theme dialogue
from the beginning and simultaneously adding a new dimension to the

Example 5.1 Haydn, Piano Concerto in D, Hob XVIII: 11, 1st movement, bars 175–85

intimate solo–orchestra engagement that characterizes the movement as a whole. The orchestra statement in bars 45–8 is answered first by an *ad libitum* bar in the piano (48) that points to solipsistic rumination rather than unencumbered dialogic engagement, but then by delicate solo and orchestra writing that re-emphasizes the intimacy of their relationship (bars 49ff.). The repeated accompanimental quavers in the lower strings (bars 45–7) migrate to the left hand of the piano (bar 49) then return to the strings (bars 50–2) where they act as understated support to the piano's beautiful sequential extension of material from bar 49 in bars 50–2.

Close dialogic engagement between soloist and orchestra in the first movement of Haydn's Trumpet Concerto in E flat, Hob. VIIe:1 (1796) – with concomitant intimate grandeur – reaches a level matched in the late eighteenth century only by Mozart's Viennese concertos. Almost every trumpet passage in the movement incorporates solo–orchestra dialogue of one type or another. Thus, in the solo exposition, part of the main

Example 5.2 Haydn, Piano Concerto in D, Hob XVIII: 11, 2nd movement, bars 45–52

theme in the trumpet is echoed in the winds and then taken up by the soloist (bars 39–41, following bars 3–5), the first tutti interjection is imitated by the trumpet (bars 44–6), march-like semiquaver/quaver figures are passed from the soloist to the orchestral trumpets and timpani (bars 49–51), thematic material is split between the trumpet and the first violin (bars 62–6) and four *forte* full-orchestra crotchets act in quick succession as imitative substance for the trumpet and as a segue between two of the soloist's phrases (bars 77–81). The development also includes protracted dialogue between the trumpet and the first violin (bars 96–106) and the recapitulation new exchanges between the trumpet and strings (for example bars 138–41, 142–9 and 152–6). Solo brilliance, of course, is by no means absent from this movement. Its continual appearance in the context of solo–orchestra exchange (in the recapitulation in particular), however, lends the orchestra a degree of participatory parity rarely witnessed in concertos of this era.

Mozart's concertos

Late eighteenth- and early nineteenth-century critics were quick to recognize not only Mozart's general status as the pre-eminent concerto composer of the era, but also his status as the genre's supreme master of orchestral writing, an essential component of the requisite balance of aesthetic characteristics. Koch and Kollmann both associate Mozart's elevated standing among concerto practitioners with orchestral as well as solo participation: Koch considers Mozart's piano concertos supreme examples of the 'passionate dialogue between the concerto player and the accompanying orchestra'; and Kollmann explains that the 'best *specimens* of good modern Concertos for the Piano-Forte, are those by *Mozart*, in which every part of the accompaniment is interesting, without obscuring the principal part'.[33] *AmZ* writers also put Mozart's orchestral writing on a pedestal. A reviewer of Breitkopf und Härtel's 'Oeuvres Complettes de Wolfgang Amadeus Mozart' in October 1800, for example, contrasts the role of the orchestra in concertos that precede Mozart with its role in Mozart's works. Before Mozart, the orchestra is completely subservient to the soloist, '[laying] aside anything of consequence' in order to provide support for the principal part. In Mozart, however, *all* instruments – orchestral and solo alike – are thoroughly worked and the soloist only the 'most striking' among them. The ritornello sections, like the solo sections, can now 'arouse expectations' and 'excite the spirit'.[34] A little over a year later in March 1802, a reviewer of the Clarinet Concerto in A, K. 622, comments in exalted fashion: 'What extraordinary effects Mozart could achieve through the most precise knowledge of all the customary instruments and their most advantageous employment; that especially *in this respect* Mozart has been equalled by *nobody*: this *everyone* knows'.[35] Even reviews of concertos by other composers occasionally pay homage to Mozart's orchestration. For example, his exemplary handling of both solo and accompanying voices – in contrast to a display-orientated piano concerto by Daniel Steibelt (1765–1823) – is 'difficult to forget'; it is unreasonable, in fact, 'to judge each modern concerto against the standard of Mozart's masterpieces in this genre'.[36]

Just as Classical critics laud an appropriately gauged level of orchestral participation in Mozart's concertos, so they also draw attention to the effective way in which virtuosity is woven into the musical fabric. Solo brilliance does not detract at all from musical quality; the Piano Concerto No. 16 in D, K. 451, is described in the *Musikalische Korrespondenz* of 1792 as 'among the most beautiful and brilliant that we have from this master' and the Piano Concerto No. 26 in D, K. 537 ('Coronation'), as 'ingenious and brilliant' in the *AmZ* of 1808.[37] Moreover, as Ernst Ludwig

Gerber explains in 1812–14, Mozart's virtuosity on the piano (including in his concertos) never relies too heavily on technical difficulties, which are always subordinated to harmonic, melodic and expressive concerns.[38] In the performance of concertos, too, Mozart's dignified *gravitas*, rather than straightforward brilliance, shines through: while a certain Mr Stein's swift, precise, fiery and brilliant performance of the Piano Concerto No. 20 in D minor, K. 466, in 1806 won the approbation of the audience, 'Mozart himself delivered this concerto with more seriousness and imposing dignity. With him the profound, rich spirit of the composition was more noticeable; with Stein, more the brilliant execution of the virtuoso'.[39]

Reviewing Mozart's Piano Concerto No. 15 in B flat, K. 450, in 1799, one *AmZ* critic integrates comments on prominent orchestral involvement and the difficulties of solo and orchestral parts in a particularly illuminating fashion:

> it is not as well crafted as some better-known and newer concertos by the same composer: on the other hand, though, its delicateness accounts for a great deal lighter and more suitable instrumental accompaniment, more practical on the whole than some of the others. It is certainly easier to find ten pianists who completely work through even the most difficult of these concertos, before one finds a single good accompanying orchestra. But in the last Allegro of the concerto in question there are also some short passages in the first oboe which, if they are to be performed well, in style and with precision, require just as much practice and assurance as any passage in the concerto part.[40]

It is significant that K. 450, written for Viennese concerts in the Trattnerhof and Burgtheater in spring 1784, is the focus of this discussion as it is the first of Mozart's self-professed 'grand' concertos featuring a 'large' rather than a 'small' orchestra.[41] Mozart explains that his earlier Viennese piano concertos, No. 11 in F, K. 413, No. 12 in A, K. 414, No. 13 in C, K. 415 (all 1782–83), and No. 14 in E flat, K. 449 (begun in 1782/3 and completed in spring 1784), can be performed in full or reduced scoring – 'either with a large orchestra with wind instruments or merely *a quattro*, viz. with two violins, one viola and violoncello' – whereas K. 450, 451 and 453 'all have [obligatory] wind instrument accompaniment'.[42] K. 450 has traditionally been described as a pivotal moment in Mozart's concerto œuvre from the point of view of orchestral deployment, especially with its newly prominent winds.[43] The intricacy of solo–orchestra engagement increases in relation to his earlier concertos as a result of the new-found textural independence of the winds; so too does the volume of virtuoso writing for the soloist. By Mozart's own admission, K. 450 and 451 are 'concertos which are bound to make the performer perspire'[44] and a straightforward comparison of the quantity

Example 5.3 Mozart, Piano Concerto in E flat, K. 449, 1ˢᵗ movement, bars 188–96

of semiquaver and triplet-quaver passage-work in the first movements of K. 449 (73 bars out of a total of 347), K. 450 (108 out of 308) and K. 451 (88 out of 325) attests – in an admittedly rudimentary way – to the greater technical difficulty of the later works. In accordance with the prevailing late eighteenth-century philosophy of aesthetic and stylistic equilibrium, Mozart simultaneously oversees an increase in intimate grandeur *and* an increase in solo brilliance in his first 'grand' concertos.

While the orchestra's interaction with the soloist in K. 449 is not as subtle as the corresponding interaction in the 'grand' concertos, it is just as significant from an aesthetic and stylistic perspective.[45] Mozart's description of K. 449 as 'a concerto of an entirely special manner'[46] is supported by a number of stylistic features unique to this piano concerto: the secondary theme appears in the dominant in the initial orchestral ritornello of the first movement; the piano's final cadential trill prior to the cadenza in the first movement does not confirm the tonic but moves abruptly to the relative minor; and the Andantino is a more complex hybrid of formal designs (rondo, concerto and ABA′) than any earlier or later slow movement. But no stylistic element of K. 449 is more remarkable or far-reaching in its originality (at least in relation to Mozart's own preceding works) than the confrontation between the piano and the orchestra in the development section of the first movement (bars 188–203; see Ex. 5.3). For the first time in one of his concertos, Mozart sets up an oppositional dialogue of sharply contrasting material – *forte* unisons in the orchestra against brilliant semiquaver writing in the piano.[47] On account of the forceful contrast, dialogue temporarily leaves the realm of intimate grandeur for the realm of emphatic grandeur; the piano and orchestra are pitted majestically against each other, thus integrating solo brilliance into a grand context.

Mozart's Piano Concerto No. 24 in C minor, K. 491 (1786), is the climactic work in his concerto sequence in terms of *both* the intimate grandeur of dialogue and the emphatic grandeur of dialogic confrontation; as such it again validates theoretical prescriptions for aesthetic and stylistic equilibrium. These two stylistic high points are starkly juxtaposed in the development and recapitulation sections of the first movement. The former includes Mozart's most momentous confrontation between piano and orchestra – a spiralling sequence of snarling, oscillating half-steps in the full orchestra and brilliant arpeggio flourishes in the piano (see bars 330–45) – and the latter the most protracted sequence of subtle, intimate dialogues witnessed in the first movements of his concertos. The second movement is scarcely less remarkable, setting brilliant writing in the winds as well as the piano (see the demisemiquaver arpeggios and scales in the flute and bassoon in bars 21–2, 29–30 and 78–9) in the context of the intimate grandeur of dialogue. There can be few better examples in Mozart's concerto repertory of 'short passages in the [winds] which ... require just as much practice and assurance as any passage in the concerto part'.

The reviewer of K. 450 for *AmZ* (1799) is not alone among late eighteenth- and early nineteenth-century writers in stressing the memorable nature of orchestration in Mozart's instrumental works. Franz Xaver Niemetschek, one of Mozart's earliest biographers, explains in 1798 that the composer judges very accurately 'the exact time and place to make his [orchestral] effect'; he 'also knew how to achieve his most magical effects with true economy, entailing the least effort, often through a single note on an instrument, by means of a chord or a trumpet blast'.[48] Mozart's father, Leopold, compliments him similarly in 1780 for writing 'with so much discernment for the various instruments'.[49] Addressing the 'dramatic interplay of dialogue' in Mozart's symphonies in the 1820s, Georg Wilhelm Friedrich Hegel also states that he is 'the great master of instrumentation' in terms of '[blending] the various kinds of string and woodwind, ... [learning] how to introduce the thunder of a trumpet-blast' and '[emphasizing] first one then another class of distinctive sounds'.[50] Indeed, the most 'magical' effects in Mozart's concertos are the result – at least in part – of inspired uses of orchestral instruments in combination with the soloist: the oboe soars gracefully over sustained strings and modest piano arpeggios to effect a mellifluous transition to the recapitulation of the first movement of the Piano Concerto No. 27 in B flat, K. 595 (see bars 235–42); the flutes, bassoons and horns, after a fourteen-bar rest, serve up a pristinely rounded final chord – in conjunction with the clarinet and strings – for the second movement of the Clarinet Concerto in A, K. 622 (bars 97–8); the sustained flutes and bassoons, strings and clarinet soloist – who alternates between low and high registers enveloping the orchestral texture – support a serene six-bar sequence in the finale of K. 622 (bars 169–74); and the one-bar wind imitations (bars 106–10) and the flute's g'' – $g\sharp''$ – a'' half-step (bars 110–11) in the transition section of the first movement of the Piano Concerto No. 19 in F, K. 459, gently converge in the ensuing piano passage which begins with the wind motif on a'' (bar 111). Such noteworthy effects are not limited to delicate moments, moreover, as the powerful confrontations between piano and orchestra in K. 449/i and K. 491/i demonstrate. Countless Mozart concerto passages could be added to those mentioned – we all have our favourites – ably illustrating the economical and seemingly effortless way (to follow Niemetschek) that Mozart achieves his memorable orchestral effects. In short, Mozart's judicious use of the orchestra is central to the aesthetic and stylistic significance of his concertos, namely the imaginative and effective ways in which they balance contrasting aesthetic phenomena.

Beethoven's concertos

Beethoven admired Mozart profoundly. Identifying him as one of music's 'great men' and regularly requesting copies of his instrumental and vocal works from publishers, Beethoven explains: 'I have always counted myself amongst the greatest admirers of Mozart and shall remain so until my last breath'.[51] This high regard for Mozart's music extends to the piano concertos and is recorded most famously in Beethoven's statement to Johann Baptist Cramer after a performance of K. 491 in 1799: 'we shall never be able to do anything like that'.[52] Beethoven saw fit to compose his own cadenzas to the first and third movements of K. 466 in *c*.1809 and also frequently to perform Mozart's piano concertos. While certainly evidence of esteem, Beethoven's cadenzas and performances of Mozart also represent clear aesthetic and stylistic departures from his predecessor. In the first-movement cadenza to K. 466, for example, the 'tunes are Mozart's, but the touch, the rhetoric, is emphatically Beethoven's'.[53] In addition, the performance style cultivated by Beethoven as a concerto soloist was very different from that cultivated by Mozart.[54] The theorist and composer Antoine Reicha, who turned pages for Beethoven during one of his performances of a Mozart piano concerto, gives a memorable account of the force and roughness of Beethoven's playing that must have been a far cry from the 'delicate and shallow touch' attributed to Mozart by Carl Czerny: 'I was mostly occupied in wrenching out the strings of the piano, which snapped, while the hammers stuck among the broken strings. Beethoven insisted upon finishing the concerto, so back and forth I leaped, jerking out a string, disentangling a hammer, turning a page'.[55] Mozart's influence on Beethoven – both in general terms and in the specific context of concertos and of Beethoven's development beyond Mozart's stylistic frames of reference – has been well documented in the critical literature.[56] What concerns us here is less Mozart's influence *per se* than the ways in which those aesthetic and stylistic qualities that are showcased in Mozart's concertos and that capture the essence of late eighteenth- and early nineteenth-century thought – grandeur, the intimate grandeur of dialogue, and brilliance – are prioritized in Beethoven's works.[57]

Beethoven's Piano Concertos No. 2 in B flat, Op. 19, begun *c.*1788 and written and revised over the next ten years and No. 1 in C, Op. 15, written in 1795 and revised in 1800, preserve much of the spirit of Mozart's concertos, but also point in new aesthetic directions.[58] For example, the dialogic alternation of contrasting orchestral and piano material in the development sections of Mozart's first and sonata-rondo movements – reaching its zenith in bars 330–45 of K. 491/i – is a relatively common occurrence in Beethoven's early concertos, but is modified in the development of Op. 19/i (bars 246–55). The piano's arpeggios contrast thematically with the quaver figures in the winds, but also act as a bridge between the strings (with which it plays) and the winds (with which it alternates), beginning and ending on or close to the lowest note in the strings and the highest in the wind. Clearly this is not a grand confrontation along the lines of those in K. 449/i and K. 491/i. By demonstrating collaborative intent instead, this interaction brings contrast into the realm of intimate grandeur. The ending of Op. 19/ii (bars 69–91) also invokes interactive procedure in Mozart's concertos, but in a context alien to Mozart's works. The orchestral segues between the piano's *con gran espressione* segments (see bars 78–9, 81–2, 83–4) and the flute's subtle reminder of the piano's b♭″ oscillations from bars 84–5 in 89–90 evince a Mozartian spirit of close piano–orchestra engagement, but the musical ingredients – an intense, emphatic orchestral tutti followed by recitative-like piano writing alternating with homophonic segments in the strings – as well as the stark juxtaposition of forceful and intimate grandeur are not features of the slow movements of Mozart's concertos.

Example 5.4 Mozart, Piano Concerto in E flat, K. 449, 1st movement, bars 230–45

Stylistic and aesthetic similarities to and differences from Mozart's works also characterize Beethoven's C major Concerto, Op. 15. This is most apparent at the end of the development and beginning of the recapitulation of the first movement (Ex. 5.5). Like Mozart at the corresponding juncture of K. 449/i in particular, Beethoven renders the transition between the two sections a moment of formal disjunction rather than smooth sectional segue (see Ex. 5.4 and Ex. 5.5).[59] Just as Mozart includes an enigmatic half-step piano ascent in the context of an indecisive ♭VI – IV⁶ – ♭VII – V⁶ progression in the run-up to the recapitulation of K. 449/i (bars 230–3) and cuts it off brusquely with the orchestra's statement of the main theme (bar 234), so Beethoven abruptly interrupts an austere, static dialogue between piano and horns (bars 334–43) with furious, *ff* semiquaver scales in the piano (bars 344–5) and an ostentatious, *ff* rendition of the main theme (bar 346); it is as if the orchestra in bar 234 of K. 449/i and the piano in bar 344 of Op. 15/i have had enough of the preceding ruminations and hastily call them to a halt. In both movements, too, the piano's re-entry in the recapitulation after an eight-bar absence forms part of a new dialogue not witnessed at the corresponding junction of the solo exposition – a split-theme exchange in K. 449/i (bars 234ff.) and an imitation of ascending semiquaver scales in Op. 15/i (bars 351–6). But Beethoven ups the ante considerably in terms of musical contrasts manifest at this 'gravely dramatic' juncture of the movement.[60] Both the piano's *ff* scales and the orchestra's rendition of

Example 5.5 Beethoven, Piano Concerto No. 1 in C, Op. 15, 1st movement, bars 334–55

the main theme – which forgoes the *pp* version from bar 1 for the *ff* version from bar 16 – wrench the music aggressively from its preceding slumber; the orchestra's entry in bar 234 of K. 449/i is mild in comparison. Indeed, Beethoven maximizes the impact of the recapitulation, not only by adopting the *ff* rather than the *pp* version of the first theme, but also by co-opting the piano unambiguously into the articulation of grand force; the piano's sweeping semiquavers pave the way majestically for the *ff* onset of the recapitulation and – in dialogue with the violins and flutes – for the ensuing ascending semiquavers (bar 347). Dialogue of a non-confrontational kind makes a decisive entry into the realm of forceful grandeur.

If Beethoven's Piano Concertos Nos. 1 and 2 mark the beginning of a new aesthetic path – especially in the increase in intensity of orchestral grandeur and in the piano's contribution to non-confrontational grand force – then the Piano Concerto No. 3 in C minor, Op. 37 (first performed in 1803), moves significantly further in this direction. Its connection to Mozart's concertos has long been a topic of discussion, even in the early nineteenth century. Explaining the development from Haydn to Mozart to Beethoven's style in December 1808, Johann Friedrich Reichardt (1752–1814) clarifies that Mozart 'placed more importance [than Haydn] in an artfully developed work, and thus built out of Haydn's charmingly imagined summerhouse his own palace. Beethoven settled down in this palace very early, and thus in order for him too to express his own nature in its own forms, he was left no choice but to build a bold and defiant tower on top of which no one could easily place anything more.'[61] Citing Reichardt's passage in his *Neues Historisches Lexikon der Tonkünstler* of 1812–14, Ernst Ludwig Gerber advises his reader to listen to Beethoven's C minor Concerto – or at least to study it through the *AmZ* review of 1805 – in order to witness this process at work, thus placing Op. 37 at a crucial nexus of stylistic evolution from Mozart to Beethoven.[62]

The closest point of connection between Beethoven's Op. 37 and Mozart's concerto repertory in tonal, thematic and affective terms is Mozart's own C minor Concerto, K. 491.[63] The orchestral ritornello of Op. 37/i, like its counterpart in K. 491/i, provides a rich variety of dialogue between and among strings and winds, but, in contrast to K. 491/i, does not foreshadow intimate engagement between piano and orchestra in the solo exposition; indeed, the piano and the orchestra do not see eye to eye in this section, aside from during the presentation of the secondary theme. The piano monopolizes the first theme and its continuation following on from its initial, assertive semiquaver scales (bar 111ff.), sets brilliant figuration directly against the orchestra's *ff* rendition of the main theme head-motif in the transition (bars 138–45), and passes up an ideal opportunity for dialogue with the clarinets and horns – again involving the head-motif – towards the end (see bars 219ff.). The first two sections of Mozart's B flat Piano Concerto, K. 450/i, are somewhat similar to the corresponding sections of Beethoven's concerto, since – unusually for Mozart – the initial wind–strings collaboration (orchestral ritornello) is replaced by piano–orchestra confrontation (solo exposition).[64] But later in K. 450/i and Op. 37/i Mozart and Beethoven respond differently to this state of affairs, revealing different aesthetic priorities. Whereas Mozart resolves confrontation wrought by the piano's domination of the main theme in the solo exposition by integrating piano, strings and winds into a collaborative three-way exchange at the nexus of development and recapitulation, subsequently bringing back a theme from the orchestral ritornello omitted in the solo exposition in three-way dialogue in order to emphasize the new-found closeness of piano and orchestral protagonists (bars 248–64), Beethoven makes no effort to address the source of the impasse between piano and orchestra from the solo exposition, namely the absence of collaborative dialogue involving the main theme. The splitting of the main theme between piano and cellos near the beginning of the development (bars 257–60) suggests that change is afoot in this respect, but no further progress is made in the recapitulation. The orchestra performs the main theme without the involvement of the piano at the opening of the section (bars 309–16); moreover, the winds and strings pass the end of the theme back and forth (bars 315–22) as the piano, re-entering with falling quaver arpeggios, again fails to partake in the exchange of this material. The confrontations from the transition are no longer present, but neither are the kinds of elaborations of piano–orchestra dialogue characteristic of the recapitulations of Mozart's first movements.[65] In addition, the exchange of the main theme between winds and strings during the first eight bars of the ritornello preceding the cadenza (403–10) only emphasizes further the piano's consistent lack of engagement with this theme in the context of solo–orchestra dialogue. For Mozart, elaboration of piano–orchestra dialogue from the solo exposition in the recapitulation – or less commonly a progression from competitive to collaborative exchange – is a standard feature of the first movements of his piano concertos; intimate grandeur thus plays a central role in defining the evolving relationship between solo and orchestral protagonists. But the same cannot be said for the first movement of Beethoven's C minor Concerto. It is not that intimate grandeur is absent – several piano–orchestra dialogues are as subtle and intimate as those typically found in a Mozart first movement – rather that its presence in a relationship-defining capacity can no longer be taken for granted. Without intimate grandeur in a pivotal role, what is more, grandeur (in terms of orchestral force and oppositional piano-orchestra dialogue) moves centre-stage.

The coda to the first movement of Beethoven's C minor Concerto, which directly follows the cadenza, captures in microcosm the changed aesthetic significance of dialogue and the pronounced emphasis on forceful grandeur.[66] As early as 1805 the long, aforementioned review of the work in the *AmZ* draws attention to distinctive solo and orchestral sounds in this section, identifying the 'uncommonly agreeable way' in which it 'excites the spirits ... through the excellent choice and treatment of the instruments', in particular the use of the timpani.[67] The piano first alternates its semiquaver flourishes with the bar 3 motif in the timpani (bars 417–24) – another example of a solo–orchestra dialogue with contrasting material that eschews forceful confrontation – and then dialogues the motif with the violas and cellos/basses (bars 425–8, Ex. 5.6), both parties subsequently adapting their material (bars 429–34, Ex. 5.6). But the principal purpose of this dialogue is not to illustrate the strong rapport between solo and orchestral protagonists, even though the progressive thematic modifications in both the piano and the lower strings demonstrate collaborative intent. The dialogue is primarily intended instead to sustain the drive to a *ff* tutti climax in bar 435, a moment of indubitable grandeur. Whereas Mozart's elaborations to piano–orchestra dialogue – both from moment to moment and from section to section – render the intimate grandeur of dialogue increasingly more intimate, Beethoven's elaborations to dialogue in this passage build to an intense tutti interjection; intimate grandeur thus serves the musical needs of forceful grandeur.

The central roles fulfilled by grandeur and brilliance in Beethoven's piano concertos, eclipsing the intimate grandeur of solo–orchestra dialogue, are also evident in the first movements of No. 4 in G major, Op. 58 (1806), and No. 5 in E flat major, Op. 73 ('Emperor') (1809). In Op. 58/i, piano–orchestra dialogues are frequent, but rarely protracted; they almost always segue immediately, moreover, to a resumption of solo brilliance (see, for example, bars 69ff., 89ff., 111ff., 134ff. in the solo exposition). As such, instances of intimate grandeur represent brief introductions to solo brilliance, rather than (as in Mozart's works) fundamental gauges of solo–orchestra relations; dialogue is a means to an end rather than an end in itself. While the main theme, passed unhurriedly from piano to strings at the famous opening of the work (bars 1–14), is an exception, its *ff* reappearance at the beginning of the recapitulation takes the piano away from intimate grandeur into the realm of solo-orientated forceful grandeur. The *ff* orchestral tutti in bars 251–2 is not simply a gesture designed 'to keep up the grandeur of the piece' (following Kollmann),[68] but is also a preparation for the piano's grand statement of the main theme (253ff.). Carrying this moment of crucial formal significance by itself and with considerable force, the piano puts itself on grand parity with the orchestra. Whereas Mozart's soloist achieved this kind of grand status only in taut dialogic

Example 5.6 Beethoven, Piano Concerto No. 3 in C minor, Op. 37, 1st movement, bars 425–37

confrontations with the orchestra, Beethoven's soloist widens its grand remit well beyond oppositional effects. Nowhere is this better illustrated, of course, than at the opening of the 'Emperor' Concerto, a passage that 'tells only of a potential for confrontation' rather than actually demonstrating it.[69] The piano's brilliant figurations are unequivocally grand, expanding the *ff* I – IV – V^7 orchestral chords into a broad, ten-bar opening salvo; the soloist simultaneously supports and is supported by the orchestra, both parties contributing equally to the work's majestic beginning. In the development, too, the piano is an equal participant in a grand dialogue (bars 304–10). Asserting its right to partake in this climactic, march-like segment of the development section with *ff* interjections of the prevailing motif, the piano presents itself as a match for the forceful wind and brass sections.

Viewed collectively, the first movements of Beethoven's five piano concertos trace a progression away from the late eighteenth-century balance of grandeur, intimate grandeur and brilliance towards a privileged status for grandeur and brilliance: the piano is assimilated as a grand participant, without having to rely on confrontation with the orchestra; brilliance becomes an important component in the articulation of grandeur, again independently of confrontation; and intimate grandeur is marginalized as a barometer of solo–orchestra relations. A parallel progression characterizes the recasting of intimacy in the slow movements. Permeating the middle movements of the first, second, third and fifth concertos, intimacy is acknowledged, albeit indirectly, in early nineteenth-century commentaries: No. 3/ii is an 'attempt at a portrait of the melancholic mood of a noble soul, depicted in the subtlest nuances. . . . [Beethoven] has brought into play here all means that this instrument possesses for the expression of gentle feelings'; No. 1/ii is 'an extremely pleasant piece, richly melodic, and . . . greatly embellished by the obbligato clarinet'; No. 2/ii contains a melody that 'must be performed softly, but with the most cantabile expression, and the simplicity of the passages must rise above the accompanying orchestra, by means of a refined tone and elegant delivery'; and No. 5/ii expresses 'holy calm and devotion'.[70] However, with the exception of the slow movements of the first two concertos, and in contrast to the middle movements of almost all of Mozart's Viennese concertos, intimacy is *not* a direct result of frequent recourse to solo–orchestra dialogue – intimate grandeur gives way to a more general atmosphere of intimacy. The middle movement of the Fourth Concerto, irrespective of scholarly controversy concerning its association with the Orpheus legend, is *sui generis* in Beethoven's concerto output – a bald confrontation (for the first half at least) of a quiet, *molto cantabile* and *molto espressivo* soloist and a loud, *sempre staccato* and rhythmically rigid string section.[71] Yet the movement also aptly symbolizes the historical and aesthetic position of Beethoven's concertos. Demonstrably 'original' in its colliding worlds of intimacy and grandeur, it continues to support the kind of carefully articulated progression to piano/orchestra intimacy – via orchestral *p* and *pp* dynamics (bar 38ff.), orchestral accommodation of the piano's lengthy soliloquy (bars 47–63) and 1st violin–piano dialogue (bars 68–70) – that is typical of Mozart's concertos.[72] For neither the first nor the last time, Beethoven dramatizes in remarkable fashion continuity with and departure from late eighteenth-century aesthetic and stylistic trends.

6 The nineteenth-century piano concerto

STEPHAN D. LINDEMAN

The piano concerto manifests a remarkable expansion during the nineteenth century in terms of the number of composers writing works in the form, and in the basic parameters of the genre itself; that is, the number of movements, size of the individual sections, instrumentation of the orchestra, and the technical demands placed on the soloist. The piano concerto is the most high-profile subspecies of the genre at this time. This chapter will investigate issues such as compositional responses to Mozart, and then Beethoven, the role of virtuosity, structural developments in the form, symphonic dimensions, and programmatic aspects of individual works.

In the early decades of the nineteenth century, composers continued to exploit the possibilities inherent in the piano concerto genre as codified by Mozart, whose twenty-three original concertos had all been published by 1806.[1] A study of almost any concerto composed during the first third of the nineteenth century (and considerably later as well) reveals the profound influence of these works. Mozart's concertos were performed by nearly every composer in the early nineteenth century (as Beethoven's would be later in the century), creating a tradition which, of course, continues to this day. The nineteenth century also saw a dramatic increase in the number of municipal concert venues and music festivals associated with the rise of the middle class in the wake of the industrial revolution, in combination with the existing venues belonging to the nobility, cities, states and countries. Orchestras were attached to many of these, and an increasing number of travelling composer-pianists developed thriving careers performing concerted works in these venues. In contrast to the older class of cultivated amateurs, this new generation 'demanded titillation by ever more spectacular virtuosity'.[2]

Composers in the nineteenth century were cognizant of their colleagues' efforts in the genre, and a great deal of cross-fertilization occurred. While maintaining certain aspects of the Mozartian approach on the one hand (particularly in the early part of the century), these composers also began to expand a number of the basic parameters of the form. This expansion – of the thematic content, harmonic vocabulary and technical demands placed on the soloist – precipitated a renegotiation of the terms of the engagement between the soloist and the orchestra. Their responses to these challenges are manifested in the changing approaches to the concerto throughout the century.

Previous writings on the nineteenth-century concerto have been organized according to activities in various important cities, geographic regions and important virtuosos. As a result of Mozart's exemplary status, some of the most important developments in the genre first occurred in the works of composers active in or originating from Vienna, Prague, Berlin and other German-speaking lands. But important developments were also occurring in London, Paris and elsewhere. It will be helpful for us to proceed from a chronological perspective, in that profound changes to the form of the concerto – particularly the first movement – begin to be seen in the second quarter of the century. And following in the wake of the radical changes of the 1830s, as manifest in the Mendelssohn and Liszt concertos in particular, an even greater variety of approaches to the genre is apparent in the second half of the century.

The piano concerto from the turn of the nineteenth century to the 1830s

One of the most important composers of concertos active at the end of the eighteenth and beginning of the nineteenth centuries was Jan Ladislav Dussek (1760–1812). The chronology of his concertos is murky; at least eighteen span nearly a third of a century. Some are lost; some specify either pianoforte or harp. Sometimes identical works were printed by different publishers with conflicting opus numbers and ordinal listings; some have no opus numbers at all. In addition, his slow movements were sometimes used interchangeably.

Dussek is probably the first important composer to omit improvised cadenzas, and their absence in many nineteenth-century concertos has been attributed to his influence. His G minor Concerto from 1801, Op. 49 (also published as Op. 50), begins with an opening tutti that is monothematic, perhaps reflecting Haydn's influence. The subsequent solo exposition, however, offers a completely fresh trinity of themes (primary, secondary and closing). The orchestra's themes are never uttered by the soloist, and vice versa. Dussek seems to establish a discrete, isolated thematic world for the soloist, removed from that of the orchestra.

Dussek's final surviving concerto, Op. 70, in E flat major, was composed in 1810, two years before his death. The gargantuan first movement numbers 570 bars (the average length of the first movements of Mozart's piano concertos is 344 bars; Beethoven's is 450 bars). As in the Op. 49 Concerto, the first movement of Op. 70 attempts to define separate worlds for the orchestra and soloist, with the protagonists sharing little. The recapitulation is substantially abridged and altered, hinting at abridgements to first-movement form that will be the subject of experimentation by other composers in subsequent years.

Dussek's younger contemporary, Johann Baptist Cramer (1771–1858), contributed eight piano concertos and one *Concerto da camera* to the genre. Excepting his final essay, the Concerto No. 8 in D minor, Op. 70, his concertos are quite conservative, especially in comparison with the work of his contemporaries, and were written over a span of more than thirty years.

Cramer's concertos that precede his Op. 70 reveal a somewhat strange combination of old and new stylistic features. On the one hand, few works include harmonic digressions to distant keys, a relatively common feature of the concertos of Cramer's younger contemporaries. Moreover, six of the concertos contain a 'fourth' ritornello to demarcate the end of the development (a characteristic that represents one of the last remnants of the Baroque conception of the form, one that is still evident in some later eighteenth-century concertos, though rarely in Mozart).[3] On the other hand, like most composers writing after 1800, Cramer did not call for improvised cadenzas; they are only found in the last two concertos, and here, written out in full. In Cramer's Eighth Concerto, the second movement features a lengthy written cadenza that functions as a transition to the finale.

Entirely shattering the Mozartian mould employed in the eight previous concerted works, the 54-year-old Cramer inexplicably demonstrated a completely new conception of the genre in his final essay, the Piano Concerto No. 8 in D minor, Op. 70 (1825). The work is cast in the traditional three-movement format; however, it is also replete with bold and original features. Proportionally, the concerto is unusual when compared to the works of his predecessors. It is heavily end-weighted with a finale of nearly 350 bars in contrast to an opening Moderato assai of 231 bars and a second movement of 107. Cramer's design includes a quasi recapitulation, in the finale, of a thematic idea first introduced in the opening movement, thereby casting a sonata-like structure across the entire span of the work; this also creates an air of organic cohesion.

The opening movement of Cramer's Op. 70 begins with discrete tutti and solo expositions. Rather than concluding the solo exposition with a closing tutti, as we would expect, the soloist initiates an abrupt move back to the tonic instead and prolongs this sonority for almost thirty bars. The movement jerks to a halt at this juncture and the Larghetto middle movement then follows in D major. With this design, Cramer jettisons the second ritornello, development, recapitulation, cadenza and concluding tutti. The formal implications of the exposition are thus unrealized in the first movement; development and resolution have become the business of the later movements.

Cramer was quite possibly influenced in his design of Op. 70 by two works, Louis Spohr's Violin Concerto No. 8, *In modo di Scena Cantante* (composed 1816 and published 1820), and the Carl Maria von Weber *Konzertstück* for Piano and Orchestra in F minor, Op. 79 (composed 1821 and published 1823). However, Cramer's Op. 70 may have been performed as early as 1819, thus clouding the issue of influence and not ruling out the possibility that he in fact influenced the other two composers. Cramer, Spohr and Weber were friends, and had relatively frequent contact at this time. In any event, something was certainly 'in the air' given the points of similarity between these works. (The Weber work is discussed briefly below.)

Johann Nepomuk Hummel (1778–1837) was active at the same time as Dussek and Cramer, and a greater influence than them on subsequent composers. Hummel's concertos may be regarded as a link between the late eighteenth-century concept of the genre, and the early efforts of the nineteenth century. Hummel composed some twenty concerted works, including (separate) concertos for bassoon, mandolin, trumpet and other instruments, a Double Concerto for Piano and Violin in G major, Op. 17 (*c*.1805, sometimes listed as 'Concerto No. 1'), and around eight concertos for piano and orchestra, including No. 2 in C major, Op. 34a, Op. 73 in G major (*Die Feyer des Geburts, oder Namenstages der Eltern*), Op. 85 in A minor (1820–1), Op. 89 in B minor (1821), Op. 110 in E major (composed and performed in 1814, but resurrected for a Paris concert in 1825, with the title *Les Adieux* appended), Op. 113 in A flat major; and the Op. posth. 1 in F major (*Dernier Concerto*).

Most important of these is a pair of concertos from the early 1820s, the Piano Concertos in A minor (Op. 85) and B minor (Op. 89). These works were concert staples in the early nineteenth century – learned, studied and performed by nearly all fledgling virtuosos, including Felix Mendelssohn, Fanny Mendelssohn Hensel, Frédéric Chopin, Robert Schumann, Clara Wieck (later Schumann), Franz Liszt, (Charles-) Valentin Alkan and many others, particularly in Russia in the second half of the century. The opening movements of Hummel's Opp. 85 and 89, although cast in an eighteenth-century Mozartian double-exposition design, are nevertheless replete with colourful chromatic juxtapositions and harmonic digressions to distant key areas, and are full of increased technical demands on the soloist that are usually forged to the needs of the form, rather than exploited simply for the purposes of technical display. The slow movements, containing much virtuoso filigree, are dominated by the soloist.

The piano concertos of Irish-born John Field (1782–1837) are of prime importance to the development of the genre in the early nineteenth century. Like Dussek's, Field's seven piano concertos were written over a lengthy period. The first movements are all cast in a double-exposition structure. Nevertheless, the works are replete with more progressive features, such as startling harmonic digressions and juxtapositions, and increased technical demands on the soloist; they also manifest some early traits of Romanticism, illustrated for example by Field's appended programmatic title for his Piano Concerto No. 5 in C major, *L'incendie par l'orage* (1815).

Field's penchant for rather shocking harmonic digressions in his concertos – a feature influential on many later nineteenth-century composers – is evident in the solo exposition of the opening movement of his Piano Concerto No. 3 in E flat major (1816), following the modulation to the dominant key area. Particularly idiomatic, this consists almost exclusively of brilliant passage-work, and confirms the new key in a series of cascading arpeggios and scales. The listener expects at this point (usually one of the more stable harmonic areas of the movement) the soloist's obligatory prolonged trill over the dominant of the new key, a clear resolution, and the commencement of the second ritornello. Instead, Field introduces a striking digression, which serves to deceive the listener as to the perception of the harmony in force, before reintroducing the 'correct' key just as quickly, and ending the exposition (and the recapitulation) in a blaze of virtuoso glory, applauded by the ensuing ritornello. This pattern becomes almost formulaic in the works of composers just after Field, frequently involving distant keys such as the flat mediant or submediant.

Quite unusually, Field's final effort, the Concerto No. 7 in C minor, is cast in only two movements, though each is very long (the first 586 bars, and the finale a gargantuan 753) and includes a number of subsections. The digressional pattern discussed above occurs in even more pronounced fashion in this work, this time involving G flat major, the flat mediant of the mediant, and a tritone away from the tonic! The subsequent development is set off by a double bar line, with key and time signatures changing to G major; the soloist ushers in a lyrical theme in sunny G major, consisting entirely of the composer's own Nocturne No. 12 in G major.

Ferdinand Ries (1784–1838), an almost exact contemporary of Field, was a prolific composer, among whose works number an early violin concerto, eight piano concertos, and other concerted works. Several of the concertos have descriptive programmatic titles, such as Op. 132 (*Farewell to London*, 1823–4), and Op. 151 (*Salut au Rhin*, 1824). In addition, the

Piano Concerto No. 3 in C sharp minor, Op. 55 (composed by 1813), provides a cogent and clever example of the digression procedure previously witnessed in the two Field concertos. In the first movement, the soloist presents the second theme in the major dominant, instead of the mediant. Following this, and in a position analogous to that of the Field concertos, Ries introduces a colourful harmonic digression, with a modulation to E major, enharmonic ♭VI of A flat major. This dramatic harmonic shift adumbrates Ries's exploitation of this same relationship in the subsequent two movements of the work, the Larghetto being cast in A major and the rondo finale including contrasting episodes in both E and A major (the flat mediant and submediant of C sharp major, the key in which the work ends).

Carl Maria von Weber (1786–1826) was born two years after Ries. In addition to a pair of clarinet concertos and a concertino, a bassoon concerto, a horn concertino and other miscellaneous concerted works, he composed two piano concertos (No. 1 in C major, Op. 11 (1810–11), and No. 2 in E flat major (1811–12)), and a highly influential work, the *Konzertstück* in F minor for Piano and Orchestra, Op. 79. Both piano concertos generally adhere to traditional formal arrangements, and are quite conservative in comparison to some of the composer's other efforts in the concerto genre. Abandoning traditional concerto form after the E flat major Piano Concerto, Weber composed no other work in the traditional format after 1812.

A number of concertos from the early nineteenth century have a programmatic basis, as we have already seen. It is likely, however, that these programmatic subtitles were usually afterthoughts, and not part of the original conception of the works in question. With Weber's Op. 79 (originally begun as a third piano concerto in 1815), however, the composer forged the programmatic conception of his piece from its very inception and was inspired by the desire to create and portray a specific dramatic story. This strikingly novel approach involved a programme that Weber described as:

> a kind of story whose thread will connect and define its character – moreover, one so detailed and at the same time dramatic that I found myself obliged to give it the following headings: Allegro, Parting. Adagio, Lament. Finale, Profoundest misery, consolation, reunion, jubilation.[4]

Setting the concerto aside for a number of years, Weber resumed work in 1821 and completed it shortly thereafter. The work, now titled *Konzertstück*, had a more extended programme, involving a medieval knight on a Middle Eastern crusade, with his loved one awaiting his return.[5]

Weber's *Konzertstück*, Op. 79, has been considered by some to be the progenitor of the Romantic concerto. Tovey regarded the work as 'the origin of the post-classical concerto form. ... The Conzertstück puts all later and more ambitious efforts to shame'.[6] Inspired by Weber's desire to portray a specific dramatic situation, Op. 79 handily offers a solution to the problems inherent in the traditional form. The composer, for example, casts off any formal gestures that he considered superfluous to the representation of the drama and connects the three movements together with transitions that weave together a seamless whole. In the first movement, Weber makes a lean, cogent and forceful presentation of the essential elements of a concerto, devoid of fluff. Separate tutti and solo expositions are excised and substituted instead with a combined presentation of primary and secondary thematic materials; there is no closing ritornello after the exposition, no development, no recapitulation of the second group, no cadenza, and no third ritornello, the latter being replaced by a combined tutti/solo coda. The overall result must have been regarded as dramatic and revolutionary by the young composers of the 1820s and 1830s. Weber had clearly pointed the way ahead for them.

Born in Prague to a German family, Ignaz Moscheles (1794–1870) was considered one of the finest virtuosos of the early nineteenth century. His eight piano concertos, composed between 1819 and 1838, reflect many of the changes apparent in the genre at this time. The first five concertos are largely cast in a late eighteenth-century guise. Among these works, Moscheles's third essay in the genre, the G minor Concerto, Op. 60 (also issued as Op. 58), is the only one of his concertos to maintain a degree of currency; published in 1820, it is still in print. The first movement of this concerto exploits a distant harmonic relationship similar to those we have encountered in the Field and Ries concertos and at the same point in the movement as well. Like Field and Ries, Moscheles employs this as a clever ruse, dramatically underscoring the exciting conclusion to the solo exposition and subsequent recapitulation and infusing this juncture of the movement with even greater virtuosic demands.

Revealing that Moscheles was a keen observer of his colleagues' respective approaches to the genre, the final three concertos that he composed in the wake of Mendelssohn's G minor Concerto, Op. 25 (published 1832), manifest a much more progressive, even radical stance than his earlier works. They each carry programmatic titles: No. 6 in B flat major, *Concerto fantastique* (1833); No. 7 in C minor, *Concerto pathétique* (1835–6), and No. 8 in D major, *Concerto pastorale* (1838). Moreover, they all follow a multi-, interconnected movement pattern, including cyclical thematic design. These later works may reveal Moscheles's awareness of the concertos of Daniel Steibelt (1765–1823), who composed eight essays in the genre, most in an unusual two-movement design (although the first movements are cast in double-exposition form). The first, in

C major, was published in 1796; the later works all carry programmatic titles, including No. 3 in E major, Op. 33, *L'orage* (published 1799), No. 5 in E flat major, Op. 64, *A la chasse* (published 1802), No. 6 in G minor, *Le voyage au Mont St Bernard* (*c.*1816), and No. 7 in E minor (scored for two orchestras), *Grand Military Concerto, dans le genre des Grecs* (*c.*1816). Some of these feature written cadenzas inserted before the secondary group. Steibelt's final, and unpublished, concerto (No. 8 in E flat major, 1820) with a *Bacchanalian Rondo* finale, stipulates an 'accompanied chorus', preceding Busoni by almost a century.

With these early nineteenth-century attempts to redefine the Mozartian model in more modern terms, the form of the concerto had, to a certain extent, broken down by the 1830s (notwithstanding later successful attempts to breathe fresh life into it). Another highly influential composition – also stemming from the 1820s, but from another genre – would greatly influence subsequent composers of piano concertos, Franz Schubert's Piano Fantasy in C major (*Wanderer*), Op. 15/D760 (1822). The title refers to his Lied 'Der Wanderer' (1816), which Schubert used as the basis for the second movement set of variations. The *Wanderer* Fantasy is cast in four sections or movements, which correspond loosely to the shape of a piano sonata: an Allegro opening; a contrasting Adagio; a Presto dance-like movement; and an Allegro finale. Unlike most sonatas composed before this date, however, the work is designed to be performed without a break between movements; transitions link the movements together. The four sections of the Fantasy suggest the outlines of a single sonata-form movement, unified by the *Wanderer* rhythmic cell (long–short–short–long). The design of the first section is intentionally 'short circuited'; a secondary key area is established, but cast in the major mediant, E, rather than the usual dominant. Following a development-like section, a retransition leads us to expect a recapitulation, but instead we are ushered into a new transition to the next movement. Here, the rarefied atmosphere of the dominant of C sharp minor, the key of the subsequent movement, leaves us suspended. Clearly, Schubert intends to shift the weight of the piece from its traditional location in the opening movement to later in the work, sweeping us along with the drama of the later movements.

The radical design of the *Wanderer* Fantasy struck a responsive chord in many early Romantic composers. Indeed, the construction of concertos by Mendelssohn, Alkan, Liszt, Wieck, Schumann, and others all imply intimate familiarity with Schubert's work. It so enamoured Liszt, for example, that he turned it into a piano concerto in the early 1850s. Moreover, the seamless weaving from one movement to the next sparked a new direction in the experiments with connecting transitions between movements, as we have seen in the Weber *Konzertstück*.

By the 1830s, in what should be regarded as a profound and revolutionary development in the evolution of the concerto genre, progressive composers began to perceive the first ritornello of the opening movement (and in some cases, nearly all formal and discrete orchestral sections) as redundant and archaic. The resulting concertos may be described as manifestations of two essentially distinct conceptions:

(a) *The concerto as an orchestral work with piano obbligato*. Here the soloist is assimilated into the society of the orchestra by downplaying the individual's special identity, making the performer work within a symphonic process and with materials that are more symphonic than pianistic. Beethoven perhaps envisioned this situation for his abandoned Sixth Piano Concerto.[7] This conception is manifest in the mature Mendelssohn and Schumann concertos among others.

In 1847, theorist Adolph Bernhard Marx described just such a conception, with concerto form no longer distinguished from that of the sonata: the former's disposition 'is that of the sonata in three movements'.[8] Tutti/solo alternation is merely a matter of orchestration, not structure. Marx, as Jane Stevens writes, is the first to understand 'the solo and orchestra solely as cooperative elements working out a single, symphonic form', with the opening tutti performing a merely introductory, and decidedly subservient, role.[9]

(b) *The concerto as a solo work with orchestral accompaniment*. In this type of concerto, the orchestra is assimilated into the soloist's world by de-emphasizing or eliminating the traditional orchestral passages. The material is now characterized by quicksilver harmonic modulations to keys far afield from the tonic and by the avoidance of a clear presentation of a 'primary theme'. Instead, the composer pervasively employs short motifs. Through this approach, typified by Liszt's works for piano and orchestra, and those of his many followers, the orchestra relinquishes its position as an equal or dominant player and adopts a supporting role in the fantasy-like world of the soloist's creation. Indeed, Liszt's creation of a concerto (1851) from the Schubert *Wanderer* Fantasy manifests this ideal.

The piano concerto in Paris

In the second third of the nineteenth century, Paris was one of the most important centres for the development of the piano concerto. In late 1831, the twenty-two-year-old Felix Mendelssohn arrived in the city for a four-month stay. During this period, he showed his new Piano Concerto No. 1 in G minor, Op. 25, still in manuscript, to the twenty-year-old Franz Liszt. Both Mendelssohn's and Liszt's conceptions of the concerto genre were profoundly influenced by Weber's *Konzertstück*, which had been a part of both of their performing repertories for some time. These two composers were good friends of Frédéric Chopin (1810–49), resident in Paris from this time until his death. His treatment of form in his two piano concertos is a special case. While both are cast in traditional three-movement design, with opening movements largely following the double-exposition paradigm, his treatment of the secondary area is quite novel in both works. His Concerto No. 1 in E minor, Op. 11 (composed in 1830 and published in 1833), has quite a curious disposition of the secondary theme throughout the movement, which Tovey dismisses as 'suicidal':[10] it is presented in the tonic major in both the tutti and the solo exposition and recurs in the mediant in the recapitulation, thus reversing the normally expected procedure. In the Concerto No. 2 in F minor, Op. 21 (1829), Chopin keeps the secondary theme in the relative major in all three presentations, another arrangement not witnessed elsewhere in the literature;[11] it never appears in the tonic. The two concertos have both been faulted by some critics for the predominance of the solo part and subservience of the orchestra (the orchestra 'merely accompanies'), while others find this a fitting setting for the gorgeous stream of lyrical melodies, and intoxicating chromatic juxtapositions. (Chopin's concertos, in this regard, echo and enrich the previously discussed formulaic harmonic digressions utilized by Field, Moscheles and Ries.) In any event, both of Chopin's concertos have consistently remained staples of the modern concert repertory, much loved by performers and the public alike.

Liszt sketched initial ideas for his Piano Concerto No. 1 in E flat major in the same month as his encounter with Mendelssohn, completing a piano score by the end of the next year (1832). As a friend of Alkan, Liszt may have informed him of his encounter with Mendelssohn's Op. 25; Mendelssohn and Alkan may also have met each other during their respective rounds of the Parisian salons. Into this environment entered the twelve-year-old prodigy Clara Wieck (later Clara Schumann), on her first concert tour to the French capital. Moving within the inner circle of the Parisian virtuosos, she met or renewed contact with most of the leading musicians of the day. Shortly after her return to Leipzig, Wieck began to formulate ideas for a first concerto of her own. And at the same time, the eighteen-year-old Alkan premièred his own initial attempt in the genre. Many works stemming from this period reveal common threads.

The concertos of (Charles-) Valentin Alkan (1813–88) are some of most progressive, even radical, responses to the problems of the genre in the mid-nineteenth century. An incredible prodigy, whom Liszt claimed to have had the 'finest technique of any pianist known to him', Alkan was admitted to the Paris Conservatoire at the age of six. By the late 1830s, his works were beginning to attract critical scrutiny, including reviews by Robert Schumann and Liszt. Alkan's compositions are thought to reflect Chopin's influence, while Alkan's 'extra-musical element and his recurrent boldness have invited comparisons with Berlioz'.[12] Alkan composed a pair of works that clearly belong to the concerto genre, and a pair of compositions that, while having some affinity with the concerto tradition, are not concertos *per se*. The former comprise the *Concerto da camera* No. 1 in A minor, Op. 10, and the *Concerto da camera* No. 2 in C sharp minor, and the latter Nos. 8–10 of the *Douze études*, Op. 39 (called the *Concerto for Solo Piano*, with a first movement cast in a massive double-exposition format), and No. 31 of the *Quarante-huit motifs (esquisse)*, Op. 63 (1861), entitled *Tutti de concerto dans le genre ancien*.

Alkan debuted his *Concerto da camera* in A minor, Op. 10, in 1832. The work is cast in a traditional three-movement structure and closely echoes two disparate works: the Hummel A minor Concerto, Op. 85, and the Cramer Piano Concerto No. 8 in D minor, Op. 70. The first movement of Alkan's Op. 10, however, is not cast in double-exposition form; there is no discrete tutti exposition, no development, no recapitulation and no cadenza. Instead, the orchestra provides a brief introduction, ushering in a combined tutti and solo exposition, which subsequently leads to the second movement; the composer here replicates the 'short-circuited' sonata-form design that we have witnessed in the first movement of the Schubert *Wanderer* Fantasy, and the Cramer Piano Concerto No. 8 in D minor, Op. 70. Alkan's second movement reveals a highly unusual disposition of keys, and his cyclical employment of thematic elements throughout all three movements reveals a desire for organic cohesion.

Alkan's *Concerto da camera* No. 2 in C sharp minor (1834) is also cast in three movements, with transitions connecting one to the next. There are no cadenzas, the work is cyclic and the writing for the soloist is extraordinarily virtuosic. The concerto is also quite brief; the three movements total a mere 176 bars and last under ten minutes.

Paris at this time was also the centre of activity for another group of piano virtuosos, including Friedrich Kalkbrenner (1775–1849), Henri Herz (1803–88), Sigismond Thalberg (1812–71) and Theodore Döhler (1814–56), who each composed several works in the concerto genre. Working in tandem with piano manufacturers who consistently strove to improve the design of pianos, these composers were known for their great pyrotechnical skill, sometimes at the expense of musical quality. Their concertos are all ostensibly cast in fairly typical, and by this point rather archaic, late eighteenth-century formal designs, artificially infused with the most extreme pyrotechnics so far conceived. The Parisian vir-tuosos were the subject of much derision in Schumann's *Neue Zeitschrift* reviews. And because these works were so popular, the critic and com-poser fretted over the future of the genre. We shall return to this topic during our discussion of Schumann's concertos.

The nineteenth-century piano concerto: Mendelssohn, Schumann, Liszt and their contemporaries

Concurrent with early nineteenth-century activities in Paris are the first important concertos by Felix Mendelssohn (1809–47). Three of his works – the Piano Concertos No. 1 in G minor, Op. 25 (1831), No. 2 in D minor, Op. 40 (1837), and the Violin Concerto in E minor, Op. 64 (1844) – are staples of the modern concerto repertory, but the remainder are less well known. Five of these are adolescent concertos written while studying with Carl Friedrich Zelter (1822–4). All are cast in a rather conventional late eighteenth-century guise, with double-exposition first movements, but are also redolent with chromatic third relations and other early nineteenth-century experimental harmonic juxtapositions and shifts.

In the early 1830s, Mendelssohn composed a pair of concerted works for piano and orchestra – the Piano Concerto No. 1, Op. 25, and the one-movement *Capriccio briliant* in B minor, Op. 22 – that were to assume considerable significance in the subsequent development of the genre. The principal features of the piano concerto include the cyclical treatment of thematic material, the unified tutti and solo exposition in the first movement, transitions between movements, and the blurring of tradi-tional structural demarcations. The influence of Weber's *Konzertstück* on Mendelssohn is profound. Before Weber, composers had run over the same ground twice, as it were, with discrete statements of the movement's thematic material by both the tutti and the soloist in their respective expositions. Mendelssohn's solution dramatically casts aside the 'redun-dant' aspect of double-exposition form, providing a cogent, closely argued presentation of unified solo–tutti thematic material. While bor-rowing from Weber, Mendelssohn nevertheless aligns himself more with the traditions of the genre than had his older colleague. The first move-ment of Op. 25 contains a nearly complete recapitulation of all thematic material introduced in the combined tutti–solo exposition. The result is a complete fusion of two forms, sonata and concerto, into a unified whole.

Other aspects of the first movement of Op. 25 demonstrate Mendelssohn's concern for balancing original, progressive ideas with the genre's more traditional features. For example, he 'bookends' a statement of the second group in the flat submediant (a key, as we have already seen, much favoured by the early Romantics) with statements in the 'right' key (the mediant). The composer's design suggests a separate harmonic world for the soloist/individual quite removed from the traditional confines of the orchestra/society, as we have also seen in some earlier efforts in the genre. Moreover, Mendelssohn's exploitation of the distant key of E major in the dreamy and lyrical world of the second movement also contributes to this goal. The ensuing finale is a traditional closing rondo. The treatment of themes is cyclical, with a return of the primary theme of the first movement in the rondo finale.

Several important concerto composers could be regarded as following closely in Mendelssohn's wake. The sixteen-year-old Clara Wieck (1819–96) premièred her Piano Concerto in A minor, Op. 7, under Mendelssohn's direction in late 1835 and the work was published the next year. The construction of Wieck's concerto is among the most radical of the time. The opening Allegro maestoso, like the first movement of Mendelssohn's Op. 25, is constructed as a unified tutti/solo presentation of the principal thematic materials. Unlike Mendelssohn's first movement, however, Wieck's is not in sonata form. Instead, it progresses rapidly, following the exposition, through a brief development-like passage and coda to a transition leading to the second-movement Romanze. The movement might therefore be regarded as a combination of the most radical features of the two designs of Wieck's predecessors: the combined tutti and solo exposition of Mendelssohn and Weber, and the 'short-circuited' design of Schubert, Cramer and Alkan. The ensuing Andante Romanze, cast in the distant key of A flat major, is intimately scored for the unusual combination of piano and solo cello. The prominence given to the cello foreshadows Robert Schumann's use of this instrument in the slow movement of his own Piano Concerto, Op. 54 (1845), and Brahms's use of it in the Andante of his Piano Concerto No. 2 in B flat major, Op. 83 (1882).

British pianist and composer William Sterndale Bennett (1816–75) composed piano concertos that are indebted to Mendelssohn, who (like Robert Schumann) was a strong supporter. Similarly, the one piano concerto by the short-lived Nobert Burgmüller (1810–36) was praised by both Mendelssohn and Schumann. In the early stages of his career, Adolf Henselt (1814–89) profoundly impressed Mendelssohn, Schumann and Liszt as one of the greatest virtuosos of his era. His Piano Concerto in F minor, Op. 16, was completed in 1844, and published three years later, but may well derive from much earlier. The work was premièred by Clara Schumann, and subsequently performed by Liszt, von Bülow, Sauer, Busoni, Gottschalk, Rachmaninov, and many others. The F minor

Concerto begins with a distinctive three-note motif very close in content and affect to the famous opening of the Rachmaninov C sharp minor Prelude. On the one hand it is cast in three movements and in Classical double-exposition design; on the other hand, cadenzas are omitted and the work is cyclical. Dramatic harmonic digressions are employed throughout, including a Mendelssohn Op. 25-like casting of the second theme in the modally borrowed flat mediant, 'bookended' with statements in the 'right' key. The development incorporates an important new theme, titled Religioso, and the movement concludes with a full recapitulation and a closing tutti. The second movement is a ternary-design Larghetto, with a *Lied ohne Worte*-type character, and an experimental harmonic disposition that parallels that of the opening movement. Three keys are prolonged – the tonic, the flat submediant (read enharmonically), and the major mediant (D♭–A–F). These key areas, a major third apart, serve to subdivide the octave symmetrically, and echo Liszt's experiments of a similar nature. The finale is a sonata rondo, with thematic material that brings to mind Mendelssohn's 'fairy' themes.

The works of Robert Schumann (1810–56) make particularly important contributions to the nineteenth-century concerto repertory. During his years with the *Neue Zeitschrift für Musik*, he personally reviewed a substantial number of concertos by his contemporaries; from this study, Schumann knew the internal workings of the concerto perhaps better than anyone else. From this vantage point, his Piano Concerto in A minor, Op. 54 (1845), his first completed essay in the form after many aborted attempts, offers a truly unique perspective on the condition of the genre. A staple of the modern concert repertory almost since its première, the concerto Op. 54 has long been regarded as Schumann's first unequivocal masterpiece in the larger forms.

During his career, Schumann conceived at least fourteen works in the category of solo instrument(s) with orchestral accompaniment, including eight piano concertos (only one of which, Op. 54, was brought to full completion), two pieces for solo piano and orchestra, a *Konzertstück* for four horns and orchestra, a violin fantasy, a cello concerto and a violin concerto.

As Leon Plantinga notes, 'of all the productions of the virtuosi Schumann liked their concertos least, because here, he felt, they were tampering with an important art form'.[13] In a review of Kalkbrenner's Fourth Concerto, Schumann particularly ridiculed the work's construction: 'I'll wager that Herr Kalkbrenner devised his introductory and internal tuttis later, and merely shoved them into place'.[14] Irritated by Theodore Döhler's cavalier treatment of the form, Schumann declaimed that 'anybody can write a jolly rondo and do it justice. But if one wants to woo a princess for his bride, it is presupposed that he must be of noble birth and disposition; or – to do away with the metaphors – if one works with so great an art form, before which even the best in the land are timid, he should know what he is doing.'[15] Whereas Schumann had once used Herz as his formal model (in his, abandoned, early F major Piano Concerto),[16] he tartly dismissed Herz's Second Concerto, Op. 74, in his 1836 review: 'Herz's Second Concerto is in C minor, and is recommended to those who liked his first'.[17]

After attempting a new concerto nearly every year from age seventeen to twenty-one, Schumann passed almost the entire decade of the 1830s without composing anything in the genre; by the end of the decade, however, he was ready to try again. In 1841, Schumann decided to make yet another attempt (his eighth) at the genre, initially creating a single-movement work, titled *Phantasie*. Adding two more movements at his publisher's request, and, after much revision over the next several years, Clara Schumann premièred the Piano Concerto in A minor, Op. 54, on 4 December 1845.

Schumann's structural conception of the A minor Concerto – nearly 550 bars for the first movement and a staggering 871 for the finale – is massive, and marks a return to the Beethovenian dimensions abandoned by many of Schumann's contemporaries. Combined with this, Schumann also responded to the latest formal developments: the work synthesizes and amalgamates some of the most progressive developments in the genre and combines them with many of the time-honoured gestures of the concerto tradition. On the one hand, Schumann employed a unified tutti and solo exposition in the first movement, wove colourful sequential harmonic digressions, employed a lengthy written cadenza, treated the material cyclically, and employed a transition between the second and third movements. On the other hand, various traditional features of the genre are retained. Schumann employs a massive development section in the first movement (transporting the listener to the remote key of A flat major, the same relationship exploited by Wieck in the first movement of her Op. 7 concerto at roughly the analogous position), capping this movement with a lengthy written cadenza; in addition both the first movement and the finale feature full-blown formal recapitulations.

The only published concerted work by Edvard Grieg (1843–1907), a student of Moscheles at the Leipzig Conservatory (founded by Mendelssohn), is the ever-popular Piano Concerto in A minor, Op. 16 (composed 1866; published 1872), one that reveals the profound influence of Mendelssohn's concertos, and, most particularly, Schumann's Op. 54 concerto in the same key. Grieg's concerto begins with the well-known descending second followed by descending-thirds motif, a gesture common in much Norwegian folk music, and utilized by the composer in other works as well. Some critics have in fact described Grieg as the 'Father of the Nationalist Concerto', with the title 'Norwegian Concerto' often appended to his A minor work.

The piano concertos of Franz Liszt offer a striking perspective on the genre *c.*1825–45, in many ways foreshadowing, and then profoundly influencing, the multiplicity of responses from composers working in the latter part of the nineteenth century. Just as Robert Schumann's Piano Concerto in A minor synthesizes and decisively sums up developments in the genre in the first half of the nineteenth century, so Liszt's numerous concerto efforts (including *Malédiction*, *Grande fantaisie symphonique* and *De profundis, psaume instrumental* in addition to the two numbered piano concertos) parallel Schumann's search for a viable solution to the problems of the genre. Like Schumann, Liszt was intimately familiar with the concertos of his predecessors and contemporaries. He experimented with many different formats of concerto design, revising two works – Nos. 1 and 2 – over a quarter of a century before producing versions with which he was content.

Though initially sketched in late 1832, Liszt's Concerto No. 1 in E flat major was not completed and performed for twenty years. Premièred in 1855, and finally published in 1857, the work had undergone at least five substantial revisions. The final, published version is cast in one large movement, with four discrete sections, including a scherzo. The first section includes a combined tutti/solo introduction and statement of primary and secondary themes, a sequential digression area leading to a closing section, no formal development, a recapitulation of the primary group an enharmonic minor third above the tonic, no restatement of the secondary theme or digression, a recapitulation of the closing section in the tonic, and a coda. Several written cadenza-like sections occur throughout the opening section. As a whole this section is difficult to comprehend in terms of traditional key-relationships, in part because quite-distant harmonic centres are boldly juxtaposed. Liszt's intent may have been to create an intoxicating wash of sound created by passages such as the sequential harmonic pattern of descending major thirds (bars 61–70) or by juxtaposing statements of the primary motif one semitone or whole-tone apart. However, it has been suggested that Liszt was creating a new manner of tonal organization, one that is not based on traditional tonic–dominant polarity, but rather on a tertian subdivision of the octave into minor or major thirds. Distant key-relationships are also in evidence in the loose ternary Quasi Adagio second section: the A section is in B major, the middle section in C major, and the return of the A section and primary theme in E major. The ensuing Allegretto vivace

(Scherzo) progresses to a transition that leads to the finale. In this final section, themes from the previous three sections are introduced in turn.

The Piano Concerto No. 2 in A major (1839; published 1861), like No. 1, is a multi-section, one-movement work, in a rhapsodic, 'continuously unfolding "cyclic" structure'.[18] The resulting design is considerably further removed from the traditions of the form, which were already blurred significantly in the First Concerto. Robert Collett has described the design as midway between the discrete divisions of the First Concerto into separate sections and a single sonata-form structure that spans one long continuous movement, as in the B minor Piano Sonata.[19] The concerto's single movement contains nearly 600 bars, and its sections are marked by many changes in tempo, metre, key signature, dynamics and texture. The beginnings of these sections are often underscored by written cadenzas. The principal unifying feature of the concerto is its thematic transformation of the primary theme, which appears in many guises, set in different tempos, keys and scorings.

While the Piano Concertos Nos. 1 and 2 are widely known, it was established by Jay Rosenblatt only in 1988 that at approximately the same time that Liszt revised the First Concerto and composed the initial version of the Second Concerto in 1839, he was also working on another Piano Concerto in E flat major, which Rosenblatt designated as *op. posth.*[20] This work is cast in one long movement (493 bars), comprising five distinct parts.

The piano concerto after 1850: Brahms, Dvořák, Saint-Saëns and Litolff

Around the middle of the nineteenth century, a number of composers came to regard Beethoven's concertos as the model to emulate. This was the result of a number of factors, including the establishment of the Bonn Beethovenhaus memorial, the prescriptions of critics and theorists such as Lenz and Marx, the writings of Berlioz and Wagner, the sketch studies of Gustav Nottebohm, Breitkopf & Härtel's edition of the Beethoven *Gesamtausgabe*, and the importance of Beethoven's works in the establishment of a repertory canon. We therefore see a return to processes used by Beethoven – especially the double-exposition format, and his experiments with introducing the soloist within the confines of the first ritornello (as in the first movements of the Fourth and Fifth Concertos, Opp. 58 and 73). Equally, though, individual composers operate flexibly, employing the traditional double-exposition form on one occasion, for example, and a unified tutti and solo exposition on another.

From this perspective, it is enlightening to witness Johannes Brahms (1833–97), who was so close to Robert and Clara Schumann, cast his own Piano Concerto No. 1 in D minor, Op. 15 (published in 1861), in the more traditional manner. Though composed in Brahms's early twenties, it is regarded as 'one of the most powerful statements after Beethoven in what Carl Dahlhaus called the *symphonic style*, which aimed for monumental effects achieved by orchestral means'.[21] It is Brahms's first work for orchestra, and, particularly in the first movement (described as Brahms's expression of grief at Schumann's suicide attempt), comparisons with Beethoven's Ninth Symphony are obvious: the use of the dramatic, throbbing pedal-point; the primary theme of Op. 15 echoing that of the Ninth in its angular construction; and the juxtaposition of the tonic and the submediant. Brahms's concerto is cast in three distinct movements, with separate tutti and solo expositions in the first (a paradigm employed in all four of Brahms's concerted works). The second movement is his self-described 'gentle portrait' of Clara Schumann, with thematic links to the first movement; there are no connecting transitions between movements. The finale, in rondo form, was closely modelled on the finale of Beethoven's Piano Concerto No. 3 in C minor, Op. 37, in a manner that 'might be called neo-classical'.[22]

Brahms's other concertos reveal a variety of approaches. Although the first movement of the Violin Concerto in D major, Op. 77 (published 1879), is also cast in double-exposition form, the work was originally conceived with the addition of a fourth (scherzo) movement. Brahms's last two concertos reveal clever manipulations of the listener's expectations with regard to the shape of the first movement. In both works, Brahms seems to have had the beginning of the Beethoven 'Emperor' Concerto in mind. In the opening of the Piano Concerto No. 2 in B flat major, Op. 83 (published 1882), the early appearance of the piano soloist in the second bar immediately engages the orchestra, even though the movement is cast in double-exposition form. (Brahms was following the cue of Beethoven's Fourth and Fifth Piano Concertos in this respect.) The fourth movement, a scherzo, contributes to the imposing dimensions of Brahms's Op. 83 and – as it had for Moscheles, Litolff and Liszt, who had preceded Brahms in this respect – brought the concerto genre closer to that of the symphony. Brahms's scherzo features a compact sonata form in D minor, followed by a D major trio. Walter Frisch states that 'it is as if the worlds of the earlier D minor Concerto and the more recent Violin Concerto are put side by side'.[23] The subsequent Andante features much writing for solo cello and piano, a texture that features prominently in the slow movement of Clara Wieck's Piano Concerto in A minor, Op. 7.

The four concertos of Antonín Dvořák (1841–1904), composed over a thirty-year span, may be seen as profoundly influenced by Brahms. The twenty-four-year-old Dvořák's first attempt was an abandoned Cello Concerto in A minor (1865). His second effort, the G minor Piano Concerto, Op. 33, was written over a decade later (1876), and was premièred in 1878. The work's debt to contemporary Czech music has often been noted by critics, particularly the finale, which incorporates a Bohemian dance, a type of material not previously encountered in a piano concerto. As the composer had written five symphonies between the abandoned Cello Concerto and the G minor Piano Concerto, he was obviously confident of his handling of formal issues and orchestration. The first movement in particular may be regarded as following Beethovenian traditions, with high technical demands placed on the piano soloist, but with the piano merged into the orchestral fabric in such a way that there is little opportunity to reveal pyrotechnical powers.

Like Dvořák, Camille Saint-Saëns (1835–1921) was one of the most popular composers of concertos in the second half of the nineteenth century, his repertory including around ten full-scale concerto works, two of which have consistently remained in the concert repertory. The solo part is highly virtuoso in all of his concertos (some commentators have described less-inspired moments as flashy, hollow and empty), with the orchestra taking an accompanimental role. The soloist almost always introduces each thematic idea, which the orchestra then restates. The first of his five piano concertos is in D major, Op. 17 (1858). A youthful work, it reflects the influence of Chopin, Liszt and Weber. The Piano Concerto No. 2 in G minor, Op. 22 (1868), now the most frequently performed of the five, was not acclaimed by the public at its première. It was apparently composed in seventeen days, and won the admiration of Liszt, who became something of a champion of Saint-Saëns's works.

Less well known than Saint-Saëns is the work of Henri Charles Litolff (1818–91), a nomadic, itinerant composer, pianist, conductor, teacher and publisher, who wrote five piano concertos, each of which he titled *Concerto symphonique*. All of these are cast in four movements, including a scherzo, and the works may be regarded as symphonies with piano obbligato. Only four of the five works survive; the first, in D minor, is now lost. The *Concerto Symphonique* No. 2 in B minor, Op. 22, was composed in 1844. It retains a double-exposition design in the first movement, follows this with a scherzo, an improvisatory Andante, and finally a Rondo Allegretto. The *Concerto Symphonique* No. 3, Op. 45 (*c.*1846), is in E flat major, subtitled *National Hollandais*, and incorporates two Dutch tunes. While the first movement is martial in character the second incorporates a children's song and the third is a simple ternary song, featuring effective orchestration for cello and horn. The finale, Mendelssohnian in its briskness and lightness, includes, for the second subject, 'Wien Netherlands bloed', widely sung in Belgium in 1830 during the uprising against the House of Orange. The *Concerto Symphonique* No. 4, Op. 102 (1851–2), is regarded by some as his greatest work. The first and last movements are cyclical and the texture of the piano is thoroughly integrated into the orchestra, manifesting the ideal of symphony with piano obbligato. The first movement is cast in double-exposition design, with thematic transformation used in both expositions; the scherzo is again second, and features expressive and effective orchestration, including triangle and piccolo; the third movement, Adagio religioso, is linked to the second, and is set in ternary design; and the Allegro impetuoso finale begins with an introduction leading to a sonata design, with several tempo changes. The final *Concerto Symphonique* No. 5, Op. 123, in C minor (1870) is much more expansive in scope, and contains Lisztian harmonic boldness in the second subject area of the first movement. The second movement, now a slow movement instead of a scherzo, is in the distant key of E major, employing a *Song without Words* character, and featuring effective scoring for cello and horn. The scherzo is reserved for the third movement, marked *Intermède*, and is demonic in affect, with an unusual trio set for pizzicato strings and bassoon. The finale, a rather eccentric sonata rondo, incorporates disparate elements of Beethoven, Mendelssohn and Liszt, and also includes a fugue in the cadenza.

The concerto in Russia

The foundation of the Russian concerto was established by the triumvirate of Anton Rubinstein, Tchaikovsky and Rimsky-Korsakov. The concertos of Anton Rubinstein (1829–94) are all cast in three movements, and, after his Piano Concerto No. 1 in E minor, Op. 25 (composed in 1850 and published in 1858), follow Mendelssohn's example of the combined tutti/solo exposition in the first movement followed by a development and a recapitulation (although frequently abridged, and with reversed restatements of the primary and second themes). Following a pair of lost adolescent piano concertos, and a third attempt, later arranged as the Octet, Op. 9, Rubinstein's first three numbered piano concertos were composed in his early twenties. The Piano Concerto No. 2 in F major (1851) contains a lengthy, fifty-six-bar solo fugato in the first half of the cadenza to the first movement, perhaps reflecting the influence of John Field's Piano Concerto No. 2 in A flat major (*c.*1811), a work of pervasive and profound influence on Chopin, Wieck and many later nineteenth-century Russian composers among others. His Second Concerto was followed soon by his most experimental work, the Piano Concerto No. 3 in G major, Op. 45 (1853–4); it was dedicated to Moscheles, a pioneer in multi-movement and cyclical design for concertos. In the exposition of the first movement, the soloist frequently interjects written cadenzas into the musical fabric, creating a rather halting effect. Norris regards the work as 'almost devoid of interesting or enduring ideas. Furthermore, the writing for the soloist is clumsy, unimaginative, and far from convincing in its efforts to support the second-rate thematic material.'[24] Although Rubinstein rejected the more radical formal experiments of Moscheles and Liszt, his Third Concerto does feature an attempt at cyclical design. Following nearly a decade later, the Piano Concerto No. 4 in D minor, Op. 70 (1864), Rubinstein's most popular and still performed on the concert stage today, is generally regarded as a dramatic step up in quality. Norris describes it as 'Rubinstein's finest work for piano and orchestra ... justly considered the first significant contribution to the genre composed by a Russian. Tchaikovsky recognized its virtues and was significantly influenced by it.'[25] In this work, the composer created a 'tightly organized thematic block',[26] probably manifesting most successfully the composer's experiments with thematic transformation. In addition a 'perceptible Russian flavor' pervades much of the finale.[27]

Many later Russian composers considered Rubinstein too much indebted to the West European (particularly German) musical tradition. Beginning with pianist and composer Mily Balakirev (1837–1910), through the influence of his teacher, Glinka, many composers attempted to integrate more inherently 'Russian' elements into their concertos (such as Eastern folk elements and Russian church melodies). Balakirev, a crucial figure in the development of Russian music, was a leader in this effort and had a strong desire to create the first Russian 'nationalist' concerto. In 1861, he began such a work, but only completed one movement. He sketched a second and third movement the next year, and apparently played the entire work for Rimsky-Korsakov at about this time. However, Balakirev laid the concerto aside, and returned to it some forty years later, completing the second movement, and sketching the finale, which was completed after his death by his disciple, Sergei Liaponov. The work was most likely influenced by Liszt's Piano Concerto No. 1 in the same key, as well as Rubinstein's Second Concerto, and Litolff's Fourth. The first movement is cast in sonata form, though with the second group initially stated in G flat major (*à la* Liszt). The recapitulation restates the primary theme a semitone down, in D major. The second movement is in the remote key of B minor, with the first theme based on a Russian Orthodox Requiem chant, and the second based on a folk song, featuring imaginative and effective orchestration. A transition connects the slow movement to the finale, which is usually regarded as the most successful of the three movements, utilizing the theme of the first movement. The initial key area of the finale recalls that of the second theme of the first movement, G flat major, serving to tie up a loose end of harmonic juxtaposition. Subsequently, the opening theme of the first movement returns, in the tonic, as we would expect. Norris has noted the influence of Rubinstein's fugato from his Second Concerto, Op. 35, on Balakirev, who employs a similar feature in both the opening and closing movements, and also describes the role of the piano as reflecting more of an influence of Litolff (supportive) than of Liszt (dominant).[28]

As a student in Anton Rubinstein's Conservatory, Pyotr Il'yich Tchaikovsky (1840–93), who composed three piano concertos, a violin concerto, and other works for piano and orchestra, was thoroughly trained in the traditions of the West; however, under the guidance and influence of Balakirev, he also produced significant works reflecting nationalistic traits. Brown sums this up as an 'interaction between the high professionalism which Rubinstein promoted and the vital Russianness (in its broadest sense) which Balakirev proclaimed produced some of the finest works of the late nineteenth-century Russian repertoire'.[29]

This combination of 'professionalism' and 'Russianness' is manifest in Tchaikovsky's first and greatest effort in the genre, the Piano Concerto No. 1 in B flat minor, Op. 23 (1874–5). The composer did not consider himself a pianist (although he was technically capable of playing all of his piano works), and was initially ambivalent about the combination of piano and strings; he had declared, in his student days, that he would never write a piano concerto, while nevertheless admiring works in the genre by Litolff and Liszt.[30] He originally intended his First Piano Concerto for Nikolay Rubinstein, who, after a first hearing, declared it to be, according to the composer himself:

> worthless, absolutely unplayable … unskillfully written … bad, trivial, common; here and there I had stolen from other people [A. Rubinstein, and Balakirev]; only one or two pages were worth anything; all the rest had better been destroyed, or entirely rewritten.[31]

N. Rubinstein later changed his view radically, recognizing the concerto as a great work. Tchaikovsky, however, subsequently dedicated it to Hans von Bülow, who performed the première in Boston, in 1875. The work was revised (primarily the soloist's passage-work) over the next decade, with the composer following the suggestions of several virtuoso pianists.[32] The piano writing in the B flat minor Concerto reflects Anton Rubinstein's influence, while the employment of Ukrainian folk songs shows the composer's nationalistic affections. The work is cast in the three traditional movements. It is compartmentalized, with the soloist and the orchestra frequently stating passages alone, perhaps stemming from the supposed Russian difficulty with handling long-term tonal structure. The first movement is unorthodox in structure and much has been remarked about the key area of the grandiose introduction and its theme, in the 'wrong' key of the relative major (D flat). That this theme never returns again after this section, and that the finely crafted exposition ends where it began, in the tonic (Eric Blom calls the D flat major theme 'one of the most baffling solecisms in the music of any great composer'[33]) has caused the spillage of an enormous quantity of critical ink. Nevertheless, as Norris notes, Soviet musicologist Alexander Alekseev has shown that Tchaikovsky actually did reintroduce the opening theme in subsequent passages of the work, 'broken up into fragments and scattered about the principal thematic material of the rest of the Concerto'.[34] Brown has also speculated that the theme may contain ciphers of the composer's name and that of Désirée Artôt, the Belgian singer to whom Tchaikovsky was briefly engaged in the late 1860s.[35] The beginning of the development is signalled with a traditional ritornello, with much subsequent thematic transformation and mutation. The first movement includes a recapitulation, with a brief written cadenza (replacing the closing area of this section). In the subsequent slow movement, Brown notes the repetitive flute melody set against changing backgrounds in the rondo (or quasi-ternary) theme, *à la* Balakirev.[36] The middle *prestissimo* section is set to a popular French chansonette. Critics have debated the form of the finale, some preferring sonata, others rondo, and still others a composite sonata rondo. In any event, the principal theme is based on a Ukrainian round dance. The composer's employment of other folk elements has also been detected. The movement concludes with a broad theme, which perhaps represents an attempt to counterbalance the grandiose opening of the first movement.

With the completion of the First Concerto, most critics regard Tchaikovsky's subsequent efforts in the piano concerto genre as disappointments. In the Piano Concerto No. 2 in G major, Op. 44 (1879–80), the disposition of the first movement is again unorthodox; the second theme is first stated in the flat submediant, and the development begins a minor third lower. The development employs two ritornelli, each followed by a written cadenza, and the recapitulation proceeds as expected. This movement is generally regarded as overly long and not ultimately successful, a fact that Tchaikovsky had himself tried to address with subsequent revisions, though the verdict still remains negative. The substantial second movement has also been criticized, in this case for its casting of three instruments – violin and cello, in addition to the piano (the solo grouping of Beethoven's 'Triple Concerto') – in equally weighted, soloistic roles.

Nikolay Rimsky-Korsakov (1844–1908), a student of Balakirev, and not a virtuoso pianist, composed a fine early Piano Concerto in C sharp minor, Op. 30 (1882–3, published 1886), in addition to concerted works in other genres. The piano concerto is cast in a single-movement structure, in four sections, with the soloist weaving written cadenzas as transitions between the sections. This work is somewhat akin to Liszt's Piano Concerto No. 2 in A major, to whom it is dedicated, and is basically a thematic transformation of one theme from a folk song published in Balakirev's seminal collection. The tune is heard first in the solo bassoon and then clarinet in a slow introduction; there follows an Allegretto (*quasi polacca*), leading to an andante middle section, and an up-tempo finale. The result of this design is that a traditional three-movement shape is still discernible. Rimsky-Korsakov's work had a profound influence on subsequent Russian composers, including Tchaikovsky (in his later efforts in the genre), as well as Glazunov, Arensky and Rachmaninov.

Building on the foundations laid by Rubinstein, Tchaikovsky and Rubinstein, Russian composers continued to refine and expand their nascent tradition, although none achieved the scope and stature of their predecessors. One such composer is Anton Arensky (1861–1906), a student of Rimsky-Korsakov who later taught Rachmaninov and Scryabin and was a close colleague of Tchaikovsky. His early Piano Concerto in F minor, Op. 2 (1882), perhaps best regarded as a student work, is nevertheless 'highly polished'[37] and reveals the strong influence of Chopin, Balakirev, Tchaikovsky and Liszt, with sparkling passage-work, and Mendelssohnian lyricism. This concerto was a favourite of the young Vladimir Horowitz.

Later nineteenth-century followers of Liszt include Xaver Scharwenka (1850–1924), a Polish-German pianist, composer and renowned pedagogue. His Piano Concerto No. 1 in B flat minor, Op. 32 (1876), was one of his most successful and popular works; it was performed by Liszt, to whom it was dedicated, and was also greatly admired by Tchaikovsky. The Piano Concerto No. 2 in C minor, Op. 56 (1881), was followed by a Third Concerto in C sharp minor, Op. 80, and by Scharwenka's last effort in the genre, the Piano Concerto No. 4 in F minor, Op. 82 (1908), which is regarded by some as his finest. Similarly to Scharwenka, Moritz Moszkowski (1854–1925) was a German pianist, composer, conductor and pedagogue of Polish descent. He composed an early concerto *c.*1875 at the age of twenty-one which, at its Berlin première, was praised by Liszt. Later in life Moszkowski also composed a Piano Concerto in E major, Op. 59 (1898), which was one of the most popular concertos in the repertory before World War I.

The piano concerto in America

The piano concerto genre in the United States is best represented by Edward MacDowell (1860–1908) and Amy Beach (1867–1944), both pianists of considerable talent. MacDowell's Piano Concerto No. 1 in A minor (1882), and its successor, the Piano Concerto No. 2 in D minor, Op. 23 (1885, published 1890), have been praised for their orchestration (and similarities with Tchaikovsky's concertos have been noted in this regard as well). The Second Concerto was dedicated to his Venezuelan teacher, Teresa Carreño (as was Amy Beach's Piano Concerto). It contains the standard three movements, although none of them are slow. The soloist begins the opening movement with a cadenza-like flourish, stating the main theme in octaves, with a virtuoso 'rippling decoration' between the hands.[38] There are also three written cadenzas interspersed throughout the movement, MacDowell perhaps taking his cue from the Liszt Piano Concerto No. 1 in E flat major, which features a similar gambit.

Amy Beach's Piano Concerto in C sharp minor, Op. 45, was composed 1898–9, and first performed in 1900 with the composer featuring as soloist with the Boston Symphony Orchestra. Cast in four movements, including a scherzo, the similarity of her conception to that of Brahms, particularly his Piano Concerto No. 2 in B flat major (which also contains a scherzo), has been noted.[39] Beach described the sonata-form first movement as 'serious in character, piano and orchestra vying with each other in the development of two principal themes'.[40] After the tutti's statement of its principal theme, the soloist enters with a fiery cadenza, followed by a lyrical restatement of this theme. The second theme follows, based on Beach's song *Jeune fille et jeune fleur*, Op. 1, No. 4. The subsequent scherzo, with the piano stating a *perpetuum mobile*, is also based on a Beach song (with a text by her husband), *Empress of the Night*, Op. 2, No. 3. The composer described the rather brief, third movement Largo as a 'dark tragic lament', based on yet another of her settings of her husband's verse, the *Twilight*, Op. 2, No. 1. The finale is joyous in mood, but from time to time also recalls thematic elements from the previous movements.

7 Nineteenth-century concertos for strings and winds

R. LARRY TODD

If the nineteenth-century piano concerto – part blend, part farrago of symphonic rigour, acrobatic virtuosity, dramatic theatrical effects, and world-weary soulful lyricism – traces its descent from Beethoven and Weber, what is the lineage of concertos for other instruments? In the case of the most prevalent non-keyboard variety, the violin concerto, a good argument could be made for the primacy of Giovanni Battista Viotti (1755–1824), whose twenty-nine concertos appeared between 1782 and 1817. Heir to the grand tradition of Baroque Italian violinists, Viotti was the prime mover in establishing the modern French violin school, the creation of which spanned the waning years of the *ancien régime* in Paris, where he worked between 1782 and 1792, and the revolutionary and Napoleonic periods.[1] Tainted by persisting associations of his music with political ideologies, owing to his earlier successes at the Concert spirituel and service to Marie Antoinette, Viotti fled Paris; then, a few years later in London, where he appeared with Haydn at Salomon's Hanover Square Concerts, he was suspected of Jacobin views and deported under the Alien Act. When the restored Bourbon monarch Louis XVIII appointed the violinist director of the Paris Opéra in 1819, the way seemed cleared for his return to former glory. But months later, an assassin dispatched the Duke of Berry on the steps of the Opéra, and Viotti's position became untenable; he resigned within two years.

Despite Viotti's prolonged retirement – after 1798 he curtailed his public performances – vivid memories of his distinctive style and virtuosity endured. In 1811 the *Allgemeine musikalische Zeitung* identified three elements: a full, rich tone; 'singing' legato; and varied bowings (facilitated by the new, resilient Tourte bow), which drew from the instrument a chiaroscuro of shadows and light.[2] The three-movement Viotti concerto became the prototype for several French musicians, chief among them Pierre Rode (1774–1830, thirteen concertos), Rodolphe Kreutzer (1766–1831, nineteen), and Pierre Baillot (1771–1842, ten). These three musicians enshrined Viotti's music at the newly established Paris Conservatoire, where they collaborated on a violin treatise;[3] the endurance of his influence is clear in Baillot's own *nouvelle méthode*, which in 1835 was still heavily dependent upon the Italian for its didactic examples.[4]

[118]

Viotti's concertos featured a fast, first movement with four orchestral tutti framing three solo sections; the opening orchestral passage, often impelled by a march-like theme, drew upon the symphonic logic of Haydn for its thematic exposition. In the slow movement, typically a lyrical Romance, Viotti approached French opera by favouring a 'singing' instrumental aria centred on the high register; here the soloist momentarily assumed the persona of an opera singer. The third movement, usually a light-hearted rondeau, adopted a popular vein that absorbed national folk tunes and dances; in the finale of Concerto No. 13 (1788), for example, Viotti introduced a polonaise, subsequently popularized in a vocal version fitted with a newly fabricated text. Viotti's disciples, in turn, often designed exotic, 'foreign' themes for their finales, as in Rode's Concerto No. 12 (*c.*1815), written for Tsar Alexander, and employing a folk song later treated by Tchaikovsky in his Fourth Symphony.

Reaching beyond French borders, Viotti's influence caught hold especially in German realms. Beethoven, who assimilated into his 'heroic', middle-period style the spirited military manner of contemporary French music,[5] was a keen student of French rescue operas and Viotti's violin concertos. What is more, Beethoven personally knew Kreutzer, Rode and Baillot.[6] The singing style of Viotti's slow movements resurfaces in Beethoven's limpid Romances for violin and orchestra in G and F major, Opp. 40 and 50. In the case of the Violin Concerto, Op. 61 (1806), the issue of French influence seems at first glance moot: the virtuoso demands on the soloist are comparatively restrained; the solo part, far from asserting its independence, is often fully integrated into the formal/thematic manipulations of the orchestra; and much of the score evinces a serenely pastoral, not military, style.[7] Nevertheless, the solo writing does exhibit French signs, as in several passages in broken octaves and sixths that recall Viotti and Kreutzer. Perhaps more telling, Beethoven's concerto begins with five timpani strokes, 'measured drumbeats, with their distant implication of military ceremony', that 'suggest a background of sternness and struggle'.[8] As Robin Stowell has shown, this compact motif infiltrates much of the movement in a variety of scorings.[9] That Beethoven indeed had in mind the topos of the march, popularized in so much French music of the period, is manifest in the cadenza to the first movement that he drafted for the 1809 piano arrangement of the concerto. Suddenly, in the middle of the solo cadenza, the timpani strokes resume, and the piano breaks into a double-step Marcia,[10] not unlike the march that begins the second act of Beethoven's *Fidelio*, based upon French rescue operas then in vogue.

Of Beethoven's German contemporaries, the versatile and prolific violinist-composer-conductor Louis Spohr (1784–1859), who in 1821 exchanged the peripatetic career of the virtuoso for the post of Kapellmeister

Example 7.1a Spohr, Violin Concerto No. 7 in E minor, Op. 38, 1st movement, bars 1–8

Example 7.1b Spohr, Violin Concerto No. 7 in E minor, Op. 38, 1st movement, bars 16–18

in Cassel, owed the greatest debt to the French violin school.[11] After hearing Pierre Rode perform in 1803, Spohr determined to master the French style, and within a year finished his first two violin concertos, modelled on Viotti and Rode. Thirteen more solo concertos appeared by 1846, of which several exhibit march-like opening themes in their first movements, and nationally imbued examples of 'local colour' in their finales (Nos. 1, 2, 3 and 12 conclude with polonaises, while No. 6 offers a *Rondo alla spagnola*).[12] An extension of Rode's pathos-laden, lyrical style, Spohr's virtuosity encompassed some new devices, including a rich use of double-stops, chromatic scales, passages in tenths, and a distinctive use of brisk staccati usually executed on an up-bow, an effect that captivated Mendelssohn.[13] On the other hand, Spohr regarded as 'unnatural' a host of special effects popularized by Paganini and the next generation of violinists, including the liberal application of artificial harmonics, rejected by the German as 'childish heterogeneous sounds',[14] and various forms of springing (*saltando*) bowings.

What set Spohr's concertos apart from those of his French predecessors were the thoroughly Germanic formal control and symphonic discipline of his first movements, strengthened by contrapuntal enrichments of the texture, and a harmonic imagination that explored distant chromatic and enharmonic relationships. His embrace of chromatic chords led Beethoven to cavil that Spohr's music depended too much on dissonances for its effect;[15] still, Spohr habitually produced well-crafted music that occasionally approached the level of greatness. The first movement of the Concerto No. 7 in E minor (1814), described as 'glowing in dark red fire',[16] shows him at the height of his powers. In the opening orchestral tutti, the brooding *pianissimo*

Example 7.2a Spohr, Violin Concerto No. 7 in E minor, Op. 38, 1st movement, bars 36–9

Example 7.2b Haydn, Andante in F minor, Hob. XVII: 6, bars 30–3

first theme, unfolding as a series of overlapping suspensions, gives way to a related transitional figure in imitative counterpoint accompanied by agitated tremolos (Ex. 7.1a–7.1b). The contrasting second theme, with its chromatic passing notes, evokes Romantic yearning, yet displays a Classical elegance that reveals Spohr as a student of Haydn (Ex. 7.2a–7.2b). And the striking entrance of the soloist, with its sweeping scale and plummeting arpeggiation against a compressed, thinned-out orchestral statement of the opening subject, introduces the virtuoso as a worthy participant in the ensuing drama.

Spohr's most famous concerto was also his most experimental – No. 8 in A minor, Op. 47 (1816), in the form of a *Gesangszene*. One of four violin concertinos with three, truncated movements linked by transitions, this work was inspired by the composer's desire to meet 'prima donnas on their own ground'[17] by writing for an Italian tour a *bravura* piece that imitated an operatic *scena*. Op. 47 actually begins with an orchestral tutti that vividly portrays another march-like introduction reminiscent of the French violin concerto. But as the orchestral procession continues, the soloist counters by interjecting phrases in a tonally and rhythmically evasive recitative style. Eventually, the orchestra abandons the march and takes up the recitative, symbolically allowing the concerto, in effect, to 'enter' the world of musical theatre. Two operatic movements follow, a cantabile Adagio linked via another recitative to a vigorous Allegro that revisits the military manner of the first movement. Here Spohr's model was the double aria (sometimes referred to as the cavatina-cabaletta pairing) being popularized at that time by Rossini and other Italian operatic composers.

While Spohr was enjoying a successful international career, a contemporary Genoese violinist was garnering accolades in Italy. The musician who revolutionized violin technique, Nicolò Paganini (1782–1840), established his dominance as the premier violinist, and anticipated Liszt's mid-century claim that virtuosity was no mere display of finger mechanics but an indispensable element of musical life.[18] Paganini's mystique owed its vitality in part to his appearance and to unending speculation about his personal life. In concert he wore black dress and struck a gaunt, pallid figure, an image reinforced by recurring health problems and, in particular, by an 1828 operation that extracted his teeth and lent his countenance a macabre, sunken quality. Rumours abounded that Paganini had been imprisoned and that he exercised satanic influences; for Goethe, the violinist projected an unmistakable demonic quality that somehow elevated his technical prowess. But gossip alone could not fully explain the mesmerizing, sensational effects of Paganini's innovative brand of virtuosity, catalogued into several categories in 1831 by the German violinist-conductor Karl Guhr:[19] experimentation with scordatura tunings to increase the brilliance and expressive gamut of the instrument (Paganini's first violin concerto of 1819, notated in D major, was originally performed in E flat major); athletic bowings, including riveting applications of ricochet; the development of rapid, left-hand pizzicati (derived from Paganini's technique as a guitarist); extensive applications of double harmonics (and all manners of multiple-stops), employing fingerings that remained a closely guarded secret;[20] playing on the G-string alone; and unprecedented leaps, facilitated by the anatomy of his hand, which permitted unusually wide lateral stretches.

In 1828 Paganini launched a European concert tour, with appearances in Vienna (1828), Berlin (1829), Paris (1831) and London (1831 and 1833). His repertory featured solo works and a handful of concertos designed to showcase his new style of virtuosity. Playing from memory (unlike many of his contemporaries), Paganini appeared in packed halls before audiences that willingly paid three times the normal ticket prices. In Vienna, Schubert compared the violinist to an angelic visitation, while in Berlin, Fanny Hensel found him a 'supernatural, wild genius' who had the 'appearance of a crazed murderer and ambled like a monkey'.[21] Paganini's Parisian debut impelled the young Liszt to explode the barriers of piano technique in the daunting first version of the *Transcendental Etudes*, teeming with keyboard extensions of Paganini's pyrotechnics. But not all reactions were positive. In London, English music lovers chafed at the inflated ticket prices, and Mendelssohn, suspicious of uninhibited virtuoso displays, was unable to warm to the musician's fabled technique.[22] Mendelssohn's father, Abraham, used a newly minted, pejorative verb – *paganinisiren* – to describe a tasteless cadenza by the Belgian violinist Charles-Auguste de Bériot.[23]

Of Paganini's six concertos, Nos. 1 and 2, and possibly No. 6 (transmitted in short score with a violin part and guitar accompaniment), were written in Italy, while Nos. 3, 4 and 5 (1828–31) were products of the European tour. To magnify the allure of his concertos, Paganini zealously guarded the orchestral parts between public performances. Indeed, Nos. 1 and 2 remained unpublished until 1851, after his death, while Nos. 3–6 awaited later, twentieth-century attempts at reconstruction. The debt of these works to the Viottian model is clear enough: the first movements usually contrast rousing, march-like rhythms of the first theme against the lyrical cantilena of the second, exposed in the violin's high register, a dramatic juxtaposition that again brings the concertos close to the world of opera, in this case to the music of Paganini's friend, Rossini. And, though the orchestral accompaniment often lapses into guitar-like chordal passages, there are effective touches in scoring – for example, the addition of sombre trombones to reinforce the 'masculine', demonic side of Paganini, the extraction of delicate colours from the winds and, in the celebrated rondo of No. 2 (*La Clochette*), the inclusion of a triangle to create a shimmering tintinnabulation Liszt later imitated in his First Piano Concerto (published 1857). But the six concertos also reveal signs of flagging inspiration. Thus, the finale of No. 5 offers a thinly veiled reworking of the familiar rondo tune from No. 2, while the first movement of No. 5 includes a somewhat stale variation of the famous A minor theme of Paganini's Capriccio Op. 1, No. 24, for violin solo. Still, the irrepressible bravura and sweep of Paganini's concertos make for compelling display; they offer effective, dramatic music, with sharply profiled thematic contrasts, in the centre of which stands the indomitable figure of the new virtuoso playing a variety of roles – now magician, now demon, now angel.

Even before Paganini's death in 1840, a younger generation of violinists was striving to emulate the new virtuosity. Chief among them was the Belgian Charles-Auguste de Bériot (1802–70, ten concertos), who adapted Paganini's style to French taste, and the Moravian Heinrich Wilhelm Ernst (1814–65), who, after witnessing Paganini's Viennese debut in 1829, pursued the Italian on his tours and sedulously imitated his showpieces with an exactitude that astonished the composer. Ernst's one-movement *Concerto pathétique*, Op. 23, in F sharp minor (1846), judged by some critics to exceed the difficulties of Paganini's music, inspired other violinists to write concertos in the same, unusual key, including Bériot's pupil, the Belgian Henry Vieuxtemps (1820–81), and the Pole Henryk Wieniawski (1835–80). These two violinists enjoyed

Example 7.3a Vieuxtemps, Violin Concerto No. 4 in D minor, Op. 31, 1st movement, bars 57–8

Example 7.3b Beethoven, Symphony No. 9 in D minor, Op. 125, 1st movement, bars 513–15

Example 7.3c Wieniawski, Violin Concerto in D minor, Op. 22, 1st movement, bars 60–5

Example 7.3d Schumann, Symphony No. 3 in E flat, Op. 97 ('Rhenish'), 4th movement, bars 1–3

highly successful touring careers that took them beyond Europe to Russia and the United States. Most of their concertos, including seven by Vieuxtemps and two by Wieniawski, are rarely heard today, yet they contain worthy music that balances the two poles of the concerto dynamic – the genre as a serious artistic statement versus a means of showcasing technical virtuosity.

Thus, Vieuxtemps's Concerto No. 4 (*c*.1850) and Wieniawski's Concerto No. 2 (1862), both in D minor, commence with complex orchestral tutti that contain telling symphonic allusions – to the first movement of Beethoven's Ninth and the fourth movement of Robert Schumann's *Rhenish* Symphony (Ex. 7.3a–7.3d). Indeed, Vieuxtemps's concerto impressed Berlioz as a 'magnificent symphony with violin solo'. In four instead of the usual three movements, the work begins with a Moderato that impresses as part fantasy, part recitative. The internal movements include a chorale-like Adagio religioso and demonic, skittish scherzo that again alludes to Beethoven's Ninth and uses caricature (Ex. 7.4), a technique that no doubt would have elicited Berlioz's

Example 7.4 Vieuxtemps, Violin Concerto No. 4 in D minor, Op. 31, Scherzo, bars 166–72

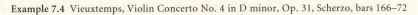

approval. The finale, introduced by a recall of the opening of the first movement, culminates in a festive march that transports the music from a spiritual to a temporal realm. Part concerto, part symphony and part programme music, Vieuxtemps's work thus crosses genres and evinces the increasingly free approaches to concept and form that became a hallmark of nineteenth-century music.

Some features of Vieuxtemps's concerto – its placement of a cadenza to prepare the recapitulation in the first movement, and use of a transition to link the first two movements – betray his interest in unifying the parts of the work and underscoring its compositional integrity. These features also suggest a determined response to what became at mid-century one of the most popular staples of the violinist's repertory – Felix Mendelssohn-Bartholdy's Concerto in E minor, Op. 64 (1844). Mendelssohn was an accomplished violinist who had studied with Pierre Baillot and Eduard Rietz, a protégé of Rode. During an illustrious career as composer, pianist and conductor, Mendelssohn came to know well leading violinists of the time, including Kreutzer, Paganini, Spohr, De Bériot, Ernst, Vieuxtemps, Ole Bull, Ferdinand David and Joseph Joachim (whom Mendelssohn introduced to English audiences in 1844 as a thirteen-year-old prodigy). Mendelssohn was thus intimately acquainted with the accelerating transformations of violin technique in the nineteenth century, yet always strove to maintain in his concertos a scrupulous balance between the structural/thematic demands of the music and the magnetism of virtuosity.

In his fourteenth and fifteenth years the composer had produced two early concertos in D minor (1822–3, for violin, and for violin and piano), but these betray the Viottian mould and Mendelssohn's conservative training; only the second gives a foretaste of the colourful Romanticism that soon washed over his maturing style in the ebullient Octet of 1825. In contrast, the Violin Concerto in E minor gestated over several years, and was the product of a composer at the height of his powers. Here Mendelssohn positioned the solo violin as an expressive agent of contrasting Romantic moods against the orchestra as guarantor of symphonic cohesion. As early as 1838, he had envisioned the haunting elegiac opening theme in E minor, suspended in the high register above tremulous strings, sustained winds and subdued timpani strokes. By 1842, however, he was contemplating instead a new piano concerto – also in E minor – for England, which, like Op. 64, would have comprised three connected movements.[24] Abandoning this effort, he then returned to the violin concerto, and incorporated into it material from the piano draft, most notably what evolved into the lyrical second theme of the first movement. But beset by self-doubt, he continued to correspond with David about nuances in the scoring, orchestral balance, registration and the cadenza in the first movement, which Mendelssohn redrafted and extended. David then premièred the work in Leipzig in March 1845, with the Danish composer Niels Gade conducting.[25]

The salient features of the concerto – the entrance of the solo near the opening and delay of the traditional orchestral tutti, the use of the soloist to accompany the second theme, placement of the cadenza to connect the development and recapitulation, the Lied-ohne-Worte-like slow movement, the trademark Mendelssohnian scherzo of the finale, and the insertion of transitions between the three movements to generate a through-composed work – are all familiar features emulated by later composers, many of whom would have been 'horrified at the notion of confessing a debt to anything so old-fashioned'.[26] But the work contains many other effective touches – for example, the co-ordinated rhythmic shifts in the first movement from quavers to quaver-triplets, semiquavers, and prestissimo quavers to sustain mounting dramatic tension, the restless tremolos midway through the slow movement that recall the agitation of the first movement, and the 'colour' cadenza late in the third movement, in which winds briefly banter against the prolonged tonic 6–4 harmony in the solo part. Permeating the work is a mercurial virtuosity contained by the structural tautness and disarmingly symmetrical tonal plan: in the first movement, two thematic groups in the tonic and mediant, E minor and G major, a development that culminates in a cadenza over a dominant B major pedal-point, and abridged recapitulation reasserting the tonic; in the second movement, a three-part song form that moves by descending and ascending thirds to the submediant and subdominant (C major–A minor–C major); and in the third movement, a hybrid sonata-rondo form that reverses the tonal trajectory of the first movement, so that it now proceeds from E major to the dominant B, mediant G major, and tonic E major.

Still much in the shadows of the Mendelssohnian warhorse are two remarkable works for violin and orchestra by Robert Schumann, the Fantasy in C major, Op. 131, and Violin Concerto in D minor (WoO 23), both from late 1853, just months before the composer's attempted suicide in February 1854. Long marginalized in the literature as products of Schumann's late period, when he 'teetered on the brink between madness and lucidity',[27] these works have merited in recent years fresh reappraisals, including a sympathetic treatment from John Daverio, who viewed the late period as re-enacting the composer's systematic exploration of music genres in the early 1840s, and projecting a variety of creative personae, including the lyric poet, story-teller and virtuoso pedagogue. The Fantasy in C major,[28] written with advice from Joachim, links two contrasting sections, a recitative-like Moderato in A minor and lively Allegro in C major, that seem to depict the familiar Eusebius-Florestan personalities populating so much of Schumann's music. Technically challenging, the work culminates in a prolonged cadenza that, in a nod to Mendelssohn's Op. 64 cadenza, spills over into arpeggiations for the violin that accompany the re-entry of the orchestra. The more ambitious Concerto in D minor, dedicated to Joachim, begins with a symphonic foray, an elevated orchestral tutti that assumes a tragic, elevated style anticipating Brahms's First Piano Concerto in the same key. The freely formed slow movement adumbrates the opening of the theme of the so-called *Geistervariationen* for piano, the 'angelic' melody that visited Schumann shortly before his plunge into the Rhine River. Lacking tonal and formal closure, the movement is elided, via a crescendo-like transition, into the finale, a stately polonaise in D major that introduces the topic of the dance and recaptures the exuberance of Schumann's early piano works such as the *Davidsbündlertänze*. But the finale was judged not virtuosic enough; after Schumann's death in 1856, Joachim withheld the concerto, and it received its première as late as 1937.

While Schumann was putting the final touches to his concerto in October 1853, he was also preparing to herald in the *Neue Zeitschrift für Musik* the young Johannes Brahms, in whose early piano sonatas Schumann had detected 'veiled symphonies', as his successor. For Brahms, as for Mendelssohn and Schumann, the concerto genre was never distinct from the symphony – Brahms's first piano concerto was conceived as a symphony, and his second piano concerto would require four movements, a plan Brahms also would consider for his Violin Concerto in D major, Op. 77, finished in 1878, after extensive consultation with Joachim.[29] Perhaps not coincidentally, this work shares its key and opening character with the Second Symphony completed the year before. And much of the concerto, especially the first movement, privileges the type of thematic elaboration and development associated with the symphonic genre, with the crucial distinction that here the 'argument is led by and concentrated in the role of the solo violin'.[30] But there is no doubt Brahms carefully situated his concerto to reflect earlier examples of the genre, including Beethoven's concerto in the same key, and Viotti's

Example 7.5a Brahms, Violin Concerto in D, Op. 77, 1st movement, bars 53–7

Example 7.5b Brahms, Violin Concerto in D, Op. 77, 1st movement, bars 349–51

Violin Concerto No. 22 in A minor, of which at least one dark passage may have influenced the first movement of Op. 77.[31] Nevertheless, the work displays several characteristically Brahmsian gestures: in the first movement, a subtle rhythmic adjustment that injects asymmetrical quintuple groupings into the triple metre, and a powerfully yearning passage for the solo violin that explores stark contrasts in register (Ex. 7.5a–7.5b); in the second movement, introduced by a graceful oboe melody with wind accompaniment, arabesques in the solo part that illustrate Brahms's art of thematic development through variation; and in a third, a rustic rondo in Hungarian style that recalls something of the *Finale alla zingara* of the *Concerto in Hungarian Style*, Op. 11, (1861) of Joachim, to whom Brahms dedicated his concerto.

Almost exactly contemporary with Brahms's Op. 77 is the concerto in the same key by Tchaikovsky, composed in the aftermath of his failed marriage and completion of the Fourth Symphony and *Eugen Onegin*. Though now a central work in the repertory, the Violin Concerto Op. 35 initially suffered a difficult reception: Leopold Auer, who succeeded Wieniawski at the St Petersburg Conservatory, declined its dedication, and in 1881 the Viennese critic Hanslick denigrated it as 'stinking music'. Traditionally, the outer movements have been judged formally diffuse and meriting cuts. That Tchaikovsky was burdened by the 'anxiety of influence'[32] is clear from several traits indebted to the Mendelssohn concerto. Thus, we encounter an extended cadenza before the recapitulation in the first movement, and linking harmonic transitions between the three movements; even the trepak-like finale (Allegro vivacissimo) occasionally approaches in its scurrying solo figuration the fleet-footed Mendelssohnian scherzo style. But there are equally distinctive qualities that stamp the concerto as Russian: in the first movement, the development that begins with a pompous orchestral *faux*-polonaise, a marker of the composer's imperial Russian style;[33] in the *Canzonetta*, the wistful, Slavonic G minor melody adapted from the composer's *Souvenir de lieu cher*, Op. 42; and in the finale, the rustic second theme, in which the soloist seems to find 'ultimate validation in the folk'.[34] There is evidence, too, of Tchaikovsky's interest in octatonic formations, an additional Russian marker that segregates the composition from its European models.[35]

The closing decades of the nineteenth century produced several other violin concertos that tested new national styles of musical expression. Among the most compelling examples was Antonín Dvořák's Violin Concerto in A minor, Op. 53, composed in 1879 for Joachim, but then withdrawn and revised. The distinctive features of its first movement include a dramatic orchestral opening, symphonic in scope, but cut short by the entrance of the soloist in the fifth bar. Departing further from tradition, Dvořák severely truncates the recapitulation, which gives way after a climactic but condensed statement of the first theme to a muted transition that introduces the deeply felt slow movement in F major. Here the singing quality of the violin reigns supreme in a formally free and harmonically exploratory context. If the first movement invokes Czech music through modally inflected melodies and characteristic harmonic progressions from the minor subdominant to dominant, the finale erupts in a celebration of folk music. Cast in a sectional rondo form – ABCADABCADA – the movement is anchored by the infectious refrain, invoking the Bohemian furiant in a vivacious A major dance with clashing, hemiola-like binary and ternary groupings, and the central D section, which introduces a lament-like dumka over a drone. The result is a compelling synthesis of virtuosity and national folk idioms.

Two other 'nationalist' works fell slightly out of the nineteenth century – both were finished in 1904 – yet remained firmly rooted in late Romantic styles: Alexander Glazunov's Slavonic, through-composed Concerto in A minor, Op. 85, and Jean Sibelius's Concerto in D major, Op. 47, which inhabited a 'brooding Nordic atmosphere'[36] even as it extended Mendelssohn's experiment by expanding the first-movement cadenza to supplant the development section. For other composers, imbuing concertos with national styles was a means of allying virtuosity with musical exoticism, of exploring musical cultures and folk idioms distinct from the mainstream European traditions. Thus, in the *Symphonie Espagnole* (1873), written for Pablo de Sarasate, the Frenchman Edouard Lalo (who also composed a *Fantaisie norvégienne* and *Concerto russe* for violin and orchestra) introduced Spanish local colour into a virtuoso violin work with symphonic pretensions. Its five movements include a sonata-form first movement, scherzo, intermezzo, slow movement and rondo-like finale, through which distinctive 'Spanish' elements gradually accumulate – cross-rhythms, quintuple patterns $(2 + 3$ and $3 + 2)$, heterophonic passages in which folksong-like themes are doubled at the octave below by the bass line in staccato, and, in the finale, the addition of a tambourine.

In the case of Max Bruch, who composed several works for violin and orchestra (three concertos, a serenade and the *Scottish Fantasy*), musical exoticism took the form of celebrating the folk songs of several countries, through direct quotation or simulation, as the wellspring of melody. Thus, the Concerto No. 1 in G minor, Op. 26 (1867), which begins with a drawn-out, Germanic Prelude that arguably rises to a Brahmsian level of lyricism, culminates in an Hungarian-styled finale probably intended as a homage to Joachim, who served as Bruch's adviser.[37] The little-known Serenade, Op. 75 (1900), dedicated to Sarasate, concludes with a stylized Spanish seguidilla, in which pizzicato strings imitate the sound of strumming guitars, while in the shorter *Kol Nidrei*, Op. 47 (1881), for cello and orchestra, Bruch produced a one-movement work based upon Hebrew melodies. Here the cello is accompanied by a harp, perhaps an allusion to its ancient role as an instrument of psalmody, in contrast to the appearance of the harp in the *Scottish Fantasy*, Op. 46 (1880), where, the composer acknowledged, it symbolizes an ancient bard. Described as a 'fantasy with free use of Scottish folk melodies', Op. 46 remains with Op. 26 Bruch's most popular work. It comprises a slow introduction and four movements, drawn from the melodies 'Auld Rob Morris', 'The Dusty Miller', 'I'm down for lack of Johnnie' and 'Scots wha' hae', and divided into two pairs of movements (slow–fast, slow–fast); a brief transition reviving material from the introduction connects the pairs. The bardic introduction, drone effects, and themes based on gapped scales lend the music a Scottish flavour, and offer a vivid example of the German Romantic fascination with Scottish culture and history.

Bruch's widely travelled contemporary Camille Saint-Saëns also explored exotic musical elements in a variety of works (for example, the *Havanaise*, Op. 83, and Spanish-influenced *Introduction and Rondo capriccioso*, Op. 28, both for violin and orchestra; the *Suite algérienne* for orchestra; and the Fifth Piano Concerto, composed in Luxor), but in the main utilized his three violin concertos to reaffirm French and German Classic-Romantic strains. The earliest of the three, No. 2 in C major, Op. 58 (1858), begins with a stiff, Classically balanced first group supported by pulsing tonic-chord tremolos, above which the solo violin indulges in figuration conspicuously outmoded for its time. When the opening yields to a second group in E major, the listener is reminded of a possible model in Beethoven's *Waldstein* Piano Sonata, Op. 53, though elsewhere Mendelssohnian turns of phrase occur, while the singular slow movement, given a sombre colour by the addition of trombones and harp, appears to pursue some type of programmatic narrative. The Violin Concerto No. 1 in A major, Op. 20 (1859), uses a telescoped formal design that absorbs a slow movement into the middle of a fast, sonata-form movement, an approach Saint-Saëns may have borrowed from Liszt. By far the most successful concerto is No. 3 in B minor, Op. 61 (1880), written, like No. 1, for Sarasate. Its three movements offer starkly contrasting characters, and an unusual tonal plan drawn from the turn-like head-motif of the impassioned first movement, springing from the pitches C♯–D–A♯–B. The leading-note, A♯, becomes the enharmonic source of the lyrical slow movement, set in the remote key of B flat major, that might be described as a barcarolle, or better yet, a siciliano, with pastoral melodies for the oboe and, at its conclusion, an eerie passage in harmonics for the violin doubled by the clarinet. The rousing third movement begins abruptly in E minor (a jolting tritone away from B flat major) with a dramatic recitative that modulates to the tonic. The movement proper then unfolds with three subjects, the third of which is an affirming (freely composed) chorale.

Surprisingly few nineteenth-century composers essayed concertos for other string instruments, and of these, only a few for cello were ultimately successful. Indeed, several works with prominent solo string parts were conceived not as concertos but as trans-generic experiments. Thus, when Paganini commissioned Berlioz to write a viola concerto, the unintended result was the programmatic symphony *Harold en Italie*, Op. 16 (1834); here the solo part, entrusted with the *idée fixe* associated with the moody Byronic hero, is actually often detached from rather than involved with the symphonic argument,[38] and the element of virtuosity requisite for a concerto is conspicuously understated. In *Don Quixote* (1897), a tone poem organized as an introduction, theme with ten free variations, and finale, Richard Strauss characterized the celebrated knight and his companion Sancho Panza through elaborate solo parts for cello and viola, but the aim was to write a series of 'fantastic variations', not a concerto. And in the neo-classic *Rococo Variations*, Op. 33 for cello and orchestra (1876), Tchaikovsky used the cello to explore variation technique and to relate his own style to that of his favourite composer, Mozart.

Of the legitimate nineteenth-century cello concertos,[39] chronological precedence goes to Robert Schumann's Concerto in A minor, Op. 129, composed in a frenetic creative burst in 1850, when he assumed his final position as municipal music director in Düsseldorf. In three connected movements, Op. 129 displays a remarkable degree of thematic cohesion.

Thus, the three introductory orchestral chords (tonic–subdominant–tonic) generate the opening motif of the first theme (E–A–B–C, entrusted to the solo cello), which recurs in several guises as a unifying device throughout the work. Schumann de-emphasizes the structural breaks within the ternary-sonata-form design, and instead interrupts the recapitulation to accommodate a compressed slow movement. Here a second cello from the orchestra joins the soloist to create a wordless duet, interpolated as a parenthetical statement within the broader narrative of the whole, and suggesting the type of quasi literary-musical digression characteristic of Schumann's music. When the transition to the finale reintroduces the opening of the first movement, and when the finale proper commences with three chords (subdominant–subdominant–dominant), the effect is of a resumption of the argument of the first movement. Near the end, the cello sketches the beginnings of a cadenza, but the incipient solo display is soon allied with dabs of orchestral colour, and leads to a stretto conclusion in the major.

Two worthy French cello concertos by Lalo and Saint-Saëns exhibit contrasting stylistic features. Composed in 1877 and 1873, they date from the years following the establishment of the *Société nationale de musique*, intended to promote French instrumental music after the crushing defeat of the Franco-Prussian War. Lalo's Concerto in D minor again has symphonic aspirations, with its Beethovenian, off-beat orchestral accents, Lisztian thematic transformations, and insertion of an Allegro presto within the central Andantino to create the effect of a four-movement work. But here the sudden appearance of a scherzo, with its drone-like prolongation of G major, magical fluttering effects in the winds, and delicate cross-rhythms, seems calculated to transport the listener south of the Pyrenees, and to cross-fertilize the composition with Spanish elements. Considerably more indebted to the German tradition is Saint-Saëns's Concerto in A minor, Op. 33, which, emulating Schumann's work in the same key, compresses that composer's three introductory orchestral chords to just one before the soloist plunges into the agitated first theme. Through-composed, the concerto experiments with a multiple formal design reminiscent of Liszt: for example, the development of the first movement proceeds not to the recapitulation but to a delicately scored minuet in neo-classical style that vitiates the need for a slow movement. And woven into the finale (Molto allegro) is considerable material from the first movement, so that the last movement also functions as the recapitulation of a sonata-form design spanning the entire composition.[40]

On several counts, the most impressive nineteenth-century work for cello was Dvořák's Concerto in B minor, Op. 104 (1895). The culmination of his American sojourn, Op. 104 is a richly hued work that summarized, near the century's end, several issues critical to the evolution of the genre. First is the relationship of the concerto to the German symphonic tradition. Throughout the work, the orchestra plays a vital role, not only in elaborating and developing thematic material, but also in the extraordinary range of orchestral colours brought to bear (including the use of trombones, tuba and, in the finale, triangle), so that the concerto is 'not so much the aggrandizement of the soloist, but an exploration of timbral combinations against a gradually evolving formal and tonal background'.[41] And when, in the peroration-like Andante near the work's conclusion, Dvořák recalls material from earlier movements – a technique also used in his celebrated Symphony No. 9 (*From the New World*) – he effectively links his concerto to a nineteenth-century symphonic tradition extending back to Beethoven.

No less significant is the question of a national style in Op. 104. Much has been made of the influence of Victor Herbert's Second Cello Concerto in E minor, Op. 30, which Dvořák heard in New York in 1894, and which left its mark on Op. 104.[42] It is tempting too to discover in Op. 104 telltale signs of Dvořák's so-called American style – pentatonic and folksong-like melodies, modal harmonies, and all the rest – and they are indeed there. Thus, the very first theme of the work displays the lowered-seventh scale-degree, a gambit also present in the opening bars of the *New World* Symphony; and much of the lyrical second theme in D major is pentatonic. But these elements, of course, are fully embedded in Dvořák's mature style, and could be ascribed to Czech influences as much as to an attempt to produce a work of distinctly American art music. Indeed, Dvořák's decision to cite in the second movement his song *Laß mich allein*, a favourite of his sister-in-law Josefina Kaunitzová (news of her fatal illness reached him in America), is sometimes taken as evidence that the concerto evinces the composer's nostalgia for his homeland. In the final analysis, the greatness of the concerto lies in its ability to admit multiple interpretations, to explore the interdependence of the concerto and symphonic traditions, and to expand the compass of Austro-German art music by positing a meaningful alternative, immaterial of whether one labels that style American or Czech.

Among Dvořák's most ardent supporters was Johannes Brahms, who, though he did not produce a cello concerto, returned to the instrument in his final orchestral work, the Double Concerto in A minor for Violin and Cello, Op. 102 (1887). Conceived as an offering to Joachim, estranged from the composer following a disagreement about Joachim's wife, the concerto was championed by the Hungarian violinist, though initially misunderstood. There are few direct precedents for it. In 1803 Spohr had

Example 7.6a Brahms, Concerto for Violin and Cello in A minor, Op. 102, 1st movement, bars 57–8

Example 7.6b Brahms, Concerto for Violin and Cello in A minor, Op. 102, 2nd movement, bars 3–4

Example 7.6c Brahms, Concerto for Violin and Cello in A minor, Op. 102, 3rd movement, bars 1–4

composed a *Concertante* in C major for violin, cello, and orchestra, which, like Op. 102, introduces the soloists only a few bars into the opening orchestral tutti, but whether Brahms knew this minor work is unclear. A more likely source to kindle his imagination was Beethoven's 'Triple Concerto' for Piano, Violin and Cello in C, Op. 56 (1804–7), which features some duetting passages for the string soloists. But much of what Brahms accomplished in Op. 102 is *sui generis*, prompting one scholar to discover in the dramatic opposition of the soloists, and in their interplay of masculine and feminine roles, an 'opera without words, and with only two protagonists'.[43] The expressive range of the two instruments is indeed remarkable: there are the separate, recitative-like cadenzas near the opening of the first movement that, following the brief orchestral review of the principal themes, combine in a dramatic display; rich homophonic passages in double-stops; lyrical duets (including the stylized 'love' duet of the slow movement); unison passages (the opening of the Andante); and, finally, passages that traverse in turn nearly the full range of the soloists, so that the two seemingly become one extended, united instrument. And, as is true of Brahms's other concertos, the symphonic rigour of the thematic construction is wedded to the soloistic display. All three movements are grounded upon themes that partition the octave into either a fifth and fourth, or fourth and fifth (Ex. 7.6a–7.6c), thereby providing a strong measure of thematic integration and coherence.

In the waning years of the century, solo concertos for violin or cello remained the dominant, non-keyboard variety of the genre, despite (or because of?) the accelerating, technological evolution of wind instruments. Indeed, throughout the century surprisingly few composers produced concerted works of lasting quality for woodwinds or brass. To take two examples, no significant new flute concertos endured into twentieth-century concert life, and of the meagre repertory for trombone, only two examples of concertini, by Ferdinand David (1837, for Carl Traugott Queisser, principal trombonist of the Leipzig Gewandhaus) and Rimsky-Korsakov[44] (1877) remained in print beyond 1900. Of these, the latter, a festive work for trombone and military band,[45] is now occasionally heard. The undated Concerto in E flat for oboe and orchestra of Bellini, which includes a brief orchestral introduction in G major, and an aria-like slow movement and *polacca* finale in E flat, resembles much more a wordless operatic scene than a full-fledged concerto. An early example of a 'legitimate' three-movement concerto for trumpet is that in E flat major of Johann Nepomuk Hummel from 1803, the year Beethoven conceived the *Eroica* Symphony. But for all its craft, Hummel's composition is a retrospective work that recalls Joseph Haydn's concerto for natural trumpet in E flat major (1796), and includes allusions in its first two movements to Mozart's *Haffner* Symphony and the slow movement of the Piano Concerto in C major, K. 467. In a similar way, Hummel's Concerto for Bassoon in F major (1805) firmly adheres to the Classical Mozartian model.

On the other hand, Carl Maria von Weber's bassoon concerto in the same key (Op. 75, 1811) treats the instrument as a quasi-operatic protagonist, with dramatic contrasts between the high and low registers in its three movements – a march-like opening movement (the bassoon's first solo is accompanied by timpani strokes), aria-like middle movement with passages bordering on recitative, and jocose, light-hearted rondo for the finale. In the more modest Concertino in E major for natural horn and orchestra (1815), Op. 45, Weber experimented with a type of through-composed, telescoped structure he later perfected in the *Konzertstück* for Piano and Orchestra. The Concertino opens with a brief introduction that gives way to an Andante theme with progressively brilliant variations, followed by a transitional recitative leading to a *polacca* finale. Much the most striking passage occurs in the cadenza of the recitative, where the soloist has to generate several simultaneously sounding pitches, by humming a pitch above or below that played by the horn, which in turn brings into audible range additional partials, thereby simulating, if only fleetingly, a complement of three or even four horns.

Weber's celebration of virtuoso effects extended to a series of brilliant works for clarinet and orchestra, including a concertino and two full-length

Example 7.7 Spohr, Clarinet Concerto No. 1 in C minor, Op. 26, 1st movement, bars 62–9

concertos in F minor and E flat major (Opp. 26, 73 and 74), all written in 1811 for Heinrich Bärmann, clarinettist at the Bavarian court in Munich. The first decade of the nineteenth century witnessed several technological modifications to the instrument, chiefly the addition of keys to facilitate chromatic passage-work and extension of range. By 1811 Bärmann's instrument had ten keys, and Weber took full advantage of its new expressive power. Thus, in the very first solo of the Concerto No. 2 in E flat major, the clarinet part plummets three octaves from a high E♭ in a dramatic entrance that looks ahead to Weber's masterpiece *Der Freischütz* (1821), where in the second-act finale Max's arrival at the Wolf's Glen is accompanied by a cascading clarinet solo. The new flexibility of the instrument encouraged the composer, ever conditiond by his operatic instincts, to treat the clarinet as a vocalizing instrument of great breadth, and to extract from it new colours and shades, especially the dark hues of the *chalumeau* register, featured in all three solo clarinet works, above all in their slow movements. Much a similar agendum motivated Louis Spohr, who composed four clarinet concertos (Opp. 26 and 57, WoO 19 and 20, 1808–28) for Johann Simon Hermstedt, virtuoso at the court of Schwarzburg-Sondershausen. Conceived violinistically and teeming with chromatic trills and runs, Spohr's concertos obliged Hermstedt to add several keys to his instrument, adjustments Spohr detailed in a list of requirements published with the first edition of Op. 26. Their effect was to give 'free rein' (*freier Lauf*) to Spohr's muse, as revealed in the first movement of Op. 26, where he exploited contrasting registers and dynamics to effect a third-related modulation from E flat to G flat major (Ex. 7.7).

Undoubtedly the most singular nineteenth-century composition to explore the technological evolution of winds was Robert Schumann's *Konzertstück* for Four Horns and Orchestra, Op. 86, completed in 1849.

Example 7.8 Schumann, *Konzertstück* in F, Op. 86, Romance, bars 15–19

In the contemporary *Adagio und Allegro* for horn and piano Op. 70, filled with chromatic arabesques for the instrument, Schumann first explored the expressive potential of the valved horn, available as early as the 1830s but only gradually introduced into European orchestras. In the *Konzertstück*, Schumann vividly juxtaposed old and new elements by including in the orchestra two natural horns opposed to the four solo valved horns, and by blending together a distinctive mixture of the old Baroque concerto grosso principle (with its discrete group of soloists pitted against an orchestra) and the modern *Konzertstück*, with its three elided movements and flexible approach to form. But the musical language and use of tonality of Op. 86 represent the composer at his most Romantic. Thus each movement (*Sehr lebhaft*, F major; *Romanze*, D minor; and *Sehr lebhaft*, F major) begins 'open-ended' away from the tonic key, and reorientates the listener to imagine that the three movements commence not at their 'beginnings' but somewhere in their middle. What is more, throughout the composition Schumann draws upon the rich symbolism of the horn in German Romantic literature and revisits topical allusions to the instrument already treated in his earlier *Lieder* and part-songs (for example *Die Lorelei* from the Eichendorff *Liederkreis* and the part-song *Im Walde*, Op. 67, No. 7). In the first movement, the dramatic horn calls enter as brilliant fanfares, while in the middle movement, the quiet echo effects produced by two horns in canon suggest a natural setting, a Romantic landscape that forms the site of some chivalric ballade or romance (Ex. 7.8). And the finale, with its insistent dactylic patterns (quaver and two semiquavers) conjures up forceful images of the hunt. Complementing the richly allusive musical language is the distinctive instrumentation, with the orchestral brass section, including two natural horns and two valved trumpets, buttressed by three trombones, so that the total complement, with the four soloists, comprises a formidable force of eleven players. Adding to their lustre is the piccolo, which often doubles the soloists two or three octaves above, reinforcing higher partials and lending the overall sound a shimmering quality.

At mid-century Schumann's *Konzertstück* represented a genuinely innovative effort. But as the nineteenth century approached its close, there were increasing signs that the concerto, especially in the case of strings and winds, was coming to symbolize a certain stylistic retrenchment, an occasion to look back upon the genre and the paradoxes of its nineteenth-century incarnation. Thus, in 1882 and 1883 the young Richard Strauss composed two nostalgically tinged works. The Violin Concerto in D minor, Op. 8, self-consciously reflected the grand tradition of Romantic violin concertos and struggled to balance virtuosity and formal cohesion (later Strauss would condemn his effort by stating that after Brahms, one should not write in such a style). The Horn Concerto in E flat major, Op. 11, assumed an even more reactionary pose; here Strauss found an opportunity to celebrate the conservative tastes of his father, the horn virtuoso Franz Strauss, who had played the most demanding valved-horn parts under Richard Wagner but preferred the natural horn. Respectfully, Franz's nineteen-year-old son scored his concerto for a *Waldhorn* and indeed, in the opening bars, assigned the instrument an energetic, triadic solo that could have been composed by Carl Maria von Weber. Notwithstanding the intensely brooding slow movement, cast in the unusual key of A flat minor, the work concludes with a buoyant rondo in another acknowledgement of a tradition extending back to the finales of Mozart's horn concertos.

Of course, by 1883, Strauss had not yet experienced his musical conversion to Liszt and Wagner; this epiphany came in 1885, when the *Zukunfstmusiker* Alexander Ritter opened Strauss to the conviction that 'new ideas must search out new forms'.[46] Significantly, when Strauss next turned to the concerto genre, in the *Burleske* for piano and orchestra (1885–6), he used the technique of parody to begin distancing himself from the nineteenth-century tradition, a creative stance he examined further a few years later in *Don Quixote*. Perhaps in 1885, Strauss was already aware that the grand tradition of the Romantic concerto was in jeopardy of losing its relevance in an increasingly un-Romantic, pre-modernist age.

8 Contrasts and common concerns in the concerto 1900–1945

DAVID E. SCHNEIDER

On 28 December 1930 American composer Henry Cowell (1897–1965) gave the first complete performance of his Piano Concerto (1928) in Havana, Cuba. The work, like the majority of concertos in the first half of the twentieth century, adheres to many earlier traditions of the genre. It consists of the standard three movements (fast–slow–fast), the first of which opens with declamatory blasts from the orchestra and contains a substantial cadenza towards the end, and the last of which opens with the piano and concludes with a rousing virtuoso display accompanied by full orchestra. Although Cowell's pianism was highly idiosyncratic, he wrote for his personal strengths as did Bartók, Britten, Copland, Dohnányi, Gershwin, Hindemith, Prokofiev, Rachmaninov, Shostakovich and Stravinsky, to name only the most prominent composers who performed their own concertos in the first half of the twentieth century. Despite a traditional approach to the broad outlines of concerto form, Cowell was best known for his radically primitive pianism. The piano part consists almost exclusively of his signature tone clusters, requiring the soloist to pound the keys with fists, palms and forearms. Cuban policemen were called in lest the performance incite riot.[1]

The incendiary nature of Cowell's Concerto might have made it a *succès de scandale* analogous to Stravinsky's *The Rite of Spring*, but violence did not erupt in Havana and Cowell's Concerto remains a footnote in music history. Indeed, few concertos have figured prominently in accounts of general musical development in the first half of the twentieth century, which have given pride of place to works in more prestigious genres (for example opera, string quartet or symphony) than the concerto – suspect in modernist circles for its conventions of acrobatic display and popular appeal. Igor Stravinsky and Alban Berg both initially resisted commissions for violin concertos in part because they distrusted virtuosos.[2] Yet, if the genre-defining requirement of athletic virtuosity mixed uneasily with high-minded modernist aesthetics, the tension between them was extraordinarily productive – Berg's Violin Concerto is not only the most popular twelve-tone concerto, it is one of the few twelve-tone works to have become staple repertory.[3]

For the most part the history of the concerto from 1900 to 1945 exemplifies the general musical trends in this period. Concertos written between 1900 and the First World War tend to be grand and effusive – characteristics that bind them to the end of a 'long nineteenth century'. Concertos of the 1920s and early 1930s tend to rebel against the expansive style of the pre-war period. As a group they are shorter, more economically scored, more rhythmically charged, and more edgily dissonant than earlier works; they frequently recall pre-nineteenth-century musical styles and/or popular music of the day. Concertos from the mid-1930s through to 1945 frequently combine characteristics of the two previous periods. They are typically longer, more lyrical and more fully scored than works of the 1920s, but are more dissonant and less lengthy than those written before the First World War.

Since this characterization of music-historical periods is easily summarized and detailed accounts of individual concertos are widely available in liner notes and other general guides, I neither follow a strict chronology nor analyse entire works here. Instead, I focus on how composers of concertos worked with elements specific to the genre, such as the relationship of the soloist and orchestra, opening and closing strategies, characteristics of the solo instruments, and relationships between individual concertos. The resulting juxtaposition of works of contrasting styles and periods illuminates ways in which the genre often united composers in spite of differing musical aesthetics.

The concerto as symphony: Dohnányi and Busoni

We begin with Ernst von Dohnányi (1877–1960) who in 1899 won the Bösendorfer competition for a piano concerto with the first movement of his Piano Concerto in E minor, Op. 5 (1898).[4] At the turn of the century the Hungarian Dohnányi was celebrated both as the heir to Brahms in compositional terms and as the greatest Hungarian pianist since Liszt. His E minor Concerto is a fine example of a Central European pre-war concerto with symphonic dimensions. Although Dohnányi's and Cowell's concertos both begin *fortissimo* in the orchestra alone, a common nineteenth-century opening that is rare in concertos from the first half of the twentieth century, the two works could hardly be more antithetical. One striking difference is that Dohnányi begins his concerto with a slow introduction – a gambit that in concertos tends to invoke other genres. The first eight bars of Dohnányi's introduction announce the symphonic aspirations of the work by recalling the opening of Brahms's First Symphony. Brahms, who was also renowned for the symphonic proportions and weight of his concertos, never began one with a slow introduction.[5] Thus, while Dohnányi's opening gesture at once pays homage to Brahms, an early promoter of Dohnányi's work, it also promises an even grander concerto than those by the recently deceased master.

Promises made at the beginnings of concertos are difficult to keep – abandoning the theme of the introduction to Tchaikovsky's First Piano Concerto in the body of the work is the most infamous example and never returning to the exquisite opening chords in Rachmaninov's Second Piano Concerto (1901) is another. Because the bravura required for the triumph of the soloist at the end of the work tends to undermine symphonic profundity, concertos rarely sustain symphonic heft throughout. Similarly, the grander the initial orchestral utterance, the more difficult it is for the solo to find a response equal to the task. Cowell's opening two orchestral blasts are minimal enough to serve as neutral curtain raisers. They demand attention and little more. The soloist responds with *fortissimo* forearm slams on the highest two octaves of the piano, a shocking gesture that soon wears thin. Dohnányi's impassioned eight-bar tutti provides a good deal more with which to grapple, but, like Cowell, Dohnányi chooses material that sharply distinguishes the soloist from the orchestra. The piano enters with a Lisztian cadenza in double, triple and quadruple octaves that wisely does not strive to match the orchestral legato. Instead, it outstrips the orchestra in range, rubato and virtuosity. The juxtaposition of weighty symphonic introduction and solo cadenza signals Dohnányi's attempt to integrate grandeur and virtuosity from the outset.

Dohnányi's slow introduction paves the way for a gentle presentation of the first theme in the Allegro. The introduction's promise of a grand symphonic movement is dutifully fulfilled by way of an extended sonata form replete with three themes – the first a transformation of the opening two bars, the second a transformation of the first phrase of the piano's initial cadenza. The most original section of the concerto and the one that most fully takes up the symphonic challenge of the slow introduction is the slow coda of the first movement, which again reaches outside the genre, this time with a nod to the symphonic poem. A deceptive cadence initiates the coda by bringing back the music of the introduction, an impassioned *fortissimo* cry abruptly cut off after only two bars.

Celestial images dominate when the coda resumes. Fragments from the third bar of the introduction drift sweetly in the woodwinds above otherworldly, *pianissimo* tremolos in the strings. A solo violin ascends to heavenly heights three times. The solo piano accompanies with gentle, harp-like arpeggios, the last of which rises from the low E pedal in the basses to the high E of the solo violin and then into the vapour above. The transformation from worldly, human struggle to divine peace is a common nineteenth-century trope, but one rarely found in concertos until the twentieth century. It requires a sacrifice – the abandonment of the soloist's virtuosity – that flew in the face of nineteenth-century conventions of the genre.

Like many concertos with brilliant openings, Dohnányi's E minor Concerto has a major flaw: it does not end after the prize-winning first movement. In the slow movement and finale, with which Dohnányi seems to have felt obliged to fulfil the formal conventions of the genre, he creates an admirable sense of organic unity through thematic transformation, but nothing in the last two movements matches the imaginative coda of the first movement. Transposed to the appropriate key, the last pages of Dohnányi's concerto could serve as a close for many a nineteenth-century concerto.

Ferruccio Busoni (1866–1924), who like Dohnányi was one of the truly great pianists of his era, identified precisely the problem to which Dohnányi succumbed:

> With the rise of virtuosity the word [concerto] became restricted to the meaning which it still commonly has – a *bravura* piece for a single instrument, for the greater glory of which the orchestra ... is subordinated.
>
> For the sake of respectability these *morceaux d'occasion* were given the outward shape of a symphony; its first movement put on the mask of a certain dignity, but in the following movements the mask was gradually dropped, until the finale brazenly displayed the grimace of an acrobat.[6]

Busoni's comments sought to justify his own Piano Concerto, Op. 39 (1904). Hoping his work would redefine the genre, he claimed to use 'concerto' in the title of his work 'in its original sense, signifying a co-operation of different means of producing sound'.[7] The notion of escaping nineteenth-century 'excess' by reverting to austere 'original' meanings would become a cliché of Stravinsky's anti-Romantic stance in the 1920s. In 1904, however, Busoni's goal was not to reject emotional expression, but to claim symphonic status for his concerto.

Busoni's Piano Concerto is a sprawling seventy-five-minute work in five movements. It could be regarded as the successor to Brahms's symphonic four-movement Second Piano Concerto, which had famously broken the three-movement mould. But, by using a chorus in the last movement to sum up the message of the work,[8] Busoni even more emphatically invokes the symphonic tradition established by Beethoven's Ninth Symphony and continued by Mendelssohn's Second Symphony, Liszt's Faust Symphony, and, in Busoni's day, by Mahler's symphonies with choral finales. In the fifth movement of his Piano Concerto, Busoni uses an off-stage, six-part male chorus to sing a *faux* oriental paean to the life-giving force of the Eternal Power on a text from the nineteenth-century Danish poet Adam Oehlenschläger's *Alladin*.

As in the coda of the first movement of Dohnányi's concerto, the turn to the divine in the last movement of Busoni's work coincides with a turn away from the earthly 'sin' of instrumental bravura, which in this concerto reached its zenith a few minutes earlier in the massive cadenza that tops off the hair-raising tarantella of the fourth movement. The piano, which accompanies thematic material in the orchestra with gentle filigree in the first pages of the fifth movement, falls completely silent for the choral entrance. Busoni's chorus, like Dohnányi's celestial solo violin, introduces a new voice to express something the piano cannot. Although the piano enters again before the chorus withdraws, it comes decidedly to the fore only in the last minute of the work. Following the chorus's last line, 'Extolling divinity, the poem falls silent', which serves as an excuse for the withdrawal of the voices, the piano and orchestra end the movement with the traditional sonorities of a piano concerto. Busoni seems to have recognized that while the piano alone could not convey the depth of expression to which he aspired, introducing a chorus ran the risk of stealing the limelight from the soloist. One suspects that Busoni had the courage to make the bulk of his finale a contemplative slow movement in part because the addition of the chorus provided the drama normally reserved for instrumental fireworks. Yet, for all this innovation, in the last twenty-one bars of the work Busoni himself yields to just the virtuoso tradition he claimed to be working against by bringing down the curtain with explosive, knuckle-busting *bravura* (Allegro con fuoco). Concertos that end slowly and softly belong to a later generation.

Although a number of substantive and important concertos (for example, Sibelius's Violin Concerto, and Rachmaninov's Second and Third Piano Concertos) appeared in the decade and a half between Dohnányi's First Piano Concerto and the beginning of the First World War, none competed in seriousness of intent or sheer size with Busoni's behemoth. Around the time Prokofiev finished his tightly knit Piano Concerto No. 1 in D flat, Op. 10, in 1912, Busoni recognized that his own concerto was the end of an era.[9] Even the Brahmsian Dohnányi seems to have registered the change in his next work for piano and orchestra. After a tumultuous introduction, the soloist enters playing the tune English speakers know as 'Twinkle, Twinkle Little Star' in simple octaves in C major. Dohnányi's *Variations on a Nursery Song*, Op. 25 (1914), his only concerted work heard with any frequency today, is a light-hearted virtuoso romp, but it contains an important historical message: even before Europe witnessed the ravages of the Great War, the idea that symphonic grandeur could be synthesized with works of solo virtuosity was under siege.

The concerto as Requiem

After Busoni, three decades passed before another composer attempted to imbue a concerto with comparable profundity. In his four-section, two-movement Violin Concerto (1935) Alban Berg (1885–1935) begins with images of birth and ends with a lament famously built around Bach's harmonization of the chorale 'Es ist genug!' ('It is enough!'). Berg's dedication 'to the memory of an angel' refers to the daughter of Alma Mahler and Walter Gropius, Manon, who died aged eighteen on 22 April 1935. As Douglas Jarman and George Perle have shown, Berg used many layers of symbolism in the work in addition to the programmatic associations of Bach's chorale: lengths of sections correspond to numbers Berg associated with himself and his lover Hanna Fuchs-Robettin and musical motifs are constructed out of the notes indicated by their initials (A–B♭, Alban Berg; B–F [B is written as H in German], Hanna Fuchs-Robettin); and the Carinthian folk song Berg weaves into the second section of the first movement has a text (un-stated in the score) that strongly suggests a hidden reference to Berg's first love affair.[10] Berg's concerto is thus at once a portrait of Manon, a secret love letter, an autobiography, and a requiem for lost youth. What makes Berg's work all the more impressive and a true violin concerto, as opposed to a symphonic poem with an exalted violin part, is that Berg uses essential properties of the solo violin as an intrinsic part of the work's dramaturgy.

As had been the case in Busoni's Piano Concerto, the slow last section of Berg's Violin Concerto lends the work special profundity. In contrast to Busoni, however, Berg extends the slow tempo and sombre mood to the final bar of his work. This difference between the works not only stems from a difference between their programmes – one a celebration of God's mystical power to endow life, the other a progression from life to death – it also exploits the different nature of the solo instruments. While the dynamic range and textural variety of the piano make it a nearly ideal match for the orchestra, as a percussion instrument, the piano is limited by its inability to play a truly seamless legato, a liability that becomes more noticeable the slower the tempo, higher the range, or softer the dynamic. This expressive limitation helps explain why Dohnányi and Busoni relegated the solo piano to secondary status and yielded to forces (solo violin and chorus) capable of sustained legato in passages analogous to the last bars of Berg's Concerto. A string instrument can not only sustain a line in a high tessitura, soft dynamic and slow tempo, it can do so without losing what Joseph Kerman has dubbed *virtù* – a term useful for describing impressive soloistic qualities that do not rely on the fireworks commonly equated with virtuosity.[11] In sum, Berg stays the distance and ends his work slowly and softly both because to do otherwise would ruin the programme and because in a violin concerto, as opposed to a piano concerto, such an ending exploits the soloist's *virtù*.

Berg's keen awareness of the dramatic potential of the innate qualities of the violin also contributes to the effectiveness of the solo entrance in the second bar of the work, a fragile arpeggio across the open strings of the instrument (G–D–A–E). The gesture, as Kerman has observed, is 'a virtually all-encompassing birth metaphor – the birth of natural acoustics, birth of the violin, birth of the twelve-tone row, birth of Manon Gropius, birth of Woman'.[12] In the last two bars of the work, as the solo violin hovers high in the heavens on its final note, the fifths return like a distant memory (Berg writes, 'wie aus der Ferne' ['as if from far away']) on the muted open strings of the orchestral violins. The superimposition of images sums up the arc of the whole work at the same time as illustrating the text of the chorale: 'I travel to my heavenly home. … My great misery remains down below. It is enough.'

Concertos for use

Berg's Violin Concerto is a rich example of a concerto that addresses death and transfiguration – a theme more often reserved for dramatic works or symphonic poems. Such works, however, form a small but important subset of concertos in the first half of the twentieth century.

Not all 'requiem concertos' are as personal as Berg's. Paul Hindemith's *Trauermusik* (Music of Mourning) for viola and string orchestra (1936) was, in line with Hindemith's anti-Romantic philosophy of *Gebrauchsmusik* (music for use), a work with a specific function. On 20 January 1936 King George V of England died, which resulted in the cancellation of Hindemith's scheduled appearance as viola soloist in Queen's Hall two days later. Instead, Hindemith was asked to participate in a memorial broadcast, for which he agreed to compose an appropriate work. In a cheerful letter to his publisher, Hindemith boasted: 'I got a furnished studio, some copyists were slowly fired up, and then, from 11 [p.m.] to 5 [a.m.], I did some rather heavy mourning'. Not one prone to sentimentality, he added: 'Shouldn't we perhaps exploit this story? … It is after all not an everyday occurrence for the BBC to have a foreigner write a piece on the death of their King and to broadcast it over their entire network. I now want to specialize in corpses.'[13]

Trauermusik is a miniature four-movement viola concerto, but the lack of generic designation in its title is telling. Works for solo instrument and orchestra that go by other names usually have a smaller range of expression than concertos proper. *Trauermusik* is no exception. While the first movement of Berg's Violin Concerto conjures images of birth, dance and folk song, Hindemith begins straightaway with death in the form of a funeral march. A memory of life peeks through only in the third movement (*Lebhaft*), which he ends with a life-sapping *ritardando*. Like Berg, Hindemith uses a chorale, 'Vor deinen Thron tret' ich hiermit' ('I step before your throne'), likely chosen both for its appropriate reference to a throne and its practical brevity, as the basis for the last movement.[14] The treatment is simple but effective. On the final note of each of the chorale's four phrases, except the last, the orchestral strings sustain a chord while the solo viola rises and falls in a gesture of imploration, each iteration successively more impassioned and wider in range. Given the circumstance, there was no possibility for bravura, but the metre-breaking fermatas and rhythmic freedom of the soloist hold the faint and, for a concerto, crucial aroma of cadenza. The final phrase for orchestral strings alone, now in complete rhythmic unison for the first time in the chorale, suggests a united community continuing without its leader. Because the dark, often strained tone of the viola is well suited to mourning, and because the last movement is concise and clear, *Trauermusik* is a rare example of 'music for use' that packs an emotional punch.

The concerto as conscientious objector

Karl Amadeus Hartmann (1905–63) learned how to end a concerto in lament from Hindemith, but adjusted Hindemith's recipe to new circumstances in the fourth and final movement of his four-movement violin concerto *Musik der Trauer* (1939), renamed *Concerto funèbre* in 1959. Hartmann, a staunch anti-fascist, addressed not the death of a foreign sovereign, but the state of the world as his German fatherland turned ever more aggressively against its neighbours and its own citizens. Like Hindemith, Hartmann alternates orchestral chorale-like phrases with solo imploration, but after the extended third outpouring from the solo violin, the mood cannot settle – first the soloist, then the orchestral violins pierce the texture with painful, glassy harmonics. The last chord, a sudden, dissonant *fortissimo* outburst, is a Munchian scream.

War, albeit viewed from a safer distance, is also the subject of Benjamin Britten's Violin Concerto, Op. 15 (1939). Completed in North America, where pacifist Britten took refuge from England bracing itself for war, his Violin Concerto is also a response to the defeat of the Republicans in the Spanish Civil War.[15] Britten's sympathy for the Spanish Republicans stemmed in part from his trip to the 1936 meeting of the International Society for Contemporary Music in Barcelona where he heard the première of Berg's Violin Concerto and collaborated with Spanish violinist Antonio Brosa, who would première Britten's concerto with the New York Philharmonic in 1940.

The last movement of Britten's three-movement work is a passacaglia, which, like the chorale for the Germans, served as a national emblem of mourning for the British. In the final section of the movement, the tone comes close to the last movement of Hartmann's Concerto, which Britten did not know, and suggests a debt both to Berg's Violin Concerto and Hindemith's *Trauermusik*, which he did.[16] In this section (Lento e solenne), the orchestra turns to a chorale-like homophonic texture with frequent fermatas over which the violin struggles in a series of rising gestures. Throughout this passage Britten effectively turns the violin into a viola (with echoes of both *Trauermusik* and Walton's Viola Concerto) by instructing the soloist to play on lower strings than those implied by the range. Britten requires the last phrase, which ends two-and-a-half octaves above middle C, to be played entirely on the violin's lowest string. The effect is one of great strain, which works against the sense of transcendence that might otherwise have been suggested by the high register. Like Hartmann, Britten at once mourns and resists.

Britten's Violin Concerto is a work of wartime, but unlike Hartmann's *Concerto funèbre* or Hindemith's *Trauermusik*, it is also a full concerto the emotional range of which resists summary in a descriptive title. Britten's opening timpani motif at once recalls the solo timpani opening of Beethoven's Violin Concerto, suggests a Spanish rhythm, and, in its alternation of pitches a perfect fourth apart (F–C), carries a martial undertone.[17] Passages composed of tattoos (figure 3ff.) and fanfare-like arpeggios (figure 4ff.) strengthen the military topic, but the primary theme of the first movement first sung *dolcissimo ed espressivo* at the entrance of the solo violin never loses its cantilena quality. Unlike Hartmann's *Concerto funèbre*, with its violent second movement, Britten's concerto never suggests a battle symphony. Britten's second movement, much indebted to the second movement of Prokofiev's Violin Concerto No. 1 in D, Op. 19, is a spiky scherzo with a trio of North African inflection and an astonishing episode in which the tuba takes the theme under *tremolo* violin harmonics and two skittering

Example 8.1 Prokofiev, Violin Concerto No. 1 in D, Op. 19, 1st movement: development of first theme in orchestra before figure 17

Example 8.2 Prokofiev, Violin Concerto No. 1 in D, Op. 19, 1st movement and Walton, Viola Concerto, 1st movement: comparison of primary themes

piccolos. While Britten's Violin Concerto is often compared to his War Requiem as an embodiment of his pacifism, it also belongs to the tradition of virtuoso concertos that finds value in ecstatic instrumental play.

Direct influences 1: Prokofiev and Walton

In addition to Hindemith and Berg, Britten's Violin Concerto betrays a debt to two intimately related works, both of which Britten first heard in 1931: the First Violin Concerto (1917) of Prokofiev, and the Viola Concerto (1929) by William Walton (1902–83), which made an especially deep impression on him.[18]

Prokofiev's First Violin Concerto is a highly original work – it may well be both the first twentieth-century violin concerto in three movements to break from the fast–slow–fast pattern, the first twentieth-century concerto to end slowly and softly, and, on a lighter note, the first concerto to contain a tuba solo (one of several details that seem to have inspired Britten). The originality of Prokofiev's First Violin Concerto extends beyond the order of movements and details of its orchestration. In the first movement Prokofiev breaks from tradition by resisting sonata form. In its place, he uses a rhapsody-like chain of freely evolving ideas rounded off with a return to the opening theme in the flute at the end of the movement. A well-disguised transformation of the slow opening theme at the most agitated point in the movement (cf. Exx. 8.1 and 8.2) is one of several subtle

Example 8.3 Prokofiev, Violin Concerto No. 1 in D, Op. 19, 1st movement,
figure 4, and Walton, Viola Concerto, 1st movement, figure 3

developmental gestures that do not significantly modify the chain-like principle of construction.

At its belated première on 18 October 1923, Prokofiev's First Violin
Concerto was paired with the première of Stravinsky's Octet.[19] In this
context, Prokofiev's Concerto (conceived in 1913 and completed in 1917)
was regarded as too conservative, 'Mendelssohnian' as one critic put it, in
comparison to Stravinsky's latest style and the sassy works of 'Les Six'.[20]
Yet beginning in 1924 when Hungarian violinist Joseph Szigeti started to
champion the work, Prokofiev's concerto gained success in more conservative venues, especially among the English.[21]

Walton's Viola Concerto, a work so pervasively modelled on
Prokofiev's First Violin Concerto that one suspects Walton had a copy
of Prokofiev's score open in front of him while composing, illustrates the
conservative streak in the post-war English concerto.[22] In addition to the
order, tempo and overall mood of the movements, and the strategy of
bringing back the first theme of the first movement accompanied by a
portion of the theme of the third movement at the end of the work,
Walton's modelling extends to numerous details. In the first movement,
the most obvious examples of close modelling on Prokofiev's concerto are
the first theme (Ex. 8.2), the gesture of departure from the first theme
(Ex. 8.3), the cadenza-like passage in double-stops leading up to the
return of the first theme, and the return of the first theme in the winds.

Given how closely Walton followed Prokofiev for the form and content of his first movement it is instructive to observe ways in which he
departed from his model. The difference is most apparent in Walton's
effort to align his concerto more closely to sonata form. Specifically,
Walton includes a warmly melodic secondary theme (figure 4), extensively infuses the fast middle section of the movement with elements of
development (cf. Exs. 8.4 and 8.2), and includes a true recapitulation that

Example 8.4 Walton, Viola Concerto, 1st movement: development of first theme

returns to both primary *and* secondary themes (figure 16). Walton's decision to recapitulate two themes necessitates breaking free of Prokofiev's model for the final bars of the movement. After the return of the first theme in the orchestra, the viola plays the second theme in an expressive singing voice. Whereas Prokofiev ends the movement with the violin dissolving *pianissimo* into the ether of its highest range, Walton does the opposite. The viola plays the return of the second theme in a comfortable singing range on the A-string followed by a passage in impassioned parallel-sixth double-stops that descends to close the movement with the viola in the meatiest part of its range.

The fundamental contrast between Walton's and Prokofiev's concertos in terms of colour and expression is already present in the orchestral introductions and emerges again emphatically in the final bars of their last movements. Prokofiev sets the mood for the initial fragile entrance of the violin with a thin, uninflected tremolo reminiscent of the opening of Sibelius's Violin Concerto, whereas Walton lays down a more robust, expressive texture to introduce the viola. Walton follows Prokofiev's lead by ending the third movement of his concerto in very nearly the same way as he had ended the first, but with the first theme of the third movement deftly reworked as accompaniment. Repeating nearly verbatim the endings of their first movements, Prokofiev ends high, Walton low. Close parallels between the two scores aside, the most important thing Walton learned from Prokofiev was that the overall tone of the concerto should grow out of an essential quality of the solo instrument. Walton's sensitivity to the nature of the viola enabled him to use Prokofiev's work as a model to create an original work that has come to be the most popular viola concerto.

The influence of Prokofiev's First Violin Concerto extended even beyond Walton's Viola Concerto, which was soon taken up by Lionel Tertis (1876–1975) and William Primrose (1904–82). In 1945 Primrose asked Béla Bartók (1881–1945) to write a concerto for him, but Bartók was reluctant to do so because of his lack of familiarity with the viola as a solo instrument. Only after hearing Primrose in a broadcast of Walton's concerto did Bartók decide to undertake the commission.[23] Because concertos by Walton, Britten and even Bartók (albeit indirectly) all owe a debt to Prokofiev's First Violin Concerto, it must be considered the seminal string concerto of its day.

Direct influences 2: Stravinsky and Bartók

Prokofiev's rival Stravinsky cast the longest shadow over keyboard concertos in 1920s and early 1930s. Echoes of his work ranging from the pre-war ballets *Petrushka* and *The Rite of Spring* to the post-war 'neo-classicism' of the Concerto for Piano and Winds (1923–4) abound in this period.[24] As soloist in his Piano Concerto, Stravinsky spread a penchant for a percussive approach to the piano and for the evocation of pre-nineteenth-century music, especially Bach, throughout Europe and the United States. Works that use Stravinsky's wind band in place of full orchestra include two string concertos: the Violin Concerto (1924) by Kurt Weill (1900–50), a big, difficult work that lies stylistically half-way between Hindemith and Schoenberg; and the light-hearted Cello Concerto (1925) by Jacques Ibert (1890–1962). Keyboard concertos that share something of Stravinsky's neo-Baroque approach include Hindemith's *Kammermusik* No. 2 (1924), the third movement of which, 'Kleines Potpourri', uses only winds; Alfredo Casella's Partita for Piano and Orchestra (1925); Ernest Bloch's Concerto Grosso for String Orchestra with Piano Obbligato (1925); and two harpsichord concertos – the first concertos for that instrument since the eighteenth century – for Wanda Landowska by Manuel de Falla (1926) and Francis Poulenc (1928). Works that exploit a percussive approach to the piano include Aaron Copland's Piano Concerto (1926) and, although it owes as much to American experimentalism, Henry Cowell's Piano Concerto discussed at the beginning of this chapter.[25] Like Stravinsky's Piano Concerto, many of the works above and others (for example piano concertos by Gershwin and Ravel) include references to popular music.

152 David E. Schneider

The most important concertos to be directly indebted to Stravinsky are Bartók's First and Second Piano Concertos (1926 and 1931).[26] Because Stravinsky had used Russian folk music in his early ballets, Bartók had long regarded Stravinsky as an ally in his fight to integrate folk music into modernist art. When Bartók emerged in the early 1920s from the isolation imposed by the First World War, he was disappointed with Stravinsky's turn away from folk music and towards a more 'objective' and ironic style. Bartók's opinion of Stravinsky's post-war style changed, however, when the Russian composer performed his Piano Concerto in Budapest on 15 March 1926. After the concert Bartók's wife reported:

> Now I know quite exactly what the new direction is. Imagine ... music in which there is no emotion, in which you can find no part that will bring tears to your eyes. You know, bare rhythm, bare timbre. The whole thing shakes one to the bone. Stravinsky is a fantastic genius, and we very much enjoyed the evening.[27]

Bartók's next works marked a change in his style towards leaner and more contrapuntal textures. His First Piano Concerto is a direct result of the Stravinskyan challenge.

The influence of Stravinsky's Piano Concerto on Bartók's First Piano Concerto can be felt in the driving quaver pulse that dominates the two outer movements, in the emphasis on wind instruments (strings are completely omitted in the second movement), in jazzy episodes in the development section of the first movement (figures 26–31), and, most important, in the percussive use of the piano. The spirit of *The Rite of Spring* comes through in the violent brutality of much of the work and in details such as the bassoon theme in the introduction (figure 2) and ostinati in the second and third movements.[28]

Stravinsky's Piano Concerto is emphatically anti-symphonic and anti-Teutonic: the *largo* introduction to the first movement is equal parts Handelian overture in the French manner and funeral march *à la* Chopin arranged for military band.[29] In a move similar to the solo entrance in Dohnányi's *Variations on a Nursery Song*, Stravinsky's entrance of the piano (Allegro) rejects the (mock) seriousness of the introduction. In contrast, Bartók begins his First Piano Concerto with a creation metaphor that makes his work (like Berg's Violin Concerto) an heir to the Germanic symphonic tradition. Dual pedal-points drummed out first in the lowest octave of the piano and the timpani gradually build in intensity until the piano erupts in the violent, repeated As that launch the first theme of the Allegro. The contrast between the topics of Stravinsky's and Bartók's introductions was intentional. While he quotes

Example 8.5 Stravinsky, Concerto for Piano and Winds, 1st movement and Bartók, Piano Concerto No. 1, 1st movement: comparison of the opening of the Allegro sections

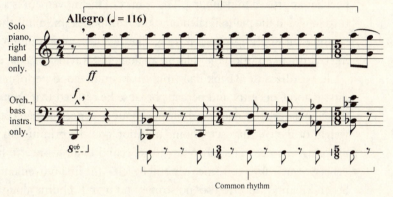

Stravinsky (compare the opening themes of the two Allegros consisting of repeated octave As with nearly identical accompanying rhythms, Ex. 8.5) Bartók was also correcting his more fashionable competitor. Bartók's approach grew out of a conflict between his desire to adopt the brilliance of Stravinsky's mechanical style and his own characteristically Central European belief in music as a deeply human art.

From the perspective of the relationship between soloist and orchestra, Stravinsky's Piano Concerto is radical in its rejection of concerto tradition. In place of melody and accompaniment, dialogue-like exchange, or tutti versus solo – types of discourse central to concertos since the eighteenth century – Stravinsky favours using the orchestra to double the solo piano, a technique possibly inspired by the late seventeenth- and eighteenth-century practice of the soloist joining the orchestra in tutti passages. With the exception of the introduction, the piano plays almost continually in the first movement of the work. The orchestra doubles the solo part (sometimes picking out only a few notes of the piano line), is silent, or carries the melody against figuration in the piano. Although orchestral duplication of the piano becomes less pervasive with each movement, the orchestra never plays accompaniment to the soloist's melody. Because in the Allegro of the first movement of the work the orchestra never opposes or engages in dialogue with the piano, it has little independent personality in the body of the movement. When the time comes for a cumulative closing gesture in the coda, Stravinsky assigns the orchestra the only music it can call its own, the introductory march, now against churning arpeggios in the piano. As Richard Taruskin has observed, the many layers of interlocking rhythmic subdivisions in this coda create a climax that revels in a subhuman mechanical quality.[30]

In contrast, while Bartók's First Piano Concerto contains a wide variety of interactions between orchestra and soloist, there is no trace of Stravinsky's peculiar approach to doubling. The climax of the movement is an orchestral tutti in which the piano is silent and the trombones sing a full-throated tune reminiscent of Hungarian folk song (figure 50ff.), an uninhibited outpouring of human emotion that has no analogy in Stravinsky's concerto.

In part because Bartók had trouble obtaining good performances of the First Piano Concerto, and perhaps because he realized that there was something incongruous and overbearing about a concerto that combined the weight of the German symphonic tradition and the primitivism of *The Rite of Spring* in a neo-classical context, his Second Piano Concerto has a lighter veneer. Stravinsky's influence can still be felt – the first movement of Bartók's Second Piano Concerto uses no strings and mainly churns along in constant quavers across shifting metres – but the levity of *Petrushka* takes the place of *The Rite*. Indeed, in the first movement of his Second Piano Concerto Bartók clearly models the first theme of the solo piano on the piano solo from the 'Russian Dance' in *Petrushka* as well as quoting from the famous closing tune of *The Firebird* in the first five notes of the opening fanfare in the trumpet. Stravinsky's shadow may also be felt when Bartók throws Bach of the two-part inventions into the mix (first movement, bars 145–71). Unlike the Stravinskyan references in Bartók's First Piano Concerto, however, those in Bartók's Second Piano Concerto are too explicit and carefree to suggest that Bartók was still having trouble navigating in Stravinsky's turbulent wake. By 1930 Bartók was no longer rewriting or correcting Stravinsky, but playing along with the Francophile Russian by using quotations of his work in much the same spirit that Stravinsky himself used Handel, Chopin and Bach to his own expressive ends.

A note on lyricism

As we have seen in the climax to the first movement of Bartók's First Piano Concerto, expressive, vocally inspired melodies are not entirely absent from concertos in the 1920s and early 1930s. At this time, however, composers tended to shy away from using lyrical themes to open concertos. Stravinsky writes achingly beautiful melodies in his Piano Concerto and Violin Concerto in D (1931), but they are hidden in internal slow movements. Likewise, the slow movement of Bartók's Second Piano Concerto contains some of Bartók's most tender vocally inspired music. Bartók uses two vocal models here: chorale in the muted strings alternates with peasant lament in the piano. The two never overlap, suggesting that the group remains oblivious to the plight of the individual. This is a rare approach to concerto discourse although there is precedent for it in the slow movement of Beethoven's Fourth Piano Concerto. Therefore, unlike Stravinsky's Baroque doubling of forces or Busoni's 'co-operation of different means of producing sound', the newness of Bartók's approach stems in part from intensifying the polarization of soloist and orchestra characteristic of late eighteenth- and nineteenth-century concertos.

George Gershwin's *Rhapsody in Blue* (1924) and Concerto in F (1925) are made almost exclusively of catchy tunes, but in Ravel's Piano Concerto (1931), a jazzy work that may be read as a corrective to Gershwin, the composer tellingly begins with a frantic march accompanied by the piano playing arpeggios in two keys simultaneously *à la Petrushka* before giving way to a blues-inflected second theme.[31] Unlike Gershwin – and herein lies a distinction between popular music with symphonic aspirations and modernist music with popular inflections – Ravel allows himself the luxury of popular lyricism only after affirming his modernist credentials. Gershwin and English composers notwithstanding, the first well-known concerto to begin with a lyrical first theme after the First World War was Prokofiev's Violin Concerto No. 2 in G minor, Op. 63 (1935). By the end of the 1930s lyricism would come to occupy a primary position in a number of important concertos. Once again, when it came to concertos, Prokofiev was in the vanguard.

Sharing the spotlight

Stravinsky's approach to doubling in his Piano Concerto may be heard as a Busonian effort to escape from the model of the concerto in which the orchestra primarily accompanies. To provide the orchestra with more equality, many composers introduce secondary soloists. The phenomenon was not new – it reaches back at least to the wind parts in Mozart's Viennese piano concertos from the 1780s – but in the first half of the twentieth century it became one of the most popular ways to invigorate the relationship between solo and accompaniment.

As the solo violin turn in Dohnányi's First Piano Concerto demonstrates, secondary soloists often carry a sustained singing line against which the primary soloist can display another aspect of instrumental *virtù*. Ravel does this famously in the slow movement of his Piano Concerto (1931). The movement opens with the piano playing a theme of aching beauty and Chopinesque languor in what may be the longest unaccompanied passage for the soloist in a concerto outside of a cadenza. The lack of accompaniment ensures no competition for the piano from instruments better able to sing. When Ravel brings back the melody after the orchestra has finally entered for a brief contrasting section, he does so in the sensuous English horn, which frees the piano to express its *virtù* in scales and trills. Similarly, in the slow movement of his First Piano Concerto, Bartók uses solo winds to sustain long melodic lines while the piano takes part in an ostinato accompaniment as an honorary member of the percussion section.

In the slow movement of his *Concierto de Aranjuez* (1939), music that like Britten's Violin Concerto is taken to lament the Spanish Civil War,[32] Joaquin Rodrigo (1901–99) reverses Ravel's strategy: the movement opens with the melody in the English horn before being taken up by the solo guitar. The ordering works in part because the guitar outshines the English horn with embellishments. More important, the guitar's inability to sustain the melody gives the lament a sobbing quality of great poignancy. Here and throughout this immensely popular concerto, Rodrigo ingeniously finds virtue (and *virtù*) in the limitations of the solo instrument.

In his concertos for flute (1926) and clarinet (1928) Carl Nielsen (1865–1931) uses secondary soloists more pervasively than any other composer of his time, an approach that helps impart to these works a variety and emotional range rarely found in wind concertos.[33] In Nielsen's Clarinet Concerto a military snare drum guards against complacency by lending a sinister undertone to lyrical passages and repeatedly prodding the volatile soloist into nervous fits. In his Flute Concerto Nielsen uses two main supporting actors, clarinet and bass trombone.

The clarinet courts the flute like a gentleman, always ready to join in dialogue, to provide a contrapuntal line, to finish a musical thought that extends below the flute's range, or (lest the flute get tired) to join in cadenzas.[34] In contrast, the bass trombone is a brute. Its aggressive, tonally unstable solo in the first movement so upsets the flute that it nervously runs itself ragged. Only after the reassurance of a heroic tutti does the flute seem to feel it is safe to return, which it does with the most beautiful music of the movement: a tender, pastoral transformation of the orchestra's heroic theme, now securely grounded in E major.

When the trombone next appears near the end of the last movement of the two-movement work, it again enters gauchely in a key (B flat minor) that clashes with the prevailing tonality (G major). After four bars, however, it turns to E major and in another two bars it suavely sings the flute's E major theme from the first movement in a supple tenor voice. The flute, smitten, joins the trombone in E major with a gently caressing countermelody unlike anything it has shared with the clarinet. Perhaps proud of its conquest, the trombone lets loose with broad *glissandi* that again elicit frightened outbursts from the flute. This time, however, the outbursts seem staged – they are short-lived and the flute quickly regains its composure. The E major coda that follows finds the flute in fine fettle. Exhilarated, one assumes from its recent encounter, it dashes exuberantly to a high E under which the trombone offers its final (post-coital?) guffaws.

Even more equality

Nielsen's reliance on secondary soloists may be seen as an offshoot of the trend to share duties more equally between soloist and orchestra that took hold in the 1920s. While Nielsen keeps his primary soloists in the lime-light, in works as diverse as Bloch's Concerto Grosso for String Orchestra and Piano obbligato and Stravinsky's Concerto 'Dumbarton Oaks' (1938), both modelled on early eighteenth-century concerti grossi, solo and ensemble duties are shared much more equitably. Webern's Concerto for Nine Instruments, Op. 24 (1931–4), is a chamber work with no primary soloist. Even in solo concertos, however, composers experimented with subsuming the soloist into the orchestra. Berg does this to haunting effect in his Violin Concerto when in the midst of the lament of the final section (bars 170–96) the solo violin, weakened with a mute, is gradually doubled by all of the upper strings. The move is explicitly dramatic – Berg states the soloist should visibly encourage the orchestral strings to join in its lament.

In contrast to Berg, American composer Roger Sessions (1896–1985), who spent the years 1925–33 in Europe absorbing the latest trends, repeatedly diffuses the dominance of the soloist in his Violin Concerto (1930–5) in a manner that weakens its dramatic force. This four-movement work is, with the exception of *Trauermusik*, the only solo concerto mentioned in this chapter that neither begins nor ends with the soloist. Although the violin part is technically demanding, Sessions rarely sets it off brilliantly, preferring to accompany with intricate contrapuntal lines often given to instruments – alto flute, bass clarinet, basset horn – the unusual timbre of which additionally draws one's attention away from the soloist. Sessions's omission of violins from the orchestra is an attempt to help the soloist stand out from the ensemble, but it is also tacit recognition that as merely a first among equals, the solo violin in many ways duplicates the traditional role of the violin section in symphonic music.

Sessions's penchant for pairing the soloist with different instruments owes a debt to Stravinsky's Violin Concerto (1931), which, like Sessions's Concerto, is in four movements without a cadenza.[35] Stravinsky's famous remark, 'I did not compose a cadenza ... because the violin in combination was my real interest', applies even better to Sessions.[36] As Kerman observes, the final chord of the third movement of Stravinsky's Concerto, in which the sound of the violin (*flautando*) merges completely with the reduced orchestra, may be heard as emblematic of Stravinsky's fusion of solo and orchestra.[37] Despite his suspicion of virtuosos, however, Stravinsky was not against showmanship. Each movement of the concerto begins with the soloist playing a bold triple-stop that Stravinsky dubbed the 'passport' to the work, and concludes with the soloist playing right up to the double bar. Even in the rare case in which the solo violin cannot be distinguished from the ensemble sound, the visual aspect of its participation is central to the effectiveness of the work as a solo vehicle. In contrast, Sessions ends his concerto with a sustained *fortissimo* chord in the flutes, trumpets and trombones punctuated by a *sforzando* hit in the other winds, timpani and bass. Sessions's decision to have the soloist stand idle for the final chord matters little for the sound of the work – the solo violin would hardly be audible as part of either closing gesture – but it is aggressively anti-dramatic.

Bartók's Violin Concerto No. 2 (1938) exemplifies the reassertion of Romantic lyricism and clear tonality in concertos that began in 1935 with Prokofiev and includes violin concertos by Bloch (1938), Barber (1939), Hindemith (1939) and Korngold (1945) – all works in three movements (fast–slow–fast) that begin with lyrical first themes. (Even the melancholy waltz with which Schoenberg begins his Piano Concerto, Op. 42 (1942), may be heard as part of the lyrical trend.) Bartók's warmly expressive writing for the violin is a far cry from that in Sessions's Violin Concerto, but Bartók also gives a prominent role to an unusual 'secondary soloist' in the first movement of the work. Here Bartók effectively pairs the solo violin with the harp in all appearances of the primary theme. For much of the movement the steady strumming of the harp effectively grounds the effusive melody, but when the violin returns to the third phrase of the primary theme after the cadenza, Bartók pulls out all the Romantic stops by allowing the harp to abandon its strumming and indulge in luxuriant *glissandi*. Given the passionate drama of Bartók's concerto, it is surprising that he nearly repeated Sessions's mistake of allowing the orchestra alone to conclude the work. Unlike Sessions, however, Bartók had second thoughts. After listening to the Brahms and Beethoven Violin Concertos, he took the advice of violinist Zoltán Székely, and rewrote the ending to include the solo violin.[38]

Gentle coda

Anthony Pople trenchantly observes that Bartók's Concerto for Orchestra (1943) is the clearest expression of the approach to the concerto as a relationship between equals.[39] It is also a return to the pre-World War I idea that symphony and concerto could be combined. Like his Concerto for Orchestra and Violin Concerto, Bartók's Third Piano Concerto (1945) reflects a trend in concerto composition. The Third Piano Concerto is Bartók's last completed work.[40] It exemplifies, like works such as the Oboe Concerto (1945) by Richard Strauss (1864–1949) and the First Violin Concerto (1939) by Walter Piston (1894–1976), a trend towards what may be called a 'gentle neo-classicism'. These works are not laments, nor do they embody profound struggle. They are works of modest proportions, generally light orchestration, and, if one discounts the extraordinary breath control needed to get through the opening bars of Strauss's oboe part, a modicum of virtuosity. Piston's concerto has a slightly jazzy inflection; Strauss's concerto is shot through with Mozart; and Bartók's abounds with historical references. In the first movement of Bartók's work, the opening theme has the dotted rhythms of *verbunkos*, a type of Hungarian dance music frequently used as a sign of national pride in Bartók's youth. In the second movement, Bartók quotes Beethoven's ode of thanksgiving *Heiliger Dankgesang* from the String Quartet Op. 130 in alternation with Bachian chorale textures, which the piano later embellishes in the style of a two-part invention. The spectre of Bach also surfaces in a fugal episode (bar 230) and a minuet (bars 392 and 473) in the third movement. Bartók's references, like Strauss's Mozartian cast and Piston's clean lines, have no trace of Stravinskyan irony.

With the deaths of Rachmaninov in 1943 and Bartók in 1945, the era of composers who regularly premièred their own concertos was effectively over. So too was the time when new concertos regularly achieved a canonical place in the repertory of their instruments. Despite a number of brilliant concertos written after the Second World War, it is hard to think of a composer in the decades after 1945 – with the exception of Shostakovich – who made as central a contribution to the concerto repertory as many of the works discussed above. The most successful concertos written between 1900 and 1945 are works that, unlike Cowell's, Sessions's, or Busoni's brilliant experiments, do not represent modernist extremes. The number and importance of such works is extraordinary. In the realm of instrumental music, no other genre better represents resilience and continuity of musical traditions in this time of radical innovation.

9 The concerto since 1945

ARNOLD WHITTALL

I

The plain fact that works called 'concerto' continued to be composed after 1945 demonstrates the failure of twentieth-century avant-garde initiatives to create a totally new musical world whose qualities and characteristics could persuade the entire community of classical composers to adopt them. Historians of culture tend to acknowledge that the very notion of an avant-garde is only meaningful in a comparative context, requiring the survival of those allegedly exhausted, conservative values and procedures that radical progressives seek to supplant: and no credible cultural history of the years since 1900 can ignore the extraordinary diversity of stylistic and structural initiatives in composition – old, new, progressive, regressive – the most profound legacy of the Romantic and modernist individualism that formed the foundations of twentieth-century culture in the widest sense.

There would nevertheless have been little point in composers after 1945 producing concertos, or any other works in such well-established genres as symphony, opera or string quartet, if institutions suited to the regular presentation of such works had not survived, and continued to prosper. In the case of the concerto the insatiable desire among concert audiences and record buyers for brilliant soloistic display must always be matched by the enthusiasm of individual virtuosos for new challenges, and while very few if any professional solo performers since 1945 have been able to make a career exclusively from the promotion of the new and the unfamiliar, the continued prominence of the concerto owes much to the supreme gifts of artists like Mstislav Rostropovich and Heinz Holliger whose advocacy of the new gained credibility by way of their evident and equal mastery of the old.

My plan in this chapter is to convey a sense of the immense variety of concerto composition since 1945, while focusing principally on those composers for whom the genre seems to have been particularly important. As in earlier times, concerto composition was not confined to works called concertos; one of the most interesting consequences of the modernist aesthetic is the play of expectation that the use – or avoidance – of a generic title can create, such as in Michael Finnissy's two concertos for solo piano

(1978–80, revised 1996 and 1980–1), or Harrison Birtwistle's *Melencolia I* for clarinet, harp and two string orchestras (1976). No less significant is the infiltration of other 'parent' genres – notably the symphony – by the kind of *concertante* elements that erode theoretically distinct generic boundaries. After 1945 Olivier Messiaen (1908–92) was a particularly inventive exponent of such ambiguity, not only in several works for piano and instrumental ensemble, but also on the largest scale in the *Turangalîla-Symphonie* (1946–8), with its virtuoso solo parts for piano and ondes martenot, as well as in *La Transfiguration de Notre Seigneur Jésus-Christ* (1965–9). The latter tends to be classified as an 'oratorio' on the grounds of its choral/orchestral forces and sacred content, but involves prominent solo parts for cello, piano and several other instruments. Only at the very end of his life did Messiaen plan a work with the plain title *Concert à quatre* (1990–2), a relatively slight four-movement piece for flute, oboe, cello, piano and orchestra in whose completion (after Messiaen's death) Yvonne Loriod, Heinz Holliger and George Benjamin all had a hand.

Composers after 1945 were as likely as their earlier twentieth-century colleagues to find as much stimulus in Baroque concerto prototypes as in Classical or Romantic models, in keeping with the twentieth-century tendency to expect a high degree of technical facility from all the members of an ensemble, even if only one or two are singled out as soloists. Twentieth-century idioms mean that an orchestral accompaniment meekly providing a discreet backdrop to the flamboyant antics of a single soloist is likely to be rare, at least outside works consciously seeking a rapprochement with Romantic traditions, such as the concertos of Shostakovich and Schnittke.

The explicit use of 'concerto' as a title is not in itself evidence of a conservative disposition: composers are just as likely to employ it to dramatize the distance of their own concepts from those of tradition as to suggest strong sympathy with that tradition. In 1950–1, for example, John Cage (1912–92) produced a *Concerto for Prepared Piano and Orchestra*, a work which not only has three separate movements but which in Cage's description sounds distinctly conventional: 'I made it into a drama between the piano, which remains romantic, expressive, and the orchestra, which itself follows the principles of oriental philosophy. And the third movement signifies the coming together of things which were opposed to one another in the first movement.'[1] But this apparent embrace of convention is countered in several fundamental ways, not least the 'preparation' of some fifty-four piano notes. This deadens their resonance to create an atmosphere of austerity and detachment fitting well with Cage's use of pre-arranged charts to determine the 'objective' deployment of musical material. Far from aspiring to the expressive world and dynamic excitement of earlier concertos, the effect, as Paul Griffiths concludes, is of 'an aimlessness quite peculiar to Cage'.[2] In the final movement the sense of randomness means that brief moments of instrumental display are as likely to occur as total silence, but such moments of display 'are bizarre bursts of activity in music marching slowly towards extinction, and apart from them the landscape is bleak indeed'.[3]

Cage had a long association with the pianist David Tudor, and added some perspective to his view of the concerto genre in the *Concert for Piano and Orchestra* (1957–8), whose basic materials are laid out for solo piano and thirteen other instruments. This is one of the many twentieth-century works in which 'all the players ... act as soloists', although the fact that 'their parts are totally independent of one another'[4] is more special to Cage. Much later, in *Fourteen*, also for piano and thirteen instruments (1990), Cage moved still further from the principle of accompanied solo display by using only the evanescent sounds of bowed piano strings.

Of other composers who shared Cage's aesthetic convictions, Morton Feldman (1926–87) was extremely consistent in his exploration of the interaction between a solo instrument and others in music of a predominantly non-dramatic, expressively restrained character. Works like *Cello and Orchestra* (1972), *Piano and Orchestra* (1975) and *Flute and Orchestra* (1978) are evidently non-concertos, or even anti-concertos, which have nevertheless not totally abandoned the basic concept of 'solo instrument and orchestra' on which 'real' concertos depend.

If the presence of an element of individual or collective display is the criterion, very few composers can be said to have avoided hints of concerto-like writing in their works; and these can appear in unlikely places. For example, the second act of Stockhausen's first opera in his *Licht* cycle, *Donnerstag* (1978–80), the purely instrumental, *Michaels Reise um die Erde* (Michael's Journey to the Earth), is in effect a trumpet concerto, and can be given separate concert performance. Even more striking, perhaps, is the emphasis on solo instrumental virtuosity – piano and trumpet – in Hans Werner Henze's purely instrumental *Requiem* (1990–2), whose subtitle 'nine sacred concertos' proclaims a specific heritage (Schütz) from which Henze's actual music no less boldly proclaims its resourceful remoteness.

II

A clear sense of both the diversity and the substance of concerto-composition after 1945 is immediately evident from a survey of a few of the most significant composers born between 1900 and 1920. At one extreme, the two works for violin (1947/8, rev. 1955, 1967) and two for cello (1959, 1966) by Shostakovich (1906–75) can be classified as the apotheosis of the traditional formal approach. These are concertos of symphonic substance, which give an intensely personal cast to what in purely technical terms are relatively conventional harmonic, melodic and formal features. A very similar point can also be made about the three-movement Cello Symphony, Op. 68 (1963), by Benjamin Britten (1913–76), which despite its title is sufficiently concerto-like to include a cadenza between the scherzo and the passacaglia-finale. At the other stylistic extreme come the concertos of Elliott Carter, born only two years after Shostakovich in 1908, with a series of early works written during the 1930s and 1940s which are as traditional as Shostakovich's in style, though rather closer to neo-classical Stravinsky than to late Romantic Mahler. All Carter's concertos were completed after 1960, however, when his approach to composition had changed radically, and he had devised the post-tonal idiom which has served him ever since. David Schiff has shrewdly noted the inevitable tension between the genre's 'dramatic character' and those 'traditions' which have made it 'somewhat alien' to Carter. According to Schiff, 'each of Carter's concertos is a subversive anti-concerto in its own way', and 'the soloist is usually cast in the role of the underdog', whose 'alienation from the orchestra is absolute'. Schiff concludes that 'by throwing the concerto tradition away and beginning anew, Carter has rediscovered the tragic implications inherent in the form'.[5]

This is most evident in Carter's concertos for piano (1963–5) and violin (1990), where the contrasting dramatic and lyrical qualities of the solo instrument are deployed to reinforce the sense of subjective alienation. And the first concerto of all, the *Double Concerto for Harpsichord and Piano with Two Chamber Orchestras* (1959–61) is full of innovative features, focusing on the idiosyncratic concept of a dialogue between disparate contenders, each supported by a separate instrumental ensemble, and achieving an uneasy coherence through emphasis on a relatively stable symmetrical design, as well as on evenly balanced differentiations between the various dualities involved. On the other hand, Carter's concertos for oboe (1987), clarinet (1996) and cello (2001), while lacking nothing in dramatic forcefulness, are not so much 'tragic' as concerned to explore an exuberant playfulness without compromising the natural intensity and concentration of Carter's musical language. In the Oboe Concerto there is interplay between the relatively delicate solo instrument and an alter ego in the form of a trombone, while in the Clarinet Concerto the soloist (in homage to Boulez's *Domaines*) is encouraged to move between various distinct groups of instruments in the accompanying ensemble before finally occupying centre-stage. Schiff notes that here, as in other late Carter scores, the composer 'purges his music of much of its anxiety'.[6]

While still nervy and volatile, it is also quirky, witty – artful in the best sense of the word.

As well as these solo concertos, Carter used the generic title for three other works. Among his most appealing late scores are the short but far from insubstantial *ASKO Concerto* (2000) for a Dutch ensemble and the *Boston Concerto* (2002), for the full-size Boston Symphony Orchestra but also, in Carter's words, 'a sort of concerto grosso'. However, Carter's grandest transmutation of the concerto grosso principle comes in his much earlier *Concerto for Orchestra* (1969), a twenty-minute New York Philharmonic commission, and a monumental achievement that is not merely 'a virtuoso symphonic work in which almost every player at some time becomes a soloist'.[7] It provides a stunning demonstration of Carter's modernism at its most resourceful, the many superimpositions of and interactions between textural and formal layers controlled and shaped with an unfailing awareness of the nature of the unfolding musical (and by no means exclusively 'tragic') drama and coherence of the work as a whole.

The stylistic middle ground of concerto composition between Shostakovich and Carter is occupied by Michael Tippett (1905–98) and Witold Lutosławski (1913–94). There is a quite pleasing symmetry between Tippett's first solo concerto (1953–5) and Lutosławski's last (1988), since both are for piano, and both involve conscious attempts to reinvent the instrument's capacity for lyrical expression in ways that recall certain works of Beethoven (Tippett) and Chopin or Rachmaninov (Lutosławski). Perhaps (at least in part) because of the complex challenges these ambitions represent, neither can be counted among its composer's best pieces: the sense of making the past 'present' is as much a constraint on invention and spontaneity as a stimulus. A further degree of symmetry between the two composers arises from aligning Lutosławski's early Concerto for Orchestra (1950–4), a superbly wrought work in relatively traditional style, with Tippett's Concerto for Orchestra (1962–3). This is one of Tippett's most radical, collage-like constructions, written at the time when his language had been transformed by the need to devise an appropriately terse and uncompromising manner for the opera *King Priam*.

Where string soloists are involved, Lutosławski's Cello Concerto (1969–70) is one of the century's finest, a brilliantly devised single-movement contest between soloist and orchestra – the composer was clear that 'the relationship is one of conflict'[8] – whose material seems to invite translation into a dramatic scenario in which a Quixotic protagonist contends with all kinds of hazards and difficulties before finding a kind of resolution. For Steven Stucky the stakes are high enough to interpret this ending, in essentially political terms, as evidence that 'the individual has survived to proclaim a message of transcendent humanism';[9] like the Shostakovich cello concertos, it was written for Rostropovich. But it is also possible to hear a note of uneasiness, a sense of isolation, alongside the apparent triumph, in keeping with the tendency of post-1945 concertos to subscribe to the aesthetic position articulated by Tippett, which questions how 'affirmation' of any kind is possible in times of such social and political unease.[10]

Tippett's own Concerto for String Trio and Orchestra (1978–9), a relatively late work, aspires to affirm by reformulating the composer's earlier lyricism, but without at the same time re-establishing the rather traditional kind of modality found in the Concerto for Double String Orchestra (1939) and the Piano Concerto. The Triple Concerto has its haunting moments, and if not all of the material is particularly memorable, the extraordinarily well-varied instrumental colours add both substance and atmosphere to the carefully balanced dialogues between soloists and orchestra. Tippett's ambivalence about the concerto genre is vividly expressed in a late essay in which he confessed that 'although I had previously written a piano concerto, I was not terribly in sympathy with the late romantic confrontation of soloist and orchestra. What interested me more was the idea of using more than one soloist, which I first tried out in the *Fantasia Concertante on a Theme of Corelli* (1953).' Of the Triple Concerto, Tippett said that 'the structure ... followed historical precedent with a fast–slow–fast sequence of movements, but included linking interludes that helped signal the change of mood within the movement to follow'.[11] He also noted that the material of the work includes allusions to the gamelan music he had encountered on a recent visit to Java and Bali – a good example of the kind of inspired eclecticism that represents the later Tippett at his best.

III

Among composers born between 1920 and 1940 there remained a strong impulse to compose large-scale instrumental and orchestral pieces, even when their musical styles were distinctly untraditional. The consistent avoidance – by Birtwistle (*b.*1934), for example – of explicit generic titles, is balanced by the easy-going pragmatics of Berio (1925–2003) and Henze (*b.*1926): to place Berio's *Il ritorno degli snovidenia* for cello and small orchestra (1976) within the same generic category as his Concerto for Two Pianos and Orchestra (1972–3), or to group Henze's *Compases para preguntas ensimismadas* for viola and twenty-two instruments (1969–70) and *Le miracle de la rose* for clarinet and chamber ensemble (1981) with the named concertos for double bass (1966), piano (1950, 1967) or violin (1947, 1971) is obviously reductive, yet it underlines the porous

boundaries between works which seem to give priority to a poetic motivation of some kind and those whose concerns appear to be more purely
formal or textural. Nevertheless, degrees of genre-bending remained part
of twentieth-century practice, as composers reacted with differing degrees
of self-consciousness to the alignments with and angles on tradition
which particular works created, and there is obviously no guarantee
that a work called, plainly, 'concerto' will not have the kind of poetic or
formal association which other compositions spell out in their titles.

Associations with particular performers (initially through solo works)
have continued to override any doctrinal reluctance a composer might
harbour with respect to the tired, staple genres of traditional concert life.
For example, Iannis Xenakis (1922–2001) wrote *Eonta* (1963), a fearsomely
challenging work for piano (Yuji Takahashi) and brass quintet, and
followed it up with larger-scale works that might be placed in the tradition
of the flamboyant nineteenth-century fantasia for a virtuoso soloist and
orchestra rather than of the concerto as a 'well-made', relatively abstract
(symphonic) conception: *Synaphaï* (1969) is a fourteen-minute piece for
piano and large orchestra, while *Keqrops* (1986), written for Roger
Woodward, is a seventeen-minute score for solo piano and 'orchestra of
92 musicians'. Xenakis also wrote comparable pieces for the violinist Irvine
Arditti (*Dox-Orkh*, 1991) and the trombonist Christian Lindberg (*Trookh*,
1991). Declaring in an interview that 'I do take into account the physical
limitations of the performers', Xenakis is clear that 'my works are to be
performed according to the score, in the required tempo, in an accurate
manner. That is how they are played by Takahashi and now by others'
including Roger Woodward and Peter Hill. 'It is very difficult,' Xenakis
acknowledged, 'but sometimes they succeed'. He also observed that 'what
is limitation today may not be so tomorrow'.[12]

By contrast, Krzysztof Penderecki (*b.*1933) has pursued an earnest
rapprochement with late Romantic style, rejecting his youthful radicalism.
But most of his concertos – No. 2 for violin (1992–5), written for Anne
Sophie Mutter, is typical – seem pale yet protracted shadows of the past
rather than positive, forward-looking reworkings of it. For concertos much
closer to earlier modes of expression and construction than Xenakis's
which nevertheless achieve a high degree of intensity and dramatic conviction one need look no further than Alfred Schnittke (1934–98). Even if the
shadow of Shostakovich looms large at times, Schnittke had the resource-
fulness, and, perhaps, the lack of self-consciousness, to make his own mark,
and his many concertos range in style from the almost melodramatic
lamenting of the Viola Concerto (1985) to an *a cappella* Concerto for
Mixed Chorus (1984–5) whose religious texts inspire a subtle retrospective
on earlier Russian sacred music, but without parody or pastiche.

While evidence of the modernist impulse to challenge generic expectations persists in the labelling by György Kurtág (*b*.1926) of *The Sayings of Péter Bornemisza* (1963–8) for soprano and piano as a 'concerto' – it is certainly a large-scale work, and makes huge technical demands on both performers – the accommodation between relatively radical techniques and a more conventional understanding of concerto form and texture can be found in two important sets of works by two quite different composers, György Ligeti (*b*.1923) and Peter Maxwell Davies (*b*.1934). Ligeti is the less 'symphonic' of the two, less concerned to follow Schoenbergian principles of reworking traditional formal and tonal templates. Indeed, his Cello Concerto (1967) is radical enough to be deemed 'virtually a non-concerto' by Richard Steinitz: it favours the 'introvert and understated', and its primary contrast is that between the 'self-denial' and 'exhibitionism' of its two movements, rather than that between the soloist and the orchestra.[13] The preference is for making the 'soloist' a first virtuoso among equals; as Steinitz describes it, the relationship of cellist and 'accompanying' ensemble 'is less that of celebrant and congregation than a collective: joining, separating and regrouping like a company of dancers'.[14] The model is Baroque, and this remains the case in both the Chamber Concerto (1969–70) and the Double Concerto for flute, oboe and orchestra (1972). Ligeti's three later concertos, for piano (1980–88), violin (1989–93) and horn (1999, rev. 2002) all had complex geneses, and have more allusive, diverse types of material than the earlier pieces, while adding new refinements to the previously featured subtle explorations of textural interaction. It is nevertheless the Violin Concerto that most merits attention as one of the finest late twentieth-century examples of the genre. It offers a remarkable conjunction between simplicity and elaboration, individuality and allusiveness to tradition. While its overriding quality is an archetypical modernist emphasis on diverse layerings and superimpositions, with many novel effects of timbre and tuning, it also includes potently direct melodic material, like that which dominates the second movement ('Aria, Hoquetus, Choral') in order to offset such ultra-expressionistic moments as the powerfully fragmented ending, with its sextuple and septuple *forte* dynamics fading suddenly to extreme *pianissimo*. Above all, Ligeti composes a properly demanding solo part without for a moment compromising the density and intensity of his musical language. There is none of the marking time or diffusion of musical energy which afflict some of the more expansive concertos by his contemporaries and successors.

Peter Maxwell Davies avoided the generic labels of both concerto and symphony in his earlier, most overtly expressionist years. But the intense thematic working – the most obvious way in which those early works explore a serialism using chant melody as its source – was always implicitly symphonic, and the kind of formal and technical concerns that he initially applied in compositions called 'Fantasia' formed the basis for the cycles of symphonies and concertos on which he embarked after 1970. During the 1980s and 1990s Davies's voluminous output included concertos for violin (1985), trumpet (1988), piccolo (1997) and piano (also 1997). But his most substantial contribution to the genre took the form of the ten 'Strathclyde' concertos (1986–96), commissioned by the Strathclyde Regional Council for the Scottish Chamber Orchestra, and moving from a sequence of eight featuring the orchestra's principals – oboe, cello, horn and trumpet, clarinet, violin and viola, flute, double bass, bassoon – to a pair of 'ensemble' concertos: No. 9 for six different woodwind instruments with string accompaniment (piccolo, alto flute, cor anglais, E flat clarinet, bass clarinet, contrabassoon); and No. 10, a Concerto for Orchestra. These works are often more immediately approachable in their material and general dimensions than many of the large-scale symphonic works that Davies was also writing during these decades, not least when using folk-like melody (the ending of No. 4 for clarinet) or alluding to seventeenth- and eighteenth-century musical styles (No. 5 for violin and viola).

IV

Composers born around and after 1940 confirm the failure of twentieth-century music to follow a single, progressive track away from tonality, traditional formal design and familiar generic categorization, in keeping with the continued institutional support for the larger-scale and the virtuosic. As with earlier generations, many works, if not literally called 'concerto', relate significantly to the traditions of Baroque, Classical or Romantic works for solo instrument(s) and orchestra (chamber or full-size), and star soloists continued to exert an influence: Colin Matthews (*b.*1946) and James MacMillan (*b.*1959) are among many from this younger generation who have written works for Rostropovich that naturally and appropriately explore the expansive expressive intensity of his style as a performer. This style is less at ease with modernistic, expressionistic fractures and technical innovations of the kind found in the Cello Concerto (1990) by Jonathan Harvey (*b.*1939), written for Frances-Maria Uitti, or his *Bird Concerto with Pianosong* for Joanna MacGregor (2001). Harvey is one of several composers to have written percussion concertos for Evelyn Glennie (1997).

As has already been shown in the earlier discussion of, in particular, Elliott Carter, composers who favour relatively complex and radical procedures are not inevitably more disposed to shun the conventional associations of the concerto than those who embrace a more 'mainstream' aesthetic. A 'genre-bending' attitude is nevertheless striking in the seven piano concertos by Michael Finnissy (*b*.1946), composed between 1975 and 1981, with some later revision, since two (Nos. 4 and 6) are for piano solo and the remainder (at least in their final versions) use only relatively small ensembles in support. As Ian Pace has noted, these distinctively original and intensely elaborate works 'represent a commentary on the nature of the piano concerto as a medium'.[15] The solo concertos are both inspired by Alkan's *Concerto for Solo Piano*, making demands on the player which – at least in the case of the twenty-minute No. 4 – veer 'towards the impossible', and 'has the performer adopt both solo and *tutti* roles, with corresponding changes of texture. There is absolutely no let-up for the pianist, who has to plough heroically through a seemingly endless series of whirling semiquavers, manage a five-part canon (with five different time signatures) in the closing section, and somehow negotiate the most hysterical of fugues.' As Pace (who has recorded these pieces) concludes, 'it is hard to imagine greater difficulties than are provided by this work'.[16]

It has long ceased to be a plausible claim that one of the attractions of minimalist music lies in its technical simplicity. While to listen to the Violin Concerto (1987) by Philip Glass (*b*.1937) immediately after a Finnissy piano concerto might have a calming effect, the accurate execution of its repeating patterns and textural shifts requires as much concentration and attention to detail as any more 'complex' score. Nevertheless, Glass's work has more in common with the Baroque concerto grosso than with the solo concerto aiming to highlight virtuoso display, and it can be argued that those composers born since 1940 who have contributed most positively and substantially to the concerto genre are those for whom the 'romantic', theatrical rhetoric of the one against the many remains a valid, vital concept, and whose concertos therefore have qualities of style and form which place them in the grand line of development from Beethoven and Liszt. To avoid the perils of copious listing and superficial commentary, I will focus on just two such composers here: John Adams (*b*.1947) and Magnus Lindberg (*b*.1958).

Adams has had huge success in demonstrating the strengths of an advance from a relatively pure minimalism into what he himself has termed a 'post-minimalist' mainstream: an 'epoch . . . in which a simple, clearly defined language has given way to another of greater synthesis and ambiguity'.[17] That there might be as much of tension as of convergence between tendencies towards synthesis and tendencies towards ambiguity is a crucial factor in giving Adams's large-scale designs the richness they need in order to hold the listener's attention and to invite repeated hearings. To this extent, 'post-minimalism' joins hands, however tentatively, with late modernism, and aligns itself with what can (no less tentatively) be called a modern classicism.[18]

1992–3 were particularly significant years for Adams in that he completed two instrumental works – a Chamber Symphony and a Violin Concerto – to which he gave traditional genre titles, having shunned traditional titles up to that time. This usage does not represent an abject collapse into the arms of historical convention – the later works for clarinet and piano with orchestra have different titles, *Gnarly Buttons* (1996) and *Century Rolls* (1997). There is a confidence in the way the Violin Concerto occupies its substantial half-hour span, subtly patterned, but with no sense of mere note-spinning, even in the toccata-style finale where the *moto perpetuo*, ostinato style inherited from 'pure' minimalism builds a cumulative, truly symphonic excitement, even without the thematic distinctiveness that powers the long first movement. The sheer drama of the soloist's confrontation and interaction with the orchestra resolves out in a startling final close-up, when a big tutti fines down to a cadence shared by soloist and timpani alone.

Much of Adams's success as a composer in large-scale genres stems from the fact that he never creates expectations of engagement with more complex aspects of contemporary practice, and the folkloric, vernacular elements of, in particular, *Gnarly Buttons* suggest that he is a successor of Copland (and Bernstein) rather than a rival to Carter. Nevertheless, depth of expression is not precluded, and the third movement of *Gnarly Buttons* is an excellent example of Adams's ability to avoid happy endings. Called 'Put your loving arms around me', it is, as he describes it, 'a simple song, quiet and tender up front, gnarled and crabbed at the end',[19] and this concluding turn to the darker side of expression indicates that each of the work's three movements is 'based on a "forgery" or imagined musical model': what starts out as warm and reassuring begins to question its own identity, and validity, in a strikingly modernistic manner. By comparison, *Century Rolls* seems rather more routine, the risks of working with allusions (from Ravel and Rachmaninov to Gershwin, Fats Waller and many others) and rhythmic mechanisms not so well alleviated by memorable material and dramatically effective forms. In his note on the work,[20] Adams refers to the seminal musical energy of Conlon Nancarrow, a vital source for Ligeti's later style, and, it must be admitted, turned to more potent use in Ligeti's concertos than in Adams's. While, not least in the Violin Concerto, Ligeti's music continues to live dangerously, and to hint at the trials and tribulations of the composer's formative years, linked as those were to an expressionistic aesthetic, Adams remains a supremely skilful, and far from superficial, entertainer, as effective in evoking feelings of stress and strain as of joy and celebration, and even admitting the occasional hint of melancholy. The 'post-minimalist mainstream', is, understandably, not a world in which ancient historical conflicts demand to be endlessly rehearsed: as Adams's post 9/11 composition, *On the Transmigration of Souls*, shows, new conflicts and new tragedies also require its response.

Adams's musical background in America was supremely eclectic, and he shares much of the pioneering minimalists' impatience with classical and 'serious' traditions. By contrast, Magnus Lindberg worked with a series of distinguished teachers outside his native Finland – Franco Donatoni, Helmut Lachenmann, Brian Ferneyhough, Gérard Grisey – whose commitment to progressive developments stemming from the post-war European avant-garde was considerable. Moreover, Lindberg's initial involvement with the kind of 'spectralism' that, in the case of Grisey, Tristan Murail and others working in France, involved complex harmonic constructions associated with electro-acoustic techniques, promoted a sequence of forcefully expressive instrumental scores between the mid-1980s and early 1990s. Since then Lindberg's music has mellowed, as he has taken increasing account of the attractions of diverse factors including popular and ethnic musics, and has allowed his harmonic thinking to evolve in the direction of focused consonance and even, to a degree, of tonality. His capacity for conceiving instrumental structures on a large scale has given his work a quality that might informally be termed 'symphonic', and a sequence of concertos shows this symphonic quality at full stretch. After the relatively early Piano Concerto (1991, revised 1994), Lindberg returned to the genre in 1999 with a Cello Concerto (in the same year he also completed *Cantigas* for orchestra with solo oboe), and has followed this up with a Clarinet Concerto (2002) and a Concerto for Orchestra (2003).

The twenty-six-minute Cello Concerto is probably the most challenging of the four for the listener, its material more radical and expressionistic, its moods darker and more intense. While in both the later concertos there are passages of relatively blank pattern-making, almost like the filling-out of a predetermined formal design with material intended to give the listener time to take stock, the pattern-like writing in the Cello Concerto contributes more positively to the large-scale evolutionary scheme; there are none of the luscious, Hollywood-style orchestral climaxes found in the Clarinet Concerto which, even if ironic in intent, show that the distance between spectrally conceived harmonic organization and technicolor bathos need not be very great. The sheer expansiveness of design and expression comes close to running out of steam in the Clarinet Concerto's later stages, and comparable reservations can be registered about the Concerto for Orchestra, even though in many respects this is an emotionally powerful and aurally enthralling experience.

It remains an open question as to whether Lindberg can manage to preserve those more immediately approachable and accessible features that have entered his music without dilution or without falling back on episodes that merely mark time. As his work illustrates as well as others in the early years of the new century, the challenge for composers of concertos who do not seek to sever all connections with the great virtuoso traditions of earlier epochs is to preserve a sense of scale and enterprise without lapsing into emptiness or tedium. The signs are that the best performers are as able as they have always been to rise to the technical challenges of contemporary styles. The question is whether composers will continue to do so, or whether they will finally and decisively abandon the particular link with the past that the concerto genre has represented so potently for so long.

PART THREE

Performance

10 The rise (and fall) of the concerto virtuoso in the late eighteenth and nineteenth centuries

CLIFF EISEN

'Virtuoso', wrote Sir George Grove, is 'a term of Italian origin, applied, more abroad than in England, to a player who excels in the technical part of his art. Such players being naturally open to a temptation to indulge their ability unduly at the expense of the meaning of the composer, the word has acquired a somewhat depreciatory meaning, as of display for its own sake. *Virtuosität* – or virtuosity, if the word may be allowed – is the condition of playing like a virtuoso. Mendelssohn never did, Mme. Schumann and Joachim never do, play in the style alluded to. It would be invidious to mention those who do.'[1]

Grove's definition more or less sums up the modern idea of the virtuoso: at least since the middle of the nineteenth century the term has been applied almost exclusively to performers and except in rare instances, the 'true' virtuoso, carries with it a whiff of disapproval, the privileging of flash over substance. But the term was not always understood in this way and did not apply exclusively to performers. Johann Gottfried Walther, following the lead of Brossard, wrote that 'Virtu [*ital.*] means that musical skill ... either in theory or in practice ... that is extraordinarily advanced. He who possesses such skill is accordingly described with the epithet *virtuoso* or *virtudioso*, and *virtuosa* and *virtudiosa*.'[2] And James Grassineau, in 1740, noted that:

> VIRTU, in *Italian*, not only means that habitude of the soul which renders us agreeable in the sight of God, and makes us act according to the rules of reason, but also that superiority of genius, address and ability, that makes us excel (either in the theory or practice of any art, & *c.*) many others who equally apply themselves thereto. From whence they form the adjective *Virtuoso* or *Virtudioso*, which often stand as substantives when used in praise of any one that Providence has blessed with that superiority or excellence: thus an excellent Painter, or an able Architect, & *c.* are called *Virtuosi*. But this epithet, says Mr *Brossard*, is oftener given to eminent Musicians, than to any other artist; and among them, rather to those who apply themselves to the theory of that art, than the practice: so that among them, to say a *Virtuoso*, would be understood an excellent Musician. The *French* have only the word *Illustre* that can answer to the *Virtuoso* of the *Italian*. We use the word *Virtuoso*, but in a more extended sense, it not being fixed to any particular art,

but is applied to any person excelling in his art, be it what it will; if it be at all
limitted among us, 'tis to the learned in physic and natural history, or
philosophy.[3]

In its earliest musical incarnation, then, a virtuoso was someone accomplished in the art, whether theoretically, compositionally or practically. And
given the word's derivation from virtue, virtuosity represents a positive
attribute. It is in this sense that Johann Mattheson, in his *Grundlage einer
Ehrenpforte*, includes a letter of recommendation for Pachelbel, written by
Daniel Eberlin, Hochfürstl. Sachsen-Eisenachischer Capellmeister und
Secretarius, as 'a *perfect* and rare Virtuoso'.[4] This kind of characterization
can be traced well into the nineteenth century. In 1802 Heinrich Christoph
Koch wrote that 'In the arts, *Virtu* means the same thing as artistic merit;
accordingly one describes as a virtuoso someone who particularly distin-
guishes himself as an artist'.[5]

The use of the term virtuoso primarily to describe performers, as
opposed to theorists, can be documented even earlier. In 1598, the
music publisher Giacomo Vincenti praised the young women of the
Venetian Ospedale della Pietà as 'virtuose giovani'.[6] And throughout
the eighteenth and nineteenth centuries the term came increasingly to
be associated exclusively with practical musicians and with performance.
Johann Georg Sulzer, who saw expression as the decisive criterion of
performance, argued that 'it is expression in performance alone that
distinguishes the master from his student and the great virtuoso from
the mediocre'[7] while Ferdinand Simon Gassner wrote that 'we divide
musical artists in two groups, the creative and the practical; the one are
composers or so-called tone-poets, the other virtuosos, that is, musicians
who perform works and accordingly have a particular facility playing an
instrument or singing. It is from this, too, that the name virtuoso is
derived (from the Italian *virtu* or the Latin *virtus*), which in the art
means merit, distinction, perfection.'[8] As late as 1873 Oskar Paul, in his
Handlexikon der Tonkunst, defined a virtuoso as 'a musician who performs a piece and has acquired complete mastery on an instrument or in
singing. This itself is called virtuosity.'[9]

Feats of virtuosity, whether in the service of expression or merely as
demonstrations of technical excellence, were usually (though not exclusively)
thought of in these terms. An anecdote told by Charles Burney about
Farinelli's vocal acrobatics during a 1722 Rome performance of an opera by
his brother, Riccardo Broschi, seems to be without a hint of censure:

> There was a struggle every night between him [Farinelli] and a famous player
> on the trumpet, in a song accompanied by that instrument: this, at first,
> seemed amicable and merely sportive, till the audience began to interest

themselves in the contest, and to take different sides: after severally swelling out a note, in which each manifested the power of his lungs, and tried to rival the other in brilliancy and force, they had both a swell and a shake together, by thirds, which was continued so long, while the audience eagerly waited the event, that both seemed to be exhausted; and, in fact, the trumpeter, wholly spent gave it up, thinking, however, his antagonist as much tired as himself, and that it would be a drawn battle; when Farinelli, with a smile on his countenance, showing he had only been sporting with him all this time, broke out all at once in the same breath, with fresh vigour, and not only swelled and shook the note, but ran the most rapid and difficult divisions and was at last silenced only by the acclamations of the audience. From this period may be dated that superiority which he ever maintained over all contemporaries.[10]

By the same token, accounts of the best-known and most widely admired performing musicians at the turn of the nineteenth century, many of them now consigned to the dustbin of history as empty technicians, generally tend to stress their virtues:

MODERN VIOLINISTS. Opinion of an eminent musician upon the great modern violinists, to the year 1831

Cramer, William.	– Born at Manheim, 1730; first performance in England, 1770. Peculiar characteristics: decision and spirit; also an excellent leader.
Barthelemon.	– Born at Bordeaux, 1741; first performance in England, 1765. Sweetness and polished taste, especially in Corelli.
Giornovichi.	– Palermo, 1745–1792. Correctness, purity of tone, and elegance.
Salomen.	– Born 1745–1781. Boldness, enthusiasm, and playfulness, particularly in Haydn's works.
Yaniewicz.	– Wilna, 1792. Delicacy and high finish, especially in quartetts.
Viotti.	– Piedmont, 1745–1790. Vigorous energy, grand bowing, extraordinary execution, and masterly style; above all, in concertos.
Vaccari.	– Modena, 1772–1823. Tenderness, exquisite taste, feeling, and refined expression.
Rode.	– Bordeaux, 1773–1794. Bold tone, vigour, and elegance.
Pinto.	– London, 1786–1798. Fire, originality, vivid fervour, and profound feeling.
Baillot.	– Paris, 1770. Sterling taste, variety, variety of manner, admirable bowing, forcible tone, and masterly command of the instrument.
Spagnoletti.	– Italy. Charming quality of tone; graceful freedom in bowing; genuine Italian taste.

Weichsel.	– Strength of tone; energy; excellent timist.
Lafont.	– Paris. Suavity and elegance, especially in cantabile movements.
Kiesewetter.	– Anpach, 1777–1821. Deep pathos in adagios, and extraordinary rapidity in allegros; fine bow-arm, and wonderfully distinct articulation.
Spohr.	– Seesen, 1784–1820. Grandeur, vigour, elevation of style, exquisite taste, purity of tone, and composer-like feeling.
Paganini.	– Genoa, 1784–1831. Everything.
Mori.	– London, 1797. Rich, full, and beautiful tone; polished taste, masterly variety of style, and extraordinary brilliancy of execution.
De Beriot.	– Belgium. Perfect intonation, grace, rich and charming tone, elegant bowing, refined taste, and wonderful execution.[11]

The heavyweights on this list, Giovanni Battista Viotti (1755–1824) and Nicolò Paganini (1782–1840), represent the *ne plus ultra* of violin playing in the late eighteenth and early nineteenth centuries, respectively. Viotti, who arrived in Paris in 1782 and remained there for ten years, cast virtually all other violinists in the shade; it was during this time, and during his early years in London after 1792, that he composed almost all of his twenty-nine extant concertos.[12] Known in particular for his full tone, smooth legato and diversity of bow strokes, Viotti inspired several generations of violinists. It seems likely, too, that his works were widely disseminated and admired: sometime between 1789 and 1791, Mozart composed additional trumpet and drum parts (K. 470a) for Viotti's E minor Concerto, No. 16.[13] Paganini's position in the pantheon of violinists can hardly be challenged. The author of five violin concertos between 1816 and 1830, his technical innovations astounded and inspired his contemporaries, including Liszt (whose own qualities as a virtuoso performer are mentioned in Chapter 12) and Chopin. Chief among these were his use of left-hand pizzicato and double harmonics as well as 'ricochet' bowing, produced by letting the bow bounce on the strings. At the same time, Paganini revived discarded techniques from the early eighteenth century, including those in Locatelli's twenty-four caprices published with twelve concertos Op. 3 as *L'Arte del Violino* (1733). According to Clive Brown, Paganini's technique depended in particular on his manner of holding the violin, with the neck of the instrument pointing down, the arms held close to the body, the thumb position some distance along the fingerboard, and one foot forward, creating a 'perfect centre of gravity'.[14]

Viotti was the inspiration for the three most important French violinists of the early nineteenth century, Pierre Rode (1774–1830 and Viotti's favourite pupil), Pierre Baillot (1771–1842) and Rodolphe Kreutzer

(1766–1831). All three toured extensively and all three were closely associated with the Conservatoire in Paris. Rode, who composed thirteen violin concertos between 1794 and about 1815, also gave the first perform-ance of Beethoven's Violin Sonata in G, Op. 96 (with Archduke Rudolph at the keyboard). Baillot composed nine concertos between 1802 and *c.*1820. And Kreutzer was the most prolific, composing nineteen concertos between 1783 and about 1810. Baillot is said to have been appalled by Paganini's harmonics and left-hand pizzicato, not surprisingly given the French violin school's predilection for clarity of execution and elevated style.[15] Other early French or French-based virtuosos included Giovanni Giornovichi (1747–1804) and Charles Philippe Lafont (1781–1839). Giornovichi, an Italian, was the most popular violinist in Paris before the arrival of Viotti and a pioneer in the unaffected French style and in the use of romance movements for his concertos, sixteen of which he composed between the early 1770s and the mid-1790s. The relatively large number of arrangements of these works for keyboard, including versions by Dussek and J. B. Cramer, attests to their popularity. Giornovichi was also active in London from 1791 to 1796 and in Hamburg from 1796 to 1802, but in Hamburg chiefly as a billiard player. Lafont, known in particular for his performance of cantabile movements, studied with Kreutzer and Rode; seven violin concertos by him are extant. Charles-August de Bériot (1802–70), who composed several concertos and was active at the Brussels conservatory from 1843 to 1852, represents the post-Rode gen-eration of violinists, strongly influenced by Paganini. Among others, de Bériot taught Henri Vieuxtemps.

London's early virtuoso violinists included the German-born Wilhelm Cramer (1746–99), the French-born François-Hippolyte Barthélémon (1741–1808), the Italian-born Paolo Spagnoletti (1773–1834), and the Polish-born Felix Janiewicz (1762–1848), who was also active in Edinburgh. Cramer, active in London from 1772 and particularly known for his off-string bowing, composed at least eight violin concertos but was better known as an orchestral leader,[16] as was Spagnoletti. Barthelemon is not known to have composed concertos at all; his fame rested on his abilities as a performer and his theatrical music.[17] Yaniewicz, on the other hand, composed at least five concertos, although it is possible these date from his time in Paris before his move to London in 1792. Nor were the finest, native English violinists prolific as concerto composers. Johann Peter Salomon (1745–1815), best known for promot-ing Haydn in London, composed a romance for violin and orchestra about 1810 and a concerto that survives only in a keyboard arrangement from 1805;[18] Charles Weichsel (1767–1850) may have composed a concerto (only sketches survive); and Nicolas Mori, a student of Barthélémon, composed several concertos none of which was published.[19]

The great early nineteenth-century German violin virtuoso was Louis Spohr (1784–1859), who was greatly influenced by Rode when he heard him play in Brunswick in 1803. Indeed, it is generally conceded that the great strength of Spohr's violin music is its combination of German and French traits and his concertos, composed between *c*.1802 and 1846, exerted a lasting influence on German violin-playing for the rest of the century, as did his *Violinschule* of 1832.[20]

Besides violinists, pianists were the most popular virtuosos of the nineteenth century, a result in no small part of the instrument's increasing prestige and its appeal to a wide-ranging bourgeois audience: not only did it represent the primary means of late eighteenth- and early nineteenth-century domestic music-making, but the increasing number and accessibility of public concerts and rapid changes in piano construction (that increased both the instrument's compass and its ability to execute rapidly), as well as marketing, gave rise to a metaphoric platform for virtuosos as Romantic heroes and as models to be emulated – models to which amateurs, especially women, could aspire. This last point in particular is explicit in a review from 1823 of a London concert, at Willis's Rooms on 6 June, by J. B. Cramer:

> The concert opened with Mozart's beautiful symphony in E flat [K. 543], after which – without mentioning in particular a song by Carafa – he [Cramer] played his sixth piano concerto in E flat with his accustomed mastery. Nothing is more uplifting than to see such a worthy artist as Cramer play year after year with undiminished fire; it is as if his talent is rejuvenated with each Spring. . . . As everyone knows, his strength lies in [the performance] of Adagios, for it is here that he finds the best opportunity to display his beautiful full tone and refined taste. Aside from the concerto in E flat, he also played a piano quintet and two piano duos for four hands, namely the lovely sonata by Hummel, Op. 92, with Mr. Kalkbrenner, and a no less praiseworthy [sonata] with Mr. Moscheles, the composer of the work. These two Duos were apparently the strongest attractions for our female pianists, for the opportunity to compare these three masters of the instrument in a display of all their skills, is no ordinary good fortune.[21]

At the time, Johann Baptist Cramer (1771–1858) was at the height of his fame. A pupil of Johann Samuel Schroeter and Clementi, Cramer had appeared on the London stage as early as the mid-1780s in performances of Mozart's concertos;[22] according to Ries, Beethoven considered Cramer the finest pianist of his day. Known for his expressive legato touch, Cramer composed nine concertos between 1795 and 1825, a relatively large number of works.[23] His concert companions, Frédéric Kalkbrenner

(1785–1849), the dedicatee of Chopin's Piano Concerto in E minor, Op. 11, and Ignaz Moscheles (1749–1870), were equally renowned. The French Kalkbrenner composed at least four concertos (three of them in minor keys) between 1823 and 1835,[24] while the Bohemian Moscheles wrote at least eight between 1819 and 1838. Something of a conservative, Moscheles deplored the *Trois nouvelles études* as evidence of Chopin's showy and effeminate virtuosity.[25] And his attraction to Beethoven's work is clear from the nicknames of two of his concertos: the 'Pathétique' Op. 93 (1835–6) and the 'Pastorale' Op. 96 (1837).

Cramer's early accounts of Mozart's concertos reflected the Viennese composer's prestige as both a performer and composer during the 1780s: unquestionably one of the most brilliant pianists of his day, Mozart's concertos not only required a highly developed technique (as, for example, his cadenzas to the D major Concerto, K. 451, show) but also set compositional benchmarks as works for budding virtuosos to perform and as compositions to be emulated when pianists wrote concertos of their own. Indeed, many young, continental virtuosos began their careers with Mozart concertos, including his pupil Johann Nepomuk Hummel (1765–1807) and Anton Eberl (1765–1807). While it is not certain that Eberl in fact studied with Mozart, it is likely he was close to the composer: in 1791 he wrote a cantata *Bey Mozarts Grabe* and in 1794 and 1795 he gave several concerts with Constanze Mozart, in Vienna and Leipzig, at which he performed Mozart concertos. His own works in the genre, two solo concertos and one concerto for two pianos, were well received; the first of them, in C major (1797), was favourably compared with (and in some circles preferred to) Beethoven's Piano Concerto No. 1 in C, Op. 15.[26] Hummel was easily the most brilliant and successful of Mozart's students: the composer of at least seven concertos between about 1805 and 1833, his later works, especially the A minor Concerto, Op. 85, and the B minor Concerto, Op. 89, are rewardingly vibrant, virtuoso flights of Romantic fantasy.[27]

Another pianist to cut his teeth on Mozart, and one who represents a tangible link between the older composer and the lion of the next generation, Beethoven, was Carl Czerny (1791–1857). Not only is Czerny said to have played part of Mozart's K. 503 for Beethoven, who then took him on as a student, but at his Augarten concert of 1800 he performed the C minor Concerto, K. 491; later, in 1806, he played Beethoven's first concerto and, in 1812, the 'Emperor'. Unlike most virtuosos of the time, Czerny travelled little. But he composed at least six piano concertos, two smaller concertinos and three cadenzas to Beethoven's Op. 15.[28]

While in some respects Czerny represents Vienna's conservative past, in other respects he represents the pianism of the future: performer of Mozart and student of Beethoven, Czerny was also a teacher of Liszt and Sigismond Thalberg (1812–71), a formidable pianist who vied with Liszt during their time together in Paris in the mid-1830s. Thalberg, who composed only one concerto, the F minor Op. 5, was better known for his fantasies on operatic themes, some of which appear in his pedagogical *L'art du chant appliqué au piano* (Paris, 1857).[29] Indeed, by the time of Thalberg and Liszt, the musical world had both expanded and contracted: the isolated virtuoso, the employee of a church or court, was now a travelling performer, well acquainted with other virtuosos and often exchanging ideas with them. Thalberg had lessons not only with Czerny, but with Hummel, Johann Peter Pixis (1788–1874 and composer of two concertos, in E flat and C major, Opp. 68 and 100, both *c.*1830),[30] Kalkbrenner and Moscheles as well. Adolf Henselt (1814–89) also studied with Hummel – his one concerto, the striking F minor Op. 16, is still sometimes performed today.[31]

Other important concerto virtuosos of the late eighteenth and early nineteenth centuries included Muzio Clementi (1752–1832), only one of whose concertos survives;[32] the Irishman John Field (1782–1837), who composed seven concertos between 1799 and about 1822;[33] Jan Ladislav Dussek (1760–1812), whose concerto in G minor Op. 49 is probably the most successful of his eighteen concertos (mostly written between 1779 and about 1813); Beethoven's pupil Ferdinand Ries (1784–1838), composer of eight concertos;[34] Daniel Steibelt (1765–1820), composer of eight concertos during the first two decades or so of the nineteenth century; and Joseph Wölfl (1773–1812), a student of Leopold Mozart and possibly Wolfgang, who around 1800 represented the only real threat to Beethoven's dominance as a pianist in Vienna. Wölfl composed seven concertos from the late 1790s to sometime in the 1810s, including 'Le calme', Op. 36, and 'Le coucou', Op. 49.[35]

Contemporaneous accounts of these pianists rarely mention specific technical devices; they usually describe the players' profound musicianship, their singing lines, propulsive passage-work or expressive playing.[36] But almost all of them had tricks up their sleeves: Dussek was known for his double thirds and consecutive octaves in both hands (for example, in the G minor Concerto), Clementi for his thirds and octave melodies,[37] Kalkbrenner for his left-hand octaves and Henri Herz (1803–88, no concertos by him are known) for his glissandos in thirds.[38] Henselt was a specialist in chords encompassing a tenth or even a twelfth as well as arpeggios with a larger stretch than an octave (for example, in the slow movement of the concerto Op. 16). And Thalberg was most famous for his 'three-hand' effects, splitting a tune situated in the middle of the keyboard between his two thumbs. Not all of these tricks were limited to traditional concertos, however. Variations with orchestral accompaniment were not uncommon: Hummel wrote variations for piano and orchestra on themes from Vogler's *Castor e Polluce* (1798) and the singspiel *Das Fest der Handwerker* (1830); Ries composed similar works based on Swedish national airs and on 'Rule, Britannia'; Field wrote a *Fantaisie sur un air favorit de mon ami N.P.* that he performed in Moscow on 6 March 1822 (the orchestral parts are now lost); and Henselt composed variations on 'Quand je quittai la Normandie' from Meyerbeer's *Robert le Diable* (published London and Leipzig, 1840). Chopin's variations on 'Là ci darem' fall into this category as well. Other, similar works include Pixis's *Fantaisie-militaire*, Op. 121 (1833), and Hummel's *Oberons Zauberhorn* (1829). A trend towards the programmatic is also evident in virtuoso concertos of the time, including Steibelt's 'Le voyage au Mont St Bernard' (*c.*1816), 'Grand Military Concerto dans le genre des Grecs' (accompanied by two orchestras) and 'L'orage' (1798, including an imitation of a storm), Wölfl's 'Le calme' and 'Le coucou', Field's 'L'incendie par l'orage', Op. 39 (1817), and Ries's 'Farewell to London', Op. 132, and 'Salut au Rhin', Op. 151. (Ries had left London in 1824 to return to his native Rhineland.) Sometimes composers worked popular tunes into their concertos, including Field, whose first concerto cites James Hook's ''Twas within a mile of Edinboro' town'.

Grassineau's 1740 characterization of a virtuoso as someone most likely to be learned in 'physic and natural history, or philosophy' points to another early, common usage of the word, a usage that resonates strongly, if implicitly, with nineteenth-century notions of musical virtuosity. The term was frequently used by members of the Royal Society of London for Improving Natural Knowledge, founded in 1662, to describe themselves; shortly after his first visit, Samuel Pepys, who was president of the society from 1684, referred to it as 'the college of vertuosoes'.[39] But the Society was also criticized and satirized for its perceived insistence on knowledge for knowledge's sake, for its collecting of facts and specimens solely for the sake of collecting. This is usually taken as the point of Thomas Shadwell's *The Virtuoso*, given at the Dorset Theatre in May 1676.[40]

This use of the word virtuoso to refer to the scientist-collector derives from a still earlier meaning of the term, specifically describing collectors and connoisseurs of *objets d'art*. John Evelyn's diary for 1 March 1644, for example, describes his visit in Paris to 'one of the greatest Virtuosas in France, for his Collection of Pictures, Achates, Medaills, & Flowers, especially Tulips & Anemonys'.[41] And at the end of the eighteenth century, an advertisement from *The Times* plays explicitly on the collecting-connoisseurship constellation:

RACKSTROW'S MUSEUM, / No. 197, near Temple-Bar, Fleet-Street / CONSISTING of the most curious Objects, no / where else to be seen, in an assemblage of wonders, in / which the works of art and nature seem to vie with each / other. Here the most elegant, ingenious, and accurate dis- / playing of the human frame ... with the most / rare natural productions the world can afford, are exhibited, / for the student to contemplate, the curious to entertain, the / artist to imitate, and the virtuoso to admire.[42]

The nineteenth-century notion of the virtuoso takes this one step further. It is not merely the collecting, contemplation and admiration of the past or present that counts, but its preservation:

> *THE ALBERT MEMORIAL.*
> TO THE EDITOR OF THE TIMES.
> Sir, – ... permit me to call your attention to an act, amounting almost to Vandalism, now being perpetrated in connexion with the alto-relievos that worthily adorn the base of the Albert Memorial. Accompanying some Italian friends there yesterday, one of them, a distinguished virtuoso, expressed his utter astonishment at the mode in which the furies were being cleansed. They were being deluged with water, possibly in combination with soap, thus presenting for the time the appearance of being whitewashed. Worse than this, the men were using, in their customary rough fashion, large bristle paint brushes. My friend remarked that if such a process of cleansing was continued, all the finer lines of the features would soon be destroyed, and within 40 or 50 years the features themselves would entirely disappear. ...
> I have the honour to be, Sir, your most obedient servant,
> J. S. Laurie. Whitehall Club, June 14.[43]

The essential point here is that Laurie's Italian virtuoso, a 'true' expert unlike those already entrusted with caring for the Albert Memorial, is a conservationist. By virtue of technique, he knows how to preserve the bas-reliefs. And by preserving their details, their contours and finely etched lines, he preserves the meaning and spirit intended by the sculptor – or 'author'. The virtuoso is therefore a custodian of some greater 'authenticity': it is not his job to promote himself but to protect the work for which he is responsible, that falls to his hands (an apt metaphor not only for a sculpture but for music as well).

If the idea that a 'true' virtuoso is the custodian of some greater good, a traditional value or even a traditional virtue, is implicit in Grassineau's definition, it is explicit in Johann Mattheson's *Der brauchbare Virtuoso* of 1720:

> Among the Italians (to whom the word belongs), virtuosos are those who excel at a particular art, for example, music, painting etc. Although this term is in fact derived from *virtus intellectualis* – from the strength or virtue of the intellect – this does not mean that *virtus moralis* – virtuous conduct in morals – is thereby excluded. Rather, this moral virtue is assumed or presupposed as something indispensable in every virtuoso even though – unfortunately! – it is

the one quality that is most lacking, and from this lack springs, in part, the most worthless virtuosos. The *virtus intellectualis* can, therefore, be entirely or partially exposed by the *virtus moralis* in a subject, and so many a man may be a virtuoso, but he is generally a disgraceful and unusable one.[44]

Within fifty years or so, Mattheson's moral imperative of virtuosity, of *virtus moralis*, was transformed into an imperative of performance, the imperative of good taste, which as an aesthetic category largely retains its roots in *virtù*. Johann Adam Hiller, discussing soloistic performance, writes that:

> The melody of a solo or concerto,[45] if indeed one can call it that, is not just a song imitative of the passions or the heart but, rather, an artistically arranged succession of sounds, according to the nature of the instrument on which it is played, whose correctness may be judged more as a matter of Art than Nature. . . . In such a piece, the artist demonstrates his skill and perfection. He seeks not so much to move as to amaze and the astonishment of the listener is the only applause he seeks. . . . In general, the inclination to amaze is a constant obstacle to Art. Good taste, which alone makes Art beautiful, founders on it and the Art loses itself in the darkness of bombast and barbarism. Deception replaces the true and instead of genuine radiance comes nothing but a false shimmer of the work of art.[46]

Taste, at least as Schubart later put it, is achieved chiefly by understanding and entering into the spirit of the composer: 'The soloist must perform either his own or another's fantasy. In both cases he must possess genius. If I play a sonata by *Bach*, I must submerge myself entirely in the spirit of this great man, so that my own ego disappears.'[47] This is Hegel's position[48] and it is the position taken by E. T. A. Hoffmann in his review of Beethoven's piano trios Op. 70: 'Many so-called virtuosos dismiss Beethoven's keyboard compositions with the rebuke: too hard! adding: and highly inconceivable! [But] as concerns their difficulty, what is needed for a correct and fitting performance of Beethoven's works is nothing less than that one . . . penetrates deep into its substance. . . . The true artist lives only in the work, which he understands in the sense of the master and now performs.'[49]

Disapproval of virtuosos who fail to enter into the spirit of the composers whose works they play, or who give themselves over to mechanical display at the expense of expression, already makes an appearance in music criticism of the late eighteenth century. A review of Viennese pianists from 1799 distinguishes between two prominent virtuosos, Mozart's pupil Josepha Auernhammer (1758–1820) and Magdalene von Kurzböck (1767–1845), a friend of Haydn: 'Madame Auernhammer: her entire endeavour is the overcoming of nearly insurmountable difficulties and so she neglects what one in the nobler sense calls "performance". Given this, she never plays truly beautifully or expressively. I cannot decide which of two usual reasons is responsible for this, whether it is a lack of feeling or a desire to shine'. Magdalene von Kurzböck, on the other hand, 'is entirely concerned with expressive, proper performance. She enters entirely into the spirit of the compositions she plays.'[50]

The obligation to be a 'true' virtuoso had always had both moral and societal dimensions. Mary Astell, in *An Essay in Defence of the Female Sex*, describes the virtuoso in this way:

> He Trafficks to all places, and has his Correspondents in every part of the World; yet his Merchandise serve not to promote our Luxury, nor encrease our Trade, and neither enrich the Nation, nor himself. A Box or two of *Pebbles* or *Shells*, and a dozen of *Wasps, Spiders* and *Caterpillars* are his Cargoe. He values a *Camelion*, or *Salamander's* Egg, above all the Sugars and Spices of the *West* and *East-Indies* . . . . To what purpose is it, that these Gentlemen ransack all Parts both of *Earth* and *Sea* to procure these *Trifles*? . . . I know that the desire of knowledge, and the discovery of things yet unknown is the Pretence; but what Knowledge is it? What Discoveries do we owe to their Labours? It is only the Discovery of some few unheeded Varieties of Plants, Shells, or Insects, unheeded only because useless; and the Knowledge, they boast so much of, is no more than a Register of their Names, and Marks of Distinction only.[51]

Not only is this similar to Mattheson's comments in *Der brauchbare Virtuos*, but the obligation had a class dimension as well: Zedler characterized musicians who played at weddings and 'beer-fiddlers and city pipers who wait at inns' as 'Musicanten' while 'the virtuosos of royal and princely chapels do not gladly classify themselves as Musicanten; rather they prefer to call themselves connoisseurs, *Musici*, virtuosos, etc.'.[52] And Heine's later formulation implicitly links the social with the economic: 'they are not virtuosos who profane music for pay, rather they [virtuosos] are apostles of the heavenly art'.[53]

It is probably not a coincidence that this constellation of 'virtuosic' needs – theory, composition or performance related, class, social value and morality – coalesces more or less over the same period as the idea of a musical canon and canonical composers. As such it not only fixes the idea of the 'true' virtuoso, one who enters into and communicates the spirit of the canonical author, but also gives rise to virtuoso performers who are themselves canonical. For some practising musicians were clearly beyond reproach. Joseph Joachim was one of them, as a notice in *The Times* (London) for 17 February 1880, comparing him with the violinist August Wilhelmj (1845–1908), makes clear: 'Herr Joachim is, no doubt, the greatest violinist of the day, looking upon his qualities in the aggregate. There may be other *virtuosi* who equal him in richness of tone or in the interpretation of a special class of music – Wilhelmj might be named among the former, Sivori among the latter – but as regards general technical mastery, combined with artistic earnestness of purpose and truly classical dignity of style, Joachim is unsurpassed. He is, indeed, not only a great *virtuoso*, but also a perfect musician, and in this fact the secret of his permanent and well-deserved success must be discovered.'[54] Joachim, it will be remembered, was one of Grove's canonical performers, together with Clara Schumann and Mendelssohn. And the description of him as 'not only a great *virtuoso*, but also a perfect musician', is nearly identical to Eberlin's description of Pachelbel.

Over the course of the eighteenth and nineteenth centuries then, the idea of the virtuoso came not only to centre on performers but also served to reinforce the authority of the composer and the authority of the work. The 'true' virtuoso was a conservationist, a guardian of traditional, authorial values. Hence the disparaging of any display that drew attention chiefly to itself, that did not worship at the altar of the great. Perhaps it is for this reason that Paganini was dismissed from the canon of 'true' virtuosos. He hardly ever played works by other composers in his public concerts because, as he told Fétis: 'I have my own special style and in accordance with this I formulate my composition. To play works of other artists I must adapt them to my style.'[55] Put another way, Paganini refused (or recognized his inability) to be the voice of some other, greater authority. By and large, this was not a concern for audiences during his lifetime: A. B. Marx noted that the violinist's audiences were captivated more by his interpretation than his acrobatics, Ludwig Rellstab claimed Paganini could make the instrument 'speak, weep and sing', and Friedrich Wieck, Clara Schumann's father, wrote that he had 'never heard a singer who had touched him as deeply as an Adagio played by Paganini'.[56] But it was a concern for canonical histories.

It is worth asking where the bulk of negative comments directed at empty virtuosity originate. To be sure, many of them derive from theorists, who more often than not had a stake in asserting their aesthetics and the authority of the theoretical systems their aesthetics gave rise to. At the same time, however, they also derive from those who had the most to lose in hand-to-hand combat with the virtuoso: the composer-performer. In his preface to his 1688 *Hortulus Chelicus*, 'Advice to Devoted Lovers of the Violin', Johann Jakob Walther takes a swipe at Biber: 'they might, as a matter of habit, use the bow in such a way that with firm and pleasing strokes, distinct purity, and pleasant melody, they delight the audience nearby, rather than offending an audience at some distance with the confusing speed of a screeching bow and of fingers leaping up and down and running over the violin, twisting variously in straight and oblique chords – as they say – or by squeaking now on two or more strings falsely tuned *ad nauseam*'.[57] And Mozart famously wrote of Clementi: '[he] plays well, so far as execution with the right hand goes. His greatest strength lies in passages in thirds. Apart from this, he has not a kreuzer's worth of taste or feeling – in short he is simply a *mechanicus*.'[58] On 4 October 1804, Beethoven wrote to Nikolaus Simrock: 'This *Kreutzer* is a dear kind fellow who during his stay in Vienna gave me a great deal of pleasure. I prefer his modesty and natural behaviour to *all the exterior*, without *any interior*, which is characteristic of most virtuosi.'[59]

Shortly after his arrival in Paris, Chopin wrote 'I really don't know whether any place contains more pianists than Paris, or whether you can find anywhere more asses and virtuoso'[60] and Liszt described the Russian musician Guskow, 'who had constructed out of wood and straw a sort of xylophone', as:

> the musical juggler who plays an infinitely large number of notes in an infinitely short period of time, and draws the most possible sound out of two of the least sonorous materials. This is the prodigious overcoming of difficulty that all of Paris is now applauding. It is greatly to be regretted that M. Guskow, the Paganini of the boulevards, has not applied his talent, one could even say his genius, to the invention of some agricultural instrument or to the introduction into his country of some new crop. He would then have enriched an entire population; instead, his talent gone astray has only produced a musical puerility, and the charlatanism of the newspapers will not succeed in endowing it with a value it cannot really have.[61]

Reviewing some of Thalberg's printed music, Liszt remarked on its 'impotence and monotony; such is, in the last analysis, what we find in the publications of M. Thalberg'.[62] It is worth noting that Liszt's review was written shortly after his return to Paris, during which time Thalberg had conquered the musical public.

Critiques of virtuosity, then, have never been disinterested, and although we now see virtuosity as a purely musical phenomenon, the idea is just as firmly rooted in notions of virtue and conservation. We extrapolate from it to other kinds of virtuosity when in fact the term calls up a wider web of interlocking historical and social meanings, many of which are now lost but that bear directly on the rich palette of relationships among music, performance, performer and audience. By understanding the essentially social nature of virtuosity, and the range of both positive and negative ideas late eighteenth- and early nineteenth-century listeners brought to virtuoso performances and virtuoso performers, we can recover, at least in part, some of the complicated aesthetic of performance at the time. At the very least, it offers a richer listening experience today, one that takes as its point of departure a complex of ideas more varied than the traditional, late nineteenth-century aesthetic of the virtuoso suggests.

11 Performance practice in the eighteenth-century concerto

ROBIN STOWELL

The concerto was a natural culmination of the opposition of solo and tutti textures that characterized much eighteenth-century music. Using it as a vehicle for virtuoso display, performers not only extended instrumental techniques but also made increasing demands on instrument-makers for better, more responsive instruments. Composers in turn exploited that potential in what proved to be a progressive cyclical relationship. The performer-composer connection was especially crucial. A composer's notated text was rarely all-embracing as regards performance practice, not least because much eighteenth-century music was disseminated in sketched rather than fully realized formats, and performers were often required to be spontaneous in their interpretations across a wide range of performance practices.

Although much can be learnt about such practices from instrumental and theoretical treatises, iconography, historical archives, letters, critiques and even anecdotal evidence, idiomatic performance is difficult to achieve across the diversity of both styles and the particular circumstances surrounding concerto composition and performance. C. P. E. Bach's concertos H471–6, for example, were written for amateurs and differ from his other concertos in that they 'are more adapted to the nature of the harpsichord, are easier both in the solo part and the accompaniment, are adequately ornamented in the slow movements and are provided with written-out cadenzas'.[1] Some concertos were written for private performance, notably Wagenseil's for the Imperial family in Vienna, while others were premièred in public concerts, notably in series such as the Concert Spirituel in Paris. Such variety of intended audience, performer and venue is reflected not only in the technical and stylistic detail of these works but also in issues relevant to eighteenth-century concerto performance (forming the focus of this chapter) such as the constitution and distribution of their ensembles, their direction, continuo usage and cadenzas. Many of these issues, of course, are not specific to the concerto but apply in most musical genres; thus, the discussion of some (national style, expression, articulation, melodic inflection, accentuation, tempo and ornamentation, for example) is of necessity quite general and unsupported by examples from the concerto repertory.

The use of period instruments

The concept of consciously performing Baroque and early Classical concertos on 'period' instruments and with due reverence to the styles and performance practices that the composer might have expected may certainly make the music sound expressive. It may also clarify what the composer actually intended, as well as re-creating some of its initial impact on the listener. Surviving 'period' instruments have been of inestimable value to modern makers of reproductions and have provided not only the vital apparatus for experiments in matters of technique, interpretation and style but also the only reliable testing ground from which to draw meaningful historical and musical conclusions. They have enabled us to tap the full intellectual and artistic potential of historically informed performance, such that audiences can appreciate the particular timbres of, say, the recorder (Nos. 2 and 4) and corno da caccia (No. 1) in three of Bach's Brandenburg Concertos, and the contrasting colours offered by the solo 'natural' horn's 'open' and 'stopped' notes in Mozart's four concertos for the instrument.[2] Compromises, though, are inevitable. The financial outlay on at least two quality instruments and three or four bows to reflect historical developments and different playing qualities during the eighteenth century is prohibitive for most string specialists. The situation with keyboard instruments is even more complex and financially draining. Wind players often meet problems with pitch, about which there is often frustratingly insufficient reliable information; and accessories such as strings, reeds and mouthpieces have also over the years required compromises regarding historical accuracy. Double and single reeds, for example, varied considerably in design from those employed nowadays, resulting also in differences in tone quality between French and German instruments/players; and several of today's period-instrument clarinettists have opted for ebonite mouthpieces, as opposed to *echt* wooden mouthpieces, because the latter tend to warp too easily.[3]

Types of instruments

It can be immensely rewarding artistically to formulate a performance on the type of instrument(s) for which the composer is known to have written. However, this does not automatically sanctify a performance; nor does playing the 'wrong' (i.e. modern) instrument invalidate an interpretation, for it can be argued that it is precisely in early music that issues of instrumentation, interpretation and performance practice are at their most flexible and diverse.[4] Furthermore, terminology is often confusing. Bach's violono grosso or violone parts in his Brandenburg Concertos, for example, seem to require a six-string contrabass viol; curiously, however, neither of the conventional tunings really suits.[5]

The cyclical relationship of composer, performer and instrument-maker facilitated such change and development that the performance practices associated with eighteenth-century music cannot be reduced to a single set of conventions that are operable throughout the entire period. Different instruments made different demands, suggested different possibilities and imposed different limits; indeed, almost every instrument had unique characteristics that could be exploited or suppressed as needed, depending on the music to be performed.

Take Haydn, for example. His early *Concerti per il clavicembalo* were clearly intended for harpsichord or organ. His Concerto in D major (Hob. XVIII:11; 1784), most likely for piano or harpsichord, dates from a period when, like Mozart, Haydn was influenced by the developments of Viennese fortepiano makers such as Stein, Schanz and Walter. It is our loss that his familiarity with the sonorous qualities of the very different English tradition of piano-making in the 1790s did not yield any concertos. However, his Horn Concerto in D (Hob. VIId:3; 1762) demands of the performer sophisticated chromatic alterations of the 'natural' horn through lipping and hand-stopping and exploits the full range of the instrument. Furthermore, his Trumpet Concerto (Hob. VIIe:1; 1796), written for the 'Organisierte Trompete', took advantage of this keyed instrument's greater flexibility in new kinds of passage-work and cantabile melody (demonstrated in the first movement, bars 115–16 and in the Andante, bars 18–22), particularly in its middle register, in exchange for some loss of sonority and tonal brilliance.[6] The background to Mozart's Clarinet Concerto in A, K. 622, written for Anton Stadler to perform on his own design of basset-clarinet that was specially constructed to extend the lower range by four semitones, demonstrates certain parallels. Mozart's autograph manuscript of the concerto is lost, and the work is heard most often in a version for clarinet in A based on an edition from 1801, in which the clarinet part was reworked to remove those four lowest notes, transposing them up an octave and resulting in some melodic contours, registers and textures atypical of the composer.[7]

The body sizes now accepted as standard for instruments of the violin family were not established until the first half of the eighteenth century. Sound-ideals eventually changed, too; the qualities of the instruments of Jacob Stainer and Nicola Amati, predominant during the first part of our period, were overtaken by those of Antonio Stradivari's instruments in the late eighteenth century. Evidence for the use of the piano rather than the harpsichord in eighteenth-century concertos is far from conclusive. Pianos were certainly known by prominent keyboard players such as Domenico Scarlatti and J. S. Bach, but whether these musicians regarded them simply as curiosities, or as serious rivals to other keyboard instruments is unclear. Eva Badura-Skoda has made a strong case for Bach's extensive use, in Leipzig at least, of the fortepiano, which he helped to develop (and market) for Gottfried Silbermann, thus questioning whether Bach's harpsichord concertos were actually written for harpsichord at all.[8]

The popularity of the piano increased right across Europe in the second half of the century; indeed, much music of the period specifies performance on the piano. However, piano models varied dramatically, along with their tone, articulation and varieties of sonority (including the moderator or the *una corda* mechanisms), and the instrument was not unanimously accepted as preferable to the harpsichord for concerto performance until at least the 1780s, largely because the harpsichord was superior in sound-projection.[9] Even Clementi, the so-called 'father of the pianoforte', is reported to have played concertos on the harpsichord rather than the piano; and it seems likely that some of Mozart's early keyboard concertos, such as K. 175, K. 238, K. 242 and K. 246, were composed for the harpsichord.[10]

'Period' performers are challenged to match not only the instrument type and techniques of playing it to the appropriate repertory but also the impact of the technical development of various instruments on national tastes and performing styles. Frédéric Kalkbrenner, amongst others, points out that the keyboard instruments constructed in Vienna and London were built to satisfy different national playing styles. He equates the precision and clarity of Viennese pianists with the instruments they played, which were 'made with mufflers up to the last high note'. The rounder sounds and heavier touch of English pianos resulted in a grander, more singing style of playing, involving frequent use of the loud pedal.[11]

David Rowland refers to national trends in instrument-making where countries that tended to use knee levers on harpsichords also tended to use them on pianos, and where countries that employed a comparatively large number of devices on harpsichords also tended to use extravagant numbers of pedals or levers on pianos.[12] Knee levers became the norm on German and Austrian pianos until replaced by pedals in the early nineteenth century.[13] Late eighteenth-century pianos by Walter seem to have a 'standard' disposition of two knee levers, one for the dampers and one for the moderator, whereas contemporary pianos by Stein normally have two knee levers for lifting the dampers but no moderator. In England, grand pianos from the mid-1770s onwards generally included two pedals (the sustaining pedal and the *una corda* pedal), but a three-lever system (operating treble dampers, bass dampers and buff) was common for square pianos and other types as well. The French relied heavily on foreign imports, initially models with hand-stops from Germany (for example by Johann Heinrich Silbermann) and later (from *c.*1770) square pianos from England, these latter providing models for native French makers.[14]

Interestingly, pedal markings were not notated in piano music until the 1790s. First used in France, they were introduced soon after in England and, somewhat later, in Vienna and the rest of Europe.[15] Nevertheless, Mozart extolled the virtues of the sustaining knee lever of Stein's pianos in 1777 and documentary evidence drawn from treatises and performance descriptions confirms their effective use, largely for imitating other instruments (for example, the harpsichord or pantaloon), for overcoming some of the tonal and other shortcomings of the instrument, or for special effect.

Instrumental techniques

While much progress has been achieved in recent years in renovating or building keyboard and orchestral instruments to historical specifications, rather less headway has been made in the cultivation of techniques appropriate to them. As Neal Zaslaw explains, 'the fortepiano ... cannot be played with a Steinway, Bechstein, or Bösendorfer technique, nor even with a harpsichord technique; it has a technique of its own, the acquisition of which requires an apprenticeship as arduous as that demanded by any other instrument'.[16] Nevertheless, Rowland remarks on the high degree of uniformity in the hand positions and other techniques adopted by keyboard players from the late sixteenth to the early nineteenth centuries, with an emphasis on quiet hand positions and techniques based on minimal curved finger movement.[17] But principles of fingering changed along with aesthetic ideals and the paired fingerings and the relatively sparing use of the thumb and fifth finger were superseded *c.*1750 by a more 'modern' fingering approach designed to achieve a more legato 'ordinary manner of playing'.

Instrumental treatises offer the most direct access to the fundamental technical instruction and interpretation of their times. Following the treatises addressed largely to educated amateur musicians in the first half of the eighteenth century and Geminiani's progressive *The Art of Playing on the Violin* (1751), four major treatises combined comparatively advanced technical instruction regarding their specialist instruments with copious details regarding general performance practice: Quantz's *Versuch einer Anweisung die Flöte traversiere zu spielen* (1752); C.P.E. Bach's *Versuch über die wahre Art das Clavier zu spielen* (2 vols., 1753, 1762); Leopold Mozart's *Versuch einer gründlichen Violinschule* (1756); and Daniel Gottlob Türk's *Clavierschule, oder Anweisung zum Clavierspielen* (1789). The information provided by these sources, however, is often retrospective and tantalizingly incomplete – many subtleties of historical performance cannot be described adequately in words and were simply passed down, unrecorded, from teacher to pupil – and performers should use it with caution and only in appropriate contexts.[18] As Humphries remarks, 'while the concertos by Mozart, Haydn, Rosetti and Punto ... were written for players who were familiar with hand-stopping, they were composed before any detailed account of the technique appeared in print'; and Rachel Brown points out that Quantz changed his mind about double tonguing and some fingerings after the publication of his *Versuch*.[19]

Throughout the eighteenth century the concerto provided a natural environment for the development of instrumental techniques whilst serving also as a vehicle for the translation of the expressive lyric qualities of the voice to an instrumental context. In the violin concerto, for example, sequences were enlivened with a variety of virtuoso figuration and arpeggiation, position-work was extended into the stratospheres of the fingerboard by the likes of Vivaldi and Locatelli, a wider variety of bow-strokes and sonorities was introduced in line with organological developments,[20] and effects such as *col legno* and left-hand pizzicato entered the genre.[21]

Continuo

The provision of an accompaniment from a thoroughbass is essential to most Baroque and much early Classical concerto performance. The continuo player(s), complying with the given bass line and harmony (normally outlined by a figured bass but sometimes inferred from the score), supplied an extempore accompaniment to support and even enhance the main melodic material. Eighteenth-century sources for continuo accompaniment comprise theoretical treatises, independent keyboard tutors, surviving examples of written-out continuo parts and critical reviews of continuo performances.[22] The treatises concern themselves chiefly with the rudiments of harmony and emphasize accuracy, discretion and fluency of harmonic support in accompaniment. Few give examples of best practice or subtleties of style in realizing a given bass-line and most are unhelpful in providing answers to questions regarding the appositeness of adding an accompaniment in certain repertories, especially those in which bass figuring is lacking.

The instruments used for thoroughbass accompaniment differed according to period, genre, nationality and even locality. They were only occasionally specified, so performers are often required to decide upon the most suitable ones to use for the particular work, circumstances and musical forces involved. By the eighteenth century, a harpsichord (or sometimes a chamber organ) with a melodic bass instrument such as a cello, violone or sometimes bassoon doubling the bass-line became standard for secular works such as concertos. According to Quantz, violone players may not have doubled all the bass notes and may well have used pizzicato more often than indicated by surviving parts.[23]

Some of the larger orchestras of the time even included two harpsichords, one combining with a cello and often a double bass to support solo singers or instrumentalists (*concertino*) and the other collaborating with a cello, double bass and even a bassoon to underpin the orchestral (*ripieno*) contribution.[24] Justification might also be made, for example, for Corelli's so-called 'church sonata' concerti grossi of Op. 6 (Nos. 1–8 inclusive) to be performed with organ continuo and the 'chamber' ones (Nos. 9–12) with harpsichord, although church and chamber styles overlap in many of these works; and there is evidence that two keyboard continuo instruments are appropriate in some of Vivaldi's concertos. The Concerto in C major RV 555, for example, includes two harpsichords in its solo ensemble, and an organ features as both a continuo and concertante instrument in some of his concertos.

The improvisatory subtleties of continuo accompaniment differ for each genre, national style, period and individual composer, as well as according to venue and other performing circumstances. Players are required to make instinctive decisions regarding taste and style; these range from questions of texture, arpeggiation, register and harmonic syntax to issues such as how much (if at all) to double the melody, how much imitation or ornamentation to add and whether to double fugal entries. Vivaldi, for example, specifically requires 'il cembalo arpeggio' in his Violin Concerto 'L'autunno' RV 293 but does not prescribe the manner of arpeggiation.

The various instruments in use inevitably result in a variety of approaches to continuo accompaniment.[25] Quantz confirms that realization in four parts was the most common type of simple keyboard accompaniment, but advises against following such a guideline too strictly.[26] Other theorists held more imaginative aspirations, sometimes involving an ornamental role, adding to rather than providing the basic harmonies and improvising melodies and imitations, and sometimes concerning textural contrast for expressive interest, with volume varied by the number of notes played and the speed of arpeggiation.[27] Quantz's views on texture and arpeggiation and his illustrative Affettuoso movement are particularly interesting, especially in relation to the treatment of dissonance.[28] Different national idioms also enter the equation, the often richly decorative, flamboyant Italian approaches contrasting sharply, for example, with the largely circumspect early French styles. In Bach's Brandenburg Concerto No. 5, the harpsichordist abandons an improvisatory continuo role for lengthy periods of written-out solo passagework, including an extended cadenza near the end of the first movement.

During the first half of the eighteenth century many composers began to thin out musical textures. Some dispensed altogether with keyboard accompaniment, while others failed to provide a figured-bass part for the keyboard player; and the *tasto solo* direction became more common, often to create dynamic differentiation. Nevertheless, the practice of basso continuo seems to have lasted in the concerto throughout the eighteenth century and well into the nineteenth, even if the extent of its use varied according to national tastes and local traditions. For example, Chappell White points out that Viotti's First Violin Concerto (now known as No. 3 in A major), as published by Hummel (Berlin, 1781), includes a figured bass, but that the same concerto was issued the following year in Paris without figures. Zaslaw notes that several orchestras during the period 1774–96 even included lute, theorbo or harp players, who may have played continuo.[29]

In genres in which full scores are rare – violin concertos, for example – guidance on continuo usage may be provided by the bass part. The presence of bass figuring or the terms 'cembalo', 'organo' or 'basso continuo' is unequivocal indication that keyboard continuo was intended. Additionally, as Chappell White observes, 'the inclusion of two bass parts in a performing set, of identical parts in which one rests during the solos, or of a single bass part with two markings, such as "violoncello e basso", all suggest the presence of continuo in the ensemble'.[30] White states that only a small proportion of bass parts incorporate figures and claims that 'the pattern of their location may be significant'. Figured basses are most common in north German sources (including the publications of Hummel in Amsterdam) and in English sources. Examples in Italian, south German, Austrian or Parisian sources are rare.

The lack of any direct evidence of continuo, however, should not be interpreted as proof of its absence. Theorists, mostly north Germans and in particular C. P. E. Bach, advocate the use of keyboard in all ensemble music, whether or not bass figuring is provided.[31] But changes in musical style during the second half of the eighteenth century and the problems involved in improvising a continuo part without exact knowledge of the melody line or the harmonic progression resulted in the keyboard continuo player's contribution becoming less significant and often superfluous. With the exception of the Violin Concerto No. 3 in A major, the autographs of Viotti's violin concertos, for example, include no reference to a figured bass. Despite the occasional occurrence of a cadential chord with a fifth and no third (see, for example, Concerto No. 7 in B flat, 1st movement, bar 150), Viotti's written-out parts are generally self-sufficient and the often sparse textures seem integral to the style. Thus, as Türk cautions, 'in doubtful cases, of which many are allowed to happen in unfigured basses, the accompanist is advised that he at least not spoil the composition, but better – that he remain silent'.[32] Furthermore, A. Peter Brown speculates that the bass line for Haydn's early concertos for organ, violin, and cello may have been performed without a cello.[33]

Despite Türk's advice, there is continued debate about the role of keyboard continuo in concerto performances, especially as to whether the soloist in late eighteenth-century piano concertos should participate in a continuo role in tutti passages. From his study of manuscript parts, Dexter Edge hypothesizes that keyboard continuo was employed only in performances of keyboard concertos in Vienna after about 1750.[34] Eva and Paul Badura-Skoda cite as evidence to support continuo practice the passages of written-out continuo in Mozart's own hand in the four early concertos K. 37, K. 39, K. 40 and K. 41, the thoroughly figured bass in the manuscripts of K. 238, K. 246 and K. 271 (possibly in Leopold Mozart's hand), the figurings in the Artaria edition of K. 413, 414 and 415, and the Salzburg copy of K. 246 with its continuo part for the tutti sections, written in Mozart's hand; but they admit that such evidence is lacking in later concertos, in which any continuo presence might counteract Mozart's delicate scoring.[35] Horst Heussner questions the Badura-Skodas's assumption, arguing that the principle that the solo instrument should be distinctive from the orchestra was beginning to counteract both the latent tradition established in early eighteenth-century keyboard concertos and the figured-bass indications provided by late eighteenth-century printers, especially in Vienna.[36]

The divide has been enlarged by Charles Rosen, who has suggested that the piano soloist should fulfil a continuo role only in the absence of wind instruments. Faye Ferguson, acknowledging that the prevalent scoring is often vital in offering clues to continuo practice, believes that no firm conclusions can be drawn, but Robert Levin and Ellwood Derr remain convinced that keyboard continuo (designated by 'col Basso') should be played with the orchestral ritornellos and occasionally even in solo sections, conceding nevertheless that *tasto solo* may be more appropriate in passages of more delicate scoring. Derr considers the piano parts to have three principal functions: to contribute solo material, obbligato accompaniment (particularly evident in Mozart's piano concertos from the 1780s), and continuo realization, now with chords, now with *tasto solo* or *unisono*. Mozart's continuo parts, he believes, not only offer an harmonic support system, but also serve as a means to heighten dissonance, enhance rhythmic precision and forward motion and 'provide cadential rhythmic or harmonic-melodic closure'.[37] Meanwhile, Tibor Szász has articulated the case for continuo practices in Beethoven's piano concertos that accurately reflect the thrust of the composer's notation.[38]

National styles

In order to formulate historically informed interpretations, performers must assimilate the diversity of idioms prevalent during the eighteenth century; these were conditioned largely by national or regional conventions and individual taste. The concept of national style concerns not only the ways in which composers wrote their music, influenced by considerations such as tradition, function, social context and even language, but also its performance. It also includes aspects of instrument construction and sound-ideals mentioned earlier.

Three principal national idioms can be distinguished during the Baroque period – Italian, French and German.[39] The free, capricious manner of Italian expression in opera also filtered into instrumental music and encouraged a trend towards virtuosity, especially in the concerto. The definitive French style was initiated by an Italian, Jean-Baptiste Lully, but its formal severity, refined precision and thoroughly ordered, mannered approach (with ornaments and detailed performance instructions prescribed and the greatest possible nuances incorporated within the smallest range) was in sharp contrast to Italian taste.

Like many writers before him, notably François Raguenet and Jean Laurent le Cerf de Viéville,[40] Quantz compares the two styles at length, directly contrasting their approaches to composition, singing and playing. With respect to the latter, he comments:

> The *Italian manner of playing* is arbitrary, extravagant, artificial, obscure, frequently bold and bizarre, and difficult in execution; it permits many additions of graces, and requires a seemly knowledge of harmony; but among the ignorant it excites more admiration than pleasure. The *French manner of playing* is slavish, yet modest, distinct, neat and true in execution, easy to imitate, neither profound nor obscure, but comprehensible to everyone, and convenient for amateurs; it does not require much knowledge of harmony,

since the embellishments are generally prescribed by the composer; but it gives the connoisseurs little to reflect upon. In a word, Italian music is arbitrary, and French is circumscribed. If it is to have a good effect, the French depends more upon the composition than the performance, while the Italian depends upon the performance almost as much as upon the composition, and in some cases almost more.[41]

The differences between the Italian and French styles were not always as clearly defined as Quantz's comparison implies. For example, some composers, such as J. S. Bach or Telemann, cultivated both French and Italian styles, as well as a distinctive German style. Telemann even incorporated some Slavonic folk influences. However, Quantz also advances the case for a 'mixed' German style that is 'universal', making 'use of the good things in all types of foreign music'.[42] The German composer Georg Muffat had already pre-empted such a synthesis of the French, Italian and German styles (as well as a blend of French suite and Italian concerto) in the twelve concerto grossi of his *Ausserlesene Instrumental-music* (1701), which paved the way for the culminating works of J. S. Bach and others.[43] Even with the emergence of a more international style in the Classical era, national preferences are often evident. The music of Haydn and Mozart, for example, involves national traits absorbed in a more cosmopolitan idiom, its more sustained, expressive lines reflecting organological developments aimed at resembling the lyricism of the human voice.

Just as the sound-ideals of the mature Antonio Stradivari differed markedly from those of Amati and Stainer, so the sound-ideals of Italian and French luthiers were strikingly different. The situation is even more striking for wind and keyboard instruments. The sound of, say, eighteenth-century Bohemian and English clarinets or French and German oboes and bassoons differed considerably,[44] affected also by national (as well as individual) preferences regarding the reed, mouthpiece or other accessories chosen by players and technical approaches cultivated by them. Oboe reeds, for instance, generally became narrower and shorter during the eighteenth century as the bore became correspondingly smaller and both tessitura and pitch rose; clarinettists normally applied the upper-lip to the reed in contrast to the present, almost universal, application of the lower-lip to the reed.

French organs had their own clearly defined characteristics, differing markedly from Italian instruments, and French and Italian traditions are observable in German organ design as they are in German music. However, German organs were not merely syntheses of other national types; Schnitger's instruments, for example, were unrivalled in comprehensiveness of pedal departments.[45] Characteristics of harpsichords generally ranged from the smooth, sweet tone of French instruments, to the more direct, brilliant sound of Flemish models, the shallow, more pronounced attack of Italian designs and the powerful, rich English instruments. The light, shallow key action, thin, bright resonance, efficient damping mechanism and clear, 'transparent' sound of Viennese pianos contrasted with 'English action' models, which were capable of greater cantabile and volume. All these factors, combined with national and regional styles of composition and performance, contributed to the wealth of practices in solo and orchestral playing.

'Period' performers thus need to assimilate the details of the various national styles of playing, composition and instrumental construction. They should be especially receptive to the details of performance style that transcend the limits of notation, not only with regard to matters of expression but also to the interpretation of rhythm and the addition of ornamentation. Furthermore, they must be prepared to adapt to a contrasting national style, should a different movement require it, in order to reflect faithfully the range of external musical influences encapsulated in, for example, Handel's Concerto Grosso Op. 6, No. 5, or Bach's Brandenburg Concerto No. 5.

Expression

Most eighteenth-century music strove to 'move' its hearers. Its language was seen as a rhetorical expression of various passions, such as fury, resolution, grief and pleasure, combining, like speech, poetic nuance with articulation between phrases and sub-phrases. The so-called 'doctrine of affections' was part of the training of every reputable musician of the time. Its Baroque unity of the central affect materializes in tonality, characteristic intervals, musical-rhetorical figures, metre, rhythm, tempo, instrumentation, dynamics, ornamentation and articulation. 'The intention of musick is not only to please the ear', Geminiani claimed, 'but to express sentiments, strike the imagination, affect the mind, and command the passions. The art of violin playing consists in giving that instrument a tone that shall in a manner rival the most perfect human voice.'[46] Such use of speech and singing as models for 'natural' procedure became common in instrumental performance throughout the eighteenth century, but the affections began to lose their objective quality as rationalized emotional states that acted as unifying devices throughout a piece, thanks largely to the desire to introduce elements of contrast and variety. By the mid-eighteenth century, Quantz demonstrates the beginnings of that doctrine's disintegration, recognizing multiple (rather than single) affects within a movement.[47]

Articulation

As a principal component of expression and phrasing (together with nuances, dynamics, tempo and other considerations), articulation is as crucial to music as it is to speech. Articulation signs appeared in scores at a relatively late stage in the history of notation. They were scarce throughout the Baroque period, but the practice of connecting notes with beams (or not, as the case may be) sometimes provided clues to phrasing and articulation. However, even in the late eighteenth century, when articulation marks of the modern, more abstract type became more common (dots, horizontal and vertical strokes, and slurs, for example), their application was inconsistent and their meaning often ambiguous. The dot seems to have been used largely to indicate a lighter, less abrupt staccato than the stroke or wedge, as Quantz and Leopold Mozart confirm; but C. P. E. Bach regards the two signs as identical.[48] Türk implicitly recognizes the notational ambiguity characteristic of this era: strokes and dots 'have the same meaning, but some would like to indicate by the strokes that a shorter staccato be played than that indicated by the dot'.[49] J. S. Bach, Haydn and Mozart, among others, were often inconsistent in their slurs, assigning different slurrings to different instruments with the same notes. Whether these differences were accidental, and should therefore be regularized, whether they were introduced intentionally, or whether they were evolutionary, refined by these composers as they went along, and should thus be regularized according to the last entry is still cause for debate.[50]

The final choice of articulation, including the interpretation of signs, depended substantially on the particular idiom and character of the work, as well as the individual taste of the performer and the qualities of the performing venue. Mattheson, for example, links detached notes with lively Allegros and slurred notes with tender Adagios.[51] Quantz, C. P. E. Bach and most eighteenth-century theorists seem to have cultivated three broad categories of articulation, with staccato and legato (indicated by a slur or *ten.*) serving as the two extremes and a semi-detached 'ordinary' manner of playing in the middleground.[52] However, an increasing reverence for a more legato style, brought to full fruition in the nineteenth century, is evident in the works of theorists such as Marpurg and Türk.[53]

The resources of articulation naturally varied with (and sometimes within) the different families of instruments and their playing techniques. Observing that flute tonguing produces a much gentler effect than recorder tonguing, and that oboe tonguing is pronounced 'a lot more strongly',[54] Hotteterre articulated most un-slurred note-patterns through the alternation of two tongue-strokes, 'tu' and 'ru', always beginning with 'tu' to emphasize the opening note. Such alternation of sharp ('tu') and

Example 11.1 Jacques Hotteterre: principal tongue-strokes, as given in
Principles of the Flute, Recorder and Oboe (1707), trans. David Lasocki
(London, 1968), p. 60

Example 11.2a Johann Joachim Quantz: single-tonguings, as given in *On
Playing the Flute* (1752), trans. Edward R. Reilly (New York, 1966), p. 77

Example 11.2b Johann Joachim Quantz: double-tonguings, as given in *On
Playing the Flute* (1752), trans. Edward R. Reilly (New York, 1966), p. 80

softer ('ru') accent often resulted in an implied inequality and certainly
helped the performer to communicate the 'good' and 'bad' notes of the bar
(Ex. 11.1).[55]

Quantz, on the other hand, recommends for the articulation of
un-slurred notes: 'ti', 'di', 'ri' and 'd'll'.[56] The appropriate tonguing for
any note was dependent largely upon the speed and character of the
movement and the position of that note in the hierarchy of the bar. 'Ti'
was the basic single-tonguing suitable for 'short, equal, lively and quick
notes', but successions of such notes involved 'ti' and 'ri', 'ti' invariably
being used for the first note or two of a phrase and 'ri' placed on the
'good' notes of paired tonguings (Ex. 11.2a).[57] 'Di' could be substituted
for 'ti' for a gentler effect or for more sustained passages, and a double-
tonguing, 'did'll', facilitated very fast passage-work (Ex. 11.2b). Similar
forms of double-tonguing persisted through the eighteenth century with
Antoine Mahaut, Lewis Granom (as 'too-tle'), Johann Georg Tromlitz (as
'ta-d'll'), and John Gunn (as, variously, 'diddle', 'teddy' or 'tiddy').[58]

Both the choice of tonguing consonant and the position of the tongue
were left to the player's taste and technical proficiency.[59] When notes

were slurred, only the first note of the group was tongued. Much early eighteenth-century French music includes slurred note-pairings to be performed connected but slightly unequally in a manner known as 'lourer', emphasizing the first of each pair. Longer slurs generally implied an equal execution of the notes they embraced, those of more than four notes often indicating that the phrase should be articulated in one breath; failing this, Quantz recommends that breath should be taken wherever possible on tied notes, between disjunctive notes of continuous semiquavers or at other equivalent moments.

For bowed stringed instruments, bow-management provided the main articulation resource and fingering principles were closely interlinked with articulation and phrasing. The natural stroke of most pre-Tourte bows was an articulated, non-legato one (especially in its upper third). Leopold Mozart writes of 'a small, even if barely audible, softness'[60] at the beginning and end of each stroke, a reference to the typical delayed attack (through only gradual take-up of hair) of pre-Tourte bows, their lightness at the tip and their balance point (closer to the hand). Unlike modern staccato, the eighteenth-century staccato stroke involved a 'breath' or articulation between notes somewhat greater than the articulation of the normal separate stroke and it was often conveyed by lifting the bow from the string after each stroke, especially in slow tempos. In fast movements the bow necessarily remained on the string in the upper half, producing an effect similar to the modern spiccato. Articulation silences often afforded players the opportunity to effect shifts of the left hand, notably on repeated notes, by the phrase in sequences, or after a lifted bow-stroke. True legato bowing with most pre-Tourte bows was achieved only by slurring, due emphasis being given to the first note of a slur and emulation of the qualities of the human voice, especially in slow movements.

Keyboard articulation depended not only on the player but also to a great extent on the nature and quality of the instrument. While François Couperin writes about the harpsichord (1716), C. P. E. Bach (1753) clearly favours the clavichord for its expressive and sustaining qualities, and Marpurg (1755) and Türk (1789) state their preference for the piano. The few surviving fingering indications in the extant keyboard manuscripts of J. S. Bach show that even in his maturity Bach largely maintained the seventeenth-century practice of playing substantial parts of white-note scales with two-finger patterns. John Butt's extensive study of articulation markings in all the Bach original materials has shown that Bach's most common slurring was this very type of two-note grouping.[61] However, as noted earlier, changes in aesthetic ideals in the second half of the eighteenth century occasioned different approaches to, and goals for, fingering.

Example 11.3 'Ordinary touch', as illustrated in Daniel Gottlob Türk, *School of Clavier Playing* (1789), trans Raymond Haagh (Lincoln, NE, 1982), p. 345

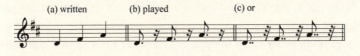

While eighteenth-century keyboard theorists concur that in 'ordinary' playing the finger must always be lifted before the next note is sounded, they disagree as to precisely when it should be lifted. Türk refuted C. P. E. Bach's theory that notes that are neither staccato nor legato nor sostenuto should be held for half their notated value, claiming that this nullified the difference between staccato and ordinary touch and resulted in a disjointed performance. His recommendations confirm the gradual change to a more legato 'ordinary' manner of performance: 'For tones which are to be played in customary fashion (that is, neither detached nor slurred [i.e. in the ordinary manner]), the finger is lifted a little earlier from the key than is required by the duration of the note. Consequently the notes in *a* [Ex. 11.3] are played approximately as in *b* and *c*, depending on the circumstances. If there are some notes intermingled which should be held out for their full value, then *ten.* or *tenuto* is written over them.'[62]

Melodic inflection

Melodic inflection was directly related to the affect(s) in the eighteenth century, as well as to national and individual taste. Some aspects were prescribed or pre-planned (for example by dynamic or articulation markings in varying degrees of detail according to period), while some were intuitive and often un-notatable. While the Italians and their adherents during the Baroque generally welcomed dynamic contrasts, the French traditionally considered such variation to be excessive and even offensive. Robert Marshall has shown that J. S. Bach used only three indications on the *forte* side of the spectrum (*forte*, *poco forte* and *mezzo forte*) but rather more refinements on the *piano* side (*piano*, *sempre piano*, *piano*, *più piano*, *poco piano* and *pianissimo*).[63] However, dynamic markings were generally sparse and the lack of a dynamic marking at the beginning of a piece or movement followed by a *piano* some way in suggests that *forte* was the preferred initial dynamic level.[64]

The dominance of two basic markings in surviving sources (*piano* and *forte*) and the rare use of crescendo and diminuendo prescriptions should not necessarily lead performers incorrectly to introduce the principle of terraced dynamics into their interpretations, contrasting large sections of music played uniformly softly and loudly.[65] Although echo effects were common in Baroque music, such interpretations ignore the fact that dynamic markings traditionally served as a framework for the structural design of a piece or movement, with either dynamic unity or dynamic contrast between sections as a prevailing feature.[66]

Among other misleading annotations is a *p* followed closely by *f*, which may, dependent upon the music's character, indicate a crescendo (and hence *f* followed closely by *p* a diminuendo) rather than any sharp dynamic contrast. The prescription *fp* was often combined with an articulation stroke and an appropriate beaming of notes to indicate emphasis or accent. Mozart's use of *sf* and *dolce* as actual dynamic markings also needs to be taken into consideration, along with the Badura-Skodas's hypothesis that Mozart's frequent use of *calando* suggests that 'becoming softer' was intended, not (as later) also 'becoming slower'.[67]

Stylish interpretation requires supplementing the notation, however sparse or dense, with subtle gradations to enhance the melodic line. Quantz advised that *forte* and *piano* should be used with 'great discernment ... not moving too vigorously from one to the other, but rather swelling and diminishing imperceptibly'.[68] Furthermore, it was natural: to play the dissonance of the appoggiatura more loudly than its resolution; to add the *messa di voce*, or swell, as an expressive ornament on long notes;[69] to crescendo a little to high notes, and diminuendo from them; and to follow the contours of the music through subtle shadings. Regional variations in the exploitation of dynamics became less distinctive over time, and careful prescription of dynamic detail involving a wider range of signs and including crescendos and diminuendos gradually became an important component of musical composition, especially from *c*.1750; the varied and abrupt dynamic changes in much Austro-German music of the time, especially that of the Mannheim composers, provide convincing supporting evidence. Some of the theories behind the application of nuances were put into practice in late eighteenth-century string playing through the cultivation of the four divisions of the bow, nuanced bowings (<; >; <>; <> <>) categorized by Leopold Mozart and widely imitated.[70] Nevertheless, performers continued to add instinctively and spontaneously to the expressive effect.

Vibrato, generally added freely by the performer, also contributed to melodic colouring. It was normally employed selectively as an expressive ornament until the late nineteenth century, despite Geminiani's exceptional recommendation of what seems essentially a continuous vibrato in the approved modern fashion. It was usually applied fairly discreetly on most instruments during the Baroque and Classical periods, although players appear to have used a range of oscillation speeds to striking effect. Flautists used both finger and chest vibrato, although the former was the more common.

Example 11.4 Degrees of accentuation, as illustrated in Daniel Gottlob Türk, *School of Clavier Playing* (1789), trans. Raymond Haagh (Lincoln, NE, 1982), p. 325

Accentuation

Accentuation contributes shape and meaning to the music (together with factors such as phrasing, articulation, nuances) and is conveyed by stress or prolongation. Accentuation conveyed by stress may result from starting a particular (usually prescribed) note assertively (accent) or making such an emphasis just after the start of the note. Accentuation by prolongation involves both adherence to the hierarchy of the bar and emphasis of important notes within phrases.

Quantz links realization of the hierarchy of the bar to good oratory, which requires 'distinct and true pronunciation' and appropriate vocal inflexions 'to arouse or still the passions'.[71] He particularly stresses the need for rhythmic flexibility and distinguishes between 'the *principal notes*, ordinarily called *accented* or in the Italian manner, *good* notes, and those that *pass*, which some foreigners call *bad* notes':

> Where it is possible, the principal notes always must be emphasized more than the passing. In consequence of this rule, the quickest notes in every piece of moderate tempo, or even in the Adagio, though they seem to have the same value, must be played a little unequally, so that the stressed notes of each figure, namely the first, third, fifth, and seventh, are held slightly longer than the passing, namely the second, fourth, sixth, and eighth, although this lengthening must not be as much as if the notes were dotted.[72]

He provides examples and mentions two exceptions: quick passages in a very fast movement, in which length and accent can be applied only to the first of every four notes; and all rapid vocal passage-work, unless it is slurred. Thus, the hierarchy of the bar was extended not only to the phrase but also to the principal sections of movements.

Türk uses dynamic indications to illustrate the degree of emphasis the various time-units should receive unless annotated otherwise[73] (Ex. 11.4). These good notes (*note buone*) were accommodated in wind playing by specific tonguings, discussed earlier, and in string playing by the traditional rule of down-bow, which required 'good' notes to be played with the stronger down-bow and the 'bad' notes with the weaker up-stroke. Geminiani refers to it as a 'wretched rule';[74] his compatriot, Tartini, also seems to have favoured greater freedom of choice regarding the use of down- and up-strokes.

Apart from the first note of a phrase, syncopated notes, a note that is longer or markedly higher or lower than its predecessors, and dissonant notes within the phrase (whether prepared or unprepared) are common instances when the agogic accent offers a flexible, inherently musical solution. Although the length of such prolongations was a matter of taste, Türk's rule that a note should not be prolonged for more than half its written value is a significant pointer to the proportional implications of this practice.[75]

Tempo

Tempo bears directly upon the effectiveness of most other interpretative issues, including expressive and technical considerations. Before Maelzel developed the metronome (1815), numerous attempts had been made to devise a convenient way of measuring time accurately, ranging from relating tempo to the human pulse (treated as averaging 80 beats per minute)[76] or to a walking pace[77] to using various forms of pendulum, but with no great reliability.[78] The use of time-words (mainly Italian and French) from the early eighteenth century onwards to give a general idea of the tempo and prevailing character of a piece or movement had often led to ambiguity. As Avison observed, 'The words Andante, Presto, Allegro, etc., are differently apply'd in … different kinds of music'.[79]

The most common Italian time-words of the Baroque were, in their most usual order from slow to fast: adagio; largo; andante; allegro; vivace; and presto.[80] However, inconsistencies in the description and inter-relationship of some time-words have caused confusion; Johann Gottfried Walther, Sébastien de Brossard and Leopold Mozart, for example, were among those who considered largo slower than adagio.[81] Nevertheless, the standard order achieved its currency because when most Baroque composers qualified these time-words, they made the adagio even slower (molto adagio, adagio assai, and adagissimo) and the largo a little less slow (larghetto, largo ma non tanto); similarly, presto when qualified became faster, and vivace slower.

The few time-words included in early Baroque music were more clearly confined to tempo and less indicative of mood than those in later music, confusion arising, for example, from Handel's seemingly contradictory time-words Andante allegro, which head the first movement of his Organ Concerto Op. 4, No. 6. These time-words may indicate either a fast-moving andante or a slowish allegro, or, more probably, a lively, cheerful andante ('allegro' translates as 'merry'). Locatelli heads the middle movement of his Concerto Op. 3, No. 10, Largo Andante, intending a flowing speed for its Siciliano-like character. A potential confusion arises, however, from putting the onus on the performer to infer an appropriate tempo from the music itself – C. P. E. Bach suggests taking its 'general mood' and its 'fastest notes and passages' chiefly into consideration[82] – even if that tempo appears to be contradicted by the time-word. Other considerations should include the harmonic rhythm, the nature and complexity of any counterpoint, the traditional mood associations coming from key or melodic make-up, compositional intent and even the size and acoustic of the performing venue.[83]

Late eighteenth-century composers used a variety of simple, (mainly) Italian terms to indicate tempo, most treatises providing clear descriptions of each time-word's particular characteristics. The commonest terms in Classical scores are andante and allegro, both of which are often qualified with clear tempo implications. However, confusion seems to have existed over the meaning of andantino, some theorists (for example Francesco Galeazzi and Jean-Baptiste Cartier) believing the term to signify a slower speed than andante, and some (such as Türk) the opposite.[84] Furthermore, many eighteenth-century treatises record that metre played a role in determining tempo, time signatures with smaller denominators normally implying faster performance than those with larger ones. Sensitivity to the crucial role played by considerations of tempo seems to have increased in the late eighteenth century, Kirnberger claiming that only the composer could establish the most appropriate tempo, that time-words were inadequate and that composers should indicate tempo by stating the ideal duration of the movement in question.[85] This perceived need to define tempo more explicitly led eventually to more extensive use of qualifying clauses, particularly by Beethoven, as well as the adoption by many of Maelzel's metronome. Beethoven and Viotti must have been among the first significant composers to issue metronome marks for many of their works. Beethoven's use is well documented.[86] Viotti evidently sent Pierre Baillot a list of metronome marks for a number of compositions that had been published before the invention of the device. Baillot recorded these and reproduced them as appropriate in his *L'art du violon; nouvelle méthode* (Paris, 1835).

Flexibility of tempo was a vital element in Baroque and Classical performance practice, allowing some freedom of expressive effect within the outlines of the pulse. The chief means of achieving such freedom was *tempo rubato* (literally 'stolen time'). Interlinked with principles of accentuation and often regarded as a species of ornament, this seems to have been applied eventually to four different expressive techniques, the most common involving a natural flexibility of the prescribed rhythm within a constant tempo, after which the ensemble between melody and accompaniment was restored.[87] Mozart was acclaimed for his exploitation of this technique. *Tempo rubato* also extended in certain cases to the modification of dynamics and/or the displacement of natural accents (resulting, for example, in unaccented 'strong' beats of the bar);[88] the expansion of the bar(s) to incorporate more notes than the time-signature theoretically allows, and a flexible yet rhythmically controlled performance of these passages;[89] or flexibility of tempo by introducing arbitrary, unwritten accelerandos or ritardandos.[90]

Ornamentation and extempore embellishment

Ornamentation

As instructions regarding the execution of specific ornaments vary greatly throughout the period, only a broad survey will be attempted here.[91] The essential ornaments, comprising primarily the appoggiatura, mordent, trill and turn, not only served as additional embellishment to a preconceived melody but formed an organic part of that melody. C. P. E. Bach considers embellishments 'indispensable ... they connect and enliven tones and impart stress and accent. ... Expression is heightened by them. ... Without them the best melody is empty and ineffective, the clearest content clouded.'[92]

Obligatory ornaments such as the cadential trill, demanded by convention and context, were not always notated, especially in most non-keyboard music,[93] and the general sign (+ or ×) was employed to indicate the possible incidence of some embellishment, the exact detail of which was undefined and left to the performer, according to mood, tempo and genre. Signs with more specific intentions were also employed, many with implied interpretative formulae relating to expression, nuance, emphasis and rhythmic subtleties. Unreliable calligraphy, ambiguous indications, casual performance, inconsistent terminology employed by theorists and a variety of different regional and personal styles combine to paint a confusing picture, from which a definitive interpretation of the *minutiae* of ornaments, often so subtle and flexible in rhythm and pitch that they defy expression in ordinary musical notation, is largely impracticable.

During the second half of the eighteenth century the three main channels of ornamental theory and practice – the French, German and Italian – gradually merged into some measure of agreement.[94] The French school's complex system of symbols was adopted with increasing thoroughness and consistency in some German schools. This was mainly the work of Quantz, Marpurg, Agricola and especially C. P. E. Bach, who, amidst the emerging homophonic *style galant*, modified and extended

French practices into a more international language of ornaments governed by the affections. This language was more harmonic than melodic, hence the quest for '*das vermischte Geschmack*', a combination of the best qualities of Italian, French and German types of ornamentation.[95] Without cataloguing signs and contexts for every ornamental figure available to the performer, C. P. E. Bach's *Versuch* became a model for numerous subsequent treatises on the subject, even though his *theoretical* inflexibility of ornamentation practice contradicts the nature and function of ornament itself. Most of his contemporary compatriots approached the issue with greater freedom and some national schools, particularly the Italian, still left ornamentation largely to the spontaneous invention of the performer.

By the end of the eighteenth century, the extraordinary variety of interpretations of ornaments and the increasing idiosyncrasy of many composers' styles resulted in a developing trend for ornaments to be indicated as precisely as possible (for example, by notating the exact value of appoggiaturas). A minimum of signs was used and all complex ornaments were written out as fully as possible in normal-sized notes as an integral part of the rhythmic scheme, in small notes extra-rhythmically, or as a compromise between the two, in such a way that their interpretation, apart from a certain rhythmic freedom, could not be doubted.[96]

A great deal of selection and taste needs to be exercised in the 'replication' of earlier approaches to ornamentation, and period performers should consider some or all of the following questions when seeking to interpret a particular ornament in a manner commensurate with the music: On what note should the ornament begin? Should it start before, on or after the beat? How fast should any repercussion be? What are the harmonic implications and how long should the dissonance (if any) last? How flexibly should the ornament be executed? Should nuances be added? Is the introduction of accidentals necessary? How should the ornament be terminated? Answers to these questions will inevitably vary according to the style, character and nationality of the music, the context and the type of ornament, and the views of those theorists whose treatises are deemed most relevant to its interpretation; but it is imperative that answers are sought and carefully considered in appropriate contexts if an informed performance is to materialize.

Extempore embellishment

Extempore embellishment was practised in varying degrees and in different forms, according to date, venue, individual preferences and national styles.[97] Vivaldi, for example, commonly employed a conventional Italian shorthand for passages of extended arpeggiation, often annotating only

the chords and leaving the style of arpeggiation to the performer's discretion. Sometimes, though, he wrote out an arpeggiated pattern in the
first bar of such a passage to serve as a guide for the realization of the
subsequent chords. In the Larghetto of his Concerto Op. 3, No. 10, for
four violins, his indication 'arpeggio battuto di biscrome' directs the solo
first violin to arpeggiate in demisemiquavers.

Improvised embellishment of a melody involved the performer in the
free and usually spontaneous addition of melodic figures that were too
variable to be indicated satisfactorily by signs – 'arbitrary' (*willkührlich*)
ornaments, as Quantz calls them – as well as some of the conventional
stereotyped ornaments such as trills, appoggiaturas and mordents
(Quantz's 'essential' (*wesentlich*) ornaments). It was confined in theory
(though apparently not always in practice) to solo contexts or passages of
ensemble music in which a solo texture prevails.[98]

Of the varying national Baroque styles, the French approach, in which
essential ornaments were usually specified and arbitrary ones played little
part, contrasted with the Italian manner, which admitted both categories
of ornament but only seldom with indication as to their application.
Italian influence was predominant in the German compromise but was
tempered by a more selective and expressive use of ornaments (both
essential and arbitrary) in keeping with the doctrine of the affections,
especially by the north German school. C. P. E. Bach deliberately refrains
from detailed discussion of improvised ornamentation, arguing that its
implementation is too variable to classify and that it was becoming
customary in his circles to write out such embellishment in full.[99]

Increasing foreign influence both before and after the Revolution of
1789 prompted significant changes in the French style. The Italian style
was championed by Rousseau and his followers; a French translation of
Tartini's treatise on ornamentation appeared in 1771; Viotti settled in
Paris (1781–2); and Italian music infiltrated French publications such as
Cartier's *L'art du violon* (Paris, 1798), disseminating the Italian style still
further. Framery confirms (1791) that French musicians tended to invent
ornaments rather more than previously, even though French composers
still consistently specified their 'essential' ornaments, thus setting limits
to the play of free ornamentation.[100] The German compromise persisted
to some extent in the late eighteenth century; however, because of their
selective and expressive approach towards ornamentation, German musicians had begun well before 1750 to notate precisely the interpretative
details of their compositions and thus to write fairly fully ornamented
melodies. Johann Adolf Scheibe famously criticized J. S. Bach for notating
embellishments in this manner, which was his common practice even in
his transcriptions of Italian works or original compositions in the Italian

style.[101] Among numerous examples of Bach's practice are the Adagio of BWV 974, a transcription of an Oboe Concerto in D minor by Alessandro Marcello, an arrangement for harpsichord solo (as BWV 973) of Vivaldi's Violin Concerto in G major RV 299, and the slow movement of Bach's own Violin Concerto in E major BWV 1042.

The design and content of the melodic elaborations are impossible to catalogue in detail because of the wide range of styles and approaches. However, guidance is at hand from the various eighteenth-century works that have survived with added embellishments; these represent a surer guide to extempore ornamental practice than most contemporary treatises. The collection of Tartini concertos at the University of California at Berkeley, for example, holds more than seventy-five embellished versions of slow movements. These demonstrate that the opening melody should be performed simply and it is possible that no ornaments were added until the repetition.[102] Viotti's improvised ornamentation, much admired by his contemporaries, is demonstrated first hand in the autograph of his Violin Concerto No. 27, which includes elaborate embellishment of the slow movement, added by the composer himself.[103] Viotti's close friend, Pierre Baillot, suggested variations for certain passages of the violin concertos in his *L'art du Violon*, and Sieber's edition of Viotti's Violin Concerto No. 15 includes an ornamented version of the solo part for the first movement, the most elaborate embellishment occurring surprisingly in the solo passage-work rather than in the lyrical, cantabile sections. Whether these legacies represent models or studies or a mixture of the two is unclear, but they certainly throw some doubt on just how extemporaneous some of these so-called improvisations actually were.

Nevertheless, such elaborations enlivened and transformed the melodic line and achieved the desired contrast of sonority. They were most prolific in slow movements, especially those written in the 'skeletal outline' manner of the Italian style; but they were by no means excluded from quick movements and also helped to sustain musical interest in repeated sections, for example, in binary form movements in which each section is repeated, in ternary form in which the first 'A' section was repeated, in rondo refrains, in reprises, and in the concerto soloist's repetitions of tutti material. Elaborations ranged from the inclusion of merely a few trills and appoggiaturas to a reworking of the entire structure. Generally, however, the embellished versions comprise a balanced variety of note-values and rhythms, exploiting some patterns consistently as a means of unification. They adhere closely to the overall melodic contour of the original, its salient structural points (cadences, principal notes, phrases, etc.) being emphasized through the addition of both stereotyped ornaments (such as appoggiaturas, trills, turns and mordents) and ornamental figures such as

Leopold Mozart's *battement, ribattuta, groppo, tirata* and *mezzo circulo,* passage-work of varying kinds or even simple arpeggios, especially at the approach to a cadence or modulation.[104] Other methods of elaboration included the use of upper and lower auxiliary notes, simple passing notes, single note repetitions, two- or three-note *Schleifer,* and scale-passages normally of no more than an octave span, the latter figures generally filling in the intervals between the notes of the given melody, especially descending leaps.

In more isolated cases, and usually at cadences, the melodic outline may be temporarily distorted and dissolved into smaller note-values faithful only to the harmonic constitution of the original. The reverse process was also exploited, involving the lengthening of note-values and condensing of melodic figuration in addition to a type of *tempo rubato,* featuring either rhythmic displacement or the accommodation of an irregular grouping of notes within the bar. *Tempo rubato* and changes of articulation, dynamic, rhythm and phrasing also played their part in the embellishing process.

Performers generally aimed to achieve a cumulative ornamental effect, a melody normally being performed as written or very simply on its first occurrence and its variations, attendant sequences or repeated passages becoming increasingly more elaborate at each recurrence. Extempore embellishment was an outlet for the performer's virtuosity; but it also served an expressive role and was intended to remain within the bounds of discretion.

With the advent of the high Classical style, the performer's freedom of extensive improvised ornamentation was curtailed. Although the practice of embellishing slow movements undoubtedly continued well beyond Tartini's generation, it seems to have declined both in importance and in the elaborateness of the ornaments as melodies became simpler and more lyrical. With the advent of the romance as a popular concerto slow movement in the early 1770s, for example, the vogue for simplicity reached its zenith. Rousseau, whose description of the vocal romance was the basis for most later writers, admonished performers against ornamenting it, and some theorists, most notably Türk, applied the ban on ornaments to instrumental romances.[105]

Well into the nineteenth century, Baillot extended the warning against ornamentation to any melody in which the charm seems to lie in its simplicity.[106] Nevertheless, we learn that Mozart and Beethoven varied their ornamental figuration in performance, especially in their slow movements. Furthermore, in answer to his sister's complaint about the sketchy form of the slow movement of his Piano Concerto K. 451, Mozart sent her an ornamented variant, implying that he expected the soloist to

Example 11.5 Mozart, Piano Concerto in D, K. 451, 2nd movement, bars 56–63

add extempore embellishment (Ex. 11.5).[107] Some of the solo leaps in the Andante of his Piano Concerto K. 453 (Ex. 11.6), the skeletal outline of the solo part in the finale of K. 482 (bars 164–72) and similar passages in K. 488 and K. 491 may also require 'filling out', as may the piano parts in tutti sections, which are sometimes only sketchily indicated.[108] Other opportunities for improvisation arise in the rondo finales of the 1770s, where, even though indications are rare, the transitions to the return of the refrain theme seem to demand embellishment, as do the repeated sections in the minuets forming the finales of Mozart's concertos in G for flute (K. 313) and in B flat major for bassoon (K. 191).

Example 11.6 Mozart, Piano Concerto in G, K. 453, 2nd movement, bars 39–42

Fermatas, cadenzas and *Eingänge*

The meaning of a fermata could range from a straightforward prolongation of the note, chord or rest thus indicated, to improvised embellishment of that note or chord in a manner appropriate to the prevalent character;[109] the fermatas at bars 127 and 315 of the first movement and bar 59 of the second movement of Mozart's Clarinet Concerto K. 622, for example, call for some modest ornamentation. A fermata could even denote an extended cadenza, whose style and content should ideally be compatible with those of the work or movement. A cadenza may also be indicated by words such as 'solo', 'tenuto' or 'ad arbitrio'.

The practice of ornamenting cadences was common in Baroque music involving vocal or instrumental soloists. In Corelli's Concerto Grosso Op. 6, No. 1, a fermata on the rests between the Largo and the Allegro suggests a short, improvised unaccompanied passage most likely contributed by the *concertino* first violinist, thus preparing for the ensuing Allegro. This type of Phrygian cadence was frequently introduced by Baroque composers at the end of movements in the relative minor key. The final chord, the dominant, is approached by the subdominant chord in first inversion, resulting in the characteristic bass movement of a descending semitone from the minor sixth scale-degree to the dominant. The cadence does not sound final, but, in its embellished form, acts as a transition to the next movement in the tonic key of the work. Among numerous other examples are the end of the Adagio of Corelli's Concerto Grosso Op. 6, No. 12, preparing for the following sarabande, and the end of the Andante of Bach's Fourth Brandenburg Concerto, the cadence preceded by a brief decorative solo passage for the first recorder. One famous curiosity is the Phrygian cadence (ending on the dominant of E minor) that comprises the Adagio between the two quick movements of Bach's Third Brandenburg Concerto. This either begs considerable embellishment from the solo first violinist or represents the concluding cadence of a movement in E minor improvised by one or more soloists.[110] Among later composers who left examples of decorated fermatas was C. P. E. Bach, notably in his *Versuch* and in some of his concertos.[111]

Derived from the vocal aria as a natural result of ornamenting cadences,[112] the cadenza was an unaccompanied solo passage of variable length and indefinite form in which a prominent cadence was embellished. The placement of cadenzas in the fast movements of Baroque concertos seems initially to have been somewhat freer and less standardized than it later became, for elaborate expansion might be undertaken at any decisive cadence. As the form became more sectional, it became customary to eliminate multiple cadenzas and to locate a single cadenza before the final recurrence of the ritornello, as an embellishment of the dominant to tonic cadence at that point. The cadenza, indicated by a pause either on the dominant of the key, or, in the case of Classical concertos, somewhat inconclusively on the tonic 6–4 chord, normally ended with a trill on the dominant chord prior to the orchestral re-entry. This convention was widespread by *c.*1770.[113]

Cadenzas were normally extemporized by performers but some were composed and written down, notably by Torelli in the passages headed 'Perfidia' in some of his concerto movements,[114] and even played a fully integrated part in the structure of the movement (as in the harpsichord 'cadenza' in the first movement of Bach's Fifth Brandenburg Concerto).

Although preceded by Tosi's rather limited survey, Quantz's account is the first extensive discussion of cadenzas.[115] He implies that Vivaldi was among the first to use the unaccompanied terminal cadenza in an Allegro movement.[116] Nine fairly lengthy cadenzas by him have survived.[117] Some of these are quite simple, comprising a succession of arpeggiated chords over a dominant pedal-point followed by a short section of modulating sequences leading to the final trill. One of the more extended cadenzas occurs in Vivaldi's Op. 11, No. 5 (RV 202). Some of the more complex examples involve reference to the thematic material of the movement or work, as in the finale of the D major Violin Concerto RV 212.[118] Not all eighteenth-century composers subscribed to the idea that the performer's musicianship and tasteful expression should be demonstrated as much as his technical prowess. The lengthy solo capriccios that appear before the final tutti of the opening and closing movements of each of Locatelli's twelve violin concertos *L'Arte del Violino*, Op. 3 (1733), are true virtuoso fare, demanding technical pyrotechnics written in a system of notation that requires decoding, and involving no thematic or motivic relationship to the main body of the movement.

Quantz charted the expansion of the largely ornamental early eighteenth-century concept of the cadenza, normally comprising non-thematic elaborations of the final cadence, into a more meaningful part of the musical design, and recommended that cadenzas should be constructed from the main motifs of the movement. His survey served as a model for Türk and for many later studies.[119] From his observation of the French style that little can be added to what the composer has written,[120] it appears that the introduction of cadenzas in eighteenth-century French music was restricted largely to works in the Italian style. Certainly, cadenzas were omitted from most Parisian Classical concertos and symphonies concertantes.

Tartini inserts cadenza opportunities into his concertos from Op. 1 onwards. Sometimes he wrote out the cadenzas himself (as in Op. 1, No. 4, in D major, D 15), but more often he preferred to indicate where they should be introduced and left the musical content to the performer. Elsewhere, he provides basic guidelines regarding cadenza construction that held wide currency, especially with singers. His recommended design involves starting with a *messa di voce*, *passaggii* or a trill, continuing with metrically free, generally fast passage-work, and progressing by step or leap to a note high in the register prior to the final trill on the supertonic.[121]

The solo cadenza was by no means an essential feature of Viotti's violin concertos; he includes one in only about half of his concerto first movements. In many cases the cadenza was left to be improvised by the soloist, but there is an increasing tendency for his later concertos to include a written-out cadenza, not least because many of these involve orchestral accompaniment (notably Nos. 22, 27, 28 and 29), demonstrating Viotti's increased interest in the integration of tutti and solo elements.[122]

The Classical era witnessed an expansion in the scope of the cadenza.[123] It normally contained meaningful musical substance and fulfilled an architectural function, with its climactic passage for the soloist balancing the orchestral exposition in the concerto structure, as well as a dramatic one, allowing the soloist free rein for unfettered solo display. Some cadenzas were written out by composers either for use in performance, as in Mozart's Piano Concerto K. 488, or as models for students to imitate, notably those by Mozart for several of his other piano concertos.[124] Mozart's cadenzas display great variety and imagination in their use of pertinent melodic material, most adopting a tripartite design (with the exception of some second and third movement cadenzas). The first (and largest) subdivision commences either with one of the principal themes of the movement (for example K. 453, first movement) or with an energetic flourish (which may also have thematic affinities; for example K. 271, first movement) emanating from the 6–4 chord. This is followed by a more reflective section, often derived from the secondary group of themes, involving sequence and passing through (but rarely establishing) a variety of close keys. A descent to a sustained chord or long note in the lower register eventually serves as a point of departure for further technical display, incorporating scales, arpeggios and suchlike, prior to the brief, normally non-thematic closing transition to the final cadential trill on the dominant seventh.[125]

Cadenza length depended to some extent on the solo instrument, Quantz claiming that 'a string player can make them as long as he likes, if he is rich enough in inventiveness', but that wind players should make their cadenzas last no longer than a single breath on the grounds that 'Reasonable brevity ... is more advantageous than vexing length'.[126] Robert Levin has calculated that Mozart's extant keyboard cadenzas are approximately 10 per cent of the length of the relevant movement.[127]

Cadenzas in concertante works for more than one soloist normally involved careful preparation and, hence, less spontaneity and freedom of invention. Quantz offers some helpful guidelines for the formulation of cadenzas in two parts and provides numerous examples of ploys such as movement in thirds and sixths, imitation, suspensions and anticipations.[128] Among the most notable extant eighteenth-century cadenzas for a double concerto are those of Mozart's Sinfonia Concertante in E flat major for Violin and Viola, K. 364, while Haydn's cadenzas for the quartet of soloists in his Symphonie Concertante in B flat are interesting models of their kind.

Eingänge or lead-ins were also indicated by fermata and generally occurred at imperfect cadences on the dominant or dominant-seventh chord and at perfect cadences in the dominant, mediant or submediant keys. Their function was to provide a brief non-modulatory transition, generally metrical but in an improvisatory style, into a new section of a work, such as the refrain of a rondo movement. They usually terminate with a second fermata. Passages that interlink with the ensuing music are normally termed *Übergänge*. Guidelines for formulating lead-ins may be found in various treatises, notably C. P. E. Bach's *Versuch* and Türk's *Clavierschule*,[129] but the use of such passages is no better demonstrated than in the finale of Mozart's Piano Concerto in E flat major K. 271, a rondeau in which *Eingänge*, notated in the score, serve as transitions between the principal divisions of the movement.

Size and distribution of the orchestra

Size

Musicians aiming to reproduce historically informed performances usually try to involve performing forces of approximately the same size as those known and written for by the composer. Traditionally, four types of evidence have been employed in analysing orchestral size: personnel lists, prescriptions in treatises, contemporary reviews and iconography.

In the first half of the eighteenth century the size and constitution of ensembles depended as much on circumstance as on the demands of the work to be performed.[130] Available players and the size of the performing venue were important factors, and so a surviving score or parts might not necessarily indicate the *ad hoc* nature in which a work was originally performed. At the Cöthen court during Bach's employment (1717–23), for example, the number of instrumentalists, between thirteen and fifteen, was relatively stable, but the specific distribution of instruments in both the string and wind sections varied from year to year and genre to genre.

Quantz's recommendations range from an orchestra with a string contingent of four violins, one viola, one cello and one double bass (plus one harpsichord) to one of 12–3–4–2 (plus four flutes, four oboes, three bassoons, two harpsichords and a theorbo, with horns added as appropriate).[131] Although Quantz emphasizes the desirability of observing certain proportions of instruments, fluidity of numbers of personnel characterized circumstances of performance even in the same location, and there were many occasions when equivalent instruments were fairly freely substituted, according to what was available. The optional nature of the forces for Corelli's concerti grossi Op. 6, as noted on the title-page, is a case in point, Muffat confirming that these works could be played equally well as trio sonatas by the *concertino* alone as by a full complement of strings and continuo;[132] and Mozart's remark to the Paris publisher Sieber that his Piano Concertos K. 413, K. 414 and K. 415 could be 'performed with full orchestra, or with oboes and horns, or merely a quattro' reflects similar flexibility of instrumentation in the 1780s.[133]

Archival and musical evidence sometimes requires imaginative and cautious interpretation. Some statistics reflect special events, others reproduce information from unreliable sources. Furthermore, we must not be too dogmatic in our reading of the evidence; thus, Zaslaw suggests studying 'an orchestra over a period of time in order to see what it had as its normal working strength'.[134] Other data such as court records often fail to account for possible instrumental doublings or available 'extra' players in the locality. In eighteenth-century Venice oboists were often flautists as well, while in Vienna oboists doubled as trombonists and in Paris those who played the horn also played the viola; furthermore, viola parts were sometimes prescribed even when no violists were apparently available and were probably played by violinists.[135]

Evidence regarding practices at the Leipzig Concert Society 1746–8 amply demonstrates the versatility of some of the twenty-seven musicians. Among the numerous identifiable doublings were those of the two horn players on viola and second violin respectively; if trumpets and drums were required, a first violinist and the second oboist played trumpet, and the first horn switched to timpani; both oboists doubled on flute, and if both oboes and flutes were needed, one of the bassoonists would help out on flute.[136]

Dexter Edge notes that the four traditional types of evidence regarding orchestral size are scanty and ambiguous for the Viennese concerto.[137] He nevertheless cites two orchestra lists that can be linked to musical academies at which concertos were performed. One, referring to the Lenten academies of 1761 suggests a potential orchestra of strings (8–8–4–4–4), one flute, pairs of oboes, English horns and bassoons, four horns, two trumpets and a timpanist; a second list, dated 1763, shows a smaller orchestra for an academy in the imperial summer palace at Laxenburg. Only one surviving list (for the academies of the Viennese Tonkünstler-Societät on 22 and 23 December 1785) is known to be directly associated with a concerto performance by Mozart (probably K. 482). The performance took place between the two parts of Dittersdorf's oratorio *Esther* and the available orchestra included strings (19–19–6–7–7), two flutes, six oboes, four bassoons, four horns, two trumpets, two trombones and a timpanist; however, it is unlikely that such a large ensemble would have been employed for the concerto. Edge suggests an orchestral size of strings (6–6–4–3–3) and pairs of winds and cites evidence from other personnel lists and manuscript concerto parts to substantiate this conjecture. He later claims that his research into manuscript parts of Mozart's piano concertos suggests that these works could conceivably have been performed with one player per string part.

Distribution

Pictorial evidence survives for a variety of orchestral placements, and there is further commentary in the theoretical works of Quantz, Carl Ludwig Junker, Johann Samuel Petri, Johann Reichardt, Galeazzi and Koch,[138] as well as other instruction books, dictionaries, autobiographies, letters and more general musical literature. Quantz's recommendations seem specific but are in fact ambiguous:

> In a composition for a large ensemble, performed either in a hall or in some other large place where there is no stage, the tip of the harpsichord may be directed towards the listeners. So that none of the musicians turns his back to the listeners, the first violins may stand in a row next to the harpsichord, with the leader on the right of the keyboard player, who has the two bass instruments playing on either side of him. The second violins may come

behind the first, and behind them the violas. Next to the violas, on the right, place the oboes in the same row, and behind this the hunting horns and the other basses. The flutes, if they have solo parts to play, are best placed at the tip of the harpsichord, in front of the first violins, or on the left side of the harpsichord. Because of the weakness of their tone, they would not be heard if they were to stand back.[139]

In general there were no standardized placements, each hall, repertory and ensemble dictating its own requirements. There was a measure of agreement that the visual as well as the acoustical should be taken into account and that the principal harpsichordist and concertmaster should be placed centrally (with any relevant continuo instruments – until about the end of the eighteenth century – positioned nearby to form a unit). Early in the eighteenth century first and second violins were generally positioned close to each other on the same side of the orchestra with no intention of creating antiphonal effect. Later, however, the two violin sections generally faced each other, with principal cello and bass either side of the harpsichord. Weak and principal melody instruments required forward placement, but the woodwind seem rarely to have been positioned together as a compact group, while trumpets and drums were distributed logically either to the rear or to one side.[140]

Gradually the Baroque arrangement of *ripieno* and *concertino* harpsichords with associated continuo instruments gave way c.1780 to use of a single keyboard. Junker echoed Quantz and Rousseau in stating that the position of the keyboard instrument normally determined the distribution of the other parts, but he failed to specify which way the keyboard should face. Like Rousseau, Junker also felt that the basses would be best situated centrally around the keyboard instrument in order better to convey the tempo. The two violin sections faced each other, with the oboes behind the first violins and the flutes behind the seconds. The violas took up a position between the basses and the oboes and the cellos between the basses and the flutes. The horns were placed behind the basses and the trumpets and timpani were positioned behind the horns. Junker reports that some orchestras of the time performed on special platforms, and that these tended to improve the ensemble and overall musical effect by offering the players better sight-lines and greater freedom. No separate mention is made of the bassoons, but one can reasonably assume that the bassoonists took an appropriate place amongst the basses.

Concert orchestras often stood to perform (except, of course, cellists, bassoonists and keyboard players) but this was not a universal practice, musicians evidently performing seated in Vienna, as Dittersdorf suggests, so that 'every player fronted his audience'.[141] Zaslaw credits Haydn with introducing an amphitheatre arrangement for the Salomon concerts in London (1791–3).[142] His hypothetical reconstruction according to a number of contemporary descriptions places the director/harpsichordist and concertmaster (and any soloist) centrally, the two violin sections opposite each other, the basses and cellos on both wings, the woodwinds and horns well forward in a ring around the higher strings with the bassoon near one flank of the other bass instruments and the trumpets and timpani at the rear. Such a plan, or a very similar distribution, is verified by Koch and Petri and was used in London's concert circles throughout much of the nineteenth century.[143]

Solo practice and concerto direction

A keyboard continuo player normally served as director of concerto ensembles in the Baroque and early Classical periods, and the benefits of having the continuo to hold the ensemble together were stressed by many writers. If the composer himself were the violin soloist, as was frequently the case in violin concertos, he would normally have assumed greater responsibility for direction.[144] In any case, as the significance of keyboard continuo diminished and larger orchestras became more common, the direction of the ensemble began to pass to, or be shared with, the concerto soloist, who was generally placed centrally within the orchestra, where he could liaise with the keyboard continuo player and/or the concertmaster and direct the performances through the very act of performance.

In the Classical concerto, as in the Baroque,[145] the soloist was not normally expected to rest while the orchestra played the various ritornello or tutti sections. As both printed and manuscript parts clearly show, any violin soloist, for example, would join with the orchestra's first violins in tutti sections and this practice extended to other instruments provided that their timbres did not contrast markedly with the other instruments in the ensemble.[146] Edge states that this reservation applies, for example, to concertos for harp, mandolin and, to a lesser extent, oboe while Lawson observes that 'one of the distinguishing features of a classical clarinet concerto is that solo involvement in tuttis has a far greater influence on tone-colour than is the case with concertos for instruments such as the violin or bassoon'. He conjectures that Anton Stadler may have played along with the orchestra 'at the very opening' of Mozart's Clarinet Concerto K. 622 '(perhaps for eight bars or so), in the concluding bars of the first movement, and at the very end of the work'. However, 'solo participation in the Adagio tuttis would clearly detract from the dialogue which lies at its very heart'.[147] Edge further points out that soloists were sometimes given unique parts in tuttis, citing as evidence a concerto for 'second horn' and bassoon in E flat by Matthias Baumgartner.

In the late eighteenth century various issues regarding modes of performance throw up interesting performing options, notably those relating to domestic concerto performances with scaled-down forces,[148] the kinds of textual alterations that were often made (for example, the omission of the opening tutti) and the 'knock-on' effects these had on concerto publication. Such practices, along with the discontinuous programming of movements of concertos, were especially relevant to performances in the 1790s and beyond and are therefore discussed in the following chapter.

Eighteenth-century styles of playing can be re-created with reference to a variety of primary source materials, but the incompleteness of the evidence makes literal reconstructions of past performance practices impossible. Furthermore, there will inevitably be occasions when particular choices reflect today's artistic culture, rather than that of a long-vanished era. Indeed, the circle of change seems to be turning again with some period ensembles nowadays adopting a middle ground between what they know of Baroque conventions and their own and their listeners' tastes. Nevertheless, historically informed attempts at faithful reconstruction are undoubtedly worthwhile; they often demonstrate more intellectual and artistic potential than their many detractors assume and inestimably enhance our comprehension and appreciation of the music.

12 Performance practice in the nineteenth-century concerto

DAVID ROWLAND

A modern audience attending a concert performance of a nineteenth-century concerto in a standard concert venue generally expects to hear an uninterrupted performance of a complete concerto in a polished performance directed by a conductor. The performers expect to play all of the notes – and no more – of a modern published score. Nineteenth-century audiences were used to something rather different. They would have been aware of a wider range of performance possibilities than we experience today. A concerto performance might comprise just one or two movements of a three-movement work. The concerto might be played as an orchestral piece, or as a chamber, or even solo work. Improvisation might play a role in the performance, not just in the cadenzas, but perhaps in a prelude, or in some embellishments to the composer's original. These and other factors would have given nineteenth-century audiences and musicians alike some strikingly different expectations to those of today. Perhaps most significant of all, these expectations would have been realized on instruments and orchestras that were fundamentally different from their modern counterparts, at least in the early part of the century.

Instruments

The nineteenth century saw very significant developments in every instrument for which concertos were written. Most individual developments were part of general trends. A brief examination of these general trends will go some way towards explaining why some instruments were more effective vehicles for solo concertos than others, especially in the first part of the century. Only a very limited amount of information on the instruments themselves can be included here: further technical details will be found in the extensive literature on instrument history.

Makers of the nineteenth century were concerned with building instruments of increasing power and projection. This had been an objective of late eighteenth-century piano makers and their instruments were already much more robustly constructed than harpsichords by *c*.1800.

However, their low string tension, small hammers and comparatively light wooden structures still produced instruments with a very limited degree of carrying power, so that composers had to provide very light orchestral writing, or no accompaniment at all, in concerto solo sections. The extent of the problem is illustrated in a review dating from 1800 of Jan Ladislav Dussek's 'Grand Military Concerto'. The review reveals a perceived balance problem in the solo passages of Wolfgang Amadeus Mozart's concertos:

> What also commends this concerto [Dussek's Grand Military Concerto] is the appropriate accompaniment to the solo part, which is so arranged throughout, that the concerto player can be well heard and understood – a circumstance that is still to be wished in Mozart's keyboard concertos, for all their remaining excellence.[1]

These comments are surprising, considering the lightness of Mozart's orchestration in solo sections, and it is quite likely that the reviewer's opinion was formed as a result of hearing the concertos on instruments other than those for which they were written. In 1828, when the same fundamental differences between 'English' and 'Viennese' pianos existed as they had in Mozart's time, Hummel remarked of 'English' pianos that:

> they are less distinguishable than ours [i.e., 'Viennese' pianos], when associated with complicated orchestral accompaniments; this, in my opinion, is to be attributed to the thickness and fullness of their tone.[2]

In any event, steps were taken throughout the first half of the nineteenth century to make pianos of all kinds more powerful. Heavier strings at higher tensions were used. In turn, the new stringing practices required bigger, heavier hammers to set the strings in motion (more layers of leather were initially used, and felt was introduced in the 1820s). The additional string tension also put a much greater strain on the frame of the instrument, resulting in ever-sturdier wooden construction with metal supports in particularly vulnerable places, and eventually the adoption of cast iron frames for grand pianos, first in the USA shortly after the middle of the century and rather later in Europe.

A great deal of attention was also given to the design of stringed instruments at the beginning of the century in order to make them more powerful. The desired results were often achieved by remodelling earlier instruments. A description, written in 1806 by Abbé Sibire in *La Chélonomie*, explains what happened:

> This is a process which does not imply the slightest deterioration and yet which virtually every old violin, no matter how well preserved it is in other ways, could not avoid: REBARRING ... Formerly it was the fashion to have

necks well elevated, bridges and fingerboards extremely low, fine strings, and a moderate tone. Then the bass bar ... could be short and thin because it was sufficient for it to have enough strength to sustain the weight of five to six pounds which the strings exerted on it ... [but now] the tilting back of the neck, the raising of the bridge, of the fingerboard, and the amplification in sound, necessitate increasing by a full third the resistant force. Repairers have only one choice: strengthening the old bar, or replacing it with a new one.[3]

Steps were also taken to increase the power of wind instruments, but rather later than the parallel changes for the piano and stringed instruments. At the beginning of the nineteenth century the nature of wind instruments remained essentially the same as in the closing decades of the eighteenth century, although metal keys were progressively added (see below). Eventually, woodwind instruments were thoroughly redesigned, resulting in an improved ability to project their sound, but these changes did not generally take place until the second quarter of the century.

As well as being made louder, the available compass of most instruments was extended in the first part of the nineteenth century. Additional keys on wind instruments extended their range by a few notes and the extended fingerboard on stringed instruments brought new possibilities in the upper register. However, the most far-reaching changes in compass took place in the design of the piano. For the second half of the eighteenth century, until about 1790, a keyboard player could expect to find about five octaves on a harpsichord, clavichord or piano. Thereafter, changes to the compass occurred at different speeds around Europe, but by about 1810 six-octave pianos were being made in most of the major centres and by the middle of the century seven octaves were standard. Experiments were made even with eight-octave pianos, but they were not successful and seven octaves remained normal until the 1870s, when an additional three notes established the compass that is found on the majority of concert grands today.[4]

Another preoccupation of nineteenth-century instrument-makers was to produce instruments capable of performing effectively in every key across the entire compass. While this was certainly a concern of piano and string instrument-makers, it was a much greater challenge for manufacturers of brass and wind instruments. The realities of the harmonic series meant that, in the absence of any slide, key or valve mechanism, brass instruments could only play scales in their upper registers – which was the case for almost all of the eighteenth century. Keys and valves enabled instruments to be fully chromatic and satisfactory systems were invented in the course of the first half of the century.

In the case of wind instruments, it had been possible to play chromatically on eighteenth-century woodwind instruments using systems of cross-fingerings. That does not mean to say, however, that those instruments were equally successful in all keys. Each woodwind instrument had strong and weak keys, some notes were difficult to tune, and the system of fingerings made some musical patterns problematic. Certain trills, for example, were very difficult, or even impossible to play. The increasing number of metal keys that were added in the late eighteenth and early nineteenth centuries helped with particular problems, but generally speaking it was not until the second quarter of the century that woodwind instruments were given the complete technical overhauls that were needed in order to make them play effectively in all keys across their compass.

In general, then, the development of the piano and members of the string family ran ahead of parallel developments in woodwind and brass instruments. It would be overstating the case to say that these changes alone accounted for the popularity of piano and violin concertos in the nineteenth century, because other social and musical factors must also have been significant; but there can be no doubt that technical developments contributed to the particular success of those instruments in concertos.

Orchestras

As recent studies of the orchestra have shown, it is very difficult to generalize about many aspects of nineteenth-century orchestras, including their size and internal balance.[5] A travelling virtuoso would have had to be more ready than his or her twentieth-century counterpart to adapt to local circumstances. One of the most important of these would have been the concert venue. Virtually all of the world's current leading concert venues were built in the nineteenth century, or later, and prior to their existence concerts took place in a mixture of halls, some of them purpose-built, as well as other venues such as theatres.

When concerts took place in purpose-built halls the musicians could expect to be arranged in such a way as to be able to hear one another, while their sound was easily projected to an audience. Orchestras were often raised a little above the level of the audience – many commentators expressed the view that the sound travelled better throughout the hall with this arrangement. In addition, the performers were often tiered in order to give good sight-lines and projection.

When concerts took place in venues that were not purpose-built the physical arrangements were adapted accordingly. Theatres were often used for one-off events such as benefit concerts. On one such occasion in 1826 Ignaz Moscheles, the piano soloist, sat on the stage with the orchestra in its customary place in the pit.[6] Whether this was the usual arrangement for concerto performances in theatres, or whether the orchestra sometimes occupied the stage, is impossible to tell from the limited evidence, but it illustrates the flexibility that was often required of the musicians.

If performance venues differed widely according to local conditions, so too did the standards of orchestras. At the beginning of the century, before the professional ethos of the new musical conservatoires and academies had taken effect, standards of orchestral discipline were often poor. Rehearsal time could be woefully inadequate and poor playing standards caused frustration to concerto soloists. Louis Spohr, for example, on tour in Italy in 1816, expressed exasperation at the standards of the local orchestras, especially in comparison with those with which he was familiar in Germany.[7] Spohr himself, however, did much to raise standards of orchestral playing by insisting on careful rehearsal, and he was not alone in his efforts. In Paris, for example, François Antoine Habeneck helped improve standards, also exerting an influence right across Europe, as reported in 1849:

> Habeneck ... brought the execution of symphonies and overtures of the great masters to a pitch of unparalleled perfection. The fire and energy of Habanek's conducting, his observance of rhythmical time, and the precision and finish which he obtained from his forces, have led to the improvement of the other great orchestras in Europe.[8]

The revolution was brought about by factors that are taken for granted today. One observer noted, for example, that the strings 'start with exactly the same bowing'.[9]

The size of orchestras was another factor that varied significantly. If questions relating to size could be assessed on the basis of average numbers one would certainly say that there had been a general enlargement of orchestras through the century. However, to present a picture of steady growth in orchestral size would be misleading. Both large and small orchestras existed at all times in the century, and there were variations in size from decade to decade in many of Europe's established orchestras. 'Large' and 'small' generally denote in the region of 100 players for the largest concerts (not including those special events for which hundreds of players were brought together) to around thirty for the smallest.[10] Having said that, by the end of the century one would almost certainly have expected to find an orchestra of around 70–100 players in a major venue.

The internal balance of orchestras varied. In the nineteenth century it was not unusual for the second violins to outnumber the firsts, the reverse of the modern pattern. It was also a feature of some orchestras, especially in Italy at the beginning of the century, to contain significantly larger numbers of double basses – both in relation to the whole string section, and in relation to the number of cellos – than we are now used to. In the first part of the century woodwinds were often doubled (that is to say two flutes playing the first flute part and two flutes playing the second, for example). Instruments now obsolete were also used, such as the ophicleide, and others such as the cornet enjoyed a popularity that is no longer in evidence.

While the piano was still in use as an instrument from which some direction took place (see below) it was positioned in the middle of the orchestra, sufficiently towards the audience to be close to other soloists, who generally stood in the same area as we are used to today, but further back than the piano is normally situated in modern concerto perform-ances. The usual arrangement of the violins for the entire century was for them to face each other, firsts on one side and seconds on the other, either side of the director. The violas, cellos and double basses were then positioned in a variety of places. Sometimes all of the cellos and basses were placed together in the centre; sometimes they were split (with basses often at the sides or back of the orchestra). Trumpets and drums were usually furthest from the audience and woodwinds usually occupied a place between the violins and the back of the orchestra.

Three different methods of orchestral direction were well known in the nineteenth century: joint direction by a pianist/director and lead violinist; direction by the lead violinist alone; and baton conducting. The first system was considered ineffective by some writers even at the beginning of the century, yet it persisted, especially in England. The Philharmonic Society's concerts were directed in this way into the 1830s, although increasingly it seems that the figure seated at the piano directed very little, or not at all, leaving the role to the lead violinist. (Presumably the pianist/director had a greater role in rehearsals, because of his awareness of the full details of the score.)

Many performances in the nineteenth century were directed by the leader who played or beat time with his bow, depending on what was required at a particular moment. The practice continued well into the second half of the century. Habeneck was one of the best-known bow-directors. Spohr also directed with his bow, but is perhaps more famous for his baton conducting, of which he was one of the most prominent early exponents. He famously rehearsed the Philharmonic Society orchestra with a baton in 1820,[11] but stepped back from doing so in the concert, preferring instead to conduct with the bow. It seems unlikely that concerto soloists on any instrument directed their own concertos. The leader of the orchestra or the conductor, depending on local tradition, would have done this.

We have become used to performances of early nineteenth-century concertos in which the piano soloist stays silent in the orchestral tuttis; an unsurprising state of affairs, since editors of modern 'Urtext' editions often suppress the notation supplied for the soloist by the composer in these sections. Nevertheless, there is strong evidence that at least some composers expected the soloists to play continuo realizations in tutti sections. Both Linda Faye Ferguson and Tibor Szász, recent authorities on the subject, argue for the presence of continuo in all of the piano concertos of Ludwig van Beethoven, who supplied detailed figured-bass parts for the pianist during orchestral tuttis (there are no figures in the *Neue Beethoven Ausgabe* or in other modern editions, but rests for both hands).[12] It seems unlikely, however, that there were universally followed practices at this time, and even if there were in fact local traditions, common sense suggests considerable flexibility in an age when continuo was in decline, and when orchestral forces were far from standard. A telling acknowledgement of a flexible approach is found in the first edition of Augustus Frederick Christopher Kollmann's Piano Concerto (*c.*1804), which, in common with other British concertos of the period, has a written-out realization of the orchestral tutti (see below). At the bottom of the first page of music is a direction that reads '[when performed] with the accompaniments [i.e. the orchestral parts], all of the Tuttis of the Piano Forte part ought either to rest, or to be play'd so that the other parts are principally heard'. Composed shortly afterwards, in 1810, the autograph score of Weber's Piano Concerto Op. 11 'contains enough evidence to support the conclusion that its composer preferred the soloist to be silent in all the tuttis'.[13] Nevertheless, more than a decade later Felix Mendelssohn was still playing discrete continuo parts in his symphonies;[14] perhaps he did so too in the tuttis of his concertos.

As will readily be seen from this brief review of orchestral practices, circumstances of nineteenth-century performance differed considerably over time and from place to place. Anyone attempting to establish performance practices for a particular work should examine the documents associated with particular composers and performers, rather than relying on suppositions about general trends.

Concert programmes and audiences

There were ample opportunities for performances of concertos in the vibrant concert environment of the nineteenth century. Every major centre of population in Europe boasted numerous public concert series and many wealthy individuals hosted private events at which instrumental groupings of various sizes could be heard.[15] Concert programmes were longer than we are used to today especially in the first half of the century, and they often included a combination of orchestral, vocal and chamber works. This trend continued into the second half of the century, although later programmes tended to be less mixed. A degree of specialization also emerged towards the middle of the century, with series devoted to chamber music and to the emergence of the solo piano recital.

While concertos were generally popular throughout the century they did not find universal favour. According to one critic in 1850, for example, London audiences were 'thoroughly nauseated' by the 'mere displays of digital activity or pulmonic strength' that they witnessed in concertos.[16] A similar sentiment was felt among the directors of London's Philharmonic Society, founded in 1813 with the intention of raising the quality of the capital's concert life. The society initially exercised a policy excluding solo concertos from its programmes.[17] Despite this policy, however, the directors relented probably as early as their first season and within a few years – certainly from the 1820s – concertos were regularly seen on the society's programmes. 'Quality' was nevertheless maintained by the directors' preference for 'symphonic' concertos, especially those by Mozart, and later those by Beethoven,[18] rather than for those concertos where the orchestra performed a more peripheral role. Other concert organizers were less particular and gave their audiences a wide range of repertory, allowing performers to play their own concertos, or the acknowledged favourites of the day, such as the Johann Nepomuk Hummel concertos with which many pianists made their names in the first half of the century.[19]

One of the major developments in programming that took place in the nineteenth century was the creation of a canon of works by composers of previous generations.[20] The Philharmonic Society's emphasis on the concertos of Mozart and Beethoven was part of this trend and similar to the situation in Paris, where concertos by both composers occupied a regular place in concert programmes.[21] Bach's concertos were also performed regularly in both cities during the middle decades of the century, although their popularity waned later on in London.[22]

The performance of concertos by earlier composers raised issues of interpretation for nineteenth-century pianists. In particular the question arose as to how far the works should be updated to suit the resources of modern instruments. In the case of Bach's works there seems to have been no question of using a harpsichord instead of a piano (despite the harpsichord's use in the 'historical concerts' of the time[23]), although some reflection of earlier performance practices might be seen in the preference shown towards performances of his concertos with very small string forces (see below). With Mozart's and Beethoven's concertos the issue that occupied pianists was whether or not to use the extended compass of the instrument. In the 1820s and 1830s, editions of Mozart's and Beethoven's works were published that adapted the right-hand parts of their concertos to use the treble notes that had progressively been added to pianos since the 1790s.[24] The low level of contemporary criticism of this approach suggests that, at the time, up-dating earlier scores was generally acceptable. There were some contrary voices, however. The reviewer of a performance of Mozart's K. 466 (a particular favourite in the nineteenth century) in 1833 made a point of praising Mendelssohn's avoidance of any additions to Mozart's text:

> The scrupulous exactness with which he [Mendelssohn] gave the author's text, without a single addition or *new reading* of his own, the precision in his time, together with the extraordinary accuracy of his execution, excited the admiration of all present.[25]

The trend of paying close attention to the composer's text grew in the middle of the century, no doubt with the growth of musical source studies and the publication of scholarly editions, and performances with additional notes appear to have been much less acceptable in the second half of the century.

Today we are used to concert performances of complete concertos. Nineteenth-century concert organizers often took a different approach. While complete concertos were programmed throughout the century, especially towards its close, significant numbers of performances took place in which only one or two movements were played. Frédéric Chopin's performances of his own E minor Concerto are typical. In Breslau in 1830 he performed only the rondo and possibly also the romance. In Paris in the years 1832–4 he gave three performances of just one or two movements of the concerto and finally, in the following year, he performed the whole work in a single performance.[26] In addition to the performance of individual concerto movements, composite concertos were played, in which works were made up of movements by different composers. John Cramer made a particular feature of this practice, performing concertos consisting of movements by himself combined with others by Mozart, for example from the Piano Concerto in C minor K. 491 and his own Concerto No. 5 in the same key.[27] Other pianists playing composite concertos include Moscheles, whose debut at the Philharmonic Society in London in 1821 included the first two movements of his own second concerto with another work of his own composition as the last.[28] The most extreme manifestation of this trend occurred when a 'Mr. Schuncke' played a concerto with a movement each by three composers: Hummel, Beethoven and Pixis according to one account and Ries, Beethoven and Pixis according to another.[29] The fashion for composite concertos peaked in the 1820s and, although accounts of it exist at other times, it should perhaps be viewed more as a curiosity than as a mainstream practice.

A final factor that militated against complete, uninterrupted performances of concertos was the behaviour of nineteenth-century audiences, who tended not to sit at concerts in reverential awe. They came in late and left early, they walked around, or ate, and generally they participated actively in the event by applauding while music was being played and by requesting encores of sections of works that they particularly enjoyed. In accounts of concerts in Italy and in Germany, Spohr noted that audiences applauded in the orchestral tuttis to such an extent that the music was drowned out.[30] The orchestral interludes in Chopin's Variations on Mozart's 'Là ci darem', Op. 2, were barely heard because of the applause at their first Viennese performance by the composer.[31] In London both Cramer and John Field had to repeat slow movements of concertos after encores were demanded by the audience.[32] Numerous examples from all over Europe and North America could be cited. Generally speaking, concert life was a much more exciting phenomenon in the nineteenth century than it is now.

Concerto arrangements

Performers of the nineteenth century were much more used to adapting the music they played to the local circumstances of the time than we are today. The absence of an orchestra did not mean that a concerto could not be performed, but rather that some other solution was sought to make a performance possible. There were several options. In the case of piano concertos the orchestral parts were often realized by a string quartet, or some other chamber ensemble. Failing even this number of accompanists a concerto could be performed as a solo, or as a piano duet. In the case of concertos for instruments other than the piano, performances were given by the solo instrument with the accompaniment of the piano.

The practice of performing keyboard concertos as chamber works was not unique to the nineteenth century. Well-known eighteenth-century examples include Mozart's Concertos K. 413–15, K. 449 and perhaps others. The *Wiener Zeitung* of 15 January 1783 noted, of K. 413–15, that 'these three concertos, which may be performed either with a large orchestra with wind instruments or merely *a quattro*, viz. with 2 violins, 1 viola and violoncello, will not appear until the beginning of April of this year'.[33] In a letter to his father Mozart wrote that K. 449 'can be performed *a quattro* without wind-instruments'.[34] Dussek's 'Œuvre Premier' concertos published by Hummel in the early 1780s were published 'avec l'accompagnement des Deux Violons, Alto et Basse. Deux Hautbois et Cors ad libitum'. The title-page of his later arrangement of a Krumpholz harp concerto advertised prices for two different collections of accompanying parts: 4 shillings for '2 Vios. & Bass' and 5 shillings for 'full Band'. In order to compensate for a crucial missing part when the work was performed in its chamber version a woodwind cue was inserted into the piano part. Even more explicitly, in the early years of the century Simrock published an edition of Beethoven's Piano Concerto in C, Op. 15, and some concertos by Mozart in which three performing options were spelled out. An introduction to each of the concertos reads:

> This concerto can be performed three different ways:
> 1st, with strings only; 2nd, with a few winds [in addition to strings]; and 3rd, with full orchestra.

1st manner: If performed without the winds, the small notes indicated in the keyboard part, and 2 violins and violas must be played. If smaller and larger notes fall in the same measure, only the first must be played. In this case, the EXTRA VIOLE is absolutely indispensable.

2nd manner: If only one or a few wind instruments are on hand, it will be easy for the [string and keyboard] players to omit those instruments present from their parts, since one always finds indicated next to the small notes in the string parts which wind instrument is represented. If larger notes fall at the same time as smaller notes which are now being played by wind instruments, the larger are thus to be played.

3rd manner: In performance with complete orchestra, leave out all smaller notes and the EXTRA Viole.[35]

A flexible pricing policy that allowed for the purchase of various combinations of performing parts became usual in the early decades of the nineteenth century, along with the inclusion of a few crucial instrumental cues. When Hummel's concerto Op. 110 was published by Welsh and Hawes in 1826 the pricing was for 'Piano Forte with Acc[ompanimen]ts. 12s – with full orchestra 18s'.[36] In order to explain the flexibility a full explanation was given further down the title-page: 'This Concerto may be performed on the Piano Forte without Accompaniments [see below] ... Also with a Quartett Accompaniment without Wind Instruments.' The parts for

Schlesinger's Paris edition of Chopin's E minor Concerto were sold as follows: the piano part alone, 12 francs; piano with quartet, 18 francs; piano with full orchestral accompaniment, 24 francs. Important cues were included in the string parts on this occasion. Many more examples could be cited and to these could be added chamber arrangements of earlier works for a mixture of stringed and wind instruments, such as Cimador's arrangement (c.1806) of Mozart's K. 503 for 'two Violins, Two Tenors, Bass and Double Bass Or A German Flute, Two Violins, Two Tenors, & Two Basses', or Cramer's and Hummel's arrangements of several of Mozart's concertos for violin, flute and cello.[37]

The consistency with which piano concertos were published with chamber accompaniments in the first half of the nineteenth century suggests that there was a considerable demand for works in this format, and therefore performance opportunities for them. We might suppose that most of the chamber performances of concertos that took place were domestic, for private audiences, or simply for the enjoyment of the players. It seems, however, that these arrangements made their way into the public domain. The *Allgemeine musikalische Zeitung* reviewer of Hummel's arrangements of Mozart's concertos for flute, violin and cello had suggested that they would be particularly suited for performances in small towns, where full orchestras were not available. In fact, there are records of them being performed in Berlin and Königsberg.[38] Similarly, there is plenty of evidence that performances of concertos with quartet accompaniment took place in Paris, especially in those concert series dedicated to chamber music that were established just before the middle of the century.[39] Chamber performances of concertos are recorded in London as, for example, when Charles Mangold performed the first two movements of Beethoven's 'Emperor' Concerto with quintet accompaniment at a benefit concert in 1842.[40] In London around the middle of the century it also seems to have been usual for performances of Bach's concertos to be given with quartet accompaniment, rather than with string orchestra.[41]

At the end of the eighteenth and beginning of the nineteenth centuries the solo parts of piano concertos were published in a variety of formats, differing particularly with regard to the notation of orchestral tutti sections.[42] Various possibilities existed. In some scores the bass line alone was printed. In others a bass line with figures was given. Occasionally a realized continuo part was printed. In many scores a reduction of the orchestral texture for two hands was included. This last option had been standard throughout the eighteenth century in Britain while a variety of formats were found on the Continent. In the early years of the nineteenth century the 'British' format was adopted as standard for piano concertos all over Europe.

The realization of the orchestral tuttis in a two-hand arrangement had a distinct advantage over other formats in that it enabled performers to play complete concertos without any form of accompaniment whatsoever. Some eighteenth-century performances of concertos as solos are recorded,[43] and occasionally one finds similar nineteenth-century accounts. On 4 April 1831, for example, Chopin appears to have played his E minor Concerto as a solo.[44] Chopin also seems to have played his 'Là ci darem' variations on a number of occasions without orchestra.[45]

Although there are only a few recorded performances of concertos being played as solos there are plenty of indications on published scores to suggest that composers expected their works to be played in this way. For example, 'This Concerto may be played without the Accompaniments', is found in J. Boosey & Co.'s edition of Cramer's Concerto No. 8 in D minor, published in 1825. The fact that only the piano part of Kollmann's Piano Concerto (*c.*1804) was printed while the orchestral parts were available in manuscript on demand suggests that the composer and/or publisher anticipated that the work would be performed mainly as a solo. In order to make such performances convincing, care was taken to include crucial orchestral material, as the note on the title-page of Hummel's Op. 110 explains: 'This Concerto may be performed on the Piano Forte without Accompaniments by playing the small Notes which are Introduced'.[46]

When concertos were played as solos some of the tutti material was evidently left out. An explicit instruction to this effect is found in Corri, Dussek & Co.'s edition of 'Dussek's Grand Concerto for the Pedal Harp or Piano Forte ... Op. 30' published in 1798. The first page of printed music bears the instruction 'NB. This Concerto when played without Accompaniments, the Tutti may be omitted'. Dussek's comments reflect what actually happened when concertos were adapted for publication as sonatas, a familiar practice at the beginning of the nineteenth century. For example, the only version of Clementi's Piano Concerto to be published in his lifetime was as a sonata (the Sonata in C, Op. 33, No. 3). The concerto version exists in manuscript and was published in the twentieth century. A comparison of the concerto and sonata versions shows that some of the concerto tutti material was removed when the work was published as a sonata.[47]

The title-page of the London edition (1782) of Haydn's Concerto Hob XVIII: G2 reads as follows:

A CONCERTO OR FAVOURITE DUETTO FOR TWO
PERFORMERS ON TWO PIANO FORTES OR HARPSICHORDS
WITH AN ACCOMPANIMENT FOR TWO VIOLINS, TWO

FRENCH HORNS & A BASS ... NOW TRANSPOSED &
ALTERED ACCORDING TO THE ENGLISH TASTE, ON TWO
PIANO FORTES OR HARPSICHORDS, WITHOUT ANY
ACCOMPANIMENT, BY GIUSEPPE DIETTENHOFER[48]

The wording here could be taken to suggest that arrangements of concertos
for two harpsichords or pianos were popular in England at the end of the
eighteenth century. If this was so, then much of the evidence for the practice
must have disappeared. We only have evidence from a much later period that
similar arrangements of other concertos were published in any numbers –
from the 1820s onwards, in fact.[49] As with other arrangements for small
forces, those who prepared the works for publication took care to ensure that
as accurate a representation as possible of the complete work was given. A
note on the first page of the solo piano part of D'Almaine's & Co's edition of
Henri Herz's *Fourth Concerto* carefully explains what is assumed in other
editions of this type (and incidentally offers evidence of another type of
chamber performance, this time for two-piano duet and quartet):

> With quartet or second piano accompaniment only, all the small notes
> representing the orchestral parts must be played – It is only with orchestral
> accompaniments or with quartet and second piano united that these notes
> can be suppressed at pleasure.[50]

Plenty of opportunities existed for two-piano duet performances of concertos in salon concerts or private gatherings. One such occasion was a
concert at the home of James Rothschild in January 1843 at which
Chopin's pupil Karl Filtsch played his teacher's E minor Concerto, the
composer supplying the orchestral parts on the second piano.[51] Twelve
years earlier the composer himself may have played the solo part of the
same concerto in a similar arrangement with Josef Stunz at the second
piano, although on this occasion it is equally possible that Chopin
performed the work as a solo.[52] Moscheles reported an occasion in 1835
on which he and Mendelssohn performed a concerto as a duet:

> We then allowed ourselves all manner of extravagances, extemporised jointly
> and alternately on two pianos – an intellectual sort of tournament. I played
> Felix's [Mendelssohn's] 'Rondo brilliant in E flat', and my 'Concerto
> Fantastique', he supplying a substitute for an orchestral accompaniment on a
> second piano.[53]

Concertos for instruments other than the piano were performed in
chamber versions too. In these cases the most convenient arrangements
were for solo instrument and piano, and publishers produced concertos
in this format from around 1830 onwards. Prior to that the situation was
rather more complex, and while arrangements of concertos for violin, etc.

certainly existed, they appeared in a variety of formats. At the end of the eighteenth century and beginning of the nineteenth a number of violin concertos were published as sonatas, but in arrangements in which the piano takes all or more of the solo role.[54] A comparison of concertos/sonatas by composers such as Giornovichi, Janiewicz, Parke and Steibelt shows that some of the tutti material was routinely cut, as with solo piano arrangements of concertos (see above). More usual than sonata versions were arrangements of violin concertos as piano concertos, as, for example, in the case of Beethoven's Violin Concerto. Sometimes, indeed, it was only the piano versions that made it to publication. Violinists did not always have their solos taken from them, however. At a chamber concert in 1812 there was a performance of the 'Adagio and Rondo from the Third Concerto, composed and performed by Drouet', and presumably accompanied on the piano by Dussek.[55]

At the beginning of the century, before the piano compass extended far beyond the reach of the harp, performers on either instrument could play from the same score. A number of Dussek's works were performed as either piano or harp works.[56] Later, some of Hummel's piano concertos were adapted for harp.[57]

All the evidence suggests that there was a widespread tradition of performing concertos in versions other than for soloist and orchestra. Not only was this a feature of informal domestic music-making; it was also an accepted concert practice.

Improvisation and embellishment

At the beginning of the nineteenth century, audiences were used to hearing performances that included improvised elements. These non-notated aspects of performance took a number of forms, ranging from complete and lengthy compositions, sometimes based on melodies supplied by the audience, through brief fragments or interludes such as preludes, cadenzas or lead-ins, to embellishments of existing melodies. The existence of such a strong culture of improvisation was perhaps to be expected in an age when many performers were themselves composers. Coincidentally or not, as fewer composers performed their own music in public, more and more performances were restricted to written musical texts, although the art of improvisation did survive to the end of the century and beyond.

A common view of improvisation is that it is a process of spontaneous creativity, and there can be no doubt that some nineteenth-century performances that fit within this category were genuinely heat-of-the-moment

affairs. More often, though, the evidence points to a high degree of premeditation, for example in Spohr's performances of previously composed
cadenzas to his concertos, or Clara Schumann's well-rehearsed preludes (see
below). For those without any inclination to exercise any degree of creativity
whatsoever there were published preludes, cadenzas and embellishments
that could be learned in advance and used as the occasion demanded.
Whatever the degree of premeditation, performances that strayed from
established scores were very much part of nineteenth-century culture, especially in the earlier part of the century.

In his *Systematic Introduction to Improvisation on the Piano*, Czerny wrote
that 'the performer should become accustomed to improvising a prelude
each time and before each piece that he studies or plays'.[58] Judging from
the number of published examples of preludes in the late eighteenth and
early nineteenth centuries it would appear that many others shared Czerny's
views on the importance of preluding. Giordani (177?), Clementi (1787),
Hummel (*c.*1814), Cramer (1818), Haslinger (1818), Moscheles (1827) and
Kalkbrenner (1827) all published sets of preludes in a variety of keys for the
use of keyboard players and it was customary for instruction books for the
piano and for other instruments to contain similar examples.[59] While the
practice became less popular as the century wore on, some performers
continued to prelude on a regular basis. Clara Schumann evidently did so
throughout her career. There are also accounts of Hans von Bülow and Anton
Rubinstein preluding, and the art continued into the twentieth century; a
recorded concert by Joseph Hofmann in 1937 includes short preludes.[60]

Although Czerny's remarks quoted above apparently recommend
preluding on all occasions, the practice was not considered appropriate
by everyone, and even those who endorsed it in general terms had
reservations about it in connection with certain types of work, or thought
that it was more appropriate in some settings than in others. Commenting
on public performances of works for piano with orchestral accompaniment
Czerny himself wrote that 'in this case all preluding must be strictly
avoided'.[61] Nevertheless, he wrote a prelude for one of Ries's concertos
and other authors sanctioned the use of preludes before concertos, especially
in private performances.[62]

Preludes varied considerably in respect of their length and nature. At
their simplest, they took the form of a spread chord or two, or a few
broken chords and arpeggios. Other preludes were lengthier and included
some working out of one or more motifs. Whatever their length, freedom
of metre was usually a feature of preludes and their structure was often
loose. Most of the published examples have no particular connection with
any work, although sometimes motifs and themes were used in order to
connect preludes with the works that followed them.

In 1828 Hummel wrote:

> In the present day, many performers endeavour to supply the absence
> of natural inward feeling by an appearance of it; for example ... by an
> overloaded decoration of the passages of melody, till the air and character
> is often no longer perceptible ... I do not by any means intend to say, that
> we may not occasionally ... introduce embellishments into an adagio; but
> this must be done with moderation, and in the proper place.[63]

Hummel's comments, while upholding the long-standing tradition of
embellishment, were aimed at the performances of the more extreme
showmen of the nineteenth century, who used every means possible to
dazzle their audiences. Liszt was among them, as he himself confessed
in 1837:

> I then frequently performed ... the works of Beethoven, Weber, and
> Hummel, and I confess to my shame that in order to compel the bravos of an
> audience always slow to grasp beautiful things in their august simplicity, I had
> no scruples against changing their tempos and intentions; I even went so far
> as insolently to add to them a host of passages and cadenzas. ... You
> wouldn't believe ... how much I [now] deplore these concessions to bad
> taste, these sacrilegious violations of the SPIRIT and LETTER, because in me
> the most absolute respect for the masterpieces of the great masters has now
> replaced the need for novelty and individuality.[64]

Despite Liszt's criticism of his earlier performances, and his respect for
the scores of the 'masters', he nevertheless continued to embellish on
occasion, sometimes extravagantly. *The Musical World* of 14 May 1840
contained a review of his performance at the Philharmonic Society three
days earlier:

> He executed about one-half *more* notes than are to be found in [Weber's]
> *Concertstück* with unfailing precision. ... We even and anon heard passages
> doubled, tripled, inverted, and *transmogrified* in all sorts of ways; merely, we
> presume, because Mr. Liszt found no sufficient difficulty in the original
> whereon to exercise his powers.[65]

Liszt made alterations to another performance of the same work in
Germany during that year, and in 1841 he amended Beethoven's
'Emperor' Concerto. On these occasions reviewers were less harsh. On
both occasions comments were made on the danger to other pianists of
the precedent Liszt had set, while conceding that Liszt's changes had been
in good taste, and impressive.[66]

Liszt was not the only pianist to embellish the 'Emperor' Concerto.
Clara Schumann, a pianist not usually associated with the more extreme
end of the nineteenth-century virtuoso tradition, is also documented as

embellishing the work in Leipzig in 1844 during one of her many perform-ances of it.[67]

What would Beethoven have thought? He grew up at a time when it was expected that every performer would be capable of adding ornament-ation to melodic lines. A passage from the *Jahrbuch der Tonkunst von Wien und Prag* of 1796, for example, reads as follows:

> There are places where it is appropriate to insert much ornamentation. This, however, must be done with care and consideration in such a way that the basic emotion does not suffer, but is enhanced. The adagio, which because of its simple melodic layout often becomes the playground of ornamentation, does not allow fast passage-work and scales, but instead well-selected chromatic lines which sigh and languish and then die out.[68]

Beethoven himself seems to have expected to embellish his own melodic lines when he played from early manuscript parts of his concertos (the autograph versions contain incomplete piano parts when compared with the first editions). However, the printed versions appear to represent Beethoven's final workings and it is unlikely that he would have tolerated much further embellishment. According to comments by two of his pupils he was very protective of the published versions of his works. Ries records that 'only in extremely rare cases would he add notes or ornamental decorations'[69] and following an occasion when Czerny had made some alterations to one of his scores Beethoven wrote to him, saying 'you must forgive a composer who would rather have heard his work performed exactly as it was written, however beautifully you played in other respects'.[70]

Beethoven may have had strong feelings about the embellishment of the melodic lines of his concertos, but that did not stop Haslinger pub-lishing editions of the concertos with embellishments a decade after the composer's death. Beethoven's concertos were not the only ones to be embellished. Weber's E flat Concerto for Clarinet, for example, was published with embellishments by its first performer, Heinrich Baermann, and in a further amended version by Baermann's son Carl.[71] Mozart's concertos were also published with embellishments; in the 1820s both Cramer and Hummel had brought out decorated versions of several of them.[72] These editions reflect what seems to have been a widespread performing practice for Mozart's concertos at the time. In an article containing many personal memories of the pianist Cipriani Potter, G. A. Macfarren wrote:

> When Potter returned to England [in 1819] he again played at the Philharmonic, and the piece in which he made his reappearance was the Concerto of Mozart in D minor. He had learnt, perhaps in Vienna, and from

the particular explanations of Attwood, who had witnessed Mozart's performance of his concertos, the fact that the printed copies are but indications of the matter which Mozart himself used to play, and he had gathered from Attwood and others what was the manner in which Mozart used to amplify the written memoranda in his performance. It almost amounted to a re-composition of the part to fill it out with such pianoforte effects as would do justices to the original intention, and it was with such amplification that Potter presented the D minor Concerto. It was in such wise that at a later time Mendelssohn made his first appearance as a pianist here with the same concerto, and with that kind of treatment of the printed sketches.[73]

Towards the end of the eighteenth century, concerto cadenzas changed from being a succession of improvisatory passages with little or no connection to the main work to more integrated sections of movements in which themes and motifs were developed.[74] At the same time composers tended increasingly to write cadenzas into the texture of the movement, supplying orchestral accompaniment and restricting the opportunities for extemporization. So, for example, only about half of Viotti's and Dussek's concerto movements provide improvised cadenza opportunities, some of them having written-out cadenzas with orchestral accompaniment. Similarly, while in his earlier years in Vienna Beethoven seems to have been content with improvisation, he later seems to have become more inclined towards pre-composed cadenzas, writing down cadenzas for his earlier concertos and, in the case of the 'Emperor' Concerto, deliberately forbidding an improvised first-movement cadenza with the words 'no si fa una cadenza' ('do not make a cadenza'). Instead, the movement contains written-out cadenzas with orchestral accompaniment. A later example of a composer who was eager to make sure that no cadenza interrupted the musical logic of a movement is Dvořák. The cellist Hanus Wihan, who offered the composer advice during the writing of his Cello Concerto and who was one of its early performers, wrote a fifty-nine-bar cadenza for insertion at bar 461 of the last movement in the first edition. Dvořák was incensed and wrote to his publisher absolutely forbidding its inclusion.[75]

Despite the tendency of nineteenth-century composers to restrict performers, plenty of opportunities for improvised cadenzas remained. Where this was so, there was a strong expectation that performers would provide their own. Potter recommended that pianists provide their own cadenzas[76] and Beethoven refused to write one for Ries, insisting instead that he should compose one for himself.[77] One consequence of this approach was that performers of earlier concertos, notably Mozart's, wrote cadenzas that were rarely in keeping stylistically with the works into which they were inserted, and a debate about stylistic propriety occasionally ensued. For example, a performance of Mozart's Concerto K. 503 with cadenzas by Frédéric Kalkbrenner was deemed unsatisfactory because the cadenzas contrasted too much with Mozart's style[78] and the *Times* critic, writing on 21 May 1850, objected to Sigismond Thalberg's cadenzas to a Mozart concerto for the same reason.

The desire to integrate cadenzas into concertos inevitably meant that performers usually gave considerable thought beforehand to what they would play. Spohr wrote out his cadenzas in full,[79] along with many other performers and composer-performers. Whether Paganini did the same is difficult to assess. No written cadenzas by him survive and it might be assumed that he improvised them. Improvisation, however, was risky for all sorts of reasons. Spohr tells the story of the violinist Alexandre-Jean Boucher, who, at an afternoon rehearsal, instructed the orchestra how to come in at the end of his improvised cadenza. During the concert, however, Boucher's cadenza got out of hand and

> some of the gentlemen put their instruments into their cases and slipped out. This was so infectious, that in a few minutes the whole orchestra had disappeared. Horrified [at the end of the cadenza, when he discovered the problem] he stared aghast around him, and beheld all the music desks abandoned. But the public, who had already prepared themselves to see this moment arrive, burst into an uproarious laughter, in which *Boucher*, with the best stomach he could, was obliged to join.[80]

Perhaps it is safer for musicians, if less entertaining for audiences, that modern performances follow patterns that are much more set than they were in the nineteenth century.

13 The concerto in the age of recording

TIMOTHY DAY

Some indication of the best-loved concertos and those most frequently performed in the concert hall in the earlier part of the twentieth century is given by Tovey in the works he selected for his famous *Essays in Musical Analysis* which appeared in the 1930s. These were originally written as programme notes for concerts given by the Reid Orchestra in Edinburgh that he founded in 1917. Tovey included a handful of concertos by Bach including the Concerto for Two Violins in D minor and the third and fourth Brandenburg Concertos, and by Handel just the Organ Concerto, Op. 7, No. 1.[1] He selected thirteen works by Mozart including five piano concertos. There is the Cello Concerto in D major by Haydn. There are all the Beethoven concertos except the Piano Concerto in B flat, Op. 19, and all Brahms's works in the genre. There is Chopin's Piano Concerto in F minor, Op. 21, Schumann's three concertos – the Violin Concerto hadn't yet been discovered – and Mendelssohn's Violin Concerto, Op. 64. There are works by Saint-Saëns and Max Bruch and Glazunov. The twentieth-century works include Stanford's Clarinet Concerto, Elgar's Cello Concerto, Delius's Violin Concerto, and Sibelius's Violin Concerto. Tovey thinks that the number of 'great works in the true concerto form is surprisingly small; far smaller than the number of true symphonies'.[2] And yet you search in vain the early record catalogues, the pre-First World War listings, to find recordings of these comparatively few canonical masterpieces.

Around 1900 the violin concertos of Beethoven and Mendelssohn were widely considered the two greatest works ever written for the violin and orchestra, and turn-of-the-century Promenade Concert programmes described the Beethoven concerto as 'one of the noblest instrumental pieces of any kind extant'.[3] And yet before the First World War there was only one recording, and this of just the Larghetto and Rondo. Juan Manén made a recording of all three movements in 1916 on four double-sided discs. There was one recording of the slow movement of Mendelssohn's Violin Concerto issued before the First World War and one of the finale, these on either side of a twelve-inch disc. The first recording of all three movements was released in 1916, again in a performance by Juan Manén. In 1924 Eddy Brown recorded the first and third movements only with the Berlin State Opera Orchestra for Parlophone, though the same company did record the middle movement with Edith Lorand and the Blüthner-Orchester. The slow movement was available only on a separate disc, however, which meant that the subtle and beautiful transition between the first and second movements was obliterated. In 1925 Josef Wolfsthal recorded the whole work, though with just piano accompaniment. The first recording of Tchaikovsky's Violin Concerto was not made until 1924, the first recording of his First Piano Concerto not until 1926. What orchestral music was being recorded in that first quarter-century? What was selling? There were thirteen records of Rossini's 'William Tell' Overture issued up to 1925. There were more than eighty versions of Strauss's 'Blue Danube Waltz'. Why was this? Why were there so few recordings made of the most famous concertos heard frequently in concert halls in the early decades of the century, and why often just separate movements?

From its beginnings in the 1890s the recording industry needed to find a mass audience for its products. There was simply no mass market for concertos by Bach or Mozart or even by Beethoven or Tchaikovsky around 1900. For one thing these early discs were very expensive. You could go to a Promenade Concert lasting three hours at Queen's Hall in London in the 1900s for a shilling (5p).[4] The standard price for a record lasting three minutes – a single-sided twelve-inch disc – was six shillings (30p). This was at a time when the average weekly wage was £1 6s 8d (£1.33). And because of the playing length of a disc and the selling cost necessary if there was to be any return on the record company's investment, longer works had to be abbreviated. Elgar's 1916 recording of his Violin Concerto lasts about a quarter of an hour, a third of the work's actual length. The recording of Bach's Double Concerto made in 1915 by Efrem Zimbalist and Fritz Kreisler cuts thirteen bars from the slow movement in order to fit on a single side of a disc.

And until 1925 the technology allowed the capture of the sounds of only a handful of instruments. So an orchestra was always an abbreviated ensemble consisting of maybe no more than thirty players and often many fewer.[5] On that 1915 recording of Bach's Double Concerto Zimbalist and Kreisler are accompanied by a string quartet rather than a body of strings. On a recording of the same work issued in 1923 Jelly d'Aranyi and Adela Fachiri play with just piano accompaniment.[6]

The arrival of the microphone in 1925 meant that a means had been found of converting acoustic energy into electrical impulses that could then be amplified. The age of 'electrical recording' – which lasted for the next quarter of a century – allowed the capture of increasingly wide frequency ranges, and so increased fidelity on playback. The microphone also permitted the recording of musicians spread over a wide area and so the recording of the orchestra in concert hall disposition.

There were single shortened acoustic versions of each of Beethoven's Piano Concertos Nos. 4 and 5; there were eleven electrical 78rpm-disc versions of the Fourth Piano Concerto and fourteen of the 'Emperor'. There were five electrical recordings of each of Chopin's piano concertos, thirteen of Mendelssohn's Violin Concerto, fourteen of Grieg's Piano Concerto, twelve of Tchaikovsky's Violin Concerto. In the age of electrical recording the standard repertory – the most important canonical works as the cognoscenti considered them at the beginning of the century – was nearly all recorded, chopped into four- or four-and-a-half-minute bits, the sound still distorted by limited frequencies and heard through varying degrees of hiss and frequent clicks, but nonetheless performances of these works were now available to be listened to and studied by an increasing number of music-lovers and those desirous of educating themselves. (For this was the time of music appreciation.)

From the 1920s onwards though, the musical experience of large numbers of people had begun to be enlarged by broadcasting. Before broadcasting, the great works of music had been 'the private preserve of a little band of people who happened to live in the places where it could be heard, and who happened to have money enough to pay to hear it'. Now, from 1925 in Britain, as one commentator explained, it was easy to hear fine performances, and it was 'dirt-cheap'.[7]

An annual radio licence in Britain in 1930 cost 10s (50p),[8] and a wireless could be bought for £5,[9] whereas in that same year the six records of Elgar's Violin Concerto cost 39s[10] (£1.95) and the discs of Beethoven's Fourth Piano Concerto were 34s[11] (£1.70). By mid-century greater spending power, increased leisure, the formation of much bigger markets through the development of public taste by the increased provision of state education and by government subsidies towards music-making and by broadcasting had gradually created bigger audiences for 'serious' music, 'permanent' music *The World's Encyclopædia of Recorded Music* called it in 1952. But it was chiefly the extraordinary impact of the long-playing record that meant that by 1961, music had become, according to a distinguished art historian in England, 'the most precious of all shared possessions, of all sources of metaphor in our culture'.[12]

An LP in the 1950s could last forty minutes, twenty minutes each side, and later LPs sometimes contained an hour's music. And they cost about £2. By the end of the decade many discs cost nearer £1 and in the 1960s there were further reductions by the cheaper classical labels. This was a decade when prices rose 49 per cent, but as average pay doubled, real income rose about 30 per cent.[13] The discs were of longer duration but also easier to handle and the sound-quality of the LP was much higher, and because of the introduction of magnetic tape and cheaper disc-pressing, an enormous investment in costly manufacturing equipment was no longer required to set up a record company. A great number of new labels suddenly appeared. In England there was Nixa and Argo and Delysé and Saga. In North America there were about a dozen record companies publishing classical music on 78rpm discs after the war; by January 1952 the *Schwann Long Playing Record Catalog* was listing over seventy companies issuing classical music, prominent among which were Westminster, Haydn Society, Lyrichord, Concert Hall Society, Period, Urania, Vox and Vanguard.

On many of these discs manufactured in the UK and in North America the performers were from continental Europe. Vox used conductors like Walther Davisson, one-time Director of the Hochschule für Musik at Frankfurt-am-Main, and Heinrich Hollreiser, conductor after the war of the Vienna State Opera, and Jascha Horenstein, who had been forced out of Germany – out of his post as director of the Düsseldorf Opera – by the Nazis. The chief reasons for the record companies using these performers – the English companies and the American ones too, as well as those in continental Europe – were economic. These men were cheaper than Toscanini or Beecham or Furtwängler. Many of the discs they recorded were made in Vienna. The exchange rates were favourable and Viennese musicians were unemployed or under-employed. The Vienna Symphony Orchestra had established a recording studio, 'Symphonia', at the end of 1948 to promote the employment of its orchestra and this studio became the recording site first for Ultraphon (Supraphon), then for Vox, Haydn Society, Westminster, Vanguard and the Society of Participating Artists – SPA – and other labels too. Alfred Brendel was telegrammed in Graz just before Christmas in 1954 and asked by SPA if he would record Prokofiev's Fifth Piano Concerto in January. The company were eager to issue the first LP of this concerto. Certainly, he said, and would they please send him the score since he'd never played the work in his life. This would be Brendel's very first disc.[14]

So what was heard on this new flood of recordings? Which concertos were being issued? The recording made in April 1958 of Tchaikovsky's Piano Concerto No. 1 played by Van Cliburn, winner of the First Prize in the First International Tchaikovsky Competition in Moscow the previous month, became the world's top-selling classical LP of its time, selling two million copies by 1965, and two-and-a-half million by 1970.[15] The disc sold because this was Tchaikovsky, but it sold too because it was played by an executant whose meteoric rise to stardom had been attended by worldwide publicity feeding off the tensions of Cold War rivalries. For the twentieth century had seen living composers displaced as the most famous musicians of the day by opera singers, conductors and instrumental virtuosos. Executants were the musical heroes of mass audiences.

For really big sales, it was the concertos by the canonical great composers and for the biggest sales of all, the handful of great Romantic warhorses by Beethoven, Brahms, Tchaikovsky, Rachmaninov and Max Bruch.

In January 2000 there were 105 CDs of Beethoven's Violin Concerto on sale in England, and also eight audio-cassettes, two video cassettes, one laserdisc, and two LPs. These were performances by fifty solo violinists. Some players had different performances available; many performances were issued on different CDs. Kyung Wha Chung was represented by two recorded versions, each issued on three different CDs. Jascha Heifetz could be bought playing with the NBC Symphony Orchestra under Toscanini in 1940, with the New York Philharmonic Symphony Orchestra in 1945, and with the Boston Symphony Orchestra under Charles Munch in 1955. That was one of the most striking aspects of commercial recordings at the end of the twentieth century. Not only were there CDs of Thomas Zehetmair in 1997 and Hilary Hahn in 1998; digital technology and sound-restoration techniques had created at least a small market for recordings made decades before. Kreisler is on the list with a 1926 recording with the Berlin State Opera Orchestra and one from 1936 with the London Philharmonic Orchestra. The same company, Biddulph, specializing in issuing old violin recordings, was selling at that time recordings of Beethoven's Violin Concerto played by Wolfsthal in 1925, Kreisler in 1926, and Enescu in 1948.[16] So with the Mendelssohn Violin Concerto: there were sixty-three soloists on 110 CDs, seven audio-cassettes, three LPs. There were four performances by Yehudi Menuhin on nine CDs. There was Maria Bachmann in 1997, and Robert McDuffie and Isabelle van Keulen in 1998, but there was also Kreisler in 1926 and 1935 and Szigeti in 1933.[17]

Larger markets meant that now, in the second half of the century, the greatest composers' works were recorded in *intégrales*, the complete output of a composer in a particular genre. In 1951 *The Record Guide* was sure that all Mozart's piano concertos 'deserve to be recorded; and, at one time or another, no fewer than sixteen of them have been available on the English lists'. It had been disheartening to see 'magnificent recordings by such artists as Schnabel, Gieseking, Fischer and Landowska vanish from the catalogues year after year for want of support'.[18] In the last decade of the century there were at least six sets of all the piano concertos available and often more, and in January 2000 complete series by Barenboim, Brendel, Schiff, Perahia, Bilson, Levin, Ashkenazy, Jandó and Shelley. In the UK that same month there were sixty-three CDs of the Piano Concerto K. 595, one audio-cassette, one laserdisc, and one VHS video cassette, which constituted performances by thirty-eight pianists, who included Schnabel and Gieseking.[19]

The small number of concertos written in the second half of the twentieth century that might be said to have entered the canon, works like, for example, the cello and piano concertos of Lutosławski, John Adams's Violin Concerto, the viola concertos of Gubaidulina and Schnittke, Ligeti's Piano Concerto, and Oliver Knussen's Horn Concerto, have indeed been commercially recorded, at least once. But this represents a small demonstration of re-creative energy compared with, say, the evidence of the 200 interpretations of Vivaldi's 'Four Seasons' that were recorded in the same period. Not only did musicians strive to imitate the exact performing forces and styles of Vivaldi's time; they also recorded arrangements of these four concertos with the solo part taken by a flute, a recorder and a trombone, and in versions in which the whole musical argument was carried by a guitar trio, a brass ensemble, a flute ensemble, a percussion ensemble, by five marimbas and by a synthesizer.[20] In 1941 Aaron Copland had the impression that audiences seemed to think that the endless repetition of a small body of entrenched masterworks was all that was required for 'a ripe musical culture'. He recognized the masterpieces for what they were but was sure that this preoccupation with the past stifled the endeavour of contemporary composers.[21] The second half of the century only emphasized this trend. Recordings of concertos certainly gave evidence of the almost hypnotic contemplation of the art of previous eras as a defining element in late twentieth-century Western culture.

Increasingly during the second half of the century concertos began to be recorded that had never been performed in concert halls, or had been unperformed for decades, or hundreds of years. In the 1970s the American pianist Michael Ponti made a substantial series of recordings for Vox of concertos by such nineteenth-century composers as Bronsart von Schellendorf, Hermann Goetz and Bernhard Stavenhagen. And in the 1980s and 90s the English independent label Hyperion explored a similar repertory in *The Romantic Piano Concerto Series* with works by composers who included Moszkowski, Paderewski, Bortkiewicz, d'Albert, Sauer, Parry and Stanford, Holbrooke and Haydn Wood, Vianna da Motta, Litolff, Moscheles and Donald Tovey, whose Piano Concerto in A minor, Op. 15, was included. But even more were earlier repertories explored by the smaller record companies. Vox was the first new American record label established after the war. It published a number of 78rpm discs – in July 1946 Klemperer recorded the Brandenburg Concertos for the label, his first records since 1931 – but it achieved a much higher profile with the coming of the LP. Vox issued the Brandenburgs again in performances directed by Jascha Horenstein as well as Handel organ concertos and concertos by Vivaldi, but there were also works by Geminiani, Locatelli, Manfredini and Albinoni. The label marked Arcangelo Corelli's 300th anniversary in 1953 with the first complete recording of his *Concerti grossi*, Op. 6. Dean Eckertson conducted the 'Corelli Tri-Centenary String Orchestra', members in fact of Toscanini's NBC Symphony Orchestra.[22]

There was only a single acoustic recording of one of Bach's Brandenburg Concertos, No. 3 in G major, and in the second quarter of the century there were nine versions of the complete set and fourteen of the most recorded, No. 4. But then the deluge. In September 1932 HMV released records of the Chamber Orchestra of the Ecole Normale of Paris playing the Third Brandenburg Concerto. The next month Columbia released the same work played by the British Symphony Orchestra. How could you choose between them? The French orchestra were on two 10-inch discs; the British orchestra on one 12-inch disc. The French cost 8s (40p), the British 6s (30p). How did you balance cost against performance against the prospect of getting out of the chair to turn the records twice or four times? One reviewer found this exasperating and thought the public had a right to grumble.[23] Twenty years later a reviewer reported that Brandenburgs were continuing to 'pour out'.[24]

In the first decade or so of the LP, Decca issued the Brandenburg Concertos played by the Stuttgart Chamber Orchestra and Münchinger, HMV the Bath Festival Orchestra and Menuhin, Columbia issued Klemperer and the Philharmonia, and Philips the Netherlands Chamber Orchestra and Goldberg. But on the small labels there was the Philomusica on L'Oiseau-Lyre and the Hamburg Chamber Orchestra on Saga; Vox put out first an instrumental ensemble conducted by Horenstein and then the Mainz Chamber Orchestra, Nixa put out the London Baroque Ensemble, Fontana put out the Stuttgart Soloists, Nonesuch released the Chamber Orchestra of the Saar, and Top Rank issued the Chamber Ensemble of the Vienna State Opera Orchestra. Deutsche Grammophon was another major label to put out a version. This was the Schola Cantorum Basiliensis under August Weinzinger, but it wasn't on their main label. It was on Archiv Produktion, the 'History of Music Division of the Deutsche Grammophon Gesellschaft'. The recording of earlier repertories had been given a great stimulus by the creation of this new specialist label, whose aim was to 'demonstrate by means of stylistically authentic performances' ('in grundlegenden Interpretationen') important landmarks in the history of music prior to the Classical period. But there were commercial reasons too for such a strategy. After the Second World War the company had faced the difficulty that some performers they would otherwise wish to engage had been tainted by Nazi associations, and some foreign artists wouldn't wish to record for a German company at that time. By using comparatively few German musicians who had begun pioneering historic performing practices before the war, men like the harpsichordist Fritz Neumeyer, the flautist Gustav Scheck, and Weinzinger, the viola da gamba player, the company was able to create a substantial and distinctive catalogue of recordings quite swiftly. Its first discs, made in September 1947, were of Bach's organ music played by Helmut Walcha on an instrument that had survived wartime destruction, the 1636 Stellwagen organ in St Jakobi's Church at Lübeck.[25] The discs were issued with lavish documentation which included details on the editions used, the sources of manuscripts, the makers and dates of the instruments being played. The LP covers and the sumptuous linen-bound boxed sets were sober and severe affairs, like library collected editions, with the composer and the works receiving prominence, not the performers: 'Research Period VIII: The Italian Settecento; Series A: The Concerto'.[26] Early on there were no notes on the performers at all, certainly no sleeve photographs of smiling soloist with carnation in button-hole, or pictures of the virtuoso's hands poised high above the keyboard, as was common on other labels at this time.

Archiv Produktion was deliberately aiming at a different market; it had a different purpose, its discs themselves envisaged as having 'high value as products of historical research'.[27] This could not fail to have an effect on the production and presentation of recordings by other labels. In March 1954 Vox began to issue a 'deluxe' series, of which its Brandenburg Concertos with Horenstein was an early example, with a reduced reprint of Boosey & Hawkes editions of the scores and a set of notes by Emanuel Winternitz, Curator of Ancient Instruments at the New York Metropolitan Museum of Art.[28]

But the Archiv performances were setting standards and changing tastes too. The soloists on the Vox set of Brandenburg Concertos were excellent; the critics recognized this. But the performances were 'not very enjoyable'; they plodded; they were earnest; they were 'determined'; they were ponderous; they sounded 'unimaginative'.[29] They disappointed by the side of the Archiv performances, and the reason seemed to be that Weinzinger had at his disposal 'an exceptionally well-trained group of musicians, conversant not only with the special technique required to play old instruments, but also with the manner of performing the music; that is, the realisation of its frequently unwritten phrasing, ornaments and rhythms'.[30] Soon Archiv were emphasizing that, quite apart from the 'scientific significance' of these recordings of the past, the works they were rescuing had an aesthetic value and were 'of engrossing interest to all music lovers'.[31]

Earlier in the century when the canon was relatively small and circumscribed, a distinguished English pedagogue pointed out that the 'immense superiority' of the concertos of Bach and Handel over such 'pioneers' as

Corelli and Vivaldi was clear if they were compared mentally. (Though it would have been 'ungracious' not to give them passing mention.[32]) Mental comparisons were no longer necessary though. Now you could listen not only to the concertos of Corelli and Vivaldi but to those of Giuseppe Torelli who continued working in this genre in Bologna after Corelli left for Rome. You could listen to the concertos of Corelli's pupils like Giovanni Mossi and Geminiani, and to Giuseppe Valentini who may well have studied with him also. By the early 1960s, there in the record catalogues were concertos by Bonporti, Boccherini, Telemann, Jean-Marie Leclair, Baldassare Galuppi, Mauro Giuliani, Pietro Nardini and Georg Monn. And soon afterwards you could listen to concertos by masters generally considered less eminent: Francesco Barsanti, for example, whose career, after modest success in Scotland in the 1730s and 1740s, ended rather obscurely as a viola player in London orchestras; and there was Revd Richard Mudge, better known in Warwickshire in the middle of the eighteenth century for his interesting sermons than for his concertos.

'*Floreat Vivaldi!*' exclaimed one reviewer in 1953: 'The cry goes up from busy little studios all over Europe and the New World, wherever a few string players can be gathered together'.[33] The first recording of Vivaldi's 'Four Seasons', in Bernardino Molinari's transcription, was issued in 1942 on six double-sided 78rpm discs. The second performance was issued in 1949 on six 78rpm discs and also on an LP performed by Louis Kaufman and a string orchestra conducted by Henry Swoboda. In 1956 alone there were four different LP versions of the 'Four Seasons' issued; there were five released in 1959, and five more new ones in 1968, and six in 1969, and nine in 1970.[34] Even then, even in 1970, it could still be very profitable: a performance by the Academy of St Martin-in-the-Fields was issued that year on the English Argo label and by 1978 it had sold over 300,000 copies.[35]

Why was it possible to record so many Baroque concertos? Why did this music sell in such large quantities? It was not considered outrageously difficult to perform; at least until the early music movement demanded special competencies of performers, it was well within the abilities of a great many orchestras of only local or regional renown. It was new: even the Brandenburg Concertos were not widely performed in concerts. Many of these Baroque concertos were not known in performance even by specialists. They spoke with such vigour and exhilarating rhythmic exuberance and a kind of inner propulsion. They possessed extravagant melodiousness, though they were clear and clean and unsentimental; they demonstrated adventurous harmonies without melodrama. They established a mood, an *Affekt*. They could be accommodated comfortably in domestic settings. They could be listened to on and off, and recordings of music of this nature and style did indeed become characterized as the 'muzak of the intelligentsia'.[36]

What did this vast archive of performance show about the general character as well as the details of performing styles over ten decades? In what ways had performances of the most frequently played concertos changed during the twentieth century? Tempos were steadier – tempo fluctuations less marked – at the end of the century. That is one of the most striking features. There are no changes of tempo indicated in the first fifty bars of the first movement of Beethoven's Violin Concerto and late twentieth-century recorded performances generally don't make many. The opening speed of the 2002 recording of the work by Viktoria Mullova[37] is $\bm{\mathsterling} = 100$; the vehement full orchestra outburst between bars 28 and 41 moves between $\bm{\mathsterling} = 98$ and 102, and the broad lyrical second subject at bar 43 is at $\bm{\mathsterling} = 108$. Compare this with a 1932 recording by Szigeti in which the performance opens at $\bm{\mathsterling} = 96$; between bars 28 and 41 the tempo reaches $\bm{\mathsterling} = 132$ and between bars 43 and 50 slows to $\bm{\mathsterling} = 112$.[38] These different kinds of tempo fluctuation are entirely characteristic of their epochs. From time to time Szigeti inadvertently brushes against strings – his playing is not impeccable – but to some listeners such squeaks and twangs may contribute to the expressiveness of the performance; they contribute a sense of strain, of strenuousness, which need not be out of place, a sense of total engagement, perhaps, mind, body and spirit. High points of phrases are lingered over; a sudden outburst is rushed – it *has* to be rushed, the listener feels. A crescendo is frequently combined with an accelerando. The phrasing, articulation and ensemble of Mullova and the Orchestre Romantique et Révolutionnaire are breathtakingly co-ordinated and exquisitely consistent. It is an almost superhuman achievement, only possible because of a multitude of social, economic, aesthetic and educational factors and not least because of the kind of detailed, objective, analytical listening that recordings made possible. It is difficult to imagine that its accomplishment would not always be recognized. Which is not to say that its particular kind of expressivity would have been admired in all epochs or indeed by all music-lovers at any time. A century before, Parry considered that the particular expressivity of the horn derived in part from its 'human fallibility'.[39]

The Mullova/Eliot Gardiner interpretation is a very literal one, accurate, correct, neutral. The performers have striven to discover all the facts about which it is possible to be certain. The conductor and the soloist prepared for the recording, the liner-note reassures us, by consulting the original scores which led them 'to incorporate a number of alternative or original readings in their interpretations of both [the Beethoven and the

Mendelssohn] concertos'.[40] In their literalness these interpretations are exceedingly characteristic of the later decades of the twentieth century, and in all their detailed nuances clearly unlike any of a century ago. It seems equally unlikely that today's interpretations resemble closely any heard in the composers' lifetimes.

This would not have concerned a performer like Wanda Landowska (1879–1959), a pianist and harpsichordist whose playing was animated by aesthetic principles and attitudes developed before the First World War. She explained her attitude towards the composer of an earlier period very clearly: 'You gave birth to it; it is beautiful. But now leave me alone with it. You have nothing more to say; go away!'[41] Landowska took the tradition as she found it and then looked within herself to unlock the mysterious force and energy, a kind of Bergsonian *élan vital*, with which succeeding generations have surrounded great musical works. In the last performance she gave of Mozart's Piano Concerto in E flat, K. 482, in a concert on 2 December 1945 there is a kind of palpitating directness as she embellishes in a highly individual and idiosyncratic way.[42]

This performance makes a dramatic comparison with a recording of this work made in November 1959 by the French pianist Robert Casadesus.[43] Casadesus was held by many in mid-century to be an ideal interpreter of Mozart and his recordings of some of the concertos made with George Szell in the 1950s considered to be models of their kind, their kind being clear, uncluttered, straightforward and cool. His interpretation is as straight and unadorned as the severe pages of the 1961 *Urtext* edition of the work. Malcolm Bilson's 1987 performance of this work[44] on a fortepiano is highly ornamented – like Landowska's – but this is the result of an attempt to reproduce eighteenth-century performing styles from the evidence of pedagogic treatises, autograph examples of ornamentation, descriptions of performances, and embellished versions of Mozart's compositions published after his death by distinguished contemporaries.

Landowska uses the text as a starting-point for her interpretation, endeavouring to 'penetrate the spirit' of the composer. The coolness of Casadesus is not the result of an impersonal positivism and literalism but of a very definite and clear neo-classical aesthetic; he was regarded as a model interpreter of Ravel as well as Mozart. Bilson sets his instincts against historical details in order to make an old work new and strange. Scrupulous transcription of the notes actually heard on these records would reveal nothing of the underlying aims and objectives and attitudes of the performers and their worlds. Recordings don't answer important questions about the history of music. But they do stimulate the formulation of new kinds of interesting questions.

Changing performing styles are perhaps most marked and the factors moulding the changes most clearly perceived in the Baroque repertory. Recordings document an ever-growing perception of the need for textural clarity and transparency. As early as 1933 the solo strings of the Pro Arte String Quartet recorded Vivaldi's A major Concerto in *L'estro armonico*.[45] Through recordings the introduction can be followed of terraced dynamics, the sudden changing of dynamic levels thought in mid-century to be particularly idiomatic, and later a relaxation of this rather relentless jagged cubist notion for something more fluid and subtle. The growth of ornamentation can be heard. A virtually unornamented performance of Vivaldi's Concerto in D major RV 428 ('Il Gardellino') recorded by the flautist Ludwig Pfersmann and the Chamber Orchestra of the Vienna State Opera Chamber Orchestra and released in 1954[46] may sound curiously flat and uninspired to listeners who were beguiled by the imaginatively embellished playing of the post-war generation of specialist recorder-players like Frans Brüggen and Bernard Krainis. In the 1970s and 1980s the record industry had made possible the development of a great number of period orchestras and certainly a consensual approach could be observed, light textures, fleet tempos, slightly mannered rhetorical gestures, in such groups as the Academy of Ancient Music, the English Concert, the Amsterdam Baroque Orchestra and the Drottningholm Baroque Ensemble.

Performances in the 1970s that attempted to re-create eighteenth-century performing styles were sometimes regarded at the time – and have been regarded increasingly since – as inhibited, careful and merely correct presentations of the notes on the page rather than true performances. But the recording studio was able to provide the opportunities for players to make new technical and expressive techniques their own and to acquire the kind of natural mastery that allows personal expressivity and musical abandon to enliven the tradition in their own ways.

After a century of recording, music-lovers could listen to a huge number of concertos, a far larger number than those frequently performed in the concert hall. At the same time it was possible to compare dozens of interpretations of the most famous works. In the middle of the century – before the age of the long-playing disc – it was still possible for pedagogues and 'appreciationists' to insist that you should listen to Beethoven's Violin Concerto, not X's or Y's interpretations of that work. The chief conductor of the summer Promenade Concerts in London was sure that the young enthusiasts who made up an important component of his audience came 'not to judge between this performance or that, not to listen to slight defects in the playing, not that [they] may be able to discourse learnedly on some small piece of interpretation'. They came, he said, to enjoy the music and to find spiritual solace in it, and they were right to do so.[47]

But the producers of LPs and CDs, for sound commercial reasons, emphasized the performance rather than the work, and the fidelity of recording technology in the second half of the century encouraged unrelenting textural accuracy – and the expectation of it in some listeners at least – and the most detailed appreciation of timbre and nuance. A reviewer in 1993 pointed out that two recordings of a Handel organ concerto fail to follow the autograph manuscript and follow an incorrect early printed source in playing two wrong notes in the soloist's left-hand part. The same reviewer questions both contemporary performing fashions and scholarly orthodoxy that lead performers in a recorded performance to approach all but the shortest trills in Handel's instrumental works with a long appoggiatura from above.[48] Another reviewer questions the use of copies of fortepianos by Anton Walter for a set of Mozart piano concertos. Instruments by this maker were certainly played by Mozart, but they have already been employed in a number of recordings. Isn't this producing 'a standardized, modern Mozart-fortepiano sound' when eighteenth-century fortepianos were remarkable for their variety of sound-quality? Why could not an instrument by Johann Andreas Stein have been used, at least for the 'Coronation' Concerto, K. 537 – 'Mozart did, after all, play on a Stein in Frankfurt on 15th October 1790'.[49]

Such concerns might be regarded as evidence that the state of affairs feared by Vaughan Williams fifty years earlier had indeed come about, that a preoccupation with the precise realization and the exact sonorities of old music would lead to the creation of an audience of specialists, connoisseurs of the most minute inflections in articulation, artificially revived and only distinguished and admired by a handful of *cognoscenti* when the great masterpieces of music should be presented, as he put it in a famous phrase, 'to everyone – not only to the aesthete, the musicologist or the propagandist, but above all to Whitman's "Divine Average"'.[50]

An interviewer of Alfred Brendel referred to the 'absurd variety' of recorded interpretations available today. In fact, neither performer nor listener who enjoys the privilege of being involved with great music, Brendel thought, need take fright at this diversity. Both will simply make up their own minds on the force and beauty of particular performances.[51] The superabundance of recordings may be a sign of impending economic disaster but it is also evidence of the stupendous creative energy in music-making in at least some areas of musical life in the later decades of the twentieth century. This legacy of a century of recordings offers opportunities for attempting to understand the economic conditions in which music flourished and of the way in which such conditions came about. But what is important about a work of art is the value-judgement we make about it, our efforts to discover meanings. All such value-judgements must inevitably be subjective. They tell us little about the work of art itself, but a lot about the listeners making the judgements, including ourselves. Recordings will enable historians to examine these changing sounds and the changing metaphors used in describing these sounds and so to understand better their significance in the individual lives and in the tribal identities of the men and women who loved this music in the twentieth century.

Notes

Introduction

1 See *Classic Morecambe and Wise, Volume Two*, VHS RDV 087–847/2 (Watershed Pictures, 1990). Born Eric Bartholomew in 1926, the comedian subsequently changed his last name to that of his home town and with Ernie Wise formed one of UK television's most successful and highly acclaimed double acts. A statue of Morecambe – unveiled in 1999 fifteen years after his death – now adorns the seafront in the northern English town of Morecambe, Lancashire.

1 Theories of the concerto from the eighteenth century to the present day

1 As given in Hélène Jourdan-Morhange and Vlado Perlemuter, *Ravel According to Ravel*, trans. Frances Tanner, ed. Harold Taylor (London, 1970), p. 87.

2 Bonavia, 'The Violin Concerto', *ML*, 8 (1927), pp. 18–19 (Beethoven Issue).

3 Quoted in John Rink, *Chopin: the Piano Concertos* (Cambridge, 1997), p. 19.

4 See, for example, Konrad Küster's recent book, *Das Konzert: Form und Forum der Virtuosität* (Kassel, 1993). Although he addresses a wide range of issues relating to the concerto genre, a large proportion of his study concerns formal and structural matters (as well as thematic working) in eighteenth-, nineteenth- and twentieth-century works.

5 See Sulzer (ed.), *Allgemeine Theorie die schönen Künste* (4 vols., Leipzig, 1771–74; reprint Hildesheim, 1969), vol. 1, p. 573, vol. 3, p. 432; Koch, *Versuch einer Anleitung zur Composition* (3 vols., Rudolstadt, 1782–93), vol. 2, p. 37, as given in Nancy Kovaleff Baker and Thomas Christensen (ed. and trans.), *Aesthetics and the Art of Musical Composition in the German Enlightenment: Selected Writings of Johann Georg Sulzer and Heinrich Christoph Koch* (Cambridge, 1995), p. 193; Triest, 'Remarks on the Development of the Art of Music in Germany in the 18th Century', trans. Susan Gillespie, in Elaine Sisman (ed.), *Haydn and His World* (Princeton, 1997), p. 370.

6 See Katharine Ellis, *Music Criticism in Nineteenth-Century France: 'La Revue et Gazette musicale de Paris', 1834–1880* (Cambridge, 1995), p. 164; Rink, *Chopin: the Piano Concertos*, p. 27; and Leon B. Plantinga,

Schumann as Critic (New Haven, 1967), pp. 157, 205. For a description of Schumann's castigation of virtuosos in general, not limited to concerto practitioners, see Plantinga, *Schumann as Critic*, pp. 196–218. For Heinrich Heine's engaging satire of virtuosos, whose 'day-long reputation . . . evaporates and dies away empty, without a trace, like a camel's wind in the desert', see Heine, 'Musical Season of 1844', given in Harry Haskell (ed.), *The Attentive Listener: Three Centuries of Music Criticism* (Princeton, 1996), pp. 115–20 (with quoted material on p. 119).

7 See Sulzer (ed.), *Allgemeine Theorie*, vol. 3, p. 432, and Koch, *Musikalisches Lexikon* (Frankfurt, 1802; reprint Hildesheim, 1964), col. 352; Rochlitz, 'Difference of Opinion about Works of Music' (1799), in Haskell (ed.), *The Attentive Listener*, p. 67; Davidson, 'A Leonine Virtuoso' (1858), in Haskell (ed.), *The Attentive Listener*, p. 130.

8 Davidson, 'Leonine Virtuoso', in Haskell (ed.), *The Attentive Listener*, p. 130.

9 Heinrich Christoph Koch, *Introductory Essay on Composition: the Mechanical Rules of Melody, Sections 3 and 4* (1787–93), trans. Nancy Kovaleff Baker (New Haven and London, 1983), p. 209.

10 Plantinga, *Schumann as Critic*, p. 204. For a different translation of this passage, see Konrad Wolff (ed.), *Schumann on Music and Musicians*, trans. Paul Rosenfeld (New York, 1946), p. 64.

11 Ellis, *Music Criticism in Nineteenth-Century France*, p. 166.

12 See Plantinga, *Schumann as Critic*, p. 157, and Glenn Gould, 'The Prospects of Recording' (1966), in Richard Kostelanetz and Joseph Darby (eds.), *Classic Essays on Twentieth-Century Music: a Continuing Symposium* (New York, 1996), p. 59. Tovey's, Carter's and Kerman's references to dialogue are discussed below.

13 Dahlhaus, *Nineteenth-Century Music*, trans. J. Bradford Robinson (Berkeley, 1989), p. 141.

14 *AmZ*, 3 (1800–01), cols. 28–9.

15 Ellis, *Music Criticism in Nineteenth-Century France*, pp. 166, 167.

16 For discussion of the confusing etymology of the word 'concerto', see Erich Reimer,

'Concerto/Konzert', in Hans Heinrich Eggebrecht (ed.), *Handwörterbuch der Musikalischen Terminologie* (Stuttgart, 1972–), vol. 1, pp. 1–17, and Siegfried Kross, 'Concerto – Concertare und Conserere', in Carl Dahlhaus (ed.), *Bericht über den internationalen musikwissenschaftlichen Kongress Leipzig 1966* (Kassel, 1970), pp. 216–20.

17 See Michael Talbot, *Vivaldi* (London, 1978), p. 139, and Ernest C. Harris (ed. and trans.), *Johann Mattheson's 'Der vollkommene Capellmeister': a Revised Translation with Critical Commentary* (Ann Arbor, MI, 1981), p. 467.

18 Walther, *Musikalisches Lexikon oder musikalische Bibliothek* (Leipzig, 1732), p. 179.

19 Kollmann, *An Essay on Practical Musical Composition* (London, 1799; reprint New York, 1973), p. 20.

20 Quantz, *Versuch einer Anweisung die Flöte traversiere zu spielen* (1752), trans. Edward R. Reilly as *On Playing the Flute* (New York, 1966), pp. 270, 280; Koch, *Introductory Essay*, p. 209.

21 Malcolm Macdonald, *The Master Musicians: Brahms* (London, 1990), p. 268, and Ellis, *Music Criticism in Nineteenth-Century France*, p. 168.

22 Given in John Warrack, *Tchaikovsky* (London, 1973), p. 164.

23 Warrack, *Carl Maria von Weber* (Cambridge, 1976), p. 147.

24 John Daverio, *Robert Schumann: Herald of a 'New Poetic Age'* (Oxford, 1997), p. 468; Jan Smaczny, *Dvořák: Cello Concerto* (Cambridge, 1999), p. 89.

25 See Kerman, *Concerto Conversations* (Cambridge, MA, 1999), pp. 61–82. For more on this topic, see Chapter 10 of this volume.

26 Given in Alistair Wightmann, *Karol Szymanowski: His Life and Work* (Aldershot and Brookfield, VT, 1999), p. 177.

27 Cooper, *Bartók: Concerto for Orchestra* (Cambridge, 1996), p. 21.

28 From Robin Stowell, *Beethoven: Violin Concerto* (Cambridge, 1998), p. 60.

29 Erik Tawarststjerna, *Sibelius, vol. 1, 1865–1905*, trans. Robert Layton (London, 1976), p. 280.

30 Dahlhaus, *Nineteenth-Century Music*, p. 141.

31 Czerny, *School of Practical Composition: Complete Treatise on the Composition of all Kinds of Music* (1848), trans. John Bishop (New York, 1979), p. 77; Tovey, 'The Classical Concerto' (1903), in *Essays in Musical Analysis: vol. 3, Concertos and Choral Works* (7th edition, London, 1981), pp. 16, 9; Tawarststjerna, *Sibelius, vol. 1*, p. 280.

32 Additional examples to those cited in this paragraph can be found in Chapter 9 of this volume, 'The Concerto Since 1945'.

33 Bryan Gilliam, *The Life of Richard Strauss* (Cambridge, 1999), p. 155; James Pritchett, *The Music of John Cage* (Cambridge, 1993), p. 62.

34 Losseff, 'The Piano Concertos and Sonata for Two Pianos and Percussion', in Amanda Bayley (ed.), *The Cambridge Companion to Bartok* (Cambridge, 2001), p. 125.

35 Jonathan Bernard (ed.), *Elliott Carter: Collected Essays and Lectures, 1937–1995* (Rochester, NY, 1997), pp. 251, 230.

36 Tovey, *Concertos and Choral Works*, pp. 6–7.

37 *Ibid.*, p. 6.

38 *Ibid.*, pp. 9, 10.

39 For Bach, see Susan McClary, 'The Blasphemy of Talking Politics in Bach Year', in McClary and Richard Leppert (eds.), *Music and Society: the Politics of Composition, Performance and Reception* (Cambridge, 1987), pp. 13–62; and Michael Marissen, *The Social and Religious Designs of J. S. Bach's Brandenburg Concertos* (Princeton, 1995). For Mozart, see Charles Rosen, *The Classical Style* (New York, 1971), pp. 185–263; McClary, 'A Musical Dialectic from the Enlightenment: Mozart's *Piano Concerto in G Major, K. 453*, Movement 2', *Cultural Critique*, 5 (1986), pp. 129–69; Joseph Kerman, 'Mozart's Piano Concertos and their Audience', in James M. Morris (ed.), *On Mozart* (Cambridge, 1994), pp. 151–68; and Simon P. Keefe, *Mozart's Piano Concertos: Dramatic Dialogue in the Age of Enlightenment* (Woodbridge and Rochester, NY, 2001).

40 Koch, *Introductory Essay*, p. 209, and *Musikalisches Lexikon* (Frankfurt, 1802; reprint Hildesheim, 1964), col. 854. Koch cites Mozart's piano concertos as paradigmatic examples of dramatic dialogue between the soloist and the orchestra in the *Musikalisches Lexikon*.

41 Kerman, 'Mozart's Piano Concertos and their Audience', p. 153; McClary, 'A Musical Dialectic', p. 138.

42 Kerman, 'Mozart's Piano Concertos and their Audience', pp. 165–8.

43 *Ibid.*, p. 167.

44 Keefe, *Mozart's Piano Concertos*, pp. 75–100.

45 McClary, 'A Musical Dialectic', p. 147.

46 *Ibid.*, p. 151.

47 For more on McClary's article, and an alternative reading of interaction in K. 453/ii, see Keefe, *Mozart's Piano Concertos*, pp. 159–61. Harold Powers also tackles

McClary's interpretation of this movement in 'Reading Mozart's Music: Text and Topic, Syntax and Sense', *Current Musicology*, 57 (1995), pp. 5–43.

48 Kerman, *Concerto Conversations* (Cambridge, MA, 1999).

49 *Ibid.*, pp. 23, 24, 41.

50 *Ibid.*, p. 50. For the Tchaikovsky discussion, see pp. 52–8.

51 Koch, *Introductory Essay*, pp. 210–13, and *Musikalisches Lexikon*, cols. 354–5.

52 See Leeson and Levin, 'On the Authenticity of K. Anh. C14.01 (297b), a Symphonia Concertante for Four Winds and Orchestra', *Mozart-Jahrbuch 1976/77*, pp. 70–96.

53 For a detailed account of the changing nature of writings on concerto form in the nineteenth century, including discussion of Czerny, Marx and Prout, see Jane R. Stevens, 'Theme, Harmony and Texture in Classic-Romantic Descriptions of Concerto First-Movement Form', *JAMS*, 27 (1974), pp. 25–60.

54 Quantz, *On Playing the Flute*, p. 311. For discussion on Riepel, see Scott L. Balthazar, 'Intellectual History and Concepts of the Concerto: Some Parallels from 1750 to 1850', *JAMS*, 36 (1983), p. 51.

55 From Balthazar, 'Concepts of the Concerto', p. 51.

56 Kollmann, *Essay*, p. 21.

57 Koch, *Introductory Essay*, p. 211.

58 *Ibid.*, p. 209.

59 Tovey, *Concertos*, p. 9.

60 *Ibid.*, p. 7.

61 Rosen, *Classical Style*, pp. 233, 197.

62 Tovey, *Concertos*, p. 17; Rosen, *Classical Style*, pp. 197, 196.

63 See Stevens, 'Theme, Harmony and Texture'.

64 Given in Baker and Christensen (ed., and trans.), *Aesthetics and the Art of Composition in the German Enlightenment*, p. 175.

65 Kollmann, *Essay*, p. 21.

66 Implied by Stevens in 'Theme, Harmony and Texture', p. 58.

67 Karol Berger, 'Toward a History of Hearing: the Classic Concerto, a Sample Case', in Wye Jamison Allanbrook, Janet M. Levy and William P. Mahrt (eds.), *Convention in Eighteenth- and Nineteenth-Century Music: Essays in Honor of Leonard Ratner* (Stuyvesant, NY, 1992), pp. 414, 421. See also Berger, 'The First-Movement Punctuation Form in Mozart's Piano Concertos', in Neal Zaslaw (ed.), *Mozart's Piano Concertos: Text, Context, Interpretation* (Ann Arbor, MI, 1996), pp. 239–59.

2 The concerto and society

1 Christopher Small, *Musicking: The Meanings of Performing and Listening* (Hanover and London, 1988). For a similar perspective, see also Howard S. Becker, *Art Worlds* (Berkeley and London, 1982).

2 Tia DeNora, *After Adorno: Rethinking Music Sociology* (Cambridge, 2003) and 'Musical Practice and Social Structure: a Toolkit', in Eric Clarke and Nicholas Cook (eds.), *Empirical Musicology* (Oxford, 2004), pp. 35–56.

3 Christoph Wolff, 'Instrumental Music', in Wolff *et al.*, *The New Grove Bach Family* (London, 1980), p. 156.

4 *Ibid.*, p. 157.

5 Susan McClary, 'The Blasphemy of Talking Politics During Bach Year', in Richard Leppert and McClary (eds.), *Music and Society: the Politics of Composition, Performance and Reception* (Cambridge, 1987), pp. 13–62.

6 *Ibid.*, p. 19.

7 *Ibid.*, pp. 22, 23.

8 *Ibid.*, p. 24.

9 *Ibid.*, p. 32.

10 *Ibid.*, p. 28.

11 *Ibid.*, p. 26.

12 *Ibid.*, p. 24.

13 *Ibid.*, p. 21.

14 Iris Murdoch, *The Good Apprentice* (London, 1985), p. 150.

15 DeNora, *After Adorno*, p. 40 and pp. 35–58 *passim*.

16 On the concept of 'do-ability', see Joan Fujimura, 'The Molecular Biological Bandwagon in Cancer Research: Where Social Worlds Meet', *Social Problems*, 35 (1988), pp. 261–83. For pragmatic perspectives on music-making, see Becker, *Art Worlds*, and Richard A. Peterson (ed.), *The Production of Culture* (Los Angeles, 1978).

17 Anthony King, *The Structure of Social Theory* (London, 2004).

18 Hans T. David and Arthur Mendel (eds.), *The Bach Reader: a Life of Johann Sebastian Bach in Letters and Documents* (London, 1966), pp. 71–5.

19 Richard D. P. Jones, 'The Keyboard Works: Bach as Teacher and Virtuoso', in John Butt (ed.), *The Cambridge Companion to Bach* (Cambridge, 1997), p. 142.

20 Wolff, 'Instrumental Music', p. 157; Malcolm Boyd, *Bach: the Brandenburg Concertos* (Cambridge, 1993), p. 16.

21 McClary, 'Talking Politics', p. 21, note 24.

22 *Ibid.*, p. 26.

23 *Ibid.*, p. 36.

24 Antoine Hennion and Joel Marie Fauquet, 'Authority as Performance: the Love of Bach in

Nineteenth-Century France', *Poetics*, 29 (2001), pp. 75–88, at p. 78.

25 See Tia DeNora, *Music in Everyday Life* (Cambridge, 2000), Chapter 2; Henry Kingsbury, 'Sociological Factors in Musicological Poetics', *Ethnomusicology*, 35 (1991), pp. 195–219; and Antoine Hennion, 'Baroque and Rock: Music, Mediators and Musical Taste', *Poetics*, 24 (1997), pp. 415–25.

26 Becker, *Art Worlds*.

27 Tia DeNora, 'How is Extra-Musical Meaning Possible? Music as a Place and Space for "Work"', *Sociological Theory*, 4 (1986), pp. 84–94.

28 See Tia DeNora, *Beethoven and the Construction of Genius: Musical Politics in Vienna, 1792–1803* (Berkeley and London, 1995), pp. 37–59. See also John A. Rice, *Empress Marie Therese and Music at the Viennese Court, 1792–1807* (Cambridge, 2003).

29 See Julia V. Moore, 'Beethoven and Musical Economics' (Ph.D. thesis, University of Illinois, Urbana-Champaign, 1987) and Norbert Elias, *Mozart: Portrait of a Genius* (Cambridge, 1993).

30 Emily Anderson (ed. and trans.), *The Letters of Mozart and His Family* (3rd edition, London, 1985), p. 872.

31 H. C. Robbins Landon, *Mozart: the Golden Years* (London, 1989), p. 140.

32 Kathrine Talbot (trans.), 'A Yearbook of the Music of Vienna and Prague, 1796 (by Johann Ferdinand von Schönfeld)', in Elaine Sisman (ed.), *Haydn and His World* (Princeton, 1997), pp. 289–331.

33 Cliff Eisen, 'The Classical Period', in 'Concerto', *NG Revised*, vol. 6, p. 247.

34 Mary Sue Morrow, *Concert Life in Haydn's Vienna* (New York, 1989), p. 158.

35 Leon Plantinga, *Beethoven's Concertos: History, Style, Performance* (New York, 1999), p. 4.

36 Nicholas Till, *Mozart and the Enlightenment* (London, 1992), p. 88.

37 See Jürgen Habermas, *The Structural Transformation of the Public Sphere: an Inquiry into a Category of Bourgeois Society*, trans. T. Burger with F. Lawrence (Cambridge, 1989) and Richard Sennett, *The Fall of Public Man* (London, 1977).

38 Till, *Mozart*, p. 92.

39 Quoted in Simon Frith, 'Afterthoughts', in Frith and A. Goodwin (eds.), *On Record: Rock, Pop and the Written Word* (London, 1990), p. 424.

40 See Simon P. Keefe, *Mozart's Piano Concertos: Dramatic Dialogue in the Age of Enlightenment* (Woodbridge and Rochester,

NY, 2001) and 'Dramatic Dialogue in Mozart's Viennese Piano Concertos: a Study of Competition and Cooperation in Three First Movements', *MQ*, 83 (1999), pp. 169–204.

41 Till, *Mozart*, p. 177.

42 On this point see DeNora, *After Adorno*, pp. 59–82, and Lucy Green, *Music, Gender, Education* (Cambridge, 1997).

43 Keefe, 'Dramatic Dialogue', p. 197.

44 Quoted above, Hennion and Fauquet, 'Authority as Performance', p. 78.

45 See Green, *Music, Gender, Education*.

46 DeNora, *Beethoven*, pp. 147–69.

47 Morrow, *Concert Life*.

48 Tia DeNora, 'Music into Action: Performing Gender on the Viennese Concert Stage, 1790–1810', *Poetics*, 30 (2002), pp. 19–33, and 'Embodiment and Opportunity: Performing Gender in Beethoven's Vienna', in William Weber (ed.), *The Musician as Entrepreneur and Opportunist, 1600–1900* (Bloomington, IN, forthcoming).

49 Quoted in Richard Leppert, *The Sight of Sound* (Berkeley and London, 1993), p. 67.

50 Plantinga, *Beethoven's Concertos*, p. 4.

51 Charles Rosen, *Piano Notes* (New York, 2002), p. 5.

52 Richard Leppert, 'Cultural Contradiction, Idolatry, and the Piano Virtuoso: Franz Liszt', in James Parakilas *et al.*, *Piano Roles: Three Hundred Years of Life with the Piano* (New Haven, 1999), p. 255.

53 Quoted in Christine Battersby, *Gender and Genius* (London, 1989), pp. 76–7.

54 Katharine Ellis, 'Female Pianists and Their Male Critics in Nineteenth-Century Paris', *JAMS*, 50 (1997), pp. 353–85, at p. 364.

55 *Ibid.*, p. 355.

56 *Ibid.*, p. 361.

57 Morrow, *Concert Life*, p. 159.

58 For example, the lyrical focus in Joe Duddell's twenty-minute concerto for percussion, *Ruby* (2002–3).

59 See Susan O'Neill, 'Gender and Music', in David Hargreaves and Adrian North (eds.), *The Social Psychology of Music* (Oxford, 1997), pp. 46–66, and Nicola Dibben, 'Gender Identity and Music', in Raymond Macdonald, David Hargreaves and Dorothy Miell (eds.), *Musical Identities* (Oxford, 2002), pp. 117–33.

60 Pierre Bourdieu, *Distinction: a Social Critique of the Judgement of Taste* (Cambridge, 1984). See also Richard A. Peterson and Albert Simkus, 'How Musical Tastes Mark Occupational Status Groups', in Michele Lamont and Marcel Fournier (eds.), *Cultivating Differences* (Chicago, 1992), pp. 152–68.

61 Lisa McCormick, 'Musical Performance as Social Performance', in Ron Eyerman (ed.), *New Directions in Arts Sociology* (Herndon, VA, forthcoming). See also Jane W. Davidson, 'The Solo Performer's Identity' in Macdonald, Hargreaves and Miell (eds.), *Musical Identities*, pp. 97–116, and Hennion, 'Baroque and Rock'.

62 See Keefe, 'Dramatic Dialogue', and Tia DeNora, 'The Biology Lessons of Opera Buffa', in Mary Hunter and James Webster (eds.), *Opera Buffa in Mozart's Vienna* (Cambridge, 1997), pp. 146–64.

3 The Italian concerto in the late seventeenth and early eighteenth centuries

1 The etymology and early uses of the term are explored in David D. Boyden, 'When is a Concerto not a Concerto?', *MQ*, 43 (1957), pp. 220–32.

2 The earliest recorded musical use occurs in the *Concerti di Andrea e di Gio[vanni] Gabrieli* (Venice, 1587).

3 As ascertained by Marc Vanscheeuwijck, whose study *The Cappella musicale of San Petronio in Bologna under Giovanni Paolo Colonna (1674–95)* (Brussels and Rome, 2003) offers an excellent introduction to the church and its music in the decades leading up to 1700.

4 The role of instrumental music in Italian churches is examined in Stephen Bonta, 'The Uses of the *sonata da chiesa*', *JAMS*, 22 (1969), pp. 58–84.

5 The reasons for dispensing with the trumpet in internal slow movements were essentially two. First, the customary contrast in key reduced the number of usable notes available to the natural brass instrument. Second, an opportunity to regain breath was welcomed by its players.

6 Johann Joachim Quantz, *Versuch einer Anweisung die Flöte traversiere zu spielen* (Berlin, 1752), p. 309.

7 Johann Mattheson, *Das neu-eröffnete Orchester* (Hamburg, 1713), pp. 193–4: 'Violin Sachen / die also gesetzet sind / daß eine jede Partie sich zu gewisser Zeit hervor thut und mit den andern Stimmen gleichsam um die Wette spielet'. In some early concertos an obbligato cello supplements or replaces the second violin in dialogues with the first violin.

8 Motto form and its evolution into ritornello form are examined in Michael Talbot, 'The Concerto Allegro in the Early Eighteenth Century', *ML*, 52 (1971), pp. 8–18 and 159–72.

9 Mattheson, *Das neu-eröffnete Orchester*, p. 194: 'wo nur die erste Partie dominiret / und wo unter viele Violinen, eine mit sonderlicher Hurtigkeit hervor raget / dieselbe / Violino concertino, genannt wird'.

10 In a nutshell, the 'church' sonata, or *sonata da chiesa*, is constructed from 'abstract' movements, the 'chamber' sonata, or *sonata da camera*, from dance movements (often with a leavening of abstract movements to lend variety).

11 In his Concerti grossi, Op. 1 (1721), Locatelli assigns the viola to the *concertino* (for the first volume of the collection he uses two viola parts).

12 Contrary to what one sometimes reads, the *tenore viola* was not a 'tenor' instrument intermediate in size between a viola and a cello but merely a part for second viola notated in the tenor clef.

13 Quantz, *Versuch*, p. 309.

14 Benedetto Marcello's elder brother Alessandro (1669–1747) was also a composer. His oboe concerto in D minor, which J. S. Bach transcribed for harpsichord around 1713–14, is evidently an early work, although its strongly Vivaldian imprint suggests that it belongs to the years immediately preceding its transcription.

15 Examples of early concertos are the violin concertos RV 275, 276 and 292, and the cello concertos RV 402, 416 and 420. ('RV' numbers are those of the standard Vivaldi catalogue by Peter Ryom.)

16 *Concerti a quattro* are fairly numerous in Vivaldi's œuvre (over forty survive), but they are basically only modernized versions, with a tighter thematic structure, of the prototype established by Albinoni. The genre lived on into the next generation – Durante and Galuppi composed some fine examples – before merging into the chamber symphony.

17 Arthur J. B. Hutchings, *The Baroque Concerto* (London, 1961), pp. 43–4. Long since superseded as a work of history, this book has not lost its capacity to inspire by its musical perception.

18 On Valentini, see Michael Talbot, 'A Rival of Corelli: the Violinist-Composer Giuseppe Valentini', in Sergio Durante and Pierluigi Petrobelli (eds.), *Nuovissimi studi corelliani. Atti del Terzo Congresso Internazionale, Fusignano, 4–7 settembre 1980* (Florence, 1982), pp. 347–65. Examples of such 'chains' occur in the first movement of the tenth concerto in B minor (RV 580).

19 This problem is discussed in Michael Talbot, *Tomaso Albinoni: the Venetian Composer and His World* (Oxford, 1990), p. 258.

20 On Alberti's concertos and their contemporary reception, see Michael Talbot, 'A Thematic Catalogue of the Orchestral Works of Giuseppe Matteo Alberti', *R. M. A. Research Chronicle*, 13 (1976), pp. 1–26.

21 'Chamber' is used here, of course, in the modern sense of 'orchestra-less', not in that of the Corellian *concerto da camera*.

22 On the Italian violin concerto after Vivaldi, see Chappell White, *From Vivaldi to Viotti: a History of the Early Classical Violin Concerto* (Philadelphia, 1992), and Jehoash Hirshberg and Simon McVeigh, *The Italian Solo Concerto 1700–1760: Rhetorical Strategies and Style History* (Woodbridge and Rochester, NY, 2004). The second book includes detailed discussion of several interesting minor figures (among them, Tessarini, Zani and Platti) who sustained the popularity of the violin concerto in the second third of the century.

23 The standard works dealing with the concertos of these two composers are Minos Dounias, *Die Violinkonzerte Giuseppe Tartinis* (Wolfenbüttel, 1935), and Albert Dunning, *Pietro Antonio Locatelli: Der Virtuose und seine Welt* (2 vols., Buren, 1981).

24 I am very grateful to Jehoash Hirshberg for reading this chapter in draft and making comments.

4 The concerto in northern Europe to *c*.1770

1 George J. Buelow, 'Dresden in the Age of Absolutism', in Buelow (ed.), *Man and Music: the Late Baroque Era* (London, 1993), pp. 254–95.

2 Meike ten Brink, *Die Flötenkonzerte von J. J. Quantz* (Hildesheim, 1995).

3 Autobiography of J. G. Walther in Johann Mattheson, *Grundlage einer Ehrenpforte* (Hamburg, 1740), ed. Max Schneider (Berlin, 1910), p. 389.

4 Werner Neumann and Hans Joachim Schulze (eds.), *Bach-Dokumente* (4 vols., Kassel, 1963–78), vol. 3, pp. 649–50.

5 Luigi Ferdinando Tagliavini, *Grosso Mogul*, in George Stauffer and Ernst May (eds.), *J. S. Bach as Organist* (Bloomington, IN, 1986), pp. 240–55 at p. 242. For a discussion of Bach's engagement with the Italian concerto, which discusses the long-held and sometimes problematic assumptions made by Bach scholarship (that is, some of the very assumptions presented in this article), see Siegbert Rampe and Dominik Sackmann, *Bachs Orchestermusik* (Kassel, 2000), pp. 65–79.

6 Jean-Claude Zehnder, 'Giuseppe Torelli und Johann Sebastian Bach. Zu Bachs Weimarer Konzertform', *Bach-Jahrbuch*, 77 (1991), pp. 33–96 at p. 34.

7 For more on Bach's engagement with the concept of the ritornello, see Laurence Dreyfus, *Bach and the Patterns of Invention* (Cambridge, MA, 1996), pp. 59–102.

8 This is of course a simplification of Vivaldi's approach to the concerto. Indeed, in *L'estro harmonico*, almost always alleged to be the formative influence on Bach, this tutti–solo dichotomy is still not fully developed. See Rampe and Sackmann, *Bachs Orchestermusik*, pp. 76–8.

9 BWV 1041 and 1043 also exist in Leipzig versions for one or two harpsichords (BWV 1059 and 1062).

10 This reading is presented by Michael Marissen in *The Social and Religious Designs of J. S. Bach's Brandenburg Concertos* (Princeton, 1995), pp. 16–35.

11 Donald Burrows, *Handel* (Oxford, 1994), p. 52.

12 Only the second movement of No. 6 was composed relatively close to the publication date; the other movements were probably written mostly between 1712 and 1723. See Hans Joachim Marx, 'The Origins of Handel's Opus 3: a Historical Review', in Stanley Sadie and Anthony Hicks (eds.), *Handel Tercentenary Collection* (London, 1987), pp. 254–70 at p. 268.

13 Willam D. Gudger, 'Handel and the Organ Concerto: What We Know 250 Years Later', in Sadie and Hicks (eds.), *Handel Tercentenary Collection*, pp. 271–8.

14 Handel later added oboes to three concertos (Op. 6, Nos. 1, 2, 5) into his autograph manuscript.

15 Donald Burrows, 'Handel as Concerto Composer', in Burrows (ed.), *The Cambridge Companion to Handel* (Cambridge, 1997), pp. 193–207 at p. 207.

16 Only the third *concerto a due cori* (HWV 334) seems to have been for the most part newly composed; the second concerto (HWV 332), for example, is made up of reworked instrumental versions of popular vocal numbers from the oratorios.

17 H. 414, 417, 428, 429, 421, 444 by C. P. E. Bach were printed in two pirated editions in London (*c*.1753–60) by Handel's publisher John Walsh.

5 The concerto from Mozart to Beethoven: aesthetic & stylistic perspectives

1 Kollmann, *An Essay on Practical Musical Composition* (London, 1799; reprint New York, 1973), p. 15; Koch, *Musikalisches*

Lexikon (Frankfurt, 1802; reprint Hildesheim, 1964), col. 854.

2 *AmZ*, 3 (1800–01), cols. 218–19.

3 *AmZ*, 7 (1804–5), col. 480.

4 *AmZ*, 9 (1806–7), col. 655.

5 *AmZ*, 4 (1801–2), col. 777.

6 *AmZ*, 7 (1804), cols. 452–3, as given in Wayne M. Senner (ed.) and Robin Wallace (trans.), *The Critical Reception of Beethoven's Compositions by His German Contemporaries* (2 vols., Lincoln, NE, 1999 and 2001), vol. 1, pp. 206, 210.

7 *AmZ*, 14 (1812), col. 8.

8 Robin Wallace characterizes Beethoven's reception in early issues of the *AmZ* in this way. See Wallace, *Beethoven's Critics: Aesthetic Dilemmas and Resolutions During the Composer's Lifetime* (Cambridge, 1986), p. 5.

9 *AmZ*, 10 (1808), cols. 490–1, given in Senner (ed.) and Wallace (trans.), *Critical Reception of Beethoven's Compositions*, vol. 2, p. 43.

10 *Wiener Theater-Zeitung*, 2 (1807), from Senner (ed.) and Wallace (trans.), *Critical Reception of Beethoven's Compositions*, vol. 2, p. 69.

11 Comprehensive, up-to-date lists of Mozart's and Beethoven's concertos, including fragments, lost works and works of doubtful authenticity, are given in Cliff Eisen and Stanley Sadie, '(Johann Chrysostom) Wolfgang Amadeus Mozart', in *NG Revised*, vol. 17, pp. 326–8, and Joseph Kerman, Alan Tyson, Scott G. Burnham, Douglas Johnson and William Drabkin, 'Beethoven, Ludwig van', in *NG Revised*, vol. 3, pp. 115–16. For an account of an unfinished Beethoven work from 1814–15, see Nicholas Cook, 'Beethoven's Unfinished Piano Concerto: a Case of Double Vision?', *JAMS*, 42 (1989), pp. 338–74.

12 For a seminal study of this concerto-related genre, see Barry S. Brook, *La symphonie française dans la seconde moitié du XVIIIe siècle* (Paris, 1962).

13 Beethoven, for example, 'withheld his concertos from the press while they were still useful for his performances, and ... only once, so far as we know, played a concerto of his that had already been published'. See Leon Plantinga, *Beethoven's Concertos: History, Style, Performance* (New York, 1999), p. 113.

14 Examples of contemporary critical acclaim for Viotti's performances in London are cited in H. C. Robbins Landon, *Haydn: Chronicle and Works. Haydn in England, 1791–1795* (London, 1976), *passim*. Beethoven's performance activities as a concerto soloist at the end of the eighteenth century are documented in Leon Plantinga, *Beethoven's Concertos*, pp. 47–56.

15 Kollmann, *Essay*, p. 24.

16 *Ibid*., pp. 24, 20–1.

17 Pierre Louis Ginguené, 'Concerto', in Ginguené and Nicholas Etienne Framery (eds.), *Encyclopédie méthodique: musique* (Paris, 1791; reprint New York, 1971), vol. 1, p. 320.

18 Koch, *Introductory Essay on Composition: the Mechanical Rules of Melody, Sections 3 and 4* (1787–93), trans. Nancy Kovaleff Baker (New Haven and London, 1983), p. 209.

19 Identifications and discussions of dialogue (the central manifestation of intimate grandeur) later in this chapter rely on understandings of the technique gleaned from eighteenth-century sources, codified in Antoine Reicha's *Traité de mélodie* of 1814. See Simon P. Keefe, *Mozart's Piano Concertos: Dramatic Dialogue in the Age of Enlightenment* (Woodbridge and Rochester, NY, 2001), pp. 24–41.

20 *AmZ*, 3 (1800–01), col. 28.

21 *AmZ*, 1 (1798–9), col. 58; *AmZ*, 13 (1811), col. 383, and *AmZ*, 2 (1799–1800), col. 781; *AmZ*, 5 (1802–3), cols. 828–9.

22 *AmZ*, 5 (1802–3), col. 665; *AmZ*, 6 (1803–4), col. 860; *AmZ*, 7 (1804–5), col. 322. Eberl, Fränzl and Rode's dates are 1765–1807, 1736–1811 and 1774–1830 respectively.

23 *AmZ*, 5 (1802–3), col. 828; *AmZ*, 6 (1803–4), col. 725.

24 *AmZ*, 1 (1798–9), col. 680.

25 *AmZ*, 11 (1808), cols. 27–8.

26 *Morning Chronicle*, 12 March 1794; given in H. C. Robbins Landon, *Chronicle: Haydn in England*, p. 242.

27 *AmZ*, 1 (1798–9), col. 654.

28 *AmZ*, 6 (1803–04), cols. 723, 837–8.

29 *AmZ*, 18 (1816), col. 359.

30 From H. C. Robbins Landon, *Haydn: Chronicle and Works. The Late Years, 1801–1809* (London, 1977), p. 423.

31 Landon, *Haydn: Chronicle and Works. Haydn at Esterhaza, 1766–1790* (London, 1978), p. 571.

32 Kollmann, *Essay*, p. 21.

33 Koch, *Lexikon*, col. 854, and Kollmann, *Essay*, p. 15.

34 *AmZ*, 3 (1800–01), col. 28.

35 As given in William McColl's translation of this *AmZ* review in Colin Lawson, *Mozart: Clarinet Concerto* (Cambridge, 1996), p. 80.

36 *AmZ*, 2 (1799–1800), col. 696.

37 See Cliff Eisen, *New Mozart Documents: a Supplement to O. E. Deutsch's Documentary Biography* (London, 1991), p. 124, and *AmZ*, 11 (1808), col. 203.

38 Gerber, *Neues Historisches Lexikon der Tonkünstler* (Leipzig, 1812–14), vol. 2, col. 496.

39 *AmZ*, 8 (1805–06), col. 729. 'Mozart selbst dies Konzert mit mehr Ernst und

imponirender Würde vortrug. Bey ihm wurde mehr der tiefe, reiche Geist der Komposition, bei Stein mehr der glänzende Vortrag des Virtuosen bemerkbar'.

40 AmZ, 2 (1799–1800), cols. 12–13. 'Zwar ist es nicht so sehr gearbeitet, als manche bereits bekanntern und neuern Konzerte desselben Verfassers: dahingegen aber sowohl wegen der schwächern als ungleich leichtern und bequemeren Instrumentalbegleitung im Allgemeinen brauchbarer als manches von diesen. Sicher findet man eher zehn Klavierspieler, die, selbst die schwersten dieser Konzerte ganz fertig durcharbeiten, ehe man ein einziges Orchester zum guten Akkompagnement dazu auftreibt. Doch sind auch in dem letzten Allegro des vor uns liegenden Konzerts in der ersten Hoboe einige Kleinigkeiten, die, wenn sie gut und in Ansehung der Manieren bestimmt und deutlich herausgebracht werden sollen, vielleicht eben so viele Uebung und Gewissheit erfordern, als irgend eine Stelle in der Konzertstimme.'

41 Anderson (ed. and trans.), The Letters of Mozart and His Family (3rd edition, London, 1985), p. 877.

42 See Mozart's announcement in the Wiener Zeitung of 15 January 1783 for the a quattro reference to K. 413, 414 and 415, given in Otto Erich Deutsch, Mozart: a Documentary Biography, trans. Eric Blom, Peter Branscombe and Jeremy Noble (London, 1965), p. 212, and Anderson (ed. and trans.), Letters of Mozart and His Family, p. 877, for the a quattro and wind-instrument references to K. 449 and K. 450/451/453.

43 Among late twentieth-century writings, see Charles Rosen, The Classical Style: Haydn, Mozart, Beethoven (London, 1971), p. 220; Leonard G. Ratner, Classic Music: Expression, Form and Style (London, 1980), p. 297; and Irving Eisley, 'Mozart's Concertato Orchestra', Mozart-Jahrbuch 1976/7, p. 9.

44 Anderson (ed. and trans.), Letters of Mozart and His Family, p. 877.

45 This paragraph is a partial summary of the article, Simon P. Keefe '"An Entirely Special Manner": Mozart's Piano Concerto in E flat, K. 449, and the Stylistic Implications of Confrontation', ML, 82 (2001), pp. 559–81.

46 Translation adapted from Anderson (ed. and trans.), Letters of Mozart and His Family, p. 877.

47 For historical explanation of oppositional/ confrontational dialogue, see Keefe, Mozart's Piano Concertos, pp. 24–41, especially pp. 32–4.

48 Niemetschek, Life of Mozart (1798), trans. Helen Mautner (London, 1956), p. 58.

49 Anderson (ed. and trans.), Letters of Mozart and His Family, p. 681.

50 See Henry Paolucci (ed. and trans.), Hegel on the Arts: Selections from G. W. F. Hegel's 'Aesthetics or the Philosophy of the Fine Arts' (New York, 1979), p. 133.

51 Emily Anderson (ed. and trans.), Letters of Beethoven (London, 1961), vol. 1, p. 75, and vol. 3, pp. 1276–7.

52 Given in Elliot Forbes (ed.), Thayer's Life of Beethoven (Princeton, 1967), p. 209. The reliability of this anecdote, however, has recently been called into question; see Barry Cooper, Beethoven (Oxford, 2000), p. 125, and Plantinga, Beethoven's Concertos, p. 141. For a brief study of Mozart's influence on Beethoven's Piano Concertos Nos. 3 and 4 and the Violin Concerto set in the context of this quotation, see Owen Jander, '"Cramer, Cramer! We shall never be able to do anything like that!": Understanding a Favorite Quotation about Mozart's Concerto in C minor, K. 491, and Mozart's Influence on Beethoven's Concertos', The Beethoven Journal, 15 (2000), pp. 57–63.

53 Richard Kramer, 'Cadenza Contra Text: Mozart in Beethoven's Hands', 19th Century Music, 15 (1991), pp. 116–31.

54 Carl Czerny's famous account of the distinguishing characteristics of Mozart's and Beethoven's piano playing is quoted and discussed in Tia DeNora, Beethoven and the Construction of Genius: Musical Politics in Vienna, 1792–1803 (Berkeley and London, 1995), pp. 131–2.

55 Given in T. Skowroneck, 'Keyboard Instruments of the Young Beethoven', in Scott Burnham and Michael P. Steinberg (eds.), Beethoven and His World (Princeton, 2000), p. 164. Czerny's comment is given in DeNora, Beethoven and the Construction of Genius, p. 131.

56 For recent literature see the following: Geoffrey Block, 'Organic Relations in Beethoven's Early Piano Concerti and the "Spirit of Mozart"', in William Kinderman (ed.), Beethoven's Compositional Process (Lincoln, NE, 1991), pp. 55–81; Bathia Churgin, 'Beethoven and Mozart's Requiem: a New Connection', JM, 5 (1997), pp. 457–77; Kramer, 'Cadenza Contra Text'; Lewis Lockwood, 'Beethoven Before 1800: the Mozart Legacy', Beethoven Forum 3 (London, 1994), pp. 39–52; Adena Portowicz, 'Innovation and Tradition in the Classic Concerto: Mozart's K. 453 (1784) as a Model for Beethoven's Fourth Concerto (1805–06)',

The Beethoven Journal, 12 (1997), pp. 65–72; Carl Schachter, 'Mozart's Last and Beethoven's First: Echoes of K. 551 in the First Movement of Opus 21', in Cliff Eisen (ed.), *Mozart Studies* (Oxford, 1991), pp. 227–51; Elaine Sisman, '"The Spirit of Mozart from Haydn's Hands": Beethoven's Musical Inheritance', in Glenn Stanley (ed.), *The Cambridge Companion to Beethoven* (Cambridge, 2000), pp. 45–63; Jeremy Yudkin, 'Beethoven's "Mozart" Quartet', *JAMS*, 45 (1992), pp. 30–74.

57 Only Beethoven's five numbered piano concertos are discussed below. His Violin Concerto in D, Op. 61 (1806), is discussed in Chapter 7 of this volume.

58 Leon Plantinga recently challenged the idea that Mozart was the predominant influence on Beethoven in Op. 19, positing that composers such as Clementi and Haydn were just as important in this respect. In addition, he concludes that 'much in the concerto is . . . quite recognizably Beethoven's own' (p. 89). See Plantinga, *Beethoven's Concertos*, pp. 86–9.

59 On the passage in K. 449/i compared to corresponding passages in K. 414/i, 415/i and 450/i, see Keefe, '"An Entirely Special Manner"', pp. 564–8.

60 This is Donald Tovey's term, given in *Essays in Musical Analysis: Concertos and Choral Works* (London, 1935–9; new edition, 1981), p. 50.

61 Given in Leo Treitler (ed.), *Strunk's Source Readings in Music History, Revised Edition* (New York, 1998), p. 1036. (Translation by Wye J. Allanbrook.)

62 Gerber, *Neues Historisches Lexikon*, vol. 1, col. 316. The review is found in *AmZ*, 7 (1804–5), cols. 445–57.

63 Michael C. Tusa explains that 'no work loomed larger in the formation of [Beethoven's] image of this key [C minor] than did K. 491' in 'Beethoven's "C Minor Mood": Some Thoughts on the Structural Implications of Key Choice', *Beethoven Forum 2* (Lincoln, NE, 1993), pp. 1–27. On Beethoven's C minor works, see also Joseph Kerman, 'Beethoven's Minority', in *Write All These Down: Essays on Music* (Berkeley and London, 1994), pp. 217–37.

64 On co-operation and competition in K. 450/i, see Keefe, *Mozart's Piano Concertos*, pp. 45–74.

65 See Keefe, *Mozart's Piano Concertos*, pp. 91–4.

66 On the possible influence of the coda of Mozart's K. 491/i on this section, see Plantinga, *Beethoven's Concertos*, pp. 140–2,

158. Charles Rosen describes Beethoven's coda as one of the work's numerous 'Mozartian reminiscences, in particular of . . . K. 491' in *Classical Style*, pp. 389–90.

67 *AmZ*, 7 (1804–5), col. 450; given in Senner (ed.) and Wallace (trans.), *Critical Reception of Beethoven's Compositions*, vol. 1, p. 208.

68 Kollmann, *Essay*, p. 21.

69 Joseph Kerman, *Concerto Conversations* (Cambridge, MA, 1999), p. 24.

70 Senner (ed.) and Wallace (trans.), *Critical Reception of Beethoven's Compositions*, vol. 1, pp. 210 and 149, and Carl Czerny (on No. 2 and No. 5), quoted in Plantinga, *Beethoven's Concertos*, pp. 103, 265.

71 On the Orpheus connection see, for example, Owen Jander, 'Beethoven's "Orpheus in Hades": the Andante con moto of the Fourth Piano Concerto', *19th Century Music*, 8 (1985), pp. 195–212; Edward Cone, 'Beethoven's Orpheus – or Jander's?' *19th Century Music*, 8 (1985), pp. 283–6; Jander, 'Orpheus Revisited: a Ten-Year Retrospect on the Andante con moto of Beethoven's Fourth Piano Concerto', *19th Century Music*, 19 (1995), pp. 31–49; Richard Will, 'When God Met the Sinner, and Other Dramatic Confrontations in Eighteenth-Century Instrumental Music', *ML*, 78 (1997), pp. 175–209, especially pp. 192–4; Plantinga, *Beethoven's Concertos*, pp. 189–94. Joseph Kerman sets his interpretation of conflict and resolution in this movement in the context of a relational progression from 'uncertainty' in the first movement to 'communal spontaneous play' in the finale, in 'Representing a Relationship: Notes on a Beethoven Concerto', *Representations*, 39 (1992), pp. 80–101. For a reading of Op. 58/ii as 'a paradigm of musical transformation, whereby the detached, objective idiom of the tutti is gradually infused with human subjectivity, won over by the power of the artistic imagination', see William Kinderman, *Beethoven* (Berkeley, 1995), pp. 112–16.

72 This applies both to those Mozart movements, such as K. 450/i and K. 482/i, that progress from competition to co-operation and the numerous others that render close solo–orchestra relations closer still later in the movement. See Keefe, *Mozart's Piano Concertos*, pp. 45–100.

6 The nineteenth-century piano concerto

1 See Ludwig von Köchel, *Chronologisch-thematisches Verzeichnis sämtlicher Tonwerke Wolfgang Amade Mozarts* (1862), ed. F. Giegling, A. Weinmann and G. Sievers (6th edition, Wiesbaden, 1964). The

Mozart piano concertos were popular in the first half of the nineteenth century, ranking third in a list of twenty in frequency of performance (behind Beethoven and Moscheles) at the London Philharmonic Society concerts through 1850 and seventh in a list of eighteen (following Hummel, Weber, Mendelssohn, Beethoven, Cramer and Moscheles) of the most frequently performed piano concertos in London, 1801–50. For more information, see Therese M. Ellsworth, 'The Piano Concerto in London Concert Life Between 1801 and 1850' (Ph.D. thesis, University of Cincinnati, 1991), pp. 103, 231.

2 Nicholas Temperley, liner notes to *Moscheles, Piano Concerto No. 21 in E-flat major; Piano Concerto No. 3 in G minor; Anticipations of Scotland, Op. 74. The Romantic Piano Concerto, vol. 29*, Howard Shelley, piano/conductor, Tasmanian Symphony Orchestra, Hyperion, CD 67276 (2002).

3 As early as 1802, theorist Heinrich Christoph Koch's *Musikalisches Lexikon* described concerto form as consisting of three tuttis rather than four. See Heinrich Christoph Koch, *Musikalisches Lexikon* (Frankfurt, 1802; reprint Hildesheim, 1964), cols 854–5.

4 Cited in John Warrack, *Carl Maria von Weber* (New York, 1968), p. 245.

5 Given in detail in Sir Julius Benedict, *Carl Maria von Weber* (London, 1894; reprint New York, 1980), p. 51.

6 Tovey, *Essays in Musical Analysis, Volume Four* (Oxford, 1936), p. 61.

7 Nicholas Cook, 'Beethoven's Unfinished Piano Concerto: a Case of Double Vision?', *JAMS*, 42 (1989), pp. 338–74. His reading has been challenged by Lewis Lockwood. See Lockwood's initial article on the work, 'Beethoven's Unfinished Piano Concerto of 1815: Sources and Problems', *MQ*, 56 (1970), pp. 624–46, reprinted in Paul Henry Lang (ed.), *The Creative World of Beethoven* (New York, 1970), pp. 122–44, and his response to Cook in 'To the Editors of Journal', *JAMS*, 43 (1990), pp. 376–82.

8 Adolph Bernhard Marx, *Die Lehre von der musikalischen Komposition, praktisch-theoretisch* (Leipzig, 1847), vol. 4, p. 439; as discussed in Jane R. Stevens, 'Theme, Harmony, and Texture in Classic-Romantic Descriptions of Concerto First-Movement Form', *JAMS*, 27 (1974), pp. 50–2.

9 Stevens, 'Theme, Harmony, and Texture', p. 51.

10 Tovey, *Essays in Musical Analysis, Volume Three: Concertos* (Oxford, 1936), p. 103.

11 Tovey allows it as 'a singular but not unsuccessful experiment in form'. See *ibid.*, p. 105.

12 Biographical information on Alkan has been culled from Ronald Smith, *Alkan, vol. 1: The Enigma* (London, 1976), p. 22; Liszt's remark on Alkan is taken from Alan Walker, *Franz Liszt, vol. 1: The Virtuoso Years* (New York, 1983), p. 187; and the comparison with Berlioz is given in Hugh Macdonald, 'Alkan', in *NG*, vol. 1, p. 262.

13 Plantinga, *Schumann as Critic* (New Haven, 1967), p. 209.

14 *Neue Zeitschrift für Musik*, 4 (1836), p. 113; as translated in Plantinga, *Schumann as Critic*, pp. 204–5 and 298.

15 *Neue Zeitschrift für Musik*, 4 (1836), p. 83; as translated in Plantinga, *Schumann as Critic*, pp. 203 and 297–8.

16 See Claudia Macdonald, 'Robert Schumann's F-Major Piano Concerto of 1831 as Reconstructed from His First Sketchbook: A History of its Composition and Study of its Musical Background' (Ph.D. thesis, University of Chicago, 1986), p. 79.

17 *Neue Zeitschrift für Musik*, 4 (1836), p. 111; as translated in Plantinga, *Schumann as Critic*, p. 205. Schumann's critique of Herz's Piano Concerto No. 2 is translated in its entirety in Henry Pleasants (trans. and ed.), *The Musical World of Robert Schumann: a Selection from His Own Writings* (New York, 1965; reprint New York, 1988), pp. 110–11.

18 Robert Collett, 'Works for Piano and Orchestra', in Alan Walker (ed.), *Franz Liszt: the Man and His Music* (New York, 1970), p. 267.

19 *Ibid.*, p. 267.

20 Jay Rosenblatt's work includes his dissertation, 'The Concerto as Crucible: Franz Liszt's Early Works for Piano and Orchestra' (Ph.D. thesis, University of Chicago, 1995). (Here he credits Michael Saffle with the first suggestion that the piece was a separate work and not related to the First Concerto, in Saffle, 'Unpublished Liszt Works at Weimar', *Journal of the American Liszt Society*, 13 (1983), p. 9.) Rosenblatt's edition, *Liszt Ferenc: Concerto for Piano and Orchestra in E-flat Major, Op. posth.* (Budapest, 1989) has been recorded commercially.

21 Walter Frisch, 'Brahms: Orchestral Works and Concertos', in Laura Macy (ed.), *Grove Music Online* (accessed 25/5/2004) http://www.grovemusic.com.

22 *Ibid.*

23 *Ibid.*

24 Jeremy Norris, *The Russian Piano Concerto, Volume 1: The Nineteenth Century* (Bloomington, IN, 1994), p. 31.

25 *Ibid.*, p. 37.

26 *Ibid.*, p. 32.

27 *Ibid.*, p. 35.

28 *Ibid.*, p. 68.

29 David Brown, *Tchaikovsky: a Biographical and Critical Study, vol. 1: The Early Years, 1840–74* (London, 1978), p. 182.

30 Norris, *Russian Piano Concerto*, p. 114, citing David Brown, *Tchaikovsky, vol. 1*, p. 71.

31 Norris, *Russian Piano Concerto*, p. 116, citing Wilson Strutte, *Tchaikovsky* (Tunbridge Wells, 1979), pp. 44–5.

32 For details on this, see Norris, *Russian Piano Concerto*, pp. 118–22. Norris's analysis of the entire work is exhaustive and exemplary.

33 Eric Blom, 'Works for Solo Instrument and Orchestra', in Gerald Abraham (ed.), *Tchaikovsky: a Symposium* (London, 1945), p. 51.

34 Norris, *Russian Piano Concerto*, p. 127, citing Alexander Alekseev, *Russkaia fortepiannaia muzika konets XIX nachalo XX veka* [*Russian Piano Music from the End of the Nineteenth to the Beginning of the Twentieth Century*] (Moscow, 1969), p. 64. Norris notes that this view has been confirmed in the West, in the writings of Edward Garden ('Three Russian Piano Concertos', *MT*, 122 (1981), pp. 238–9), and Brown, *Tchaikovsky, Volume 2: The Crisis Years* (London 1978), pp. 22–4.

35 Norris, *Russian Piano Concerto*, p. 127, citing Brown, *Tchaikovsky, Volume 1*, pp. 197–200.

36 Norris, *Russian Piano Concerto*, p. 184.

37 *Ibid.*, p. 78.

38 Michael Thomas Roeder, *A History of the Concerto* (Portland, OR, 1994), p. 417.

39 *Ibid.*, p. 418.

40 Given by Adrienne Fried Block in liner notes to *Amy Beach: 'Gaelic' Symphony; Piano Concerto*, Alan Feinberg, piano, Nashville Symphony Orchestra, conductor Kenneth Schermerhorn, Naxos American Classics, CD 8.559139 (2003).

7 Nineteenth-century concertos for strings & winds

1 For studies of Viotti's career and influence, see Boris Schwarz, 'Beethoven and the French Violin School', *MQ*, 44 (1958), pp. 431–47; Chappell White, *From Vivaldi to Viotti: a History of the Early Classical Violin Concerto* (Stuyvesant, NY, 1992), and White (ed.), *G. B. Viotti: Four Violin Concertos* (Madison, WI, 1976), Preface.

2 *AmZ*, 13 (1811), col. 452.

3 Rode, Kreutzer and Baillot, *Méthode de violon* (Paris, 1803).

4 Baillot, *L'art du violon* (Paris, 1835); trans. Louise Goldberg as *The Art of the Violin* (Evanston, IL, 1991).

5 On Beethoven's interest in French music, see, most recently, Robin Stowell, *Beethoven: Violin Concerto* (Cambridge, 1998), pp. 11–19; and Lewis Lockwood, *Beethoven: the Music and the Life* (New York, 2002), pp. 151–6.

6 He dedicated the Violin Sonata in A minor, Op. 47, to Kreutzer and composed the Violin Sonata in G, Op. 96, for Rode.

7 See Leon Plantinga, *Beethoven's Concertos: History, Style, Performance* (New York, 1999), pp. 217–18.

8 *Ibid.*, p. 218.

9 Stowell, *Beethoven: Violin Concerto*, pp. 70–3.

10 See further Lewis Lockwood, *Beethoven*, p. 246, and Plantinga, *Beethoven's Concertos*, pp. 249–50.

11 Regarding Spohr, see in particular Clive Brown, *Louis Spohr: a Critical Biography* (Cambridge, 1984).

12 There are also several concertos for multiple soloists, including violin and cello, violin and harp, two violins, and string quartet and orchestra.

13 Employed by Spohr in the Concertino in E major, Op. 92; see Brown, *Spohr*, pp. 231–3.

14 In Spohr's *Violinschule* of 1832, cited in *ibid.*, p. 212.

15 A. W. Thayer, *Life of Beethoven*, ed. Elliot Forbes (Princeton, 1970), p. 956.

16 *AmZ*, 19 (1817), col. 327.

17 Brown, *Spohr*, p. 109.

18 Liszt, 'Clara Schumann (1855)' in L. Raman (ed.), *Gesammelte Schriften* (Leipzig, 1882; reprint Hildesheim, 1978), vol. 4, p. 194.

19 Guhr, *Über Paganinis Kunst die Violine zu spielen* (Mainz, 1830), pp. 7, 10, 15, 30, 47, 50.

20 See Warren Kirkendale, 'Segreto communicato da Paganini', *JAMS*, 18 (1965), pp. 394–407.

21 Diary entry for 9 March 1829. Fanny Hensel, *Tagebücher*, ed. H.-G. Klein and Rudolf Elvers (Wiesbaden, 2002), p. 9.

22 See R. Larry Todd., *Mendelssohn: a Life in Music* (New York, 2003), p. 275.

23 Abraham Mendelssohn-Bartholdy, letter of 9 June 1833, in H.-G. Klein, 'Abraham Mendelssohn Bartholdy in England: Die Briefe aus London im Sommer 1833 nach Berlin', *Mendelssohn Studien*, 12 (2001), pp. 71–2.

24 See Todd, *Mendelssohn: a Life in Music*, pp. 479–80, and Todd, 'An Unfinished Piano Concerto by Mendelssohn', *MQ*, 68 (1982), pp. 80–101.

25 For a comparison of the two versions of the violin concerto, see my forthcoming edition of Op. 64 (Kassel, 2005).

26 Donald Francis Tovey, *Essays in Musical Analysis* (London, 1981), vol. 2, p. 157.

27 John Daverio, *Robert Schumann: Herald of a 'New Poetic Age'* (New York and Oxford, 1997), p. 457.

28 Available in a new edition by Joachim Draheim (Wiesbaden, 2002).

29 See Boris Schwarz, 'Joseph Joachim and the Genesis of Brahms' Violin Concerto', *MQ*, 69 (1983), pp. 503–26.

30 Malcolm MacDonald, *Brahms* (New York, 1990), p. 269.

31 Boris Schwarz, *Great Masters of the Violin* (New York, 1983), p. 146.

32 As was his colleague at the Moscow Conservatory, Nikolay Rubinstein, whose Violin Concerto in G major, Op. 46 (1858) shows clear signs of Germanic influence.

33 Joseph Kerman, *Concerto Conversations* (Cambridge, MA, 1999), p. 54; Richard Taruskin, 'Chaikovsky and the Human: a Centennial Essay', in *Defining Russia Musically: Historical and Hermeneutical Essays* (Princeton, 1997), pp. 281–90.

34 Raymond Knapp, 'Passing – and Failing – in Late-Nineteenth-Century Russia: or Why We Should Care about the Cuts in Tchaikovsky's Violin Concerto', *19th Century Music*, 26 (2003), p. 222.

35 See Knapp ('Cuts in Tchaikovsky's Violin Concerto') who also reads into the octatonicism a symbol for the composer's homosexuality.

36 James Hepokoski, 'Sibelius', in *NG Revised*, vol. 23, p. 329.

37 See Wilhelm Lauth, 'Entstehung und Geschichte des Ersten Violinkonzertes Op. 26', in Dietrich Kämpfer (ed.), *Max Bruch-Studien* (Cologne, 1970), pp. 57–66.

38 See Mark Evan Bonds, *After Beethoven: Imperatives of Originality in the Symphony* (Cambridge, MA, 1996), pp. 28–72.

39 For a list, see Robin Stowell, *The Cambridge Companion to the Cello* (Cambridge, 1999), pp. 95–9. To these should be added a concerto evidently sketched or drafted during the 1840s by Mendelssohn for the Italian cellist Alfredo Piatti, although nothing has survived of this work.

40 A somewhat related experiment is the Violin Concerto in A minor of Anton Arensky (1891), in one continuous movement, with the exposition and reprise separated by a slow movement and a waltz.

41 Jan Smaczny, *Dvořák: Cello Concerto* (Cambridge, 1999), p. 68.

42 See *ibid.*, 10ff.

43 MacDonald, *Brahms*, p. 322.

44 Appointed inspector of Naval Bands in 1873, Rimsky-Korsakov also wrote two minor works with orchestral accompaniment for clarinet and for oboe.

45 The finale contains examples of the *faux-polonaise* rhythms employed in Tchaikovsky's contemporaneous Violin Concerto to suggest a Russian imperial style.

46 See further R. Larry Todd, 'Strauss before Liszt and Wagner: Some Observations', in Bryan Gilliam (ed.), *Richard Strauss: New Perspectives on the Composer and His Work* (Durham, NC, 1992), pp. 3–40.

8 Contrasts and common concerns in the concerto 1900–1945

1 Nicolas Slonimsky, *Music Since 1900* (5th edition, New York, 1994), p. 330.

2 Igor Stravinsky, *An Autobiography* (New York, 1936), p. 166; Anthony Pople, *Berg: Violin Concerto* (Cambridge, 1991), pp. 26–7.

3 Christian Tetzlaff, one of the few violinists to play Arnold Schoenberg's twelve-tone Violin Concerto (1936) with any frequency, estimates that he performs the work only once for every twenty times he performs Berg's Violin Concerto. See Allan Kozinn, 'A German Violin Virtuoso with a Casual Attitude Toward the Violin', *The New York Times* (21 May 2004), B4.

4 Although Dohnányi completed the short score of the work in 1898, he submitted only the first movement of it to the competition because he was unable to finish the orchestration of the second and third movements in time. See Bálint Vázsonyi, *Dohnányi Ernő* (2nd revised edition, Budapest, 2002), p. 65.

5 At an early stage in its planning, Brahms had thought that the material that he eventually used for his First Symphony might be used for a piano concerto.

6 Translation by Edward J. Dent, quoted in Larry Sitsky, *Busoni and the Piano* (New York, 1986), p. 92.

7 *Ibid.*

8 Busoni states that 'the music has taken us through so manifold a variety of human feelings that the words of a poet are necessary to sum them up in conclusion'. *Ibid.*, p. 93.

9 *Ibid.*, p. 95.

10 See Douglas Jarman, 'Secret Programmes', in Anthony Pople (ed.), *The Cambridge Companion to Berg* (Cambridge, 1997), pp. 171–5; and George Perle, *The Operas of Alban Berg, vol. 2: Lulu* (Berkeley, 1988),

pp. 255–7. This information is also summarized in Pople, *Berg: Violin Concerto*, pp. 60–4.

11 Joseph Kerman, *Concerto Conversations* (Cambridge, MA, 1999), p. 67.

12 *Ibid.*, pp. 51–2.

13 Letter to Willy Strecker (23 January 1936) in Dieter Rexroth (ed.), *Paul Hindemith Briefe* (Frankfurt am Main, 1982), p. 159. A different translation of this letter appears in Geoffrey Skelton (ed. and trans.), *Selected Letters of Paul Hindemith* (New Haven, 1995), p. 91. (Translations are my own unless otherwise noted.)

14 The tune of 'Vor deinen Thron tret' ich hiermit' is well known in the English-speaking world as the 'Old Hundredth', but Hindemith was unaware of this at the time he composed *Trauermusik. Ibid.*

15 Interview with Antonio Brosa first broadcast on 18 April 1980, BBC Radio 3. Cited in John Evans, 'The Concertos', in Christopher Palmer (ed.), *The Britten Companion* (Cambridge, 1984), p. 415.

16 Donald Mitchell and Philip Reed (eds.), *Letters from a Life: the Selected Letters and Diaries of Benjamin Britten 1913–1976* (Berkeley, 1991), vol. 1, p. 409.

17 Hindemith's Violin Concerto similarly recalls Beethoven by opening with a timpani solo.

18 Mitchell and Reed (eds.), *Letters from a Life*, vol. 1, pp. 169, 201–2, 204 and 206–7. After hearing Lionel Tertis play Walton's concerto under the composer on 10 September 1931 Britten wrote in his diary that it 'stood out as a work of genius' and later reported that no works of the previous generation of British composers could be compared to it.

19 Stephen Walsh, *Stravinsky: a Creative Spring* (New York, 1999), p. 372.

20 Harlow Robinson, *Sergei Prokofiev* (New York, 1987), p. 179.

21 Joseph Szigeti, *With Strings Attached* (2nd revised edition, New York, 1967), p. 105.

22 In 1972 Walton admitted that he used Prokofiev as a model. See Stephen Lloyd, *Walton: Muse of Fire* (Woodbridge and Rochester, NY, 2002), p. 94, note 20.

23 Malcolm Gillies (ed.), *Bartók Remembered* (London, 1990), pp. 190–1. Because at the time of his death Bartók left only a sketchy draft of his Viola Concerto, performing versions of it should not be taken as authoritative. See László Somfai's commentary to *Béla Bartók: Viola Concerto: Facsimile Edition of the Autograph Draft* (Homosassa, FL, 1995). The fact that Primrose habitually transposed fast passages in

Walton's Concerto up an octave further confuses the tangled history of the genesis of Bartók's Viola Concerto. See Michael Steinberg, *The Concerto: a Listener's Guide* (Oxford and New York, 1999), p. 496.

24 Commentators frequently describe Stravinsky's inclusion of string basses in the orchestra of his Piano Concerto as an 'addition' to the wind band, but the double bass has been a regular member of wind ensembles since the eighteenth century and therefore should not be considered in this way.

25 In 1930 Darius Milhaud (1892–1974) became the first to place percussion front and centre in his Concerto for Percussion and Small Orchestra.

26 I discuss the relationship between Bartók and Stravinsky in greater detail in 'Bartók and Stravinsky: Respect, Competition, Influence, and the Hungarian Reaction to Modernism in the 1920s', in Peter Laki (ed.), *Bartók and His World* (Princeton, 1995), pp. 172–99.

27 Béla Bartók Jr. (ed.), *Bartók Béla családi levelei* [Béla Bartók's family letters] (Budapest, 1981), p. 375.

28 That Bartók first got to know *The Rite of Spring* in 1917 in the reduction of the work for two pianos helps to explain its influence on his First Piano Concerto.

29 For all Stravinsky's philosophizing about the suitability of wind instruments for his 'objective style', one suspects that he got a special satisfaction from the lowly associations of military bands.

30 Richard Taruskin, 'The Pastness of the Present and the Presence of the Past', in Nicholas Kenyon (ed.), *Authenticity and Early Music* (Oxford, 1988), p. 176.

31 David Schiff suggests Ravel's Piano Concerto as a corrective to Gershwin in *Gershwin: Rhapsody in Blue* (Cambridge, 1997), p. 75. The key of the piano right hand (G major) is the key of the first theme. The key of the piano left hand (F sharp major) is the key of the second theme.

32 Christopher Headington, 'The Concerto in Modern Times', Part 3, 'Italy, Spain and Latin America', in Robert Layton (ed.), *A Guide to the Concerto* (Oxford, 1996), p. 302.

33 Jacques Ibert's Flute Concerto (1933) and Ralph Vaughan Williams's and Richard Strauss's Oboe Concertos (1944 and 1945) are important works for their instruments, but less successful in going beyond the expressive limitations of a solo wind instrument than Nielsen's concertos.

34 Kerman sees the role of the clarinet similarly. See *Concerto Conversations*, p. 87.

35 Since Sessions was living in Berlin at the time, it is probable that he heard the première of Stravinsky's Violin Concerto there on 23 October 1931.

36 Igor Stravinsky and Robert Craft, *Dialogues* (Berkeley, 1982), p. 47.

37 Kerman, *Concerto Conversations*, p. 89.

38 Claude Kenneson, *Székely and Bartók: the Story of a Friendship* (Portland, OR, 1994), p. 186.

39 Anthony Pople, *Berg: Violin Concerto*, p. 8.

40 Only the last seventeen bars of Bartók's Third Piano Concerto remained to be orchestrated at the time of his death.

9 The concerto since 1945

1 James Pritchett, *The Music of John Cage* (Cambridge, 1993), p. 62, citing John Cage, *For the Birds* (Salem, NH, and London, 1981), p. 41.

2 Paul Griffiths, *Cage* (Oxford, 1981), p. 23.

3 *Ibid.*, p. 24.

4 Pritchett, *John Cage*, p. 112.

5 David Schiff, *The Music of Elliott Carter* (London, 1998), p. 234.

6 *Ibid.*, p. 273.

7 *Ibid.*, p. 290.

8 Tadeusz Kaczynski, *Conversations with Witold Lutosławski*, trans. Yolanta May, with additional material trans. Dorota Kwiatkowska-Rae (London, 1994), p. 84. Cited by Arnold Whittall, 'Between Polarity and Synthesis: the Modernist Paradigm in Lutosławski's Concertos for Cello and Piano', in Zbigniew Skowron (ed.), *Lutosławski Studies* (Oxford, 2001), p. 247.

9 Steven Stucky, *Lutosławski and His Music* (Cambridge, 1981), p. 177.

10 Michael Tippett, 'Archetypes of Concert Music', in Meirion Bowen (ed.), *Tippett on Music* (Oxford, 1995), pp. 96–8.

11 *Ibid.*, pp. 101, 103–4.

12 Bálint András Varga, *Conversations with Iannis Xenakis* (London, 1996), pp. 64–5.

13 Richard Steinitz, *György Ligeti: Music of the Imagination* (London, 2003), p. 139.

14 *Ibid.*

15 Ian Pace, 'The Piano Music', in Henrietta Brougham, Christopher Fox and Ian Pace (eds.), *Uncommon Ground: the Music of Michael Finnissy* (Aldershot, 1997), p. 71.

16 *Ibid.*, pp. 72–3.

17 John Adams, booklet with TELARC CD-80494 (1999) p. 5.

18 See Arnold Whittall, *Exploring Twentieth-Century Music* (Cambridge, 2003), pp. 180–5.

19 John Adams, note with Nonesuch CD, 79465–2 (1998).

20 John Adams, note with Nonesuch CD, 79607–2 (2000).

10 The rise (and fall) of the concerto virtuoso in the late eighteenth and nineteenth centuries

1 George Grove, *A Dictionary of Music and Musicians* (4 vols., London, 1899), vol. 4, p. 313.

2 Johann Gottfried Walther, *Musikalisches Lexikon oder musikalische Bibliothek* (Leipzig, 1732), p. 638: 'Virtu [*ital.*] bedeutet diejenige Musicalische Geschicklichkeit . . . entweder in der Theorie, oder in der Ausübung, etwas ungemeines zum Voraus hat. Der oder die solche besitzen, werden daher mit dem *Epitheto*: *virtuoso* oder *virtudioso*, und *virtuosa* oder *virtudiosa* belegt.'

3 James Grassineau, *A Musical Dictionary* (London, 1740), p. 330.

4 Johann Mattheson, *Grundlage einer Ehrenpforte* (Hamburg, 1740), p. 245: 'ein *perfecten* und raren Virtuosen'.

5 Heinrich Christoph Koch, *Musikalisches Lexikon* (Frankfurt, 1802), col. 1699: '*Virtu*, bezeichnet im Fache der Kunst eben so viel, wie Künstlerverdienste; man nennet daher denjenigen Virtuos, der sich als Künstler vorzüglich ausgezeichnet'.

6 Jane L. Baldauf-Berdes, *Women Musicians of Venice: Musical Foundations 1525–1855* (Oxford, 1993), p. 107. Giovanni Battista Sfondrino's *Trattenimento virtuoso disposto in leggiadrissime sonate per la chitarra* (Milan, 1637) apparently appeals to all possible positive meanings of 'virtuoso': it is entertaining (according to the title), technically advanced and compositionally wide ranging, including most major genres of the day.

7 'Vortrag', in Johann Georg Sulzer (ed.), *Allgemeine Theorie der schönen Künste* (4 vols., Leipzig, 1774; reprint Hildesheim, 1969), vol. 4, p. 706: '. . . ist est der Ausdruck allein, der bey dem Vortrag des nämlichen Stüks den Meister von seinem Schüler, den großen Virtuosen von dem mittelmäßigen, unterscheidet'; cited in Erich Reimer, 'Der Begriff des wahren Virtuosen in der Musikästhetik des späten 18. und frühen 19. Jahrhunderts', *Basler Jahrbuch für historische Musikpraxis*, 20 (1996), p. 63.

8 Ferdinand Simon Gassner, *Universal-Lexikon der Tonkunst* (Stuttgart, 1849), p. 871: 'wir theilen in der Musik die Künstler ein in zwei Hauptclassen, in dichtende und ausübende; jene sind die Componisten oder sogenannten Tondichter und Tonsetzer (s.d.),

diese die Virtuosen, d.h. diejenigen Musiker, welche die componirten Tonstücke vortragen, und deshalb sich auf irgend einem Instrumente oder im Gesange eine besondere Fertigkeit aneignen. Daher auch der Name, denn das italienische *virtu* oder lateinische *virtus*, wovon der Name Virtuos abstammt, bedeutet in der Kunst so viel als Vollkommenheit, Verdienst, Auszechnung u.s.w.'

9 Oskar Paul, *Handlexikon der Tonkunst* (Leipzig, 1873), vol. 2, p. 560: 'der Musiker, welcher, von Tonstücke vor zutragen, sich auf einem Instrumente oder im Gesange eine vollkommene Fertigkeit angeeignet hat. Diese selbst nennt man Virtuosität'.

10 Charles Burney, *The Present State of Music in France and Italy* (London, 1773), pp. 213–14.

11 *The Times* (London), 20 July 1836, p. 7, col. A.

12 See Chappell White, *Giovanni Battista Viotti (1755–1824): a Thematic Catalogue of His Works* (New York, 1985); and White, *From Vivaldi to Viotti: a History of the Classical Violin Concerto* (Philadelphia, 1992).

13 See Manfred Hermann Schmid, 'Ein Violinkonzert von Viotti als Herausforderung für Mozart und Haydn', *Mozart-Studien*, 5 (1995), pp. 149–71.

14 Robin Stowell, 'Nicolo Paganini (1782–1840): the Violin Virtuoso *in excelsis?*', *Basler Jahrbuch für historische Musikpraxis*, 20 (1996), pp. 76–7.

15 In general, see Arthur Pougin, *Notice sur Rode* (Paris, 1874); Boris Schwarz, 'Beethoven and the French Violin School', *MQ*, 44 (1958), pp. 431–47; and Jean Mongrédien, *La musique en France, des lumières au romantisme: 1789–1830* (Paris, 1986).

16 See Simon McVeigh, 'The Professional Concert and Rival Subscription Series in London, 1783–1793', *R. M. A. Research Chronicle*, 22 (1989), pp. 1–135; and McVeigh, *The Violinist in London's Concert Life, 1750–1784: Felice Giardini and His Contemporaries* (New York, 1989).

17 Marc Pincherle, 'Sur François Barthélémon' in *Mélanges de musicologie offerts à M. Lionel de La Laurencie* (Paris, 1933), pp. 235–45.

18 Friedrich Rochlitz, 'Johann Peter Salomon', *AmZ*, 18 (1816), pp. 132–7; McVeigh, *The Violinist in London's Concert Life, 1750–1784.*

19 'Messrs. Mori, Spohr, and Kiesewetter', *Quarterly Musical Magazine and Review*, 3 (1821), pp. 323–7.

20 Louis Spohr, *Selbstbiographie* (Kassel, 1860–1); Folker Gothel, *Thematisch-bibliographisches Verzeichnis der Werke von Louis Spohr* (Tutzing, 1981); Clive Brown, *Louis Spohr: a Critical Biography* (Cambridge, 1984).

21 *AmZ*, 25 (1823), cols. 588–9: 'Es wurde mit der schönen Mozart'schen Symphonie in Es eröffnet, worauf, eines Zeischengesanges von Carafa nicht zu erwähnen, der Concertgeber sein sechstes grosses Pianoforte-Concert in Es dur mit seiner bekannten Meisterschaft vortrug. Nichts ist herzerhebender als einen so hochverdienten Künstler wie unsern Cramer Jahr aus Jahr ein mit unvermindertem Feuer auftreten zu sehen; es ist, als verjünge sich sein Talent mit jedem Frühling, und es war gewiss nur Eine Stimme, dass er noch nie so schön gespielt habe als diessmal. Seine Stärke liegt bekanntlich im Adagio, denn hier findet er am besten Gelegenheit, seinen schönen, vollen Ton und feinen Geschmack im Bortrage zu zeigen. Ausser jenem Concert in Es spielte er noch ein Pianoforte-Quintett und zwey Pianoforte-Duos zu vier Händen, nämlich die schöne Sonate von Hummel Op. 92. Mit Hrn. Kalkbrenner, und eine nicht minder gerühmte mit Hrn. Moscheles, dem Verfasser derselben. Diese beyden Duos waren offenbar die mächtigen Anzeihungen für unsere Klavierspielerinnen; denn, die drey grössten Meister auf diesem Instrumente in dem Aufwande all ihrer Fähigkeiten vergleichen zu können, ist kein alltägliches Glück.'

22 See Cliff Eisen, *New Mozart Documents: a Supplement to O. E. Deutsch's Documentary Biography* (London, 1991), pp. 140–3.

23 See Wilhelm von Lenz, *Die grossen Pianoforte-Virtuosen unserer Zeit aus persönlicher Bekanntschaft* (Berlin, 1872); Thomas B. Milligan, *The Concerto and London's Musical Culture in the Late 18th Century* (Ann Arbor, MI, 1983); and Milligan, *Johann Baptist Cramer (1771–1858): a Thematic Catalogue of His Works* (Stuyvesant, NY, 1994).

24 'Memoir of Mr. Frederick Kalkbrenner', *Quarterly Musical Magazine and Review*, 6 (1824), pp. 499–513; Antoine F. Marmontel, *Les pianistes célèbres: silhouettes et médallions* (Paris, 1878), pp. 97–115; Hans Nautsch, *Friederich Kalkbrenner: Wirkung und Werk* (Hamburg, 1983).

25 See Emil Smidak, *Isaak-Ignaz Moscheles: das Leben des Komponisten und seine Begegnungen mit Beethoven, Liszt, Chopin, Mendelssohn* (Vienna, 1988).

26 In general, see Franz Josef Ewens, *Anton Eberl: ein Beitrag zur Musikgeschichte in Wien um 1800* (Dresden, 1927).

27 See Joel Sachs, *Kapellmeister Hummel in England and France* (Detroit, 1977); Kurt Thomas, *Johann Nepomuk Hummel und Weimar* (Weimar, 1987); Hanns Schmid (ed.), *Johann Nepomuk Hummel, ein Komponist zur Zeit der Wiener Klassik: Eisenstadt 1987* (Eisenstadt, 1989).

28 Carl Czerny, *Erinnerungen aus meinem Leben*, ed. Walter Kolneder (Strasbourg, 1968); and Czerny, *On the Proper Performance of all Beethoven's Works for the Piano, with excerpts from Czerny's Memoirs and Anecdotes and Notes about Beethoven*, ed. Paul Badura-Skoda (Vienna, 1970). See also George Barth, *The Pianist as Orator* (Ithaca, 1992).

29 See Marmontel, *Les pianistes célèbres.*

30 See Lucian Schiwietz, *Johann Peter Pixis: Beiträge zu seiner Biographie, zur Rezeptionshistoriographie seiner Werke und Analyse seiner Sonatenformung* (Frankfurt, 1994).

31 For Henselt, see Wilhelm von Lenz, *Die grossen Pianoforte-Virtuosen unserer Zeit aus personlicher Bekanntschaft: Liszt, Chopin, Tausig, Henselt* (Berlin, 1872).

32 See Leon Plantinga, *Clementi: his Life and Music* (London, 1977); Simon McVeigh, *Concert Life in London from Mozart to Haydn* (Cambridge, 1993).

33 For Field, see Marmontel, *Les pianistes célèbres*, pp. 96–105; Cecil Hopkinson, *A Bibliographical Thematic Catalogue of the Works of John Field* (London, 1961).

34 For Ries, see Cecil Hill, *The Music of Ferdinand Ries: a Thematic Catalogue* (Armidale, New South Wales, 1977).

35 On Wölfl's competition with Beethoven, see Tia DeNora, 'The Beethoven–Wölfl Piano Duel', in David Wyn Jones (ed.), *Music in Eighteenth-Century Austria* (Cambridge, 1996), pp. 259–82.

36 A contemporaneous report on Clementi, Dussek and Cramer, published in the *AmZ*, 5 (1802–3), cols. 196–7, is typical: 'If I had to attempt to characterize the playing of these three true masters, I would say the following: all three accomplish an admirable amount on their instrument. ... Clementi's greatest strength lies with the characteristic, pathetic Allegro, less with the Adagio; Dussek plays brilliant Allegro movements of enormous difficulty quite excellently, but performs Adagios as well in a delicate, agreeable and engaging manner; Cramer may not master so much difficulty, but he plays everything extremely neatly and clearly; there is also something peculiar, rare and piquant in his performance that can be felt instantaneously, but cannot be described in words'. Translation

from Katalin Komlós, *Fortepianos and their Music: Germany, Austria, and England, 1760–1800* (Oxford, 1995), p. 140.

37 Leon Plantinga, 'Clementi, Virtuosity, and the "German Manner"', *JAMS*, 25 (1972), pp. 303–30.

38 For an account of some of Herz's travels as a virtuoso, see his *Mes voyages en Amérique* (Paris, 1866), trans. Henry Bertram Hill as *My Travels in America* (Madison, WI, 1963).

39 'Virtuoso', in *Dictionary of the History of Ideas* (New York, 1973–4), vol. 4, p. 487; see also Walter E. Houghton, Jr., 'The English Virtuoso in the Seventeenth Century: Part I', *Journal of the History of Ideas*, 3 (1942), pp. 51–73.

40 But see Joseph M. Gilde, 'Shadwell and the Royal Society: Satire in The Virtuoso', *Studies in English Literature, 1500–1900*, 10 (1970), pp. 469–90, who argues that the Royal Society is not the object of Shadwell's satire but that it provides a standard for judging the useless science of the play's two main characters, Sir Nicholas Gimcrack and Sir Formal Trifle. There is no question, however, that Molière's *Les femmes savantes* is directly specifically at *virtuose*, who were also prominent at the time, not only in France but at the Royal Society as well. Molière's play was adapted by Thomas Wright and produced in 1693 as *The Female Vertuosos*. It was for this production that Purcell wrote the duet 'Love, Thou Art Best'; see *The Works of Henry Purcell. Volume XX: Dramatic Music, Part II* (London, 1916), pp. 7–10.

41 'Virtuoso' in *Dictionary of the History of Ideas*, vol. 4, p. 486.

42 *The Times* (London), 24 March 1790, p. 4, col. A.

43 *The Times* (London), 17 June 1873, p. 8, col. A.

44 Johann Mattheson, *Der Brauchbare Virtuoso, welcher sich (nach belibiger Uberlesung der Vorrede) mit Zwölf neuen Kammer = Sonaten /' af der Flute Traversiere, der Violine und dem Klavier bey Gelegenheit hören lassen mag* (Hamburg, 1720), pp. 2–3: '*Virtuosi* heissen bey den Italiänern (denen das Wort zugehöret) diejenigen so in einer gewissen Kunst / Z.E. in der Music a) Mahlerey / &c. *excelliren*. B) Ob nun zwar diese Benennung ihren Ursprung eigentlich *a virtute intellectuali*, von der Krafft oder Tugend des Verstandes hernimmt; so ist doch deswegen die *virtus moralis*, oder das tugendliche Wesen in den Sitten so wenig ausgeschlossen daß es vielmehr als etwas Unaussetzliches bey jedem *Virtuoso* voraus gesetzt oder *praesupponirt* wird ob es gleich / leider! Daran am meisten fehlet und aus diesem Mangel die

unbrauchbaresten *Virtuosi* zum Theil erwachsen. ... Die *Virtus intellectualis* kan demnach bey einem *Subjecto* gäntzlich / oder zum Theil von der *morali* entblösset seyn / und so ist mancher zwar ein *Virtuoso*, aber gemeiniglich ein schändlicher und unbrauchbarer.' I am indebted to Stewart Spencer for the translation of this passage.

45 Here Hiller defines a 'solo' as a work for a single voice with basso continuo and a 'concerto' as a work with several accompanying voices. The implication is that, except for the accompanying ensemble, the two kinds of works are comparable.

46 Hiller, 'Von der Nachahmung der Natur in der Musik', in Friedrich Wilhelm Marpurg (ed.), *Historisch-kritische Beyträge zur Aufnahme der Musik* (Berlin, 1754), vol. 1, pp. 537–8: 'Die Melodie des Solo oder Concerts, wenn man es allemal eine nennen kann, ist nicht so wohl ein nachgeahmter Gesang der Leidenschaften und des Herzens, als vielmehr eine nach der Schaffenheit des Instruments, worauf gespielt wird, eingerichtete künstliche Berbindung der Töne, von deren Richtigkeit man mehr die Kunst als die Natur muß urtheilen lassen. ... Der Künstler will durch dergleichen Stücke seine Stärke und die Vollkommenheit seines Instruments zeigen. Er sucht nicht so wohl zu bewegen, als bewundert zu werden. Das Erstaunen der Zuhörer ist allein der Beyfall den er verlanget. ... Ueberhaupt ist die Neigung zum Wunderbaren beständig eine gefährliche Klippe für die Künst gewesen. Der gute Geschmack, durch den sie allein schön waren, scheiterte gar bald daran, und die Künste verlorren sich in eine Nacht von Schwulst und Barbarey. Lauter Blendwerk kam an die Stelle des Wahrhaften; und an statt des ächten Glanzes umgab nichts, als ein falscher Schimmer die Werke der Kunst.'

47 Christian Friedrich Daniel Schubart, *Ideen zu einer Ästhetik der Tonkunst* (Vienna, 1806), p. 295: 'Der Solospieler muss entweder seine eignen oder fremde Phantasien vortragen. In beyden Fällen muss Genie sein Eigenthum seyn. Will ich eine Sonate von *Bach* vortragen, so muss ich mich so ganz in den Geist dieses grossen Mannes versenken, dass meine Ichheit wegschwindet.'

48 Georg Wilhelm Friedrich Hegel, *Vorlesungen über die Ästhetik*, in Eva Moldenhauer and Karl Markus Michel (eds.), *Werke* (Frankfurt, 1970), vol. 15, pp. 219–20.

49 *AmZ*, 15 (1813), cols. 153–4: 'Mancher sogenannte Virtuos verwirft die B.sche Flügel-Composition, indem er dem Vorwurfe: Sehr schwer! noch hinzufügt: Und höchst undenkbar! Was nun die Schwierigkeit betrifft, so gehört zum richtigen, bequemen Vortragen B.scher Compositionen nichts Geringeres, als dass man ihn begreife, dass man tief in sein Wesen eindringe zu treten. ... Der ächte Künstler lebt nur in dem Werke, das er in dem Sinne des Meisters aufgefasst hat und nun vorträgt.'

50 *AmZ*, 1 (1798–9), cols. 523–4: 'Madame Auernhammer: Ihr ganzes Bestreben geht auf Überwindung fast unüberwindlicher Schwierigkeiten, dabey vernachläsigt sie das, was man im edlern Sinn Vortrag nennet, und wird es, bey diesem Umständen niemals zum wirklich schönen und ausdrucksvollen Spiel bringen. Ich will nicht entscheiden, welche von den beyden gewöhnlichen Ursachen dieser Erscheinung – ob Mangel an seinem Gefühl, oder Begierde glänzen zu wollen, bey dieser Virtuosin hieran Schuld sind.' 'Sie [Kurzböck] ist ganz mit dem Ausdrucksvollen und Angenehmen des Vortrags beschäftigt, denkt sich immer ganz in den Sinn der Kompositionen, die sie vorträgt, hinein.'

51 Mary Astell, *An Essay in Defence of the Female Sex* (2nd edition, London, 1696), pp. 97–9, 102–3.

52 'Musicanten', in Johann Heinrich Zedler, *Universal Lexikon* (Leipzig and Halle, 1739), vol. 22, pp. 1386–7: 'in den Dorff- und Bier-Schencken aufwartenden Stadt-Pfeiffer, und Bierfiedler' and 'die in Königlichen und Fürstliche Capellen befindliche[n] Virtuosen sich nicht gerne unter die Classe der Musicanten rechnen; sondern [wollten] vielmehr lieber Musick-Verständige, Musici, Virtuosen etc. heissen'; cited in Erich Reimer, 'Der Begriff des wahren Virtuosen', p. 62.

53 See Jacob and Wilhelm Grimm, *Deutsches Wörterbuch* (Leipzig, 1951), vol. 12, part 2, p. 374: 'das sind keine Virtuosen / die entweiht jemals für Lohnungunst / die Musik, sie blieben stets / die Apostel heil'ger Tonkunst'.

54 *The Times* (London), 17 February 1880, p. 7, col. D. Sivori is the Italian violin virtuoso Camillo Sivori (1815–95).

55 See Robin Stowell, 'Nicolo Paganini', p. 84.

56 *Ibid.*, p. 86.

57 Johann Jakob Walther, 'Advice to Devoted Lovers of the Violin', in Leon Sherer (ed.) *Hortulus Chelicus* (New York, 1981), introduction to facsimile edition, n.p.

58 Emily Anderson (trans. and ed.), *The Letters of Mozart and His Family* (3rd edition, London, 1985), p. 792 (letter of 12 January 1782). Concerning Mozart's piano duel at court with Clementi on 24 December 1781, see Katalin Komlós, 'Mozart and Clementi: a

Piano Competition and its Interpretation',
Historical Performance, 2 (1989), pp. 3–9.
59 Emily Anderson (trans. and ed.), *The
Letters of Beethoven* (London, 1961), vol. 1,
p. 120.
60 B. E. Sydow, S. Chainaye and D. Chainaye,
Correspondance de Frédéric Chopin (Paris,
1981), vol. 2, p. 39.
61 Franz Liszt, 'Lettres d'un bachelier ès
musique', cited in Paul Metzner, *Crescendo of
the Virtuoso* (Berkeley, CA, 1998), p. 144 (from
articles in *La Revue et gazette musicale de Paris*,
1837–9).
62 Metzner, *Crescendo of the Virtuoso*, p. 145.

11 Performance practice in the eighteenth-century concerto

1 As given in Cliff Eisen *et al.*, 'Concerto', *NG
Revised*, vol. 6, p. 247.
2 See John Humphries, *The Early Horn: a
Practical Guide* (Cambridge, 2000), pp. 87–8.
3 See Colin Lawson, *The Early Clarinet: a
Practical Guide* (Cambridge, 2000), pp. 35–6.
4 See, for example, Lawson's discussion (*ibid.*,
pp. 81–2) of the issues encountered in
determining the type of clarinet most
historically appropriate for a performance of
Stamitz's Clarinet Concerto in B flat.
5 See Jon W. Finson, 'The Violone in Bach's
Brandenburg Concerti', *Galpin Society
Journal*, 29 (1976), p. 105.
6 See Reine Dahlquist, *The Keyed Trumpet
and its Greatest Virtuoso, Anton Weidinger*
(Nashville, TN, 1975).
7 See Colin Lawson, *Mozart: Clarinet
Concerto* (Cambridge, 1996). See also Colin
Lawson (ed.), *The Cambridge Companion to
the Clarinet* (Cambridge, 1995) for details of
the various designs of early clarinet.
8 Eva Badura-Skoda, 'Komponierte J. S. Bach
"Hammerklavier-Konzerte"?' *Bach-Jahrbuch*,
77 (1991), pp. 159–71.
9 See David Rowland, *A History of Pianoforte
Pedalling* (Cambridge, 1993), pp. 11ff.
10 Interestingly, K. 466 and K. 467 were
probably composed for a fortepiano with a
pedalboard. See David Rowland, *Early
Keyboard Instruments: a Practical Guide*
(Cambridge, 2001), pp. 101–2.
11 Frédéric Kalkbrenner, *Méthode pour
apprendre le pianoforte* (Paris, 1830; English
trans. London, 1862), p. 10.
12 Rowland, *Pianoforte Pedalling*, pp. 14–25.
See also Kenneth Mobbs, 'Stops and Other
Special Effects on the Early Piano', *EM*, 12
(1984), pp. 471–6.
13 Mozart's Walter piano (early 1780s) in the
Internationale Stiftung Mozarteum in

Salzburg has three hand-stops, two for raising
the dampers and one for the moderator, but
also has two knee-levers which perform the
same function as the two damper-raising
stops. It may not, however, be in its original
state. See Michael Cole, *The Pianoforte in the
Classical Era* (Oxford, 1998), pp. 208–11.
14 Much of this information is indebted to
Rowland, *Pianoforte Pedalling*, to which the
reader should refer for further detail.
15 Rowland, *Pianoforte Pedalling*, pp. 52–81.
16 Neal Zaslaw, 'Toward the Revival of the
Classical Orchestra', *PRMA*, 103 (1976–7),
pp. 158–9. Zaslaw's argument can be extended
to most other instruments. See, for example,
Ingrid Pearson's chapter 'Playing Historical
Clarinets', in Lawson, *The Early Clarinet*,
pp. 41–62.
17 Rowland, *Early Keyboard Instruments*,
pp. 58–60.
18 See Colin Lawson and Robin Stowell, *The
Historical Performance of Music: an
Introduction* (Cambridge, 1999), pp. 22–5.
19 Humphries, *The Early Horn*, p. 5; Rachel
Brown, *The Early Flute: a Practical Guide*
(Cambridge, 2002), p. 7.
20 See Robin Stowell, *The Early Violin and
Viola: a Practical Guide* (Cambridge, 2001),
pp. 38–48.
21 For example, Mozart uses *col legno*
('coll'arco al roverscio') in the orchestral
string parts of the finale of his Violin Concerto
in A major, K. 219. Whether or not he intends
left-hand pizzicato in the *ossia* for bars 277–80
or in bars 382–4 of the finale of his G major
Violin Concerto, K. 216, is a contentious
matter.
22 The major treatises are reviewed
extensively in Frank Thomas Arnold, *The Art
of Accompanying from a Thorough-Bass as
Practised in the Seventeenth and Eighteenth
Centuries* (London, 1931) and Peter Williams,
Figured Bass Accompaniment (Edinburgh,
1970).
23 Johann Joachim Quantz, *Versuch einer
Anweisung die Flöte traversiere zu spielen*
(Berlin, 1752), trans. Edward R. Reilly as *On
Playing the Flute* (New York, 1966), pp. 249–50
and Table xxiii.
24 See Georg Muffat's detailed account of
Corelli's concerto practices in his *Ausserlesene
Instrumental-Musik* (Passau, 1701). Charles
Avison (*An Essay on Musical Expression*
(London, 1752), pp. 132–3) remarks that if
only one keyboard is employed, it should not
participate in the *concertino* sections.
25 See Peter Williams's survey in *NG Revised*,
vol. 4, pp. 691–8.
26 Quantz, *On Playing the Flute*, p. 223.

27 C. P. E. Bach states that 'accompaniment may be in one, two, three, four, or more parts'. See *Versuch über die wahre Art das Clavier zu spielen* (Berlin, vol. 1, 1753, revised 1787; vol. 2, 1762, revised 1797), trans. William J. Mitchell as *Essay on the True Art of Playing Keyboard Instruments* (New York, 1949), p. 175. Johann David Heinichen (*Der General-Bass in der Composition, oder Neue und gründliche Anweisung* (Dresden, 1728), pp. 131–2) recommends a many-voiced accompaniment texture, specifically with the harpsichord in mind.

28 See Quantz, *On Playing the Flute*, pp. 250–65.

29 Chappell White, *From Vivaldi to Viotti: a History of the Early Classical Violin Concerto* (New York, 1992), p. 53; Zaslaw, 'Toward the Revival', p. 179.

30 White, *From Vivaldi to Viotti*, p. 49.

31 See C. P. E. Bach, *Playing Keyboard Instruments*, Part II.

32 Daniel Gottlob Türk, *Anweisung zum Generalbassspielen* (Leipzig, 1791; 2nd enlarged edition, Leipzig, 1800), p. 324; English translation in White, *From Vivaldi to Viotti*, p. 50.

33 A. Peter Brown, 'Performance Practice: 5. Orchestral Music', in David Wyn Jones (ed.), *Oxford Composer Companion: Haydn* (Oxford, 2002), pp. 283–4.

34 Dexter Edge, 'Manuscript Parts as Evidence of Orchestral Size in the Eighteenth-Century Viennese Concerto', in Neal Zaslaw (ed.), *Mozart's Piano Concertos: Text, Context, Interpretation* (Ann Arbor, MI, 1996), pp. 427–60. Lawson (*Mozart: Clarinet Concerto*, p. 78) similarly doubts if a fortepiano would contribute usefully to the texture of Mozart's Clarinet Concerto, K. 622.

35 Eva and Paul Badura-Skoda, *Mozart-Interpretation* (Vienna, 1957), trans. Leo Black as *Interpreting Mozart on the Keyboard* (London, 1962), pp. 197–8.

36 Horst Heussner, 'Zur Musizierpraxis der Klavierkonzerte im 19. Jahrhundert', *Mozart-Jahrbuch*, 15 (1967), pp. 165–75.

37 Charles Rosen, *The Classical Style: Haydn, Mozart, Beethoven* (London, 1971), pp. 189–96; Faye Ferguson, 'The Classical Keyboard Concerto: Some Thoughts on Authentic Performance', *EM*, 12 (1984), pp. 437–45; Ferguson, 'Mozart's Keyboard Concertos: Tutti Notations and Performance Models', *Mozart-Jahrbuch, 1984/85*, pp. 32–9; Robert Levin, 'Improvisation and Embellishment in Mozart Piano Concertos', *Musical Newsletter*, 5/2 (1975), pp. 3–14; Ellwood Derr, '*Basso Continuo* in Mozart's

Piano Concertos: Dimensions of Compositional Completion and Performance Practice', in Zaslaw (ed.), *Mozart's Piano Concertos*, pp. 393–410.

38 See Tibor Szász, 'Beethoven's *Basso Continuo*: Notation and Performance', in Robin Stowell (ed.), *Performing Beethoven* (Cambridge, 1994), pp. 1–22; Szász, 'Figured Bass in Beethoven's "Emperor" Concerto: Basso Continuo or Orchestral Cues?', *Early Keyboard Journal*, 6–7 (1988–9), pp. 5–71.

39 English and other national practices largely comprised a synthesis of Italian, Spanish, Dutch, German and French customs, the English most closely approximating the Italians for sheer impulsiveness, expressive freedom and richness of fantasy.

40 François Raguenet, *Parallèle des Italiens et des Français en ce qui regarde la musique et les opéras* (1702), in Oliver Strunk (ed.), *Source Readings in Music History* (New York, 1950), pp. 473–88; Jean Laurent le Cerf de Viéville, 'From the "Comparaison de la musique italienne et de la musique française"' (1704), in Strunk (ed.), *Source Readings*, pp. 489–507.

41 Quantz, *On Playing the Flute*, pp. 334–5.

42 *Ibid.*, pp. 342 and 338.

43 Several of these concerti grossi are based on Muffat's collection of 'sonatas' entitled *Armonico Tributo* (1682); Nos. 2, 4, 5 and 11 are reworkings respectively of sonatas Nos. 3, 2, 1 and 4, while Nos. 11 and 12 use material from the Fifth Sonata.

44 David Ross ('A Comprehensive Performance Project in Clarinet Literature with an Organological Study of the Development of the Clarinet in the Eighteenth Century' (Ph.D. thesis, University of Iowa, 1985)) concludes that the relatively small amount of undercutting in eighteenth-century English clarinets contributed to their lighter timbre, while the larger tone-holes of the Bohemian clarinets of Mozart's time, especially at their lower end, resulted in a fuller tone in the chalumeau register.

45 See Peter Williams, *A New History of the Organ* (London, 1980); Fenner Douglass, *The Language of the Classical French Organ* (New Haven, 1969).

46 Francesco Geminiani, *The Art of Playing on the Violin* (London, 1751; facsimile edition, London [1952]), Preface, p. 1.

47 Quantz, *On Playing the Flute*, p. 107.

48 *Ibid.*, pp. 223, 232; Leopold Mozart, *Versuch einer gründlichen Violinschule* (Augsburg, 1756), trans. Editha Knocker as *A Treatise on the Fundamental Principles of Violin Playing* (London, 1948), p. 45; C. P. E. Bach, *Playing Keyboard Instruments*, p. 154. For

further information on the meaning of dots and strokes, see Clive Brown, 'Dots and Strokes in Late 18th-Century and 19th-Century Music', *EM*, 22 (1993), pp. 593–610; Robert D. Levin, 'The Devil's in the Details: Neglected Aspects of Mozart's Piano Concertos', in Zaslaw (ed.), *Mozart's Piano Concertos*, pp. 29–32.

49 Daniel Gottlob Türk, *Clavierschule oder Anweisung zum Clavierspielen* (Leipzig and Halle, 1789), trans. Raymond Haagh as *School of Clavier Playing* (Lincoln, NE, 1982), p. 342.

50 See Dene Barnett, 'Non-Uniform Slurring in 18th-Century Music: Accident or Design?', *Haydn Yearbook*, 10 (1978), pp. 179–99; Georg von Dadelsen, 'Die Crux der Nebensache – Editorische und praktische Bemerkungen zu Bachs Artikulation', *Bach-Jahrbuch* (1978), pp. 95–112.

51 Johann Mattheson, *Der vollkommene Capellmeister* (Hamburg, 1739), p. 151. See also Frederick Neumann, 'Mattheson on Performance Practice', in George J. Buelow and Hans Joachim Marx (eds.), *New Mattheson Studies* (Cambridge, 1983), pp. 257–68.

52 C. P. E. Bach, *Playing Keyboard Instruments*, pp. 154–6; Quantz, *On Playing the Flute*, pp. 216–20, 230–2.

53 Friedrich Wilhelm Marpurg, *Anleitung zum Clavierspielen* (Berlin, 1755); Türk, *School of Clavier Playing*.

54 Jacques Hotteterre, *Principes de la flûte traversière* (Paris, 1707), trans. and ed. David Lasocki as *Principles of the Flute, Recorder and Oboe* (London, 1968), p. 63.

55 *Ibid.*, pp. 59–65.

56 See Quantz, *On Playing the Flute*, Chapter 6. 'Ti' and 'ri' are the equivalents of Hotteterre's 'tu' and 'ru'. There was disagreement about the syllables that the horn player, for example, should use for articulation purposes. Giovanni Punto (*Etude ou Exercice Journalier Ouvrage Périodique pour le Cor* (Offenbach, 1801), pp. 4–10) recommended 'daon' for strong tonguing, 'ta' for staccato and 'da' for softly tongued notes in more sustained passages. By contrast, Heinrich Domnich (*Méthode de Premier et de Second Cor* (Paris, 1807), p. 31) suggested 'tou' and 'dou'.

57 See 'Accentuation' (below).

58 Antoine Mahaut, *Nieuwe manier om binnen korten tijd op de dwarsfluit te leeren speelen* (Amsterdam, 1759); Lewis Granom, *Plain and Easy Instructions for Playing on the German Flute* (4th edition, London, 1766); Johann Georg Tromlitz, *Ausführlicher und gründlicher Unterricht die Flöte zu spielen* (Leipzig, 1791); John Gunn, *The School of the German Flute* (London, 1792).

59 See Brown, *The Early Flute*, pp. 50–1. Brown's survey of articulation (pp. 49–67) is an excellent digest of flute theorists' views, as is Ingrid Pearson's for the clarinet in Lawson, *The Early Clarinet*, pp. 47–51.

60 Leopold Mozart, *Fundamental Principles of Violin Playing*, p. 97.

61 John Butt, *Bach Interpretation: Articulation Marks in Primary Sources of J. S. Bach* (Cambridge, 1990), pp. 94–6.

62 Türk, *School of Clavier Playing*, p. 345.

63 Robert L. Marshall, 'Tempo and Dynamic Indications in the Bach Sources: a Review of the Terminology', in Peter Williams (ed.), *Bach, Handel, Scarlatti: Tercentenary Essays* (Cambridge, 1985), pp. 259–76.

64 Hans-Peter Schmitz, *Prinzipien der Aufführungspraxis Alter Musik* (Berlin, 1950), pp. 22–3.

65 See David Boyden, 'Dynamics in Seventeenth- and Eighteenth-Century Music', in *Essays in Honor of Archibald Thompson Davison by His Associates* (Cambridge, MA, 1957), pp. 185–93.

66 Sometimes the dynamic appears in the movement heading – for example Handel's Concerto Grosso Op. 6, No. 2, third movement (Larghetto andante, e piano) – with no dynamic markings notated.

67 See Levin, 'The Devil's in the Details', in Zaslaw (ed.), *Mozart's Piano Concertos*, pp. 32–5. Eva and Paul Badura-Skoda, *Interpreting Mozart*, p. 22.

68 Quantz, *On Playing the Flute*, p. 140.

69 See John O. Robison, 'The messa di voce as an Instrumental Ornament in the Seventeenth and Eighteenth Centuries', *Music Review*, 43 (1982), pp. 1–14.

70 Leopold Mozart, *Fundamental Principles of Violin Playing*, pp. 97–9.

71 Quantz, *On Playing the Flute*, p. 119.

72 *Ibid.*, p. 123. As the 'quickest notes' Quantz includes the crotchet in 3/2 metre, the quaver in 3/4 and the semiquaver in 3/8, the quaver in alla breve, and the semiquaver or demisemiquaver in 2/4 or common duple time.

73 Türk, *School of Clavier Playing*, p. 325.

74 Geminiani, *The Art of Playing*, Ex. VIII, p. 4.

75 Türk, *School of Clavier Playing*, pp. 325–7, 340–1, 327–9.

76 Quantz, *On Playing the Flute*, pp. 283–94. Quantz's system is a late version of the old fixed-tactus theory; see Neal Zaslaw, 'Mozart's Tempo Conventions', in Henrik Glahn, Søren Sørenson and Peter Ryom (eds.), *International Musicological Society: Report of the Eleventh Congress, Copenhagen 1972* (Copenhagen, 1974), vol. 2, pp. 720–33.

77 Michel de Saint Lambert, *Les Principes du clavecin* (Paris, 1702), trans. and ed. Rebecca Harris-Warwick as *Principles of the Harpsichord by Monsieur de Saint Lambert* (Cambridge, 1984), Chapter 8, p. 44.

78 See Rosamund Harding, *The Metronome and its Precursors* (London, 1938); Eugène Borrel, 'Les indications métronomiques laissés par les auteurs français du 18e siècle', *Revue de Musicologie* (1928), pp. 149–53; Ralph Kirkpatrick, '18th-Century Metronomic Indications', *Papers of the American Musicological Society* (1938), pp. 30–50.

79 Avison, *An Essay on Musical Expression*, p. 107. See also Rosamund Harding, *Origins of Musical Time and Expression* (London, 1938), Chapter 2; Quantz, *On Playing the Flute*, pp. 283–94.

80 All six words were qualified as required, Vivaldi being especially prolific in the variety and detail of his descriptions. See Walter Kolneder, *Aufführungspraxis bei Vivaldi* (1955), trans. A. de Dadelsen as *Performance Practices in Vivaldi* (Winterthur, 1979), p. 19.

81 Johann Walther, *Musikalisches Lexicon* (Leipzig, 1732); Sébastien de Brossard, *Dictionnaire de Musique* (Paris, 1703); Leopold Mozart, *Fundamental Principles of Violin Playing*, p. 51.

82 C. P. E. Bach, *Playing Keyboard Instruments*, p. 151.

83 See Quantz, *On Playing the Flute*, p. 200.

84 Francesco Galeazzi, *Elementi teorici-pratici di musica con un saggio sopra l'arte di suonare il violino analizzata, ed a dimostrabili principi ridotta* (2 vols., Rome, 1791–6), vol. 1, p. 36; Jean-Baptiste Cartier, *L'art du violon* (Paris, 1798), p. 17; Türk, *School of Clavier Playing*, p. 106.

85 Johann Philipp Kirnberger, in Johann Georg Sulzer (ed.), *Allgemeine Theorie der schönen Künste* (4 vols., Leipzig, 1771–4), vol. 1, p. 157. Türk later cited Kirnberger's idea.

86 See Peter Stadlen, 'Beethoven and the Metronome', *ML*, 48 (1967), pp. 330–49.

87 See, for example, C. P. E. Bach, *Playing Keyboard Instruments*, pp. 150–1; Leopold Mozart, *Fundamental Principles of Violin Playing*, p. 224; Türk, *School of Clavier Playing*, pp. 363–4.

88 See Türk, *School of Clavier Playing*, pp. 364–5.

89 C. P. E. Bach, *Playing Keyboard Instruments*, pp. 160–1.

90 See Heinrich Koch, 'Ueber den technischen Ausdruck Tempo rubato', *AmZ*, 10 (1808), pp. 513–19.

91 For detailed surveys of eighteenth-century ornaments, see Frederick Neumann, *Ornamentation in Baroque and Post-Baroque Music with Special Emphasis on J. S. Bach* (Princeton, 1978); and Neumann, *Ornamentation and Improvisation in Mozart* (Princeton, 1986).

92 C. P. E. Bach, *Playing Keyboard Instruments*, p. 79.

93 *Ibid.*, p. 82.

94 Such national divisions were not necessarily as clear-cut as my statement implies; for Austro-German ornamental practice was itself a hybrid mixture of national customs, some parts (for example Celle) being primarily French-influenced, and others (such as Salzburg) Italian-influenced.

95 C. P. E. Bach, *Playing Keyboard Instruments*, p. 85; Quantz, *On Playing the Flute*, pp. 341–2.

96 See, for example, Johann Peter Milchmeyer, *Die wahre Art das Pianoforte zu spielen* (Dresden, 1797), p. 37.

97 See Quantz, *On Playing the Flute*, p. 113.

98 See John Spitzer and Neal Zaslaw, 'Improvised Ornamentation in Eighteenth-Century Orchestras', *JAMS*, 39 (1986), pp. 524–77.

99 C. P. E. Bach, *Playing Keyboard Instruments*, pp. 79–80.

100 Nicholas Etienne Framery, Pierre Louis Ginguené and Jérôme-Joseph de Momigny (eds.), *Encyclopédie méthodique* (Paris, 1791), vol. 1, p. 182, s.v. 'Broderies'.

101 See Scheibe's criticism of Bach's approach and Birnbaum's defence of it in Hans T. David and Arthur Mendel (eds.), *The Bach Reader* (New York, 1945), pp. 238–48.

102 See Minnie Elmer, 'Tartini's Improvised Ornamentation, as illustrated by Manuscripts from the Berkeley Collection of 18th-Century Italian Instrumental Music' (Ph.D. thesis, University of California, Berkeley, 1962).

103 The autograph is housed in the British Library (Add. MS 28970). A scholarly modern edition has been prepared by Chappell White. See White (ed.), *Giovanni Battista Viotti: Four Violin Concertos* (Madison, WI, 1976).

104 Leopold Mozart, *Fundamental Principles of Violin Playing*, pp. 209–14. See also Joan E. Smiles, 'Directions for Improvised Ornamentation in Italian Method Books of the Late Eighteenth Century', *JAMS*, 31 (1978), pp. 495–509.

105 Jean-Jacques Rousseau, *Dictionnaire de Musique* (Paris, 1768), 'Romance'; Türk, *School of Clavier Playing*, p. 391.

106 Baillot, *L'art du violon; nouvelle méthode* (Paris, 1835), p. 158.

107 Reported by Reinecke, as quoted in Robert Haas, *Aufführungspraxis der Musik* (Leipzig, 1931), p. 259. See also Robert Levin, 'Improvisation and Embellishment in Mozart Piano Concertos', *Musical Newsletter*, 5/2 (1975), pp. 3–14; Henry Mishkin, 'Incomplete Notation in Mozart's Piano Concertos', *MQ*, 61 (1975), pp. 345–59.

108 Eva Badura-Skoda (in Zaslaw (ed.), *Mozart's Piano Concertos*, pp. 365–71) writes more fully about improvised embellishments, referring to the finale of K. 482 as well as to the interpretation of some sketchy notation in the left-hand part of numerous bars of the so-called 'Coronation' Concerto in D, K. 537.

109 See Mishkin, 'Incomplete Notation in Mozart's Piano Concertos'.

110 An example of such an improvised movement is given in Gerhard Krapf, *Bach: Improvised Ornamentation and Keyboard Cadenzas: an Approach to Creative Performance* (Dayton, OH, 1983), pp. 77–8.

111 Brown (*The Early Flute*, p. 104) gives examples from a manuscript collection housed in the library of the Brussels Conservatoire.

112 *Cadenza* is Italian for 'cadence'.

113 As White indicates (*From Vivaldi to Viotti*, p. 264), a few composers such as Giuseppe Demachi annotated numerous fermatas which beg cadenza-like improvisations (White counted no fewer than fifteen fermatas in Demachi's Op. 12), while some, notably Viotti, omitted cadenza markings altogether.

114 See Franz Giegling, *Giuseppe Torelli* (Kassel, 1949), pp. 27ff.

115 Pier Francesco Tosi, *Opinioni de' cantori antichi e moderni, o sieno osservazioni sopra il canto figurato* (Bologna, 1723), trans. and ed. John Ernest Galliard as *Observations on the Florid Song* (London, 1742), pp. 128–9; Quantz, *On Playing the Flute*, pp. 179–95.

116 Quantz, *On Playing the Flute*, p. 179. On the early history of cadenzas, see Heinrich Knödt, 'Zur Entwicklungsgeschichte der Kadenzen im Instrumental-Konzert', *Sammelbände der Internationalen Musikgesellschaft*, 15 (1914), pp. 375–419, and Arnold Schering, *Geschichte des Instrumental-Konzerts* (Leipzig, 1905), pp. 111–13.

117 Kolneder, *Aufführungspraxis bei Vivaldi*, p. 123.

118 This and another cadenza are included in Walter Kolneder, *Antonio Vivaldi: Dokumente seines Lebens und Schaffens* (Wilhelmshaven, 1979), pp. 52ff. The discussion of Vivaldi's cadenzas in Kolneder's *Aufführungspraxis bei Vivaldi* also includes some interesting examples.

119 Türk, *School of Clavier Playing*, pp. 297–309.

120 Quantz, *On Playing the Flute*, p. 328.

121 Giuseppe Tartini, *Traité des Agréments* (1771), ed. Erwin Jacobi (Celle and New York, 1961), pp. 117–25.

122 In the booklet notes for a recent compact disc of Viotti's Violin Concertos Nos. 2 and 18 (Bongiovanni GB5133–2), the anonymous writer refers to the recent discovery of Viotti's *Souvenirs de Violon*, a 'technical-musical journal' of his career that includes, either as studies or caprices, a collection of cadenzas for his concertos.

123 For a detailed discussion of the Classical cadenza, see Philip Whitmore, *Unpremeditated Art: the Cadenza in the Classical Keyboard Concerto* (Oxford, 1991). See also Neumann, *Ornamentation and Improvisation in Mozart*, pp. 257–63; Eva and Paul Badura-Skoda, *Interpreting Mozart*, pp. 214–34.

124 See Christoph Wolff, 'Zur Chronologie der Klavierkonzert-Kadenzen Mozarts', *Mozart-Jahrbuch 1978/9*, pp. 235–46.

125 Among the most successful attempts to compose stylish cadenzas for concertos by Mozart are those of Marius Flothius (for the Piano Concertos K. 466, 467, 482, 491, 503 and 537, the Flute Concertos K. 313 and 314, the Flute and Harp Concerto K. 299 and the Violin Concertos K. 211, 216, 218 and 219) and Robert Levin (for the Violin Concertos K. 207, 211, 216, 218 and 219). Paul Badura-Skoda's *Kadenzen, Eingänge und Auszierungen zu Klavierkonzerten von Wolfgang Amadeus Mozart* (Kassel, 1967) and the efforts of Hans Henkemans are also admirable, if less attuned to the *minutiae* of Mozart's vocabulary.

126 Quantz, *On Playing the Flute*, p. 185. For examples of original woodwind cadenzas see David Lasocki and Betty Bang Mather, *The Classical Woodwind Cadenza* (New York, 1978).

127 In Howard Mayer Brown and Stanley Sadie (eds.), *Performance Practice: Music after 1600* (London, 1989), p. 280.

128 Quantz, *On Playing the Flute*, pp. 186–92.

129 C. P. E. Bach, *Playing Keyboard Instruments*, pp. 143–6; Türk, *School of Clavier Playing*, pp. 289–96.

130 See Daniel Koury, *Orchestral Performance Practices of the Nineteenth Century* (Ann Arbor, MI, 1986), pp. 5–28.

131 Quantz, *On Playing the Flute*, p. 214. Quantz assumed 'that the harpsichord will be

included in all ensembles, whether large or small'.

132 Muffat, *Ausserlesene Instrumentalmusik*.

133 Letter of 26 April 1783, in Emily Anderson (ed.), *The Letters of Mozart and His Family* (3rd edition, London, 1985), p. 846. Mozart later claimed that his Piano Concerto K. 449 could be played 'a quattro'.

134 Zaslaw, 'Toward the Revival', p. 180. On pp. 171–7, Zaslaw provides a useful tabular overview of the size and composition of orchestras 1774–96, gathered (and verified wherever possible) from nineteenth- and twentieth-century sources.

135 Zaslaw ('Toward the Revival', p. 170) cites the example of the court orchestra at Donaueschingen, as reported in Friedrich Schnapp, 'Neue Mozart-Funde in Donaueschingen', *Neues Mozart-Jahrbuch* (1942), pp. 211–23.

136 Koury, *Orchestral Performance Practices*, pp. 38–9. On p. 15, he tabulates the constitution of various eighteenth-century orchestras. See also Brown, 'Performance Practice: Orchestral Music', in Jones (ed.), *Oxford Composer Companion: Haydn*, pp. 282–4.

137 Dexter Edge, 'Manuscript Parts as Evidence of Orchestral Size in the Eighteenth-Century Viennese Concerto', in Zaslaw (ed.), *Mozart's Piano Concertos*, pp. 427–60.

138 Quantz, *On Playing the Flute*; Carl Ludwig Junker, *Zwanzig Componisten: eine Skizze* (Bern, 1776); Carl Ludwig Junker, *Einige der vornehmsten Pflichten eines Kapellmeisters oder Musikdirektors* (Winterthur, 1782); Johann Samuel Petri, *Anleitung zur practischen Musik* (Lauban, 1767); Johann Reichardt, *Über die Pflichten des Ripien-Violinisten* (Berlin and Leipzig, 1776); Heinrich Koch, *Musikalisches Lexikon* (Frankfurt am Main, 1802).

139 Quantz, *On Playing the Flute*, pp. 212–13; the text is illustrated by a seating plan. The ambiguity of Quantz's instructions – it is unclear what he meant by 'on the left side of the harpsichord' – has caused Koury to deduce a different physical arrangement from the text. See Koury, *Orchestral Performance Practices*, pp. 36 and 38.

140 Koury, *Orchestral Performance Practices*, p. 56. At the turn of the century, Friedrich Rochlitz ('Bruchstücke aus Briefen an einen jungen Tonsetzer', *AmZ*, 2 (1799–1800), col. 59) complained that placement of orchestras had not been changed to reflect new compositional procedures, for example with regard to bassoons, trumpet and drums.

141 Koury, *Orchestral Performance Practices*, p. 38, note 23.

142 Zaslaw, 'Toward the Revival', p. 165 (includes illustration).

143 Heinrich Koch, *Musikalisches Lexikon* (Frankfurt, 1802), 'Stellung', cols. 1435–8; Petri, *Anleitung zur practischen Musik* (2nd edition, Leipzig, 1782), p. 188.

144 For more evidence on solo practices and direction, see Koury, *Orchestral Performance Practices*.

145 See Joseph Adolph Scheibe, *Critischer Musikus*, 69 (22 December 1739), p. 631.

146 Edge, 'Manuscript Parts as Evidence of Orchestral Size', in Zaslaw (ed.), *Mozart's Piano Concertos*, p. 445.

147 Lawson, *Mozart: Clarinet Concerto*, p. 78.

148 Mozart's flexibility regarding the instrumentation of the accompanying forces for K. 413, K. 414 and K. 415 has already been mentioned.

12 Performance practice in the nineteenth-century concerto

1 *AmZ*, 2 (1799–1800), col. 781.

2 Johann Nepomuk Hummel, *A Complete Theoretical and Practical Course of Instructions on the Art of Playing the Pianoforte* (London, 1828), Part 3, p. 65. Pianos made in southern Germany and Austria are generally referred to as 'Viennese'. They differ in several important respects from their northern European counterparts, which are usually referred to as 'English'. The action and construction of the two types are fundamentally different, as are their playing characteristics. The sound of 'Viennese' pianos is bright and their playing mechanism easily facilitates a clearly articulated style. The 'English' pianos have a somewhat duller sound, but they are powerful and rich, particularly in the bass, and are well suited to a more cantabile style.

3 As given in David Boyden, Peter Walls *et al.*, 'Violin', in *NG Revised*, vol. 26, p. 716.

4 David Rowland (ed.), *The Cambridge Companion to the Piano* (Cambridge, 1998), pp. 32–3, 46.

5 An account of the most relevant issues will be found in Daniel J. Koury, *Orchestral Performance Practices in the Nineteenth Century: Size, Proportions, and Seating* (Ann Arbor, MI, 1986), from which much of the general information for this section is taken.

6 A. D. Coleridge (trans.), *Life of Moscheles with Selections from His Diaries and Correspondence by His Wife* (London, 1873), vol. 1, p. 125.

7 Clive Brown, *Louis Spohr: a Critical Biography* (Cambridge, 1984), p. 111.

8 *Illustrated London News* (17 February 1849).

9 Gisella Selden-Goth (ed. and trans.), *Felix Mendelssohn: Letters* (London, 1946), p. 191.

10 Koury, *Orchestral Performance Practices*, p. 161, gives sample figures for the size of orchestras throughout the nineteenth century.

11 Brown, *Louis Spohr*, pp. 131–2.

12 Linda Faye Ferguson, '"Col basso" and "Generalbass" in Mozart's Keyboard Concertos: Notation, Performance Theory, and Practice' (Ph.D. thesis, Princeton University, 1983); Tibor Szász, 'Beethoven's *basso continuo*: Notation and Performance', in Robin Stowell (ed.), *Performing Beethoven* (Cambridge, 1994), pp. 1–22.

13 Szász, 'Beethoven's *basso continuo*', p. 22.

14 *Ibid.*

15 For some accounts of concert life in the nineteenth century, see the following: Otto Biba, 'Concert Life in Beethoven's Vienna', in Robert Winter and Bruce Carr (eds.), *Beethoven, Performers, and Critics* (Detroit, 1980), pp. 77–93; Peter Bloom, *Music in Paris in the Eighteen-Thirties* (Stuyvesant, NY, 1987); Jeffrey Cooper, *The Rise of Instrumental Music and Concert Series in Paris, 1828–1871* (Ann Arbor, MI, 1983); Theresa Marie Ellsworth, 'The Piano Concerto in London Concert Life between 1801 and 1850' (Ph.D. thesis, University of Cincinnati, 1991); Alice M. Hanson, *Musical Life in Biedermeier Vienna* (Cambridge, 1985); Mary Sue Morrow, *Concert Life in Haydn's Vienna: Aspects of a Developing Musical and Social Institution* (Stuyvesant, NY, 1989); Janet Ritterman, 'Piano Music and the Public Concert, 1800–1850', in Jim Samson (ed.), *The Cambridge Companion to Chopin* (Cambridge, 1992), pp. 11–31; William G. Weber, *Music and the Middle Class: the Social Structure of Concert Life in London, Paris, and Vienna between 1830 and 1848* (London, 1975).

16 *The Examiner*, 9 March 1850.

17 Cyril Ehrlich, *First Philharmonic: a History of the Royal Philharmonic Society* (Oxford, 1995), p. 4.

18 Ellsworth, 'The Piano Concerto in London Concert Life', Chapter 2.

19 *Ibid.*, pp. 57ff.

20 Jim Samson, 'Canon', *NG Revised*, vol. 5, pp. 6–7.

21 Cooper, *The Rise of Instrumental Music and Concert Series in Paris*, Chapter 4.

22 Ellsworth, 'The Piano Concerto in London Concert Life', pp. 148–9; Cooper, *The Rise of Instrumental Music and Concert Series in Paris*, Chapter 4.

23 Harry Haskell, *The Early Music Revival* (London, 1988), pp. 19ff.

24 Eva Badura-Skoda, 'Performance Conventions in Beethoven's Early Works', in Winter and Carr (eds.), *Beethoven, Performers, and Critics*, pp. 60–1; David Grayson, 'Whose Authenticity? Ornaments by Hummel and Cramer for Mozart's Piano Concertos', in Neal Zaslaw (ed.), *Mozart Piano Concertos: Text, Context, Interpretation* (Ann Arbor, MI, 1996), pp. 373–91.

25 *The Harmonicon*, 11 (1833), p. 135.

26 John Rink, *Chopin: the Piano Concertos* (Cambridge, 1997), pp. 14–19.

27 Ellsworth, 'The Piano Concerto in London Concert Life', pp. 30, 77.

28 *Ibid.*, p. 86.

29 *Ibid.*, p. 94.

30 Brown, *Louis Spohr*, pp. 111, 173.

31 William G. Atwood, *Fryderyk Chopin: Pianist from Warsaw* (New York, 1987), p. 23.

32 Ellsworth, 'The Piano Concerto in London Concert Life', pp. 77, 81.

33 Otto Erich Deutsch, *Mozart: a Documentary Biography*, trans. Eric Blom, Peter Branscombe and Jeremy Noble (London, 1990), p. 212.

34 Emily Anderson (ed.), *The Letters of Mozart and His Family* (3rd edition, London, 1985), p. 877; Mozart's letter of 15 May 1784.

35 Translated in Ferguson, '"Col basso" and "Generalbass" in Mozart's Keyboard Concertos', pp. 239–40.

36 *Grand Concerto for the Piano Forte with full Orchestral Accompaniments (called 'Les Adieux de Paris') . . . Op. 110* (London, 1826).

37 Grayson, 'Whose Authenticity?', in Zaslaw (ed.), *Mozart's Piano Concertos*, pp. 373, 384.

38 *Ibid.*, p. 387 (note 5).

39 Cooper, *The Rise of Instrumental Music and Concert Series in Paris*, pp. 52ff.

40 Ellsworth, 'The Piano Concerto in London Concert Life', p. 139.

41 *Ibid.*, especially pp. 139–40.

42 David Rowland, 'Clementi and the British Concerto Tradition', in Roberto Illiano, Luca Sala and Massimiliano Sala (eds.), *Muzio Clementi: Studies and Prospects* (Bologna, 2002), pp. 179–90.

43 Rowland, 'Clementi and the British Concerto Tradition', p. 183.

44 Atwood, *Fryderyk Chopin*, p. 43.

45 Michael Thomas Roeder, *A History of the Concerto* (Portland, OR, 1994), p. 222.

46 *Grand Concerto for the Piano Forte, Op. 110*, title-page.

47 Rowland, 'Clementi and the British Concerto Tradition', pp. 187–8.

48 Anthony van Hoboken, *Joseph Haydn: thematisch-bibliographisches Werkverzeichnis* (Mainz, 1957), vol. 1, p. 825.

49 Ferguson, '"Col basso" and "Generalbass" in Mozart's Keyboard Concertos', p. 36.

50 *Fourth Concerto, for the Piano Forte with Accompaniment for an Orchestra or for a Second Piano Forte . . . Op.131* (London, 1843).

51 Atwood, *Fryderyk Chopin*, pp. 150, 243.

52 *Ibid.*, pp. 48, 218.

53 *Life of Moscheles*, vol. 1, pp. 329–30.

54 Rowland, 'Clementi and the British Concerto Tradition', p. 187.

55 *AmZ*, 51 (1849), cols. 707–10 and 741–4. See Howard Allen Craw, 'A Biography and Thematic Catalogue of the Works of J. L. Dussek (1760–1812)' (Ph.D. thesis, University of Southern California, 1964).

56 See, for example, Dussek's concertos Opp. 17 (C.53) and 30 (C.129), which exist in authentic versions for either harp or piano.

57 Ellsworth, 'The Piano Concerto in London Concert Life', p. 172.

58 Carl Czerny, *A Systematic Introduction to Improvisation on the Pianoforte*, Op. 200 (1829), trans. and ed. Alice L. Mirchell (New York and London, 1983), p. 15.

59 Tommaso Giordani, *Preludes for the Harpsichord or Piano Forte in all the Keys flat and sharp* (London, 177?); Muzio Clementi, *Clementi's Musical Characteristics, or a Collection of Preludes and Cadences for the Harpsichord or Pianoforte . . . Op. 19* (London, 1787); Johann Nepomuk Hummel, *Vorspiele vor Anfang eines Stückes aus allen 24 Dur und Mol Tonarten* (Vienna, *c.*1814); Johann Baptist Cramer, *Twenty-Six Preludes or short Introductions in the principle major and minor Keys* (London, 1818); Tobias Haslinger, *XXX Vorspiele in den gebräuchlichsten Dur und Moll Tonarten* (Vienna, 1818); Ignaz Moscheles, *50 Preludes in the major and minor Keys . . . Op. 73* (London, 1827); Frédéric Kalkbrenner, *Twenty-Four Preludes for the Piano Forte, in all the major and minor Keys* (London, 1827). See also Betty Bang Mather and David Lasocki, *The Art of Preluding, 1700–1830* (New York, 1984), which contains examples of preludes for non-keyboard instruments.

60 Valerie Woodring Goertzen, 'By Way of Introduction: Preluding by 18th- and Early 19th-Century Pianists', *JM*, 14 (1996), pp. 299–337, and 'Setting the Stage: Clara Schumann's Preludes', in Bruno Nettl and Melinda Russell (eds.), *In the Course of Performance: Studies in the World of Musical Improvisation* (Chicago and London, 1998), pp. 237–60.

61 Carl Czerny, *Complete Theoretical and Practical Pianoforte School, Op.500* (London, 1839), Part 3, p. 87.

62 Goertzen, 'By Way of Introduction', p. 307.

63 Hummel, *A Complete Theoretical and Practical Course*, Part 3, p. 40.

64 Dennis Libby *et al.*, 'Improvisation', *NG*, vol. 9, p. 49.

65 *The Musical World*, 13, no. 217 (new series, vol. 6, no. 124), 14 May 1840, p. 305.

66 Goertzen, 'By Way of Introduction', p. 335.

67 Goertzen, 'Setting the Stage', p. 253.

68 Translated in Badura-Skoda, 'Performance Conventions in Beethoven's Early Works', p. 58.

69 Badura-Skoda, 'Performance Conventions in Beethoven's Early Works', p. 61.

70 Emily Anderson (ed.), *The Letters of Beethoven* (London, 1961), vol. 2, p. 560; Beethoven's letter to Czerny of 12 February 1816.

71 Colin Lawson, *The Early Clarinet: a Practical Guide* (Cambridge, 2000), p. 90.

72 Grayson, 'Whose Authenticity?', in Zaslaw (ed.), *Mozart's Piano Concertos*, pp. 373–91.

73 G. A. Macfarren, 'Cipriani Potter: his Life and Work', *PRMA*, 10 (1884), p. 46.

74 The most complete modern discussion is found in Philip Whitmore, *Unpremeditated Art: the Cadenza in the Classical Keyboard Concerto* (Oxford, 1991).

75 Jan Smaczny, *Dvořák: Cello Concerto* (Cambridge, 1999), pp. 89–90.

76 Ellsworth, 'The Piano Concerto in London Concert Life', p. 50.

77 Badura-Skoda, 'Performance Conventions in Beethoven's Early Works', p. 56.

78 *The Musical World*, 17 July 1845, p. 345.

79 Brown, *Louis Spohr*, p. 45.

80 *Louis Spohr's Autobiography* (London, 1865), vol. 2, pp. 71ff.

13 The concerto in the age of recording
There is no single authority, either published printed catalogue or database, which gives details of classical recordings from the whole of the century. For a list of the principal sources, see Timothy Day, *A Century of Recorded Music: Listening to Musical History* (New Haven and London, 2000), pp. 260–1.

Where labels and numbers of acoustic shellac 78rpm discs cited are not given they may be found in Claude Graveley Arnold, *The Orchestra on Record: an Encyclopedia of Orchestral Recordings Made by the Acoustical Process* (Westport, CT, and London, 1997).

Details of the electrical 78rpm discs cited are given in Francis F. Clough and G. J. Cuming, *The World's Encyclopædia of Recorded Music* (London, 1952). The record numbers given here for commercial discs are those that recordings carried on their first release. '78rpm' indicates a coarsegroove shellac disc (not necessarily playing at 78rpm). 'Digital' indicates that the master recording was digitally encoded.

1 Donald Francis Tovey, *Essays in Musical Analysis Volume 2: Symphonies, Variations and Orchestral Polyphony* (London, 1935).

2 Donald Francis Tovey, *Essays in Musical Analysis Volume 3: Concertos* (London, 1936), p. 3.

3 From a note in a Queen's Hall Promenade Concert programme by Edgar F. Jacques for Friday, 2 October 1896, and reproduced in numerous other Promenade Concert programmes at that time; *British Library shelfmark* h.5470.

4 London Promenade Concert programmes; *British Library shelfmark* h.5470.

5 Robert Philip, *Performing Music in the Age of Recording* (London, 2004), pp. 26–30.

6 Vocalion D 62107 (12" double-sided acoustic 78rpm disc issued in 1923).

7 Percy Scholes, *Everybody's Guide to Broadcast Music* (London, 1925), p. 10.

8 Asa Briggs, *The Golden Age of Wireless* (Oxford/New York, 1965/1995), p. 512.

9 Andrew Crisell, *An Introductory History of British Broadcasting* (London, 1997), p. 17.

10 *The Gramophone*, vol. 7, no. 80 (January 1930), p. 357.

11 *The Gramophone*, vol. 8, no. 91 (December 1930), p. 339.

12 E. H. Gombrich, 'The Tradition of General Knowledge' (Oration delivered at the London School of Economics and Political Science on 8 December 1961), *Ideals and Idols: Essays on Values in History and in Art* (London, 1979), pp. 16–17.

13 Guy Routh, *Occupation and Pay in Great Britain 1906–79* (London, 1980), pp. 166, 168.

14 Alfred Brendel, *The Veil of Order: Conversations with Martin Meyer* (London, 2002), p. 22.

15 RCA Victor RB 16073 (UK); RCA Victor LM-2252 (US) (12" 33⅓ rpm mono discs released 1958); Robert and Celia Dearling with Brian Rust, *The Guinness Book of Recorded Sound* (Enfield, 1984), pp. 153, 205.

16 *R.E.D.Classical 2000 Catalogue: Master Edition 1* (London, 1999), p. 119.

17 *Ibid.*, pp. 714–15.

18 Edward Sackville-West and Desmond Shawe-Taylor, *The Record Guide* (London, 1951), p. 383.

19 *R.E.D.Classical 2000 Catalogue: Master Edition 1*, p. 760.

20 Udo Zilkens, *Antonio Vivaldi: Zwischen Naturalismus und Pop: Die vier Jahreszeiten im Spiegel ihrer Interpretationen durch Musiktheoretiker und Musiker in Bearbeitungen und auf Plattencovern* (with a discography by Roger-Claude Travers) (Cologne-Rodenkirchen, 1996), p. 90.

21 Aaron Copland, *Our New Music: Leading Composers in Europe and America* (New York and London, 1941), p. 133.

22 Vox PL 7893 (three 12" 33⅓ rpm mono discs).

23 Compton Mackenzie, 'Editorial', *The Gramophone*, vol. 10, no. 114 (November 1932), p. 198.

24 Andrew Porter in Alec Robertson (ed.), *Music 1952* (Harmondsworth, 1952), p. 166.

25 Stephan Bultmann, 'Bach and Potatoes: Archiv Produktion's Early Years', *International Classical Record Collector* (Autumn 1998), pp. 54–8.

26 See, for example: Archiv Produktion APM 14097 (12" 33⅓ rpm mono disc released 1957).

27 Archiv Produktion, 1963 catalogue, p. 8; British Library.

28 Jerome F. Weber, 'Vox Productions – a Short History', *International Classical Record Collector* (November 1995), p. 24.

29 Andrew Porter, review of Vox DL 122, *The Gramophone*, vol. 33, no. 391 (December 1955), p. 268.

30 Denis Stevens, review of Archiv Produktion APM 14011–12, *The Gramophone*, vol. 32, no. 383 (April 1955), p. 485.

31 Archiv Produktion, 1963 catalogue, p. 8.

32 R. O. Morris, *The Structure of Music* (London, 1935), pp. 59–60.

33 Andrew Porter, *The Gramophone*, vol. 31, no. 361 (July 1953), p. 44.

34 Udo Zilkens, *Antonio Vivaldi: Zwischen Naturalismus und Pop*, pp. 84–5.

35 Harley Usill, 'A History of Argo: Problems of a Specialist Record Company', *Recorded Sound*, 78 (July 1980), pp. 40–1 (edited transcript of a talk given at the British Institute of Recorded Sound on 23 May 1978; *British Library shelfmark* Tape T2049).

36 Harry Haskell, 'Interpretations on Record: Antonio Vivaldi', BBC Radio 3, 30 December 1996; *British Library shelfmark* Tape H8233.

37 Viktoria Mullova with the Orchestre Révolutionnaire et Romantique conducted by John Eliot Gardiner; Philips 473 872-2 (digital stereo CD released 2003).

38 Robert Philip, *Early Recordings and Musical Style: Changing Tastes in Instrumental Performance 1900–1950* (Cambridge, 1992), pp. 16–17.

39 Vaughan Williams, 'How Do We Make Music?', *National Music and Other Essays* (2nd edition, London, 1987), p. 223.

40 Programme book to Philips 473 872-2, p. 3.

41 Wanda Landowska, 'Being an Interpreter', in Denise Restout (ed. and trans.) assisted by Robert Hawkins, *Landowska on Music* (London, 1965), p. 408.

42 International Piano Archives IPA 106–7 (two 12" $33\frac{1}{3}$ rpm mono discs released 1976).

43 Columbia ML 5594/MS 6194 (12" $33\frac{1}{3}$ rpm mono/stereo disc released 1961).

44 Archiv Produktion 4276522 AH (digital stereo CD released 1989).

45 HMV DB 2148; Victor 8827 (78rpm shellac discs, recorded on 12 December 1933). See EMI Music Archive microfilm: reel 377 (at the British Library).

46 Nixa PVL 7018; Vanguard BG 538; Amadeo AVRS 6002 (12" $33\frac{1}{3}$ rpm mono discs).

47 Sir Malcolm Sargent, recorded on 25 July 1952; BBC Sound Archives MP 18192 (track 3) *British Library shelfmark* 1SE0061325.

48 Terence Best, review of Hyperion CDA 66633 and Sony Classical SK52 553, *EM*, 21 (1993), pp. 649–52.

49 Bernard Harrison, review of Archiv Produktion 427 846-2, *EM*, 18 (1990), pp. 681–2.

50 Ralph Vaughan Williams, 'Bach, the Great Bourgeois', in *National Music and Other Essays*, p. 176.

51 Brendel, *The Veil of Order*, pp. 199–200.

Selected further reading

The following citations – taken for the most part from readily available sources – represent a diverse range of starting points for those wishing to pursue specific interests. Subsections in 'Secondary literature on specialized topics' correspond to the topics of chapters in this volume. Readers are encouraged to survey the bibliography in its entirety, rather than limiting their line of enquiry to literature listed under a single topic.

General works

Hill, Ralph (ed.). *The Concerto*, Harmondsworth, Penguin Books, 1952.

Layton, Robert (ed.). *A Guide to the Concerto*, Oxford University Press, 1988.

Roeder, Michael Thomas. *A History of the Concerto*, Portland, OR, Amadeus Press, 1994.

Steinberg, Michael. *The Concerto: a Listener's Guide*, New York, Oxford University Press, 1998.

Tovey, Donald Francis. *Essays in Musical Analysis: vol. 3, Concertos and Choral Works*, 7th edition, London, Oxford University Press, 1981.

Secondary literature on specialized topics

Theories of the concerto

Balthazar, Scott L. 'Intellectual History and Concepts of the Concerto: Some Parallels from 1750 to 1850', *JAMS*, 36 (1983), pp. 39–72.

Berger, Karol. 'Toward a History of Hearing: the Classic Concerto, a Sample Case', in Wye Jamison Allanbrook, Janet M. Levy and William P. Mahrt (eds.), *Convention in Eighteenth- and Nineteenth-Century Music: Essays in Honor of Leonard Ratner*, Stuyvesant, NY, Pendragon, 1992, pp. 405–29.

Kerman, Joseph. *Concerto Conversations*, Cambridge, MA, Harvard University Press, 1999.

Koch, Heinrich Christoph. *Introductory Essay on Composition: the Mechanical Rules of Melody, Sections 3 and 4* (1787–93), trans. Nancy Kovaleff Baker, New Haven and London, Yale University Press, 1983.

Küster, Konrad. *Das Konzert: Form und Forum der Virtuosität* (Bärenreiter Studienbücher Musik, Band 6), Kassel, Bärenreiter, 1993.

Plantinga, Leon B. *Schumann as Critic*, New Haven and London, Yale University Press, 1967.

Reimer, Erich. 'Concerto/Konzert', in Hans Heinrich Eggebrecht (ed.), *Handwörterbuch der Musikalischen Terminologie*, Stuttgart, Fritz Steiner Verlag, 1972– , vol. 1, pp. 1–17.

Stevens, Jane R. 'Theme, Harmony and Texture in Classic-Romantic Descriptions of Concerto First-Movement Form', *JAMS*, 27 (1974), pp. 25–60.

Tovey, Donald. 'The Classical Concerto' (1903), in *Essays in Musical Analysis: vol. 3, Concertos and Choral Works*, 7th edition, London, Oxford University Press, 1981, pp. 3–27.

The concerto and society

Becker, Howard S. *Art Worlds*, Berkeley and London, University of California Press, 1982.

DeNora, Tia. 'Music into Action: Performing Gender on the Viennese Concert Stage, 1790–1810', *Poetics: Journal of Empirical Research on Literature, the Media and the Arts*, 30/2 (2002), pp. 19–33 (Special Issue on 'New Directions in Sociology of Music', guest editor T. Dowd).

After Adorno: Rethinking Music Sociology, Cambridge University Press, 2003.

Green, Lucy. *Music, Gender, Education*, Cambridge University Press, 1997.

Hargreaves, David and Adrian North. *The Social Psychology of Music*, Oxford University Press, 1997.

Keefe, Simon P. *Mozart's Piano Concertos: Dramatic Dialogue in the Age of Enlightenment*, Woodbridge and Rochester, NY, The Boydell Press, 2001.

Macdonald, Raymond, David Hargreaves, and Dorothy Miell (eds.). *Musical Identities*, Oxford University Press, 2002.

McClary, Susan. 'The Blasphemy of Talking Politics During Bach Year', in Richard Leppert and McClary (eds.), *Music and Society: the Politics of Composition, Performance and Reception*, Cambridge University Press, pp. 13–62.

Morrow, Mary Sue. *Concert Life in Haydn's Vienna: Aspects of a Developing Musical and Social Institution*, Stuyvesant, NY, Pendragon Press, 1989.

O'Neill, Susan. 'Gender and Music', in David Hargreaves and Adrian North (eds.), *The Social Psychology of Music*, Oxford University Press, 1997.

Small, Christopher. *Musicking: the Meanings of Performing and Listening*, Hanover and London, Wesleyan University Press, 1998.

Till, Nicholas. *Mozart and the Enlightenment: Truth, Virtue and Beauty in Mozart's Operas*, London and Boston, Faber & Faber, 1992.

The Italian concerto in the late seventeenth and early eighteenth centuries

Allsop, Peter. *Arcangelo Corelli: New Orpheus of Our Times*, Oxford University Press, 1999.

Dunning, Albert. *Pietro Antonio Locatelli: Der Virtuose und seine Welt*, 2 vols., Buren, Frits Knuf, 1981.

Dunning, Albert (ed.). *Intorno a Locatelli. Studi in occasione del tricentenario della nascita di Pietro Antonio Locatelli (1695–1764)*, 2 vols., Lucca, Libreria Musicale Italiana, 1995.

Everett, Paul. *Vivaldi, The Four Seasons and Other Concertos, Op. 8*, Cambridge University Press, 1996.

Giegling, Franz. *Giuseppe Torelli: Ein Beitrag zur Entwicklungsgeschichte des italienischen Konzerts*, Kassel, Bärenreiter, 1949.

Heller, Karl. *Antonio Vivaldi: the Red Priest of Venice*, Portland, OR, Amadeus Press, 1997.

Hutchings, Arthur J. B. *The Baroque Concerto*, London, Faber & Faber, 1961.

McVeigh, Simon, and Jehoash Hirshberg. *The Italian Solo Concerto 1700–1760: Rhetorical Strategies and Style History*, Woodbridge and Rochester, NY, Boydell & Brewer, 2004.

Selfridge-Field, Eleanor. *Venetian Instrumental Music from Gabrieli to Vivaldi*, 3rd edition, New York, Dover, 1994.

Talbot, Michael. 'Albinoni's Oboe Concertos', *The Consort*, 29 (1973), pp. 14–22.

'Anna Maria's Partbook', in Helen Geyer and Wolfgang Osthoff (eds.), *Musica agli Ospedali/Conservatori veneziani tra il Seicento e Ottocento*, Rome, Edizioni Storia e Letteratura, 2004.

'The Concerto Allegro in the Early Eighteenth Century', *ML*, 52 (1971), pp. 8–18 and 159–72.

Tomaso Albinoni: the Venetian Composer and His World, Oxford, Clarendon Press, 1990.

Vivaldi, 2nd edition, London and New York, Dent, 1993.

White, Chappell. *From Vivaldi to Viotti: a History of the Early Classical Violin Concerto*, Philadelphia, Gordon & Breach, 1992.

The concerto in northern Europe to *c.*1770

Bolen, Jane. 'The Five Berlin Cembalo Concertos P390 of Johann Christian Bach: a Critical Edition', Ph.D. thesis, Florida State University, 1974.

Boyd, Malcolm. *Bach: the Brandenburg Concertos*, Cambridge University Press, 1993.

Burrows, Donald. 'Handel as Concerto Composer', in Burrows (ed.), *The Cambridge Companion to Handel*, Cambridge University Press, 1997, pp. 193–207.

Drummond, Pippa. *The German Concerto: Five Eighteenth-Century Studies*, Oxford, Clarendon Press, 1980.

Kross, Siegfried. *Das Instrumental Konzert bei Georg Philipp Telemann*, Tutzing, Hans Schneider, 1969.

Marissen, Michael. *The Social and Religious Designs of J. S. Bach's Brandenburg Concertos*, Princeton University Press, 1995.

Palisca, Claude. *Baroque Music*, Englewood Cliffs, NJ, Prentice-Hall, 1968.

Rampe, Siegbert and Dominik Sackmann. *Bachs Orchestermusik*, Kassel, Bärenreiter, 2000.

Sadie, Stanley. *Handel Concertos*, London, BBC Music Guides, 1972.

Schwarze, Penny. 'Styles of Composition and Performance in Leclair's Concertos', Ph.D. thesis, University of North Carolina, 1983.

Stevens, Jane. *The Bach Family and the Keyboard Concerto: the Evolution of a Genre*, Warren, MI, Harmonie Park Press, 2001.

Wade, Rachel. *The Keyboard Concertos of Carl Philipp Emanuel Bach*, Ann Arbor, MI, UMI Research Press, 1981.

The concerto from Mozart to Beethoven

Irving, John. *Mozart's Piano Concertos*, Aldershot and Burlington, VT, Ashgate, 2003.

Jander, Owen. 'Beethoven's "Orpheus in Hades": the Andante con moto of the Fourth Piano Concerto', *19th Century Music*, 8 (1985), pp. 195–212.

Keefe, Simon P. *Mozart's Piano Concertos: Dramatic Dialogue in the Age of Enlightenment*, Woodbridge and Rochester, NY, The Boydell Press, 2001.

'"An Entirely Special Manner": Mozart's Piano Concerto in E flat, K. 449, and the Stylistic Implications of Confrontation', *ML*, 82 (2001), pp. 559–81.

'A Complementary Pair: Stylistic Experimentation in Mozart's Final Piano Concertos, K. 537 in D and K. 595 in B♭', *JM*, 18 (2001), pp. 658–84.

Kerman, Joseph. 'Representing a Relationship: Notes on a Beethoven Concerto', *Representations*, 39 (1992), pp. 80–101.

Koch, Heinrich Christoph. *Introductory Essay on Composition: the Mechanical Rules of Melody, Sections 3 and 4* (1787–93), trans. Nancy Kovaleff Baker, New Haven and London, Yale University Press, 1983.

Kollmann, August Frederick Christopher. *An Essay on Practical Musical Composition*, London, 1799; reprint New York, Da Capo Press, 1973.

Kramer, Richard. 'Cadenza Contra Text: Mozart in Beethoven's Hands', *19th Century Music*, 15 (1991), pp. 116–31.

Lawson, Colin. *Mozart: Clarinet Concerto*, Cambridge University Press, 1996.

Plantinga, Leon. *Beethoven's Concertos: History, Style, Performance*, New York, Norton, 1999.

Rosen, Charles. *The Classical Style: Haydn, Mozart, Beethoven*, London, Norton, 1971.

Senner, Wayne M. (ed.) and Robin Wallace (trans.). *The Critical Reception of Beethoven's Compositions by his German Contemporaries*, 2 vols., London and Lincoln, NE, University of Nebraska Press, 1999 and 2001.

Whitmore, Philip. *Unpremeditated Art: the Cadenza in the Classical Keyboard Concerto*, Oxford, Clarendon Press, 1991.

Zaslaw, Neal (ed.). *Mozart's Piano Concertos: Text, Context, Interpretation*, Ann Arbor, MI, University of Michigan Press, 1996.

The nineteenth-century piano concerto

Ellsworth, Therese M. 'The Piano Concerto in London Concert Life Between 1801 and 1850', Ph.D. thesis, University of Cincinnati, 1991.

Koch, Juan Martin. *Das Klavierkonzert des 19. Jahrhunderts und die Kategorie des Symphonischen. Zur Kompositions-und Rezeptionsgeschichte der Gattung von Mozart bis Brahms* (Musik und Musikanschaug im 19. Jahrhundert: Studien und Quellen, Band 8), Sinzig, Studio Verlag, 2001.

Koiwa, Shinji. *Das Klavierkonzert um 1830: Studien zur formalen Disposition* (Berliner Musik Studien 26), Sinzig, Studio Verlag, 2003.

Küster, Konrad. *Das Konzert: Form und Forum der Virtuosität* (Bärenreiter Studienbücher Musik, Band 6), Kassel, Bärenreiter, 1993.

Lindeman, Stephan D. *Structural Novelty and Tradition in the Early Romantic Piano Concerto*, Stuyvesant, NY, Pendragon, 1998.

Mäkelä, Tomi. *Virtuosität und Werkcharakter: Eine analytische und theoretische Untersuchung zur Virtuosität in den Klavierkonzerten der Hochromantik* (Berliner Musikwissenschaftliche Arbeiten, Band 37), Munich and Salzburg, Emil Katzbichler, 1989.

Mies, Paul. *Das Konzert im 19 Jahrhundert: Studien zu Formen und Kadenzen*, Bonn, Bouvier, 1972.

Norris, Jeremy. *The Russian Piano Concerto, vol. 1: The 19th Century*, Bloomington, IN, Indiana University Press, 1994.

Plantinga, Leon. *Schumann as Critic*, New Haven, CT, Yale University Press, 1967.

Stevens, Jane R. 'Theme, Harmony, and Texture in Classic-Romantic Descriptions of Concerto First-movement Form', *JAMS*, 27 (1974), pp. 25–60.

Rink, John. *Chopin: the Piano Concertos*, Cambridge University Press, 1997.

Weber, William. *Music and the Middle Class: the Social Structure of Concert Life in London, Paris, and Vienna between 1830–1848*, London, Croom Helm, 1975.

Nineteenth-century concertos for strings and winds

Bonds, Mark Evan. *After Beethoven: Imperatives of Originality in the Symphony*, Cambridge, MA, Harvard University Press, 1996.

Botstein, Leon (ed.). *The Compleat Brahms*, New York, Norton, 1999.

Brown, Clive. *Louis Spohr: a Critical Biography*, Cambridge University Press, 1984.

Daverio, John. *Robert Schumann: Herald of a 'New Poetic Age'*, New York, Oxford University Press, 1997.

Emans, Reinmar and Matthias Wendt (eds.). *Beiträge zur Geschichte des Konzerts: Festschrift Siegfried Kross zum 60. Geburtstag*, Bonn, G. Schröder, 1990.

Fiske, Roger. *Scotland in Music: a European Obsession*, Cambridge University Press, 1983.

Kerman, Joseph. *Concerto Conversations*, Cambridge, MA, Harvard University Press, 1999.

Knapp, Raymond, 'Passing – and Failing – in Late-Nineteenth-Century Russia; or Why We Should Care about the Cuts in Tchaikovsky's Violin Concerto', *19th Century Music*, 26 (2003), pp. 195–234.

MacDonald, Malcolm, *Brahms*, New York, Schirmer Books, 1990.

Schwarz, Boris, *Great Masters of the Violin*, New York, Simon and Schuster, 1983.

'Joseph Joachim and the Genesis of Brahms's Violin Concerto', *MQ*, 69 (1983), pp. 503–26.

Smaczny, Jan. *Dvořák: Cello Concerto*, Cambridge University Press, 1999.

Stegemann, Michael. *Camille Saint-Saëns and the French Solo Concerto from 1850 to 1920*, trans. Ann C. Sherwin, Portland, OR, Amadeus Press, 1991.

Stowell, Robin, *Beethoven: Violin Concerto*, Cambridge University Press, 1998.

Stowell, Robin (ed.). *The Cambridge Companion to the Violin*, Cambridge, Cambridge University Press, 1992.

The Cambridge Companion to the Cello, Cambridge University Press, 1999.

Struck, Michael. *Die umstrittenen späten Instrumentalwerke Schumanns*, Hamburg, K. D. Wagner, 1984.

Todd, R. Larry. *Mendelssohn: a Life in Music*, New York, Oxford University Press, 2003.

Warrack, John. *Carl Maria von Weber*, New York, Macmillan, 1968.

Weiss-Aigner, Günter. *Johannes Brahms: Violinkonzert D-dur*, Munich, Fink, 1979.

Weston, Pamela. *Clarinet Virtuosi of the Past*, London, Hale, 1971.

The early twentieth-century concerto

Evans, John. 'The Concertos', in Christopher Palmer (ed.), *The Britten Companion*, Cambridge University Press, 1984, pp. 411–24.

Howes, Frank. *The Music of William Walton*, London, Oxford University Press, 1965.

Kerman, Joseph. *Concerto Conversations*, Cambridge, MA, Harvard University Press, 1999.

Kroó, György. *A Guide to Bartók*, trans. Ruth Pataki and Mária Steiner, Budapest, Corvina Press, 1974.

Pople, Anthony. *Berg: Violin Concerto*, Cambridge University Press, 1991.

Rimm, Robert. *The Composer-Pianists: Hamelin and The Eight*, Portland, OR, Amadeus Press, 2002.

Schiff, David. *Gershwin: 'Rhapsody in Blue'*, Cambridge University Press, 1997.

Schneider, David E. 'Bartók and Stravinsky: Respect, Competition, Influence, and the Hungarian Reaction to Modernism in the 1920s', in Peter Laki (ed.), *Bartók and His World*, Princeton University Press, 1995, pp. 172–99.

Simpson, Robert. *Carl Nielsen: Symphonist*, London, Kahn & Averill, 1993.

Sitsky, Larry. *Busoni and the Piano: the Works, the Writings, and the Recordings*, New York, Greenwood Press, 1986.

Szigeti, Joseph. *With Strings Attached*, 2nd edition, New York, Alfred A. Knopf, 1967.

Taruskin, Richard. 'The Pastness of the Present and the Presence of the Past', in Nicholas Kenyon (ed.), *Authenticity and Early Music*, Oxford University Press, 1988, pp. 137–207.

White, Eric Walter. *Stravinsky, the Composer and his Works*, 2nd edition, Berkeley, University of California Press, 1979.

The concerto since 1945

Bowen, Meirion (ed.). *Tippett on Music*, Oxford, Clarendon Press, 1995.

Brougham, Henrietta, with Christopher Fox and Ian Pace (eds.). *Uncommon Ground: the Music of Michael Finnissy*, Aldershot, Ashgate, 1997.

Clarke, David. *The Music and Thought of Michael Tippett: Modern Times and Metaphysics*, Cambridge University Press, 2001.

Cross, Jonathan. *Harrison Birtwistle: Man, Mind, Music*, London, Faber & Faber, 2000.

Fay, Laurel E. *Shostakovich: a Life*, New York and Oxford, Oxford University Press, 2000.

Henze, Hans Werner. *Bohemian Fifths: an Autobiography*, trans. Stewart Spencer, London, Faber & Faber, 1998.

Ivashkin, Alexander. *Alfred Schnittke*, London, Phaidon Press, 1996.

Osmond-Smith, David. *Berio*, Oxford University Press, 1991.

Pritchett, James. *The Music of John Cage*, Cambridge University Press, 1993.

Rae, Charles Bodman. *The Music of Lutosławski*, 3rd edition, London, Omnibus Press, 1999.

Schiff, David. *The Music of Elliott Carter*, London, Faber & Faber, 1998.

Skowron, Zbigniew (ed.). *Lutosławski Studies*, Oxford University Press, 2001.

Steinitz, Richard. *György Ligeti: Music of the Imagination*, London, Faber & Faber, 2003.

Varga, Bálint András. *Conversations with Iannis Xenakis*, London, Faber & Faber, 1996.

Whittall, Arnold, *Exploring Twentieth-Century Music*, Cambridge University Press, 2003.

The rise (and fall) of the concerto virtuoso in the late eighteenth and nineteenth centuries

Ellis, Katharine. 'Female Pianists and their Male Critics in Nineteenth-Century Paris', *JAMS*, 50 (1997), pp. 353–85.

Hamilton, Kenneth. 'The Virtuoso Tradition', in David Rowland (ed.), *The Cambridge Companion to the Piano*, Cambridge University Press, 1998, pp. 7–74.

Metzner, Paul. *Crescendo of the Virtuoso: Spectacle, Skill, and Self-Promotion in Paris during the Age of Revolution*, Berkeley, University of California Press, 1998.

Milliot, Sylvette. 'Le Virtuose international: une création du 18 siècle', *Dix-huitième siècle*, 25 (1993), pp. 55–64.

Reimer, Erich. 'Die Polemik gegen das Virtuosenkonzert im 18. Jahrhundert', *Archiv für Musikwissenschaft*, 30 (1973), pp. 235–44.

Schonberg, Harold C., *The Great Pianists*. New York, Simon & Schuster, 1963.

Stowell, Robin. 'The Nineteenth-Century Bravura Tradition', in Robin Stowell (ed.), *The Cambridge Companion to the Violin*, Cambridge University Press, 1992, pp. 61–78.

Wangermée, Renée. 'Tradition et innovation dans la virtuosité romantique', *AM*, 42 (1970), pp. 5–32.

Performance practice in the eighteenth-century concerto

Bach, Carl Philipp Emanuel. *Versuch über die wahre Art das Clavier zu spielen*, Berlin, Henning, 1753; trans. William J. Mitchell as *Essay on the True Art of Playing Keyboard Instruments*, New York, Norton, 1949.

Badura-Skoda, Eva and Paul. *Mozart-Interpretation*, Vienna, Eduard Wancura Verlag, 1957; trans. Leo Black as *Interpreting Mozart on the Keyboard*, New York, St. Martin's Press, 1962.

Brown, Clive. *Classical and Romantic Performance Practice 1750–1900*, Oxford University Press, 1999.

Burton, Anthony (ed.). *A Performer's Guide to Music of the Baroque Period*, London, ABRSM Publishing, 2002.

A Performer's Guide to Music of the Classical Period, London, ABRSM Publishing, 2002.

Brown, Howard Mayer and Stanley Sadie (eds.). *Performance Practice: Music after 1600*, London, Macmillan, 1989.

Kolneder, Walter. *Aufführungspraxis bei Vivaldi*; trans. Anne de Dadelsen as *Performance Practices in Vivaldi*, Winterthur, Amadeus-Verlag, 1979.

Koury, Daniel. *Orchestral Performance Practices of the Nineteenth Century: Size, Proportions, and Seating*, Ann Arbor, MI, UMI Research Press, 1986.

Lawson, Colin, and Robin Stowell. *The Historical Performance of Music: an Introduction*, Cambridge University Press, 1999.

Mozart, Leopold. *Versuch einer gründlichen Violinschule*, Augsburg, 1756; trans. Editha Knocker as *A Treatise on the Fundamental Principles of Violin Playing*, Oxford University Press, 1948.

Neumann, Frederick. *Ornamentation in Baroque and Post-Baroque Music with Special Emphasis on J. S. Bach*, Princeton University Press, 1978.

Ornamentation and Improvisation in Mozart, Princeton University Press, 1986.

Quantz, Johann Joachim. *Versuch einer Anweisung die Flöte traversière zu spielen*, Berlin, J. F. Voss, 1752; trans. Edward R. Reilly as *On Playing the Flute*, New York, Schirmer, 1966.

Rowland, David. *A History of Pianoforte Pedalling*, Cambridge University Press, 1993.

Türk, Daniel Gottlob. *Clavierschule oder Anweisung zum Clavierspielen*, Leipzig, Schwickert, 1789; trans. Raymond Haagh as *School of Clavier Playing*, Lincoln, NE, University of Nebraska Press, 1982.

Whitmore, Philip. *Unpremeditated Art: the Cadenza in the Classical Keyboard Concerto*, Oxford, Clarendon Press, 1991.

Zaslaw, Neal. 'Toward the Revival of the Classical Orchestra', *PRMA*, 103 (1976–7), pp. 158–87.

Zaslaw, Neal (ed.). *Mozart's Piano Concertos: Text, Context, Interpretation*, Ann Arbor, MI, University of Michigan Press, 1996.

Performance practice in the nineteenth-century concerto

Bloom, Peter. *Music in Paris in the Eighteen-Thirties*, Stuyvesant, NY, Pendragon Press, 1987.

Cooper, Jeffrey. *The Rise of Instrumental Music and Concert Series in Paris 1828–1871*, Ann Arbor, MI, UMI Research Press, 1983.

Ellsworth, Theresa Marie. 'The Piano Concerto in London Concert Life between 1801 and 1850', Ph.D. thesis, University of Cincinnati, 1991.

Goertzen, Valerie Woodring. 'By Way of Introduction: Preluding by 18th- and Early 19th-Century Pianists', *JM*, 14 (1996), pp. 299–337.

Grayson, David. 'Whose Authenticity? Ornaments by Hummel and Cramer for Mozart's Piano Concertos', in Neal Zaslaw (ed.), *Mozart Piano Concertos: Text, Context, Interpretation*, Ann Arbor, MI, University of Michigan Press, 1996, pp. 373–91.

Hanson, Alice M. *Musical Life in Biedermeier Vienna*, Cambridge University Press, 1985.

Koury, Daniel J. *Orchestral Performance Practices in the Nineteenth Century: Size, Proportions, and Seating*, Ann Arbor, MI, UMI Research Press, 1986.

Milligan, Thomas B. *The Concerto and London's Musical Culture in the Late Eighteenth Century*, Ann Arbor, MI, UMI Research Press, 1983.

Plantinga, Leon. *Beethoven's Concertos*, New York, Norton, 1999.

Rowland, David. 'Clementi and the British Concerto Tradition', in Roberto Illiano, Luca Sala and Massimiliano Sala (eds.), *Muzio Clementi: Studies and Prospects*, Bologna, Ut Orpheus Edizioni, 2002, pp. 179–90.

Szász, Tibor. 'Beethoven's *basso continuo*: Notation and Performance', in Robin Stowell (ed.), *Performing Beethoven*, Cambridge University Press, 1994, pp. 1–22.

Weber, William. *Music and the Middle Class: the Social Structure of Concert Life in London, Paris, and Vienna between 1830 and 1848*, London, Croom Helm, 1975.

Winter, Robert and Bruce Carr (eds.). *Beethoven, Performers, and Critics*, Detroit, Wayne State University Press, 1980.

The concerto in the age of recording

Butt, John. *Playing with History*, Cambridge University Press, 2002.

Chanan, Michael. *Repeated Takes: a Short History of Recording and its Effects on Music*, London, Verso, 1995.

Day, Timothy. *A Century of Recorded Music: Listening to Musical History*, New Haven and London, Yale University Press, 2000.

Haskell, Harry. *The Early Music Revival*, New York and London, Dover Publications, 1996.

Horowitz, Joseph. *Understanding Toscanini: a Social History of American Concert Life*, London, Faber & Faber, 1987.

Marco, Guy A. *Encyclopedia of Recorded Sound in America*, New York and London, Garland Publishing, 1993.

Philip, Robert, *Early Recordings and Musical Style: Changing Tastes in Instrumental Performance 1900–1950*, Cambridge University Press, 1992.

Performing Music in the Age of Recording, New Haven and London, Yale University Press, 2004.

Rink, John. *Musical Performance: a Guide to Understanding*, Cambridge University Press, 2002.

Taruskin, Richard. *Text and Act*, New York, Oxford University Press, 1995.

Index

Cambridge Companions to Music

Topics

The Cambridge Companion to Blues and
Gospel Music
Edited by Allan Moore

The Cambridge Companion to the
Concerto
Edited by Simon P. Keefe

The Cambridge Companion to Conducting
Edited by José Antonio Bowen

The Cambridge Companion to Grand
Opera
Edited by David Charlton

The Cambridge Companion to Jazz
Edited by Mervyn Cooke and David Horn

The Cambridge Companion to the Lied
Edited by James Parsons

The Cambridge Companion to the Musical
Edited by William Everett and Paul Laird

The Cambridge Companion to the
Orchestra
Edited by Colin Lawson

The Cambridge Companion to Pop and
Rock
Edited by Simon Frith, Will Straw and John
Street

The Cambridge Companion to the String
Quartet
Edited by Robin Stowell

Composers

The Cambridge Companion to Bach
Edited by John Butt

The Cambridge Companion to Bartók
Edited by Amanda Bayley

The Cambridge Companion to Beethoven
Edited by Glenn Stanley

The Cambridge Companion to Berg
Edited by Anthony Pople

The Cambridge Companion to Berlioz
Edited by Peter Bloom

The Cambridge Companion to Brahms
Edited by Michael Musgrave

The Cambridge Companion to Benjamin Britten
Edited by Mervyn Cooke

The Cambridge Companion to Bruckner
Edited by John Williamson

The Cambridge Companion to John Cage
Edited by David Nicholls

The Cambridge Companion to Chopin
Edited by Jim Samson

The Cambridge Companion to Debussy
Edited by Simon Trezise

The Cambridge Companion to Elgar
Edited by Daniel Grimley and Julian
Rushton

The Cambridge Companion to Handel
Edited by Donald Burrows

The Cambridge Companion to Haydn
Edited by Caryl Clark

The Cambridge Companion to Liszt
Edited by Kenneth Hamilton

The Cambridge Companion to
Mendelssohn
Edited by Peter Mercer-Taylor

The Cambridge Companion to Mozart
Edited by Simon P. Keefe

The Cambridge Companion to Ravel
Edited by Deborah Mawer

The Cambridge Companion to Rossini
Edited by Emanuele Senici

The Cambridge Companion to Schubert
Edited by Christopher Gibbs

The Cambridge Companion to Sibelius
Edited by Daniel M. Grimley

The Cambridge Companion to Verdi
Edited by Scott L. Balthazar

Instruments

The Cambridge Companion to Brass
Instruments
Edited by Trevor Herbert and John Wallace

The Cambridge Companion to the Cello
Edited by Robin Stowell

The Cambridge Companion to the Clarinet
Edited by Colin Lawson

The Cambridge Companion to the Guitar
Edited by Victor Coelho

The Cambridge Companion to the Organ
Edited by Nicholas Thistlethwaite and
Geoffrey Webber

The Cambridge Companion to the Piano
Edited by David Rowland

The Cambridge Companion to the
Recorder
Edited by John Mansfield Thomson

The Cambridge Companion to the
Saxophone
Edited by Richard Ingham

The Cambridge Companion to Singing
Edited by John Potter

The Cambridge Companion to the Violin
Edited by Robin Stowell